HEALTH LAW AS PRIVATE LAW

Health Law as Private Law delves into the complex relationship between private law and health care. During the COVID-19 pandemic, the importance of public ordering and state-created rules was evident, yet this work reveals the equally important role of private agreements in shaping health care policy. The volume's five sections – theory and structure, reproductive care, costs and financing, innovation and institutions, contracts and torts – include innovative conceptualizations and approaches to applying private law to health law. Chapters authored by leading experts explore how private law can be utilized to address significant health care and public health problems, and to achieve much-needed health care reform. Comprehensive and timely, *Health Law as Private Law* opens new pathways that will influence future policy, jurisprudence, and regulation. This title is also available as Open Access on Cambridge Core.

I. Glenn Cohen is the James A. Attwood and Leslie Williams Professor of Law and a Deputy Dean at Harvard Law and the Faculty Director of Petrie-Flom Center for Health Law Policy, Biotechnology & Bioethics. He is one of the world's leading experts on the intersection of bioethics and the law, as well as health law. He also teaches civil procedure. He is the author of more than 200 articles and the author, editor, or coeditor of more than twenty books.

Susannah Baruch is the Executive Director of the Petrie-Flom Center for Health Law Policy, Biotechnology, and Bioethics at Harvard Law School. She previously held key leadership roles in nonprofit organizations, academia, and government. Her research focuses on reproductive health law policy and issues surrounding genetics and genomics.

Wendy Netter Epstein is Vincent de Paul Professor of Law at DePaul University College of Law and an expert in health care law and policy, with an emphasis on the financing and delivery of health care, and matters of health equity. She has authored dozens of articles and coauthored *Contracts: Law in Action* (5th ed).

Christopher Robertson is N. Neal Pike Scholar and Professor of Law and Public Health at Boston University. He is an expert in health law, institutional design, and decision-making. Robertson has been published in *JAMA*, *NEJM*, and *Science*.

Carmel Shachar is Assistant Clinical Professor of Law and the Faculty Director of the Health Law and Policy Clinic at Harvard Law School. She previously served as the Executive Director of the Petrie-Flom Center for Health Law Policy, Biotechnology, and Bioethics at Harvard Law School. Shachar is the coeditor of several other volumes including *Transparency in Health Care* and *Disability, Law, Health, and Bioethics*.

Health Law as Private Law

PATHOLOGY OR PATHWAY

Edited by

I. GLENN COHEN
Harvard Law School

SUSANNAH BARUCH
Harvard Law School

WENDY NETTER EPSTEIN
DePaul University College of Law

CHRISTOPHER ROBERTSON
Boston University

CARMEL SHACHAR
Harvard Law School

CAMBRIDGE
UNIVERSITY PRESS

CAMBRIDGE
UNIVERSITY PRESS

Shaftesbury Road, Cambridge CB2 8EA, United Kingdom

One Liberty Plaza, 20th Floor, New York, NY 10006, USA

477 Williamstown Road, Port Melbourne, VIC 3207, Australia

314–321, 3rd Floor, Plot 3, Splendor Forum, Jasola District Centre, New Delhi – 110025, India

103 Penang Road, #05-06/07, Visioncrest Commercial, Singapore 238467

Cambridge University Press is part of Cambridge University Press & Assessment, a department of the University of Cambridge.

We share the University's mission to contribute to society through the pursuit of education, learning and research at the highest international levels of excellence.

www.cambridge.org
Information on this title: www.cambridge.org/9781009480451

DOI: 10.1017/9781009480468

When citing this work, please include a reference to the DOI 10.1017/9781009480468

First published 2025

Cover image: Alexander Calder, Untitled, 1967. Gouache and ink on paper, 30 3/4″ × 22 3/4″
© 2024 Calder Foundation, New York / Artists Rights Society (ARS), New York

A catalogue record for this publication is available from the British Library

A Cataloging-in-Publication data record for this book is available from the Library of Congress

ISBN 978-1-009-48045-1 Hardback
ISBN 978-1-009-48049-9 Paperback

I. Glenn Cohen: To Michael Boudin.

Susannah Baruch: To my excellent menfolk, for supporting me in this new adventure.

Wendy Netter Epstein: To my family for both pushing me and supporting me, and to my coeditors and all the writers for making this project such a pleasure.

Christopher Robertson: For my friend and mentor, David Rosenberg.

Carmel Shachar: To Daniel, who encourages me to spread my wings and fall down rabbit holes, even when it means more work for him.

Contents

Contributors

Susannah Baruch, Harvard Law School

Ximena Benavides, Yale Law School

Asees Bhasin, University of Maryland Francis King Carey School of Law

Valarie K. Blake, University of Tennessee College of Law

Cindy L. Cain, The University of Alabama at Birmingham

I. Glenn Cohen, Harvard Law School

Alberto De Diego-Habel, UCLA School of Law

Wendy Netter Epstein, DePaul University College of Law

Barbara J. Evans, University of Florida Levin College of Law; University of Florida Herbert Wertheim College of Engineering

Barry R. Furrow, Drexel University Kline School of Law

Erin C. Fuse Brown, Brown University School of Public Health

Mark A. Hall, Wake Forest University

Jill R. Horwitz, UCLA School of Law

Jaime S. King, University of Auckland, Auckland Law School

Maanasa Kona, Georgetown University McCourt School of Public Policy

Craig Konnoth, University of Virginia School of Law

Myrisha S. Lewis, William & Mary Law School

Jessica Mantel, The University of Houston Law Center Faculty

Elizabeth Y. McCuskey, Boston University School of Public Health; Boston University School of Law

Christine H. Monahan, Georgetown University McCourt School of Public Policy

Madeline O'Brien, Georgetown University Law Center

Christopher Robertson, Boston University

Daniel B. Rodriguez, Northwestern Pritzker School of Law

Lauren R. Roth, Touro University Jacob D. Fuchsberg Law Center

William Sage, Texas A&M University

Enrique Santamaría Echeverría, Erasmus University Rotterdam

Carmel Shachar, Harvard Law School

Barry Solaiman, Hamad Bin Khalifa University College of Law; Weill Cornell Medicine – Qatar

James Toomey, University of Iowa College of Law

Jackson Williams, Dialysis Patient Citizens

Thomas W. Williams, American University Washington College of Law

Rebecca E. Wolitz, The Ohio State University Moritz College of Law

Megan S. Wright, Penn State Law

Acknowledgments

A book like this is the result of the hard work of many. We thank our student line editors, Oceania Eshraghi (lead line editor), Gwen Byrne, Rebekah Ninan, and Carli Sley, for their meticulous work. We are grateful to Laura Chong and Chloe Reichel for their administrative support in organizing the conference that gave rise to this book. We are also grateful for Laura Chong's hard work, shepherding all the many pieces of this manuscript. We thankfully acknowledge the Petrie-Flom Center for Health Law Policy, Biotechnology, and Bioethics at Harvard Law School, with support from the Oswald DeN. Cammann Fund and the Lynde and Harry Bradley Foundation for conference sponsorship. Finally, of course, we thank the contributors for their thoughtful and important scholarly contributions.

Introduction

Susannah Baruch, I. Glenn Cohen, Wendy Netter Epstein, Christopher Robertson, and Carmel Shachar

Health care today is the most regulated industry in America. Statutes and regulations govern everything from licensing and insurance to privacy and emergency care. In pursuit of the iron triangle of improved access, better quality, and lower cost, health law scholars have long focused on "public law," or law that involves governmental action, including action by administrative agencies at both the state and federal levels.

At the same time, US health care is substantially governed by private relations and dependent on operation of the private market. Two-thirds of Americans are covered by private health insurance. Private insurers even play an important role in administering public programs like Medicare and Medicaid. Hospitals and nursing facilities are largely privately owned.

Hospital mergers and private equity acquisitions affect the delivery of care and the prices patients pay for that care. Medical debt continues to be a wide-ranging problem affecting the everyday lives of Americans, a problem worsened by the high price of pharmaceuticals sold by private manufacturers. Private employers also play an important role in health care, making decisions about benefits that can impact, for instance, whether employees can access reproductive services or gender-affirming care.

"Private law" classically refers to the law circumscribing relations between individuals and institutions behaving as private actors, for instance, the law that governs when one person reaches an agreement with another person for a given set of services and at a given price. The state's role is in the background to enforce the parties' agreement.

Although private law plays a central role in the delivery of health care, the intense focus on public law as the right mechanism to fix our health care system stems from two main conceits. The first is that government oversight is essential when it comes to something as crucial as the health and well-being of our citizens. The second is that the private market is subject to clear market failures in health care, including agency problems, collective action problems, and information problems.

In this volume, twenty-seven contributors take a fresh look at private law approaches to issues in health law, focusing on the US context. The chapters that follow consider whether private law is a pathology of or a potential fix for the US health care system. They interrogate in what ways private law might be used as a catalyst for health care reform, separate from federal or state initiatives. And they also explore the limits of private law approaches.

In Part I, *What Is Private Law? Theory and Structure*, the first chapter by William Sage, *Public Funds, Public Functions, Private Actors*, describes a cognitive dissonance at the heart of the American health care system: Private actors and private contractual relationships, fueled by large amounts of money, seem in constant conflict with public needs and struggling public health care systems. Barbara J. Evans engages with these assertions in *Private Ordering Is Ubiquitous in Health Care, but Why?* arguing that in the United States private ordering has been central as a practical necessity, in the face of constitutional constraints on government regulation of the health care system. In *Abandoning Fiduciaries in Health Care*, Lauren R. Roth uses game theory and game strategy to show how health fiduciaries are not adequately constrained in the face of conflicts of interest in the health care system. The part concludes with a comparative chapter, *European Distinctions between Private and Public Law in Health Care and the Emerging Influence of Private Lobbies* in which Barry Solaiman explores how private law and private entities operate in European health care systems, focusing on the United Kingdom.

Part II, *Tools of Private Law: Torts, Contracts, and Property as Vehicles of Health Policy*, reintroduces these three traditional tools of private law. Editor Wendy Netter Epstein's introduction asks us to consider how these tools might or might not address our most pressing problems. In his chapter, *Adaptation of Tort Law to Modern Health Care Delivery in the Restatement of Medical Malpractice*, Mark A. Hall explores medical liability. He sees tort law as capable of evolving with medical practice but not the right tool to effect change itself. Next, in *Pandemic Harms and Private Law's Limits: A Proposal for Tort Replacement*, Alberto De Diego-Habel, Jill R. Horwitz, and Daniel B. Rodriguez consider tort law in the context of the Covid-19 pandemic, arguing for a public tort replacement social insurance system to provide both compensation to those harmed and clarity to businesses. Turning to contract law, in *States as Contractor*, Christine H. Monahan, Maanasa Kona, and Madeline O'Brien describe how states can function as private actors and use contracting power to control costs. Craig Konnoth's chapter, *Data Transparency, ERISA Preemption, and Freedom of Contract*, argues that state laws to improve transparency in health care can serve a public regulatory function while also supporting private market functioning, which might encourage courts to reject ERISA preemption challenges. Finally, in *The Human Body Commons*, Enrique Santamaría Echeverría explores how private law might advance the right to health by supporting both open public access to scientific knowledge and innovation.

In Part III, "Russian Dolls, Reproduction, and Private Law," Editor I. Glenn Cohen introduces the relationship between private law and reproductive health care policy by describing a "nesting doll" structure like Russian *matryoshka* dolls. Even as private and public law influence each other, watershed events such as the 2022 decision in *Dobbs v. Jackson Women's Health Organization*[1] can still upend the project. Valarie K. Blake and Elizabeth Y. McCuskey's chapter, *Employer-Sponsored Abortion Coverage*, demonstrates how private employers have become policymakers on abortion access in America through both the health insurance they provide employees and their coverage decisions that impact care. Myrisha Lewis' chapter on *Reproductive Innovation and Reproductive Exceptionalism* focuses on family formation through reproductive technologies and the great variety of coexisting public laws and private employer policies that are still evolving. In *Business Responses to* Dobbs, Asees Bhasin looks critically at corporate gap-filling and private law itself, noting that corporate responses lack enforceability and prioritize profit maximization. Finally, Thomas Williams' chapter, *Privatizing the Creation of Equity in Women's Health*, looks at how private law (especially corporate law and contract law) and private equity influence "Femtech" – technologies aimed at promoting women's health and reproductive health.

In Part IV, *Controlling Costs: Private Law's Impact on Health Care Financing and Pricing*, Editor Christopher Robertson's introduction focuses on the centrality of private law – in a broader market largely dominated by the federal government – to issues of cost, who pays, and how physicians and insurers operate. Erin C. Fuse Brown's chapter, *Federalism, Private Law, and Medical Debt*, explores the issue of medical debt and the interplay between federal and state laws, which provide limited protection, noting that private enforcement mechanisms like Unfair and Deceptive Acts or Practices (UDAP) might bring increased accountability. In *Paying for Health Care and Private Law's Internal Point of View*, James Toomey focuses on opaque pricing in health care, noting that traditional contract law enforces agreed-upon prices while exploring the idea that contract law could draw from tort law's use of "reasonableness." In *Health Law's Sheathed Sword*, Jackson Williams finds high health care costs based on legal contracts are hard to solve with civil litigation and considers approaches such as class actions, involvement of state attorneys general, and lawsuits sponsored by foundations, unions, or other employee-based groups. In *The Canary in the Coal Mine*, Jamie S. King argues antitrust enforcement in health care has not kept pace with market changes, suggesting private actors could bring cases challenging problematic practices and potentially lowering prices. Finally, Jessica Mantel's chapter, *Health Care Finance Law's Relational Bias*, considers how to align the incentives of the provider with the interests of the patient,

1 597 U.S. 215 (2022).

exploring Multi-Payor Alignment Incentives and ultimately arguing for a public law framework.

Part V, *Private Law Applied: The Pharmaceutical Industry, Nursing Homes, and the End of Life*, is introduced by Editor Carmel Shachar, who notes that while the chapters examine different aspects of health care, they reveal commonalities. In *Private Equity Firms and Digital Clinical Trials*, Ximena Benavides considers the role of private equity and private actors in pharmaceutical research, and the need for a greater sense of moral responsibility. Rebecca E. Wolitz, in *Shareholder Resolutions and Access to Medications*, notes that while managers and directors of pharmaceutical companies believe investors expect profit maximization, shareholder resolutions – a private law tool – reveal investors' concerns about high drug pricing. In *The Hollowed-Out American Nursing Home*, Barry Furrow argues that although private equity's focus on short-term returns for its investors means low-quality care for nursing home residents, a private law model of robust fiduciary duty could create meaningful protections. Finally, in *Health Care Organization Policies about the California End of Life Option Act*, Megan S. Wright and Cindy L. Cain show that despite implementation of medical aid in dying (MAiD) in California as a public policy, few individuals can meet its requirements because the private choices of health care organizations to opt out or limit its use undermine the policy.

As our society considers the experience and lessons of Covid-19 and the ongoing challenges in health care, it is a unique moment to document the interplay of public policy and private action in health law. Perhaps we may take solace in the possibility that openness to revised approaches, including theories of private law, may lead us toward a more effective legal framework.

PART I

What Is Private Law?

Theory and Structure

1

Public Funds, Public Functions, Private Actors

The Cognitive Dissonance of US Health Law

William Sage

1.1 INTRODUCTION

It is commonplace for critics of the US health care system to observe that it is neither a system nor focused on health.[1] This fundamental confusion is a feature, not a bug. Because of cultural resistance to government control and the political power of physicians, the American health care system tends to utilize private actors to perform public functions with (lavish) public funding, supposedly under the ethical and scientific direction of the self-governing medical profession. Consequently, "private law" plays an outsized role in American health governance, often – if not necessarily – working against rather than for what in other countries are incontrovertibly "public law" goals.[2]

US health care constitutes an extraordinarily large commitment of financial resources, currently exceeding US$5,000,000,000,000 annually (writing the word "trillion" does not do justice to an expenditure of this magnitude) and comprising over one-sixth of the national economy. Counting explicit exclusions from otherwise taxable funds as well as direct spending, more than half of the financing comes from public monies, representing as large a public per capita contribution as one would find in any other country – to which the United States adds a roughly equal private financial contribution. As a general matter, the same set of corporate organizations serving as intermediaries operate both the public (Medicare/Medicaid) and the private (employer-sponsored) health insurance systems, which process payment to the same private health professionals, health care facilities, and suppliers of medical

[1] Wendy Netter Epstein, The Healthcare System Misnomer, 82 Ohio St. L.J. 409 (2021); Farshad Marvasti & Randall S. Stafford, From "Sick Care" to Health Care: Reengineering Prevention into the U.S. System, 367 New Eng. J. Med. 889 (2012).

[2] Michel Rosenfeld, Rethinking the Boundaries between Public Law and Private Law for the Twenty First Century: An Introduction, 11 Int'l J. Con. L. 125 (2013), https://doi.org/10.1093/icon/mos053.

products, which in turn meet standards set by the same professional self-regulatory entities.

Efforts at "systemness" are further challenged by the deference of nearly all health law to the personal and collective judgments of the American medical profession, which tend to emphasize discrete services by identifiable physicians to individual patients.[3] As cataloged in 1982 by sociologist Paul Starr and confirmed in subsequent years, medical interests have repeatedly managed to defeat efforts to bring full public accountability to health care while simultaneously keeping massive amounts of public money flowing.[4] Although organized medicine chafes at "corporatization" as well as "socialized medicine," corporate lobbying power reinforces the system's transactional bias because the most extensive legal frameworks in US health care center on the generation and payment of often-lucrative clinical claims.

In essence, American health care can be thought of as a giant system of lawful money laundering, the result of which is to conceal massive public financial obligations that serve indisputably public purposes by embedding them in what appear to be private commercial transactions that arise largely from decentralized patient care encounters.[5]

Laundering public money through these private actors, many of whom are trusted physicians or nonprofit hospitals, results in more resources being made available than would be the case were health care deliberately designed for collective benefit and financed through explicit taxation and direct spending. Because of its reliance on medical professionalism, the laundered system also results in a lower degree of formal regulatory oversight and a less enforceable pledge of social solidarity or equity, substituting for those features the appearance if not often the reality of effective market competition.[6]

The entities involved in the laundered system and the relationships among them tend to be governed by private law. This creates space for diverse parties to pursue advantage using diverse arguments in diverse forums that create, refine, interpret, and adjudicate legal interests – most of which at some level involve claims on resources that would not be available absent the aforementioned public commitments. As a result, health law can involve any combination of judicial decision-

[3] Einer Elhauge, The Fragmentation of U.S. Health Care: Causes and Solutions (2010) (online ed., https://doi.org/10.1093/acprof:oso/9780195390131.001.0001).

[4] Paul Starr, The Social Transformation of American Medicine: The Rise of a Sovereign Profession and the Making of a Vast Industry (1982).

[5] Robert I. Field, Mother of Invention: How the Government Created Free-Market Health Care 24–25 (2014).

[6] William M. Sage, Explaining America's Spendthrift Health Care System: The Enduring Effects of Public Regulation on Private Competition, in The Law and Policy of Healthcare Financing 17–36 (Wolf Sauter et al. eds., 2019); William M. Sage, Antitrust Law and Competition Policy in U.S. Health Care, in Oxford Handbook of U.S. Health Law 606–36 (I. Glenn Cohen et al. eds., 2016).

making, legislation, administrative regulation, medical professional self-regulation, and enforceable entitlements (i.e., payment guarantees).

Private law acts as a conservative – if not always an obstructionist – force in pursuing consensus goals regarding access to affordable medical care, which in turn makes it more difficult to promote collective health and well-being across the range of social sectors that must share public investment. Put bluntly, the cognitive dissonance between the private orientation we ascribe to US health care and the public funds that its specialized, very "medical" activities consume implies that (largely private) health law often acts at cross-purposes with (necessarily public) health policy.[7] This cognitive dissonance also implies that the laws most relevant to health, especially at the population level, involve fundamental social commitments to equity and opportunity that are not what we usually consider health law.[8]

This chapter begins with the evolution of American medicine from a "sovereign" self-regulating profession focused on direct patient service to a large industry that serves the social sector but that, because of its professional heritage, receives extensive public subsidies without equivalent public accountability. Next, the chapter identifies regulatory dynamics in American health care governance that structurally discourage movement from the prevailing, if dissonant, private law framework to one explicitly grounded in public law. The chapter concludes by highlighting the challenges and opportunities inherent in a private law approach to what is intuitively a public law domain.

1.2 HEALTH LAW AND THE JOURNEY FROM SELF-REGULATING PROFESSION TO SUBSIDIZED INDUSTRY

1.2.1 *Medicare and Medicalization*

Common retellings of American legal history situate a more fully formed sense of national identity across states in the post-Civil War period, the origins of the federal administrative state in Progressive Era responses to industrialization, and a centrally funded social safety net in New Deal and Great Society commitments. Medicare, enacted in 1965, was seen by many as the medical completion of Social Security's promise of income support for workers reaching retirement age.[9]

7 William M. Sage, Relating Health Law to Health Policy: A Frictional Account, in Oxford Handbook of U.S. Health Law 3–28 (I. Glenn Cohen et al. eds., 2016).

8 Elizabeth Tobin-Tyler & Joel B. Teitelbaum, Essentials of Health Justice: A Primer (2019); Dayna Bowen Matthew, Just Medicine: A Cure for Racial Inequality in American Health Care (2015); Lindsay F. Wiley, From Patient Rights to Health Justice: Securing the Public's Interest in Affordable, High-Quality Health Care, 37 Cardozo L. Rev. 833 (2016).

9 David Blumenthal & James A. Morone, The Heart of Power: Health and Politics in the Oval Office (2010).

By channeling massive, permanent financial support to the American medical profession and those who supply its work, Medicare heralded a golden era of patient care. For achieving broader public goals of individual and population health, however, "Gilded Age" may better describe the Medicare half-century.[10] Medicare's political settlement with organized medicine reconstructed US health care governance around a precarious balance of national industrial support and deference to professional judgment. Compromise was accomplished in part by replicating forms of private health insurance that were unthreatening to physicians – which amplified organized medicine's longstanding fetishization of "choice" on both the doctor's and the patient's side of the therapeutic relationship and set in legislative stone a fragmented form of health care delivery inattentive to nonmedical drivers of health, especially those shared within communities and populations.[11]

This pragmatic approach continued up to and beyond the Patient Protection and Affordable Care Act of 2010 (ACA or Obamacare). Aroused by both partisan and interest group politics, voters did not challenge the framing of health care as a private matter by the ACA's opponents. Rationing through "death panels" and similarly false or exaggerated accusations of intended government incursion on private medical decisions became routine parts of public discourse. For fear of backlash, even the Obama administration never came closer to social solidarity than informed consumerism in its pro-ACA messaging.[12] As a result, the ACA's sweeping ambitions of remaking health care delivery and improving underlying health in addition to expanding coverage for medical services remain unfulfilled.[13]

Conceptually, the US health care system operates as an extrapolation to the population level of individual clinical encounters between skilled, ethical physicians and suffering, vulnerable patients. Roughly US$3 trillion in annual "health" expenditures derive from the services, orders, referrals, and recommendations of licensed medical professionals. From this perspective, large public investments in health are legitimate only insofar as they fit within the medical model, and there are strong incentives to "medicalize" social problems in order to let those who would help solve them cross into better-funded territory.[14] Law, particularly private law

[10] William M. Sage, Adding Principle to Pragmatism: The Transformative Potential of "Medicare-for-All," 20 Yale J. Health Pol'y L. & Ethics 1 (2021).

[11] Charles D. Weller, "Free Choice" as a Restraint of Trade in American Health Care Delivery and Insurance, 69 Iowa L. Rev. 1351, 1356 (1984).

[12] President Barack Obama, Remarks by the President on the Supreme Court's Ruling on the Affordable Care Act (June 25, 2015), https://obamawhitehouse.archives.gov/the-press-office/2015/06/25/remarks-president-supreme-courts-ruling-affordable-care-act (https://perma.cc/NW89-RRFZ).

[13] William M. Sage, Putting Insurance Reform in the ACA's Rear-View Mirror, 51 Hous. L. Rev. 1082 (2014).

[14] William M. Sage & Jennifer E. Laurin, If You Would Not Criminalize Poverty, Do Not Medicalize It, 46 J.L. Med. & Ethics 573 (2018); Craig Konnoth, Medicalization and the New Civil Rights, 72 Stan. L. Rev. 1165 (2020).

governing the organizational and financial relationships among private parties, is constitutive of this health policy orientation.

As a policy matter, the dense matrix of legal obligation in which US health care is embedded perpetuates inefficiency, trapping within medical practice organizations and the nonprofit sector massive economic value that could be redeployed both privately (as lower prices for consumers) and publicly (as explicit commitments to health beyond medical services).[15] An important question for policymakers today is whether the recent, large-scale engagement of "private equity" firms with the rapidly consolidating health care sector is mobilizing and appropriating these economic reserves, and whether – if that is the case – any of it can be reclaimed for public purposes.

1.2.2 *Physician Primacy and the Paradox of Hospitals*

Legal governance of the US health care system still relies heavily on a fiduciary model of professional service, applying self-regulatory standards to clinicians' dedication and skill, often construing equity as a matter of ethics and charitable obligation, basing payment on properly coded point-of-service claims for disaggregated care processes, and requiring a multitude of complex contracts among individuals, nonprofit organizations, and business corporations to both enable performance and assure compliance.[16]

Post-Medicare industrialization, technological innovation, and financial opportunism have added to legal complexity and potential conflict in multiple domains, often making physicians feel exploited or marginalized.[17] The nursing profession faces even greater risks of "burnout" as the COVID-19 pandemic recedes.[18] But the fundamental legal grounding of the health care system remains relational (i.e., private and professional), not regulatory (i.e., public and collective) – and therefore is subject primarily to private legal action and resolution.[19]

15 William M. Sage, Fracking Health Care: The Need to Safely De-Medicalize America and Recover Trapped Value for Its People, 11 N.Y.U. J. L. & Liberty 635 (2017).

16 William M. Sage, Assembled Products: The Key to More Effective Competition and Antitrust Oversight in Health Care, 101 Cornell L. Rev.609 (2016); Rand E. Rosenblatt, The Four Ages of Health Law, 14 Health Matrix 155 (2004).

17 Nat'l Acads. of Sci., Eng'g, and Med., Taking Action Against Clinician Burnout: A Systems Approach to Professional Well-Being (2019), https://doi.org/10.17226/25521.

18 Nat'l Acads. of Sci,, Eng'g, and Med., The Future of Nursing 2020–2030: Charting a Path to Achieve Health Equity (Mary K. Wakefield et al. eds., 2021), https://doi.org/10.17226/25982 (https://perma.cc/RK45-X5SC); Allison Squires et al., "Should I Stay or Should I Go?" Nurses' Perspectives about Working during the COVID-19 Pandemic's First Wave in the United States: A Summative Content Analysis Combined with Topic Modeling, 131 Int. J. Nurs. Stud. (July 2022), www.ncbi.nlm.nih.gov/pmc/articles/PMC9020864/.

19 Lindsay F. Wiley, The Struggle for the Soul of Public Health, 41 J. Pol., Pol'y & L. 1083 (2016); William M. Sage, Relational Duties, Regulatory Duties, and the Widening Gap between Individual Health Law and Collective Health Policy, 96 Geo. L.J. 497 (2008).

American hospitals, which comprise trillions of dollars of asset value and generate hundreds of billions of dollars of annual income, are emblematic of the cognitive dissonance inherent in the US health care system. Acute care hospitals in the United States are redoubtable facilities replete with advanced technology and specialized, trained professionals who perform delicate procedures and administer sophisticated medication to patients with serious illnesses and injuries. If "private" were in fact an accurate descriptor, hospitals would be integrated enterprises within a market-based system that produce these complex clinical services and deliver them at competitive prices. Although some US hospital companies operate abroad more or less on this model, virtually none do so here at home.[20]

Instead, US hospitals have served variously as fee-free workshops for loosely affiliated physicians, as community resources, or as hubs for education and technology-driven research. The most financially successful hospitals thrive on nonoperating income, including charitable donations that support ever larger and more lavish physical facilities. With respect to operating income, hospitals focus intently on generating revenues, which on the private side typically originate from pass-through organizations that administer claims for coverage sponsored by self-insured employers, rather than from hard-nosed buyers purchasing for their own accounts. Because government coverage (Medicare and Medicaid) applies "administered prices" that offer hospitals less money for clinical services than do private payers, a favorable or unfavorable "payer mix" rather than managing production costs or offering higher quality services typically makes the difference between success and financial failure.

The longstanding legal partition of most hospitals from the physicians who practice within their walls has further drained hospitals of both motivation and authority to manage the cost and quality of the care they offer. For decades, physicians kept hospitals under their control, aided by state case law and statutes prohibiting physician employment as the "corporate practice of medicine," and by other laws declaring that patient care decisions, including the awarding of "privileges" to use hospital resources, be made by self-governing "medical staffs" legally independent of hospital executives. It is a major point of hypocrisy for physicians who routinely oppose "socialized medicine" that, for generations, they have paid nothing to utilize surgical suites, diagnostic services, and hospital facilities for patient care that generates lucrative professional fees.[21]

At the same time, US hospitals have little systematic public accountability – even though public subsidy through grants, tax-favored charitable contribution, and tax-exempt bond financing has been primarily responsible for hospital construction and

[20] I. Glenn Cohen, Patients with Passports: Medical Tourism, Law, and Ethics (2014).

[21] Uwe Reinhardt, Wanted: A Clearly Articulated Social Ethic for American Health Care, 278 JAMA 1446 (1997) (letters to the editor and author's reply at 279 JAMA 745 (1998)).

capital expansion, and even though clinical revenues from public payers support major chunks of their operating budgets. Outside of intermittent allegations of financial malfeasance involving government programs ("fraud and abuse"), emergency care access obligations under the Emergency Treatment and Labor Act (EMTALA), and rare instances of criminal prosecution involving patient care, hospitals are seldom charged with violating explicit public duties.

Hospitals respond mainly to reputational concerns and the commercial and legal risks associated with particular patients, physicians, payers, and business partners. As a result, hospitals have been drawn repeatedly into transactions and disputes governed by private law – usually as a by-product of their relationships with physicians. Hospitals are frequently defendants in antitrust lawsuits brought by physicians denied medical staff privileges or by other parties alleging anticompetitive activities. And hospitals expend extraordinary resources negotiating payment agreements with their own suppliers and with third-party payers for care they deliver (i.e., private health insurers), which takes account of physicians' continuing professional authority without running afoul of intricate and ever-changing rules concerning potential fraud or abuse.

Malpractice claims against physicians often implicate hospitals because the riskiest, most technologically advanced, and most expensive care takes place in hospital settings. Disputes over insurance coverage of services that have been recommended to patients by physicians center on hospitals for similar reasons. Hospitals also must navigate legally and ethically complicated situations involving care at the beginning and end of life, few of which have been governed by public law.

Today, hospitals are on a steep learning curve with respect to their post-pandemic workforces. The very different management approaches and financial incentives that they historically have applied to physicians, nurses, and other staff are now converging on an employment model, with private law doing most of the work defining and adjusting that model.[22]

1.3 REGULATORY DYNAMICS AS STRUCTURAL REINFORCERS OF PRIVATE HEALTH LAW

Given the intimacy associated with medical need and the substitution of professional for familial caregivers at times of greatest personal vulnerability, a governance model drawn from private law that assigns primacy to physicians might be psychologically appealing whatever the government's actual role. Still, identifiable regulatory dynamics tend to perpetuate confusion about how much public funding the

[22] Carol K. Kane, Policy Research Perspectives: Updated Data on Physician Practice Arrangements: For the First Time, Fewer Physicians Are Owners than Employees, Am. Med. Ass'n, 6 (2019), https://www.ama-assn.org/system/files/2019-07/prp-fewer-owners-benchmark-survey-2018.pdf (https://perma.cc/8ZD4–5XZD).

health care system absorbs and what that sizeable investment should accomplish – which the country's prevailing political polarization, including urban–rural divides within many states, exacerbates.

1.3.1 *Federalism*

In brokering a compromise on the constitutionality of the ACA's "individual mandate" (and, in related language, its Medicaid expansion) in 2012, Chief Justice John Roberts offered a familiar conservative defense of American federalism as protecting individual freedom. "The Commerce Clause," he stated, "is not a general license to regulate an individual from cradle to grave, simply because he will predictably engage in particular transactions. Any police power to regulate individuals as such, as opposed to their activities, remains vested in the States."[23] Even as nationally important and expensive a project as health care could not constitutionally be declared a federal matter.

One cannot overstate the extent to which state law has centered the health care system on private therapeutic relationships. During the late nineteenth and early twentieth centuries, the traditional "police powers" of state government to regulate health and safety were applied increasingly through licensing of individuals and facilities, largely disconnecting medical care from public hygiene, and entrusting the former to professional self-regulation. State health law is therefore presumptively oriented toward private physicians and their patients, while relying on professionally controlled licensing boards to define misconduct and on state courts to enforce professionally based standards of care in specific cases of alleged harm.

The national role in health governance, by contrast, has primarily involved payment for services authorized to be prescribed or delivered under state law (with the Food and Drug Administration's [FDA's] national authority over the safety and effectiveness of drugs and medical devices the exception that proves the rule). Federal intervention is also almost entirely a product of the half-century since Medicare was enacted under professional pressure as a passive, blank-check form of "socialized medicine" – whereas state health law has a much longer and more intrusive history. Medicare regulation has grown substantially over the years, but much of it operates indirectly through state-based oversight processes and national self-regulatory entities such as the Joint Commission.

It is true that Medicare payment policy today sets the tone for payment under employer-based private coverage. It is equally true, however, that Medicare has generally stayed in the lane defined for it by the conventional health insurance model of physician-dictated, medically coded claims – again conceptualizing health care as an aggregation of private transactions rather than a public commitment in service of public goals. Medicare has almost never directly challenged state health

[23] Nat'l Fed. of Indep. Bus. v. Sebelius, 567 U.S. 519 (2012).

laws to better serve its beneficiaries and the public – such as by liberalizing scope of practice or improving hospitals' response to medical errors.[24]

1.3.2 *Fiscal Politics*

Politicians who raise taxes or promote "big government" usually lose elections. Even legislators who vote for popular (and, to nearly all economists, necessary) aid packages during times of acknowledged economic crisis such as the Great Recession of the late 2000s or the COVID-19 pandemic risk the public turning against them when normalcy returns.

When Medicare was enacted in 1965, the federal Budget Control Act was nearly a decade in the future and the fiscal infrastructure of government policymaking was minimal. The votes that passed Medicare were motivated by the merits of Medicare. By the time the Clinton administration's health reform proposal was defeated in 1994, however, extensive budget control requirements had been placed in both federal law and the procedural rules of Congress. Since then, legislation in essence has to secure passage twice – once on its substance, and again on its effects on federal financial obligations as "scored" by the Congressional Budget Office (CBO).[25]

Politicians of both parties therefore have strong incentives to hide public spending on health care behind a curtain of ostensibly private conduct. One sees this not only in the US health care system's reliance on tax-subsidized, employer-based coverage and private nonprofit hospitals but also in how budget-strapped public schools and health departments try to offload financial responsibility for care delivery onto premium dollars that flow through the health insurance sector. Similar considerations lead legislators to shift money in other off-budget ways, such as by changing rules regarding market exclusivity for intellectual property (e.g., prescription drugs). A side-effect of these strategies is to expand the importance of private law in determining how health insurers, health care providers, suppliers, and a host of intermediaries transact business.

President Clinton's proposed Health Security Act never even reached a vote. It died on the day that the CBO concluded (reluctantly, as its rules were not intended for evaluating such major changes in national policy) that requiring private employers to transfer funds to private health plans through regional nonprofit "alliances" should be considered an exercise of sovereign power – immediately

[24] William M. Sage & Eleanor D. Kinney, Medicare-Led Malpractice Reform, in Medical Malpractice and the U.S. Health Care System 318–49 (William M. Sage & Rogan Kersh eds., 2006).

[25] Timothy M. Westmoreland, Invisible Forces at Work: Health Legislation and Budget Processes, in The Oxford Handbook of U.S. Health Law 873–91 (I. Glenn Cohen et al. eds., 2017).

converting the dollar value of all existing private coverage into a massive, politically intolerable federal tax hike.[26] The ACA avoided a similar fate in CBO scoring through artful drafting and a bit of luck, but in return incurred a high degree of litigation risk because it placed greater obligations on private parties and politically diverse states. That tradeoff was responsible in large part for the ACA's prolonged and repeated scrutiny in the US Supreme Court.[27]

1.3.3 *Interest Groups*

Redistribution of public resources is part of nearly every major government decision and is greater in US health care than in any other context except overall tax policy. The Medicare program alone contributes approximately 24 percent of total national health care spending, with Medicaid adding another 19 percent. The vast majority of this spending supports private activities that (unlike, say, defense spending) are used by members of the public rather than by government itself, and very little is subject to competitive bidding.

The most pronounced, and clearly inflationary, transfers are from tax revenues (or equivalent borrowing) to medical special interest groups – what has sometimes been called the "medical-industrial complex."[28] Because the recipients of government payments for medical goods and services are generally reputable private health care providers, suppliers, and insurance intermediaries, these transfers have a side benefit of increasing political support for what might otherwise be viewed as excessive or misguided charity. Moreover, the absence of a coherent national health insurance or care system in the United States means that there is no collective political interest in questioning aggregate expenditures or weighing the comparative benefit of spending on medical care versus other areas.

Medical interest groups expend enormous energy (and funds) to secure their slice of this very large pie and to resist efforts by others to wrest it away. Having one's services covered by Medicare (and, therefore, also by private insurers), and having Medicare pay a generous price, is the sine qua non of success among private health care providers – and, to be fair, among patient groups seeking the best-trained specialists and most advanced technologies for diagnosis and treatment. Medicare "payment reform" is therefore an endless and often fruitless endeavor – as the

26 Robert D. Reischauer, Testimony of the Director of the Congressional Budget Office to the House Energy Committee, Subcommittee on Health and the Environment, regarding the Clinton Health Plan (Feb. 10, 1994).

27 William M. Sage & Timothy M. Westmoreland, Following the Money: The ACA's Fiscal-Political Economy and Lessons for Future Health Care Reform, 48 J.L. Med. & Ethics 434 (2020).

28 William M. Sage, Minding Ps and Qs: The Political and Policy Questions Framing Health Care Spending, 44 J.L. Med. & Ethics 559 (2016); Bruce C. Vladeck, The Political Economy of Medicare, 18 Health Affs. 22 (Jan.–Feb. 1999).

enduring power of Medicare's physician-dominated Relative-Value Update Committee (RUC) to "recommend" generous payment for specialty services using the American Medical Association's (AMA's) own copyrighted CPT codes amply attests.[29] In addition, Medicare's interest-group politics tend to freeze in place state law because Medicare funding relies so heavily on the distinctions that state law makes among health care professionals and between those professionals and health care facilities.

The politics of drafting statutes and regulations in the United States gives these private parties and their lobbyists a very strong voice in forming ostensibly public law, which they deploy for their private advantage, and which carries over to their private agreements and disputes. Private jockeying for public financial support also co-opts much of the informational infrastructure of the US health care system. Information in the health care system is collected primarily to secure payment for codable claims, and only incidentally for safety, quality, cost management, or community/population health improvement. Health-related social services suffer particularly because they seldom fit a clinician-driven, professionally coded, claims-based model.

1.3.4 *Constitutionalism*

American constitutionalism tends to reinforce perceptions of US health care as private. A Constitution that emphasizes – both structurally and in the Bill of Rights – protection against restrictions imposed by government rather than receipt of assistance from government can seem (and may be) inhospitable to efforts that seek to formalize health care as a collective investment and health as a collective asset. This bias includes the state-federal divisions of authority that the Constitution imposes – which perpetuate deference to professional self-regulation at the state level and empower state courts of general jurisdiction to make what are effectively public policy decisions based on the facts and equities in private lawsuits.

The ACA survived constitutional review by the skin of its teeth, suffering significant if not irreparable harm to its core purposes of universalizing coverage, streamlining care, and improving population health. Moreover, the legal-political process of litigating the ACA on both constitutional and statutory grounds resulted in a substantial strengthening by a conservative Supreme Court majority of individual and states' rights.[30] The backlash against public health mandates during the COVID-19 pandemic led to even stricter judicial limits on collective health strategies as exceeding federal administrative authority or as infringements of individual

[29] Miriam Laugesen, Fixing Medical Prices: How Doctors Are Paid (2016).

[30] Nat'l Inst. of Family and Life Advocs. v. Becerra, 585 U.S. 755 (2018); Burwell v. Hobby Lobby Stores, Inc., 573 U.S. 682 (2014).

rights of speech and religion (though not of arguably parallel rights regarding reproductive freedom).[31]

Private law governance sidesteps many, if not all, of these constitutional concerns. For example, private entities, including hospitals and universities, can attempt to address health care misinformation and disinformation in ways that government itself, including professional licensing boards, generally cannot.[32] In addition, private employers sponsoring insurance coverage are usually governed by the federal Employee Retirement Income Security Act (ERISA), potentially preempting conflicting state laws regarding controversial clinical services such as abortion or transgender care.[33]

1.4 CONCLUSION

About fifteen years ago, I speculated that the US health care system might never shift from a relational to a regulatory footing absent a severe shock such as an economic collapse or a crisis of communicable disease.[34] We have had both events since then, with at least a partial public response. There probably would have been no ACA without the global recession that preceded it, nor would so many people retain health insurance coverage today absent the COVID-19 pandemic.

But fundamental change has proved elusive – in part because those who profit from existing arrangements cloak themselves in the undoubted virtue of skilled physicians and nurses while younger generations of those professionals have yet to convey a sense of ethical urgency to the public.[35] The COVID-19 pandemic revealed many unfortunate truths about the US health care system's dependence on private pathways to serve public purposes, but even that tragedy has failed to generate much productive policy debate.[36] The cognitive dissonance remains, along with the flaws it perpetuates.

I therefore end on a sober note. Private law in the current health care environment is not necessarily forward-looking and offers no assurances of solidarity, of justice, or even of progress in the vital project of maintaining America's health in the face of population aging, climate change, and political or economic instability. Even the pronounced trend since the Great Recession, in both scholarship and

[31] Roman Catholic Diocese of Brooklyn v. Cuomo, 141 S.Ct. 63 (2020).

[32] Hoeg v. Newsom (E.D. Cal. Jan. 25, 2023), https://nclalegal.org/wp-content/uploads/2023/01/Hoeg-v.-Newsom-PI-Decision.pdf; William M. Sage & Y. Tony Yang, Reducing "COVID Misinformation" While Preserving Free Speech, 327 JAMA 1443 (2022), https://jamanetwork.com/journals/jama/fullarticle/2790859.

[33] Brendan S. Maher, Pro-Choice Plans, 91 Geo. Wash. L. Rev. 446 (2023).

[34] William M. Sage, Solidarity, in Connecting American Values with American Health Care Reform 10–12 (Thomas H. Murray & Mary Crowley eds., 2009); Sage, supra note 19.

[35] Donald M. Berwick, The Moral Determinants of Health, 324 JAMA 225, 225–26 (2020).

[36] William M. Sage, What the Pandemic Taught Us: The Health Care System We Have Is Not the System We Hoped We Had, 82 Ohio St. L.J. 857 (2021).

practice, to make explicit the public responsibilities of the corporate sector now faces a backlash.[37] On the other hand, as many authors in this volume explain, private law presents a variety of opportunities for decentralized improvements (which, after all, is the central premise of the "Triple/Quadruple Aim") as well as creating some possibilities for systematic effect.[38] We should make the most of them.

37 Compare Donald C. Langevoort, The Social Construction of Sarbanes-Oxley, 105 Mich. L. Rev. 1817 (2007) to Marc Andreesen, The Techno-Optimist Manifesto (Oct. 18, 2023), The Techno-Optimist Manifesto | Andreessen Horowitz (a16z.com).

38 Rishi Sikka, Julianne M. Morath & Lucian Leape, The Quadruple Aim: Care, Health, Cost and Meaning in Work, 24 BMJ Quality & Safety 608 (2015).

2

Private Ordering Is Ubiquitous in Health Care, but Why?

Barbara J. Evans

2.1 INTRODUCTION

Twenty years ago, Lester Salamon noted "the extent to which actual public problem solving has come to embrace the collaborative actions of government . . . and private organizations – both for-profit and nonprofit."[1] He traced these "alternative instruments of public action," which engage private actors in the work of governance, back "at least two decades,"[2] corresponding to about 1980. At that time, there was growing disenchantment with top-down governmental command-and-control rule-setting amid energy shortages, environmental degradation, and concern that regulated industries sometimes capture their regulators.[3] Research overseen by the US Public Health Service had, by the early 1970s, produced shocking revelations about the Tuskegee Syphilis Study, undermining people's faith that the government is any better at protecting individual rights than private-sector Institutional Review Boards (IRBs) would be.[4] An expansion of social programs in the mid-twentieth century stretched the role of the state far beyond its traditional governmental functions,[5] making it plausible that lessons from the private sector might be relevant to public governance.

All these factors fueled the rise of private ordering, which Steven Schwarcz defines as a "broad spectrum" of alternatives to having "rules of law originated and

[1] Lester M. Salamon, The Tools of Government: A Guide to the New Governance vii (Lester M. Salamon ed., 2002).

[2] Id.

[3] José A. Gómez-Ibáñez, Regulating Infrastructure: Monopoly, Contracts, and Discretion 41–48 (2003).

[4] Kayte Spector-Bagdady, Governing Secondary Research Use of Health Data and Specimens: The Inequitable Distribution of Regulatory Burden between Federally Funded and Industry Research, 8 J.L. & Biosciences 2–3, 6–8 (Jan.–June 2021).

[5] See, e.g., 49 U.S.C. § 40125(a)(2) (defining "governmental functions" as including activities such as national defense, intelligence gathering, law enforcement, and firefighting).

put into force by sovereign governments."[6] Health care, as a heavily regulated industry, offers fertile soil for privately ordered alternatives to governmental regulation, and William Sage observes that "'private law' in its many forms plays an outsized role in American health governance."[7] This raises a question: Why? Does private ordering in US health care simply mirror a trend that swept many economic sectors after 1980, or is the trend uniquely amplified in health care? Does it reflect, as Professor Sage suggests, a "cognitive dissonance" between health care's lusty appetite for public financing and its deep distaste for public control?[8] Is it a charade that helps politicians conceal vast "public spending on health care behind a curtain of ostensibly private conduct"?[9] Is it, perhaps, required by constitutional constraints on what government actors can do?

This chapter explores this last possibility but discounts the role federalism plays in forcing private ordering. Courts have generally proved unreceptive to arguments that the federal government lacks power to regulate the practice of medicine.[10] Even if courts were receptive to such arguments, federalism merely divides responsibilities between federal public ordering and state public ordering; it is agnostic on whether private ordering is superior to both those alternatives. Federalism thus cannot explain the outsized role private ordering plays in health care. This chapter focuses instead on constitutional speech protections, which bind the federal and state governments alike and which leave room for private actors to oversee medical speech and information flows in ways public agencies cannot do.

2.2 THE PREVALENCE AND VARIETY OF PRIVATE ORDERING SOLUTIONS IN HEALTH CARE

Health care displays a striking diversity of private ordering solutions that engage private actors in the work of governance. Some of the variants seen in health care predate the post-1980 rise of private ordering, making health care one of the early proving grounds for private ordering models. This section samples health care's breathtaking array of private ordering solutions as a prelude to Section 2.3, which explores sector-specific considerations that favor private ordering.

It is useful to state what private ordering is *not*. As conceived in this chapter, private ordering is not the same thing as decisional privacy, which connotes "a realm of personal liberty which the government may not enter,"[11] wherein individuals are

6 Steven L. Schwarcz, Private Ordering, 97 Nw. U. L. Rev. 319, 325 (2002).
7 Chapter 1 in this volume, at 7.
8 Id. at 9.
9 Id. at 15.
10 David G. Adams, The Food and Drug Administration's Regulation of Health Care Professionals, in 2 Fundamentals of Law and Regulation: An In-Depth Look at Therapeutic Products 423, 424–25 (David G. Adams et al. eds., 1999).
11 Planned Parenthood of Southeastern Pennsylvania v. Casey, 505 U.S. 833, 847 (1992).

free to make decisions in line with their own consciences and without governmental interference. Decisional privacy is a regime without externally imposed rules, leaving individuals to make whatever decisions they prefer (e.g., to consent or not to consent to share their data, to pierce or not to pierce their navels, or to seek or not to seek an abortion) in a cherished realm of private disorder. Private ordering, in contrast, is a framework for creating binding rules that at times may constrain individual choice. It differs from traditional governmental rule-setting by enlisting private actors to help set those rules. Once established, privately made rules sometimes call on individuals to do things they would prefer not to do, or demand that they refrain from actions they view as desirable – as also happens with government-set rules. Private ordering gives private actors a voice in setting the rules but does not leave them free to do whatever they please.

A well-known instance of private ordering is the role private accreditation bodies play in determining whether health care facilities qualify to receive payments under the Medicare and Medicaid programs.[12] The Centers for Medicare and Medicaid Services (CMS), which administers these programs, allows hospitals and other health care facilities to establish eligibility to participate in them by undergoing accreditation by private bodies that CMS approves.[13] Accredited health care facilities do not need to undergo formal governmental regulatory inspections.[14] When challenged in court, this arrangement was held not to be an improper delegation of governmental authority to private actors, because the Secretary of the US Department of Human and Health Services (HHS) retains ultimate authority over decisions to certify or decertify participation in the Medicare and Medicaid programs.[15] In practice, however, the Secretary rarely, if ever, asserts this theoretical authority to override private accreditors' decisions. Timothy Stoltzfus Jost traces this reliance on private accreditation bodies back to the early years of the Medicare program, when heavy resistance from health care providers threatened to derail the program.[16] Private accreditation, as a form of industry self-regulation, seemed less intrusive than direct federal control of Medicare-eligible facilities and elicited their buy-in. It was, in Professor Sage's phrase, a "political settlement."[17]

[12] Schwarcz, supra note 6, at 320–21; Clark C. Havighurst, Foreword: The Place of Private Accrediting among the Instruments of Government, 57 Law & Contemp. Probs. 647 (Autumn 1994).

[13] See Karen S. Rieger, Medical Staff Fundamentals, in 1 Health Law Practice Guide §§ 2:5–2:10 (Alice G. Gosfield et al. eds., 2d ed. 2021).

[14] Id. § 2:6.

[15] Cospito v. Heckler, 742 F.2d 72, 87–88 (3rd Cir. 1984), 471 U.S. 1131 (1985) (cert. denied).

[16] Timothy Stoltzfus Jost, Medicare and the Joint Commission on Accreditation of Healthcare Organizations: A Healthy Relationship?, 57 Law & Contemp. Probs. 15, 23–24 (Autumn 1994).

[17] Chapter 1 in this volume, at 10.

CMS also administers the Clinical Laboratory Improvement Amendments of 1988 (CLIA)[18] regulations,[19] which govern clinical laboratories that perform diagnostic tests used in clinical health care. CLIA is intriguing because it lets regulated entities choose how much public or private ordering they prefer. Nonexempt[20] laboratories conducting moderate- and high-complexity tests can, at their discretion, elect to pursue either a certificate of compliance or a certificate of accreditation.[21] Those choosing a certificate of compliance follow government-set standards and undergo periodic inspections by state agencies to which CMS delegates local inspection responsibilities.[22] Those choosing a certificate of accreditation follow standards set by various CMS-approved private accreditors, which carry out inspections to ensure compliance.[23]

It is wrong to assume private regulation is laxer than its governmental counterpart. At times, private ordering is more stringent. For example, CLIA's concept of high-complexity testing arguably understates the true complexity of genetic and genomic tests. In 1997, a federal advisory body urged the Clinical Laboratory Improvement Advisory Committee (CLIAC), which advises CMS on CLIA matters, to consider creating specialty requirements for genetic testing,[24] and CMS received citizens' petitions supporting this idea.[25] CMS rejected these calls, leaving this superlatively complex type of testing under the same general rules that govern other high-complexity tests. Private accreditation bodies such as the College of American Pathologists have worked to fill this gap in public regulation by developing private standards specifically addressing genetic and genomic testing.[26] Unfortunately, some

[18] Pub. L. No. 100-578, 102 Stat. 2903 (codified as amended at 42 U.S.C. § 263a).

[19] 42 C.F.R. § 493.

[20] See List of Exempt States under the Clinical Laboratory Improvement Amendments (CLIA), Ctrs. for Medicare & Medicaid Servs. (May 30, 2022), https://www.cms.gov/regulations-and-guidance/legislation/clia/downloads/exemptstateslist.pdf (exempting clinical laboratories in Washington and New York from CLIA because CMS deems their state laboratory regulations to satisfy CLIA's requirements).

[21] Types of CLIA Certificates, Ctrs. for Medicare & Medicaid Servs. (May 29, 2005), https://www.cms.gov/regulations-and-guidance/legislation/clia/downloads/types_of_clia_certificates.pdf.

[22] Clinical Laboratory Improvement Amendments (CLIA) State Agency Contacts, Ctrs. for Medicare & Medicaid Servs. (Dec. 18, 2023), https://www.cms.gov/regulations-and-guidance/legislation/clia/downloads/cliasa.pdf.

[23] List of Approved Accreditation Organizations under the Clinical Laboratory Improvement Amendments (CLIA), Ctrs. for Medicare & Medicaid Servs. (May 30, 2022), https://www.cms.gov/regulations-and-guidance/legislation/clia/downloads/aolist.pdf.

[24] National Institutes of Health-Department of Energy Working Group on Ethical, Legal & Social Implications of Human Genome Research, Task Force on Genetic Testing, Promoting Safe and Effective Genetic Testing in the United States 30 (N. A. Holtzman & M. S. Watson eds., 1997).

[25] Kathy L. Hudson, Petition Requesting a Genetic Testing Specialty and Standards for Proficiency Testing, Public Citizen (Sept. 26, 2006), https://www.citizen.org/article/petition-requesting-a-genetic-testing-specialty-and-standards-for-proficiency-testing.

[26] Nazneen Aziz et al., College of American Pathologists' Laboratory Standards for Next-Generation Sequencing Clinical Tests, 139 Archives of Pathology & Lab'y Med. 481–93 (2015).

laboratories conduct genomic tests under a CLIA certificate of compliance and are governed by less rigorous public standards.[27]

Private ordering spans a spectrum of approaches. At the more formal end of the spectrum are examples, including those just given, that Steven Schwarcz describes as rules "put into force by private actors pursuant to governmental delegation."[28] Professor Schwarcz recognizes a second, somewhat less formal type of private ordering where the rules are "originated by private actors but put into force by sovereign governments."[29] Health care offers many examples. For example, hospitals and vendors negotiate private contracts but look to courts (public bodies) to enforce them. Courts look to medical experts (private actors) to establish the standard of care that courts (public bodies) enforce in medical malpractice actions.

An instructive example is the US Food and Drug Administration's (FDA) reliance on independent advisory committees, created by statute or at the discretion of the Secretary of HHS and staffed with individual experts, to prepare recommendations on scientific, technical, and policy matters.[30] These committees allow the agency to tap a breadth of sector-specific expertise that may not exist among civil servants. While their advice is not binding on the agency, a recent study of prescription drug decisions found that the agency follows advisory committee votes 88 percent of the time.[31] The 88 percent of advisory committee recommendations that the FDA chooses to implement become privately ordered rules "originated by private actors and put into force by"[32] the FDA, but the agency retains discretion to reject recommendations and does so 12 percent of the time. Not all private recommendations become rules in this private ordering scheme.

In the same way, not all private contracts are enforceable in health care – for example, you cannot sell your newborn or your kidney, even if you are a willing seller and find a willing buyer. Private contracts play a major role in governance of health care just as they do in all industries, but health care exhibits a constant tug-of-war between freedom of contract and welfare-enhancing public constraints on that freedom. Thus, the states limit physicians' freedom to ask patients to waive their right to bring malpractice suits, either through restrictions that state medical practice acts impose on the use of medical liability waivers or through judicial determinations that waivers are coercive and void as against public policy.[33] The Health

[27] Barbara J. Evans et al., How Can Law and Policy Advance Quality in Genomic Analysis and Interpretation for Clinical Care?, 48 J.L. Med. & Ethics 44, 53 (2020).

[28] Schwarcz, supra note 6, at 325.

[29] Id.

[30] Advisory Committees, U.S. Food & Drug Admin., https://www.fda.gov/advisory-committees.

[31] C. Joseph Ross Daval et al., Association of Advisory Committee Votes with US Food and Drug Administration Decision-Making on Prescription Drugs, 2010–2021, 4 JAMA Health Forum e231718 (July 2023).

[32] Schwarcz, supra note 6, at 325.

[33] See, e.g., Tunkl v. Regents of the University of California, 60 Cal.2d 92, 383 P.2d 441 (1963).

Insurance Portability and Accountability Act[34] (HIPAA) Privacy Rule[35] requires health care providers to sign Business Associate Agreements and Data Use Agreements providing contractual privacy protections for data they share with certain data users, but it leaves the specific terms of those agreements largely open to private negotiations between the provider and the data recipient.[36] Federal laws addressing Medicare fraud limit health care providers' ability to enter various contractual arrangements (such as agreeing to give and receive discounts on services provided) that would be perfectly normal and uncontroversial in other business settings.[37] Health care's ambivalence about contractual ordering reflects the reality that individuals operating in the health care sector, however autonomous they may be, are engaged in activities that may leave some of the parties vulnerable or implicate broader public interests (such as keeping Medicare expenditures within reasonable bounds).

At the least formal extreme of private ordering, Professor Schwarcz recognizes rules that are "adopted by private actors without governmental sanction or enforcement."[38] These call to mind Robert Ellickson's work on sources of control, other than governments, that can create rules and incentives to comply with them.[39] Professor Ellickson's "controllers" include (1) ethical principles that foster internal self-control (e.g., voluntary codes, such as the American Medical Association's Code of Medical Ethics,[40] to which members of a professional community bind themselves); (2) contractual rules formed through interpersonal negotiations (e.g., a Data Use Agreement requiring special privacy protections and restricting how a researcher can use health data supplied by a hospital),[41] (3) norms that emerge from social forces (e.g., standard practices, customs, and professional etiquette in clinical care settings); and (4) organizational rules (e.g., institutional policies that hospitals voluntarily adopt to protect patients and research participants in ways that go beyond what law requires).[42] All of these sources of nongovernmental control are at work in health care.

Depending on the type of private ordering scheme, compliance may be more or less of a problem. When, as in Professor Schwarcz's first two private ordering schemes, the private rules are "put into force by" governments or "made pursuant

34 Health Insurance Portability and Accountability Act of 1996, Pub. L. No. 104–191, 110 Stat. 1936 (codified as amended in scattered sections of 18, 26, 29, and 42 U.S.C.).

35 45 C.F.R. pts. 160, 164.

36 Barbara J. Evans, The HIPAA Privacy Rule at Age 25: Privacy for Equitable AI, 50 FSU L. Rev. 741, 802 (2023).

37 Medicare Fraud and Abuse (Anti-kickback) Statute, 42 U.S.C. § 1320a-7b; Physician Self-referral Law (Stark Law), 42 U.S.C. § 1395nn.

38 Schwarcz, supra note 6, at 325.

39 Robert G. Ellickson, Order without Law: How Neighbors Settle Disputes 126 (1991).

40 AMA, Code of Medical Ethics, https://code-medical-ethics.ama-assn.org/.

41 See 45 C.F.R. § 164.514(e)(3)(i), (e)(4).

42 Ellickson, supra note 39, at 126–27.

to" a formal governmental delegation,[43] the state's "monopoly on official use of force"[44] lurks in the background to help ensure compliance with the privately made rules. However, when private rules are made "without governmental sanction or enforcement,"[45] there is a crucial institutional challenge to craft private decision-making structures with sufficient authority and legitimacy to induce compliance with norms that at times may go against individual preferences. Despite this, private rules that arise spontaneously without any governmental involvement often work better than one would expect, possibly because such rules tend to be welfare-enhancing (otherwise, people would not have spontaneously embraced them in the first place).[46] This is not always the case, however.

One final example hints that private ordering schemes struggle for legitimacy in situations where competing interests force private decision-makers to make difficult trade-offs. The HIPAA Privacy Rule regulates permissible flows of clinical health data and sets rules governing when personal data can be shared for various purposes. It respects decisional privacy, but in an asymmetric manner: Individuals can *authorize* the sharing of their data however they wish,[47] but they cannot *refuse* to share their data for certain uses that serve broader public interests.[48] The regulation identifies twenty-three "national priority"[49] data uses that offer sufficient benefit to society that access to personal data may be justified even without individual authorization – for example, to track epidemics, regulate medical product safety, detect domestic violence, acquit accused suspects whose defense turns on medical evidence, and promote health care quality and equity.[50]

For each of these twenty-three data uses, the regulation specifies who, precisely, is empowered to authorize unconsented data sharing in a particular instance.

43 Schwarcz, supra note 6, at 325.

44 Jonathan R. Macey, Public and Private Ordering and the Production of Legitimate and Illegitimate Legal Rules, 82 Cornell L. Rev. 1123, 1133 (1997) (citing Robert D. Cooter, Law from Order, in A Not-So Dismal Science: A Broader and Brighter Approach to Economies and Societies (J. Mancur Olson & S. Kahkonen eds., 1998)).

45 Schwarcz, supra note 6, at 325.

46 Macey, supra note 44, at 1132–33.

47 45 C.F.R. §§ 164.502(a)(1)(iv), 164.508.

48 The Privacy Rule only requires individual authorization, in the sense of treating it as a precondition of data sharing, in a few instances where the balance of public and private interests tips in favor of the individual, either because the individual's interest in privacy is unusually high (e.g., psychotherapy notes, see 45 C.F.R. § 164.508(a)(2)) or because the data use provides low benefits to society (e.g., selling data or using it for marketing). See id. §§ 502(a)(5)(ii)(B)(1), 164.508(a)(4)(i) (data sales), 164.508(a)(3) (marketing).

49 Off. of the Assistant Sec'y for Plan. & Evaluation, Confidentiality of Individually Identifiable Health Information: Recommendations of the Secretary of Health and Human Services, Pursuant to Section 264 of the Health Insurance Portability and Accountability Act of 1996, U.S. Dep't Health & Hum. Servs. § I.I (Sept. 10, 1997).

50 Evans, supra note 36, at 749–51 tbl. 1 (listing twenty-seven norms allowing patients health data to be shared under the HIPAA Privacy Rule, of which twenty-three allow unconsented access to support specific data uses deemed to offer large benefits to society).

For example, legislatures, by enacting laws, can decide that your data can be accessed, even against your wishes, for various public health uses (public ordering).[51] Courts and administrative law judges can decide that your data can be shared without consent for judicial and regulatory uses (another type of public ordering).[52] Licensed medical professionals can decide to share your data with other licensed professionals to inform the treatment of patients with similar illnesses[53] or if they believe, in good faith and consistent with medical ethical standards, that data sharing will avert serious threats to the public or to other individuals – the so-called *Tarasoff* exception (private ordering).[54] Institutional Review Boards or HIPAA Privacy Boards (together, "IRBs") can authorize unconsented research use of your data by approving a waiver (again, private ordering).[55]

Certain things can be inferred from the way the HIPAA Privacy Rule allocates authority to approve each type of unconsented data use. When a data use is especially important to society (such as tracking epidemics or ensuring accurate administration of justice), HIPAA generally favors public ordering and lets legislatures and courts decide whether an unconsented data use serves the public's interests. Individuals "consent" to the rules these bodies set in a Blackstonian sense, by consenting to be governed by the rule of law.[56] Unfortunately, public ordering is not very nimble and cannot accommodate the thousands (millions?) of granular, day-to-day decisions about specific data uses in a modern health care system. Codifying fixed legal rules to resolve all possible trade-offs in all possible circumstances is probably impossible. This reality creates a need to delegate some day-to-day decisions to local – and often private – actors such as IRBs and licensed medical professionals. The HIPAA Privacy Rule constrains the private decision-making power it grants, either by setting its own standards (such as the criteria IRBs must follow when authorizing research pursuant to a waiver)[57] or by reference to external standards (such as state laws and ethical standards that place physicians under strong fiduciary duties to handle patients' data carefully).[58]

The drafters of the HIPAA Privacy Rule undoubtedly worked hard to strike an appropriate balance between public and private ordering of these fraught data access

51 45 C.F.R. §§ 164.512(a)–(c).

52 45 C.F.R. § 164.512(e).

53 45 C.F.R. § 164.502(a)(1)(ii); see also 512 – May a provider disclose information about an individual to another provider, U.S. Dep't Health & Hum. Servs. (Jan. 13, 2009), https://www.hhs.gov/hipaa/for-professionals/faq/512/under-hipaa-may-a-health-care-provider-disclose-information-requested-for-treatment/index.html (clarifying that, except for psychotherapy notes, a HIPAA-covered doctor may disclose a patient's information to another doctor without individual authorization for use in treating "another patient" – not necessarily a family member of the patient whose data are shared).

54 45 C.F.R. § 164.512(j); Tarasoff v. Regents of the University of California, 551 P.2d 334 (1976).

55 45 C.F.R. § 164.512(i).

56 Barbara J. Evans, Much Ado about Data Ownership, 25 Harv. J.L. & Tech. 69, 126 (2011).

57 45 C.F.R. §§ 164.512(i)(2)(ii)(A)–(C).

58 See Barry R. Furrow et al., Health Law 117 (8th ed. 2018).

decisions. Even so, the HIPAA Privacy Rule is the poster child for the perils of private ordering in situations where governance requires tough trade-offs between individual rights and public interests. Privacy advocates abhor the power IRBs and other private actors wield to approve unconsented data access,[59] while there are ongoing complaints that IRBs block important research and public health data uses that would benefit society.[60] There may be strong pragmatic reasons to rely on private ordering, but there is ongoing discomfort with it. Why, in spite of this discomfort, is private ordering so prevalent in health care?

2.3 THE ROOTS OF PRIVATE ORDERING IN HEALTH CARE

The sheer variety of private ordering schemes in health care thwarts easy generalizations about why they are so prevalent. Each instance of private ordering is a response to different concerns about regulatory efficiency, buy-in from regulated entities, or the benefits of private-sector expertise to help with specific tasks. No single principle explains them all. Some instances, no doubt, reflect political compromises or follow the post-1980s fad of private ordering in all regulated industries. However, others are responses to a special problem that confronts all health care regulators, state and federal: Regulating health care easily crosses the line into regulating scientific and medical speech.

Centuries before the term "informational medicine" entered the modern lexicon, the practice of medicine has always been mainly an informational service. It involves a few activities that constitute conduct – notably, surgery, inserting catheters, and so forth – but most of the practice of medicine consists of communication: gathering and curating information relevant to a patient's case, rendering a diagnosis, recommending a treatment plan, writing prescriptions, counseling patients and their families. The practice of medicine, at its core, is a physician analyzing relevant parts of the general medical knowledge base (all the knowledge and experience gained through centuries of clinical health care and biomedical research) along with patient-specific medical information and knowledge about a patient's "predicaments, rights, and preferences"[61] to develop tailored communications customized for each particular patient.

[59] Inst. of Med., Beyond the HIPAA Privacy Rule: Enhancing Privacy, Improving Health Through Research 66 (Sharyl J. Nass et al. eds., 2009), http://www.nap.edu/catalog/12458.html.

[60] William Burman & Robert Daum, Grinding to a Halt: The Effects of the Increasing Regulatory Burden on Research and Quality Improvement Efforts, 49 Clinical Infectious Diseases 328, 328 (2009) (arguing that the role of IRBs has slowed research); Sarah L. Cutrona et al., Validation of Acute Myocardial Infarction in the Food and Drug Administration's Mini-Sentinel Program, 22 Pharmacoepidemiol Drug Safety 40, 44 (2013) (describing IRB interference with public health data uses).

[61] David L. Sackett et al., Evidence Based Medicine: What It Is and What It Isn't, 312 BMJ 71, 71–72 (1996).

As the Supreme Court confirmed in the 2018 case, *National Institute of Family and Life Advocates, dba NIFLA v. Becerra*,[62] the First Amendment affords strong protection to physicians' professional speech – the recommendations and advice licensed medical professionals utter to patients during clinical treatment encounters. The case did not resolve how strong – strict versus intermediate scrutiny – because the court felt the challenged regulation failed under either standard.[63]

Private ordering circumvents impermissible speech regulation by state actors. Moreover, it upholds a 175-year-old cultural tradition dating back to the 1847 Code of Ethics of the American Medical Association (AMA).[64] The 1847 Code conceived medicine as a knowledge-based profession, distinct from the ill-trained quacks holding themselves out as doctors in that day.[65] Claudia Haupt defines a profession as a self-governing "knowledge community" sharing "common knowledge and experience as a result of training and practice," with "shared notions of validity and a common way of knowing and reasoning."[66] From 1850 through the end of the Progressive Era, the AMA entered an uneasy collaboration with legislatures and supported state regulation of medical practice as a necessary tool to oust ill-trained healers.[67] The resulting state regulatory scheme "is commonly described as a system of self-regulation because the entities, often called 'boards,' which implement the applicable statutes are generally dominated by members of the licensed profession and often rely on customary practice of the profession for standards."[68] Since the 1850s, a self-governing medical staff has remained a central principle of US health law, featured in numerous state and federal statutes.[69] This is not just a cultural tradition or a political compromise, however. It is at times a constitutional necessity, because medical professionals can regulate medical speech, information flows, and evidentiary standards in ways government agencies cannot do.[70]

First Amendment concerns also shaped modern biomedical research oversight. In 1944, President Roosevelt sought to extend wartime research funding into

62 Nat'l Inst. of Family and Life Advoc., dba NIFLA v. Becerra, 138 S.Ct. 2361 (2018).

63 Id. at 2375.

64 See Jeffrey F. Chase-Lubitz, The Corporate Practice of Medicine Doctrine: An Anachronism in the Modern Health Care Industry, 40 Vand. L. Rev. 445, 448 n.14 (1987); James G. Burrow, Organized Medicine in the Progressive Era: The Move Toward Monopoly (1977).

65 See supra note 64.

66 Claudia E. Haupt, Professional Speech, 125 Yale L.J. 1238, 1250–51 (2016).

67 Chase-Lubitz, supra note 64, at 448; see generally Burrow, supra note 64 (describing the AMA's work with state legislatures).

68 Furrow, supra note 58, at 33; Sylvia R. Cruess & Richard L. Cruess, The Medical Profession and Self-Regulation: A Current Challenge, 7(4) Virtual Mentor: Ethics J. of the Am. Med. Ass'n 1, 1–5 (2005), https://journalofethics.ama-assn.org/sites/journalofethics.ama-assn.org/files/2018-06/oped1–0504.pdf.

69 1 Health Law Practice Guide, Ch. 2 (Medical Staff Fundamentals) (2022).

70 See NIFLA, supra note 62.

ongoing federal financing of medical and other scientific research.[71] To allay concerns that federal funding would undermine constitutionally protected freedom of scientific inquiry, the National Institutes of Health embraced its privately ordered scheme of peer-review "study sections" to select projects for funding.[72] When the Tuskegee Syphilis Study came to light in 1973, it sparked calls for greater research regulation amid concerns that regulators might infringe scientific freedom.[73] In 1974, Congress empowered a National Commission to design the research regulations now known as the Common Rule,[74] and its 1978 report recommended a significant oversight role for private IRBs.[75] While courts had not previously found a "First Amendment 'right to research,'" the Commission felt that the freedom of scientific inquiry would be likely to receive constitutional protection "if a case arose."[76] The Commission noted that "an institution may empower the IRB to apply both content and manner restrictions" on its employees as a condition of employment or receipt of research funds, "whether or not such a system would be constitutional if directly imposed by the state on nonfunded research."[77]

In the medical products area, the FDA has repeatedly faced First Amendment constraints on its power to protect patients from unsafe medical products.[78] While manufacturers cannot actively promote off-label uses of their products, FDA allows them to respond to unsolicited queries from health care professionals by sending peer-reviewed literature about off-label uses.[79] This policy appoints private actors (medical journals and their peer reviewers) to police the boundaries of acceptable speech. In the US legal system, private actors can do things that governments are not allowed to do – and these are, at times, important things that need to be done by

[71] Donald S. Fredrickson, Asilomar and Recombinant DNA: The End of the Beginning, in Committee to Study Decision Making, Inst. of Medicine, Biomedical Politics 258, 259–60 (K. E. Hanna ed., 1991).

[72] Id. at 260; see Nat'l Inst. of Health, Ctr. for Scientific Review, Study Sections (Apr. 4, 2022), https://public.csr.nih.gov/StudySections; see Lori B. Andrews, Is There a Right to Clone? Constitutional Challenges to Bans on Human Cloning, 11 Harv. J.L. & Tech. 643, 661 (1998) (grounding freedom of scientific inquiry in the First and Fourteenth Amendments); Natalie Ram, Science as Speech, 102 Iowa L. Rev. 1187, 1198 (2017) (arguing that research produces knowledge that is the basis for speech, warranting First Amendment protection).

[73] John D. Edsall, Scientific Freedom and Responsibility (1975).

[74] 45 C.F.R. pt. 46, subpt. A.

[75] U.S. Dep't of Health, Educ., & Welfare, Protection of Human Subjects: Institutional Review Boards: Report and Recommendations of the National Commission for the Protection of Human Subjects of Biomedical and Behavioral Research, 43 Fed. Reg. 56,174, 56,192 (Nov. 30, 1978).

[76] Id.

[77] Id.

[78] See Nathan Cortez, Can Speech by FDA-Regulated Firms Ever Be Non-Commercial?, 37 Am. J.L. & Med. 388 (2011) (summarizing a body of twenty-four cases in which FDA-regulated firms claimed First Amendment protection, often successfully).

[79] Michelle M. Mello et al., Shifting Terrain in the Regulation of Off-label Promotion of Pharmaceuticals, 360 New Engl. J. Med.1557–66 (2009).

someone in order to ensure a well-functioning health care system. When public regulation hits constitutional limits, private ordering helps fill regulatory gaps.

2.4 CONCLUSION

Private ordering has been baked into the fabric of US health laws dating back to their origins in the nineteenth century. This is not an aberration but a central fact of US health care oversight. Constitutional constraints on the government's power to regulate some aspects of health care make private ordering a practical necessity in certain contexts. This reality does not alter our sense of unease that health care is a vitally important economic sector posing delicate trade-offs between individual rights and competing interests. Private ordering will always make us a little uncomfortable, even if we acknowledge that it can be effective, efficient, and – at times – legally necessary. This book aims to clarify the opportunities and concerns that accompany private ordering in its many manifestations in the modern health care system.

3

Abandoning Fiduciaries in Health Care

Lauren R. Roth

3.1 INTRODUCTION

Justice Cardozo wrote that when serving as a fiduciary, "thought of self [is] to be renounced, however hard the abnegation."[1]

The American health care system's reliance on fiduciary principles accelerated with the passage of the Employee Retirement Income Security Act of 1974 (ERISA).[2] After the failure of many employer pension plans in the 1950s and 1960s, Congress passed ERISA to protect workers.[3] ERISA did not require employers to offer employee benefits. Instead, ERISA incentivized the private sector to provide these benefits. However, the statute left employers with control over not only whether and how to provide benefits but also how any such benefits plans were to be administered. Through ERISA, legislators attempted to constrain employer power with statutory fiduciary duties by, for example, requiring plan fiduciaries (employed directly or contractually by the employer) to act "solely in the interest of the participants and beneficiaries" and with "the exclusive purpose of (i) providing benefits … and (ii) defraying reasonable expenses of administering the plan."[4]

In the following years, however, the Supreme Court effectively gutted any restraints that existed by providing employers and their affiliates serving as fiduciaries with a highly deferential standard of review when participants (i.e., employees) challenged their decisions.[5] Sections 502 and 514 of ERISA have allowed employee benefit plans (which provide more than half of Americans with health insurance) to

[1] Meinhard v. Salmon, 164 N.E. 545, 548 (N.Y. 1928).

[2] Employee Retirement Income Security Act of 1974 ("ERISA"), P.L. 93-406, 29 U.S.C. 1001 et seq.

[3] James A. Wooten, The Employee Retirement Income Security Act of 1974: A Political History (2004).

[4] 29 U.S.C. 1104(a)(1).

[5] See Lauren R. Roth, A Failure to Supervise: How the Bureaucracy and the Courts Abandoned Their Intended Roles under ERISA, 34 Pace L. Rev. 216, 244–66 (2014).

opt in to that deferential standard of review when they deny benefit claims.[6] ERISA preemption spread the illusion that fiduciary duties could protect workers – but it went beyond their finances to their health.[7] However, fiduciary protections over health are a mirage. Employers pretend they can act in the best interests of employees when maintaining health plans – even though they pay (directly or indirectly) for claims.

Physicians and other providers are also considered fiduciaries.[8] They are obligated to act in the best interests of patients, regardless of financial incentives to reduce their standard of care. Though providers have always had an incentive to see more patients, the consolidation of health care has increased the risk of systemic conflicts because of reduced competition. Physicians pretend they can act in the best interests of patients – even when hospitals and group practices pressure them to see more patients and spend less time with them, and even though physicians and their employers are incentivized to order expensive tests and procedures. Cardozo's fiduciary ideal has become even more strained because of corporate consolidation in health care and the pressure of skyrocketing health insurance costs.

But what if, instead of ignoring these conflicts of interest, the American health care system abandoned the fiduciary fallacy? Building on recent scholarship showing that targeted legislation, regulation, and self-policing by stakeholders – rather than reliance on broad fiduciary duties – better manage these conflicts, this chapter uses game theory to analyze different behavioral scenarios involving the actors responsible for financing and providing care.

In Section 3.2, I review the literature addressing the role of fiduciary duties in health care and how game theory has been used to study strategic behavior and legal constraints. In Section 3.3, I explain the "game" as it currently exists, recognizing that the game I present is a substantially simplified version of reality – though one that highlights why fiduciary duties do not adequately constrain providers and payors. Finally, in Section 3.4, I show how abandoning fiduciary duties in this context is paradoxically more likely to result in providers and payors behaving in the best interests of patients using the same, simple game.

My goal is to advance scholarship arguing that fiduciary duties are inadequate to address conflicts in health care, while also proposing paths forward. Proposals to better resolve conflicts in health care should incorporate how rational actors are likely to behave and react to different restrictions designed to constrain their behavior. Laws restricting specific financial conflicts, in combination with financial incentives based on patient outcomes, advance the goal.

6 See Wooten, supra note 3, at 281–83.

7 Carmel Shacher, The Preemption Clause That Swallowed Health Care: How ERISA Litigation Threatens State Health Policy Efforts, Health Affs. (Oct. 15, 2020), https://www.healthaffairs.org/do/10.1377/forefront.20201013.533063/.

8 Sam Halabi, Against Fiduciary Utopianism: The Regulation of Physician Conflicts of Interest and Standards of Care, 11 U.C. Irvine L. Rev. 433, 443–45 (2020).

3.2 LITERATURE REVIEW

3.2.1 *Abandoning Fiduciary Duties*

Recent work by Sam Halabi argues against "fiduciary utopianism," or the idea that fiduciary law is the best way to regulate relationships of trust.[9] Recently, fiduciary protections have expanded beyond private relationships that impact "public or quasi-public interests – e.g., attorneys and clients, directors and shareholders, guardians and wards" to juries, taxpayers, and friends. Scholars have argued that fiduciary protections can "benefit [] those locked out or marginalized by prevailing economic and political structures."[10] However, the fiduciary framework may be largely aspirational because fiduciaries in health care are hopelessly conflicted.

Moving beyond critiques seeking to limit the application of fiduciary duties in specific cases,[11] Halabi "argues that the application of fiduciary duties to more legal relationships distracts from lawmaking and law-enforcement processes that lead to more effective solutions to the problems that fiduciary duties are asserted to solve."[12] In other words, fiduciary duties are the wrong tool in many relationships. In lawsuits not subject to ERISA preemption, common law tort and contract claims are preferred over fiduciary claims for their clarity and judicial conservatism (e.g., compensatory damages in a malpractice action over disgorgement for a fiduciary breach).[13]

Moreover, fiduciary duties do not deter bad behavior. In fact, instead of acting as a deterrent, fiduciary duties "may instead encourage [misbehavior] by weakening executives' internal moral constraints."[14] Fiduciary duties change the calculation of human decision-making because (1) otherwise immoral acts move within the range of justifiable action if not prohibited by fiduciary duties (including due to lack of enforcement), and (2) people engage in self-interested behavior by (roughly) weighing costs and benefits when choosing an action within that range.[15] As courts allow more self-interested behavior in spite of statutory or common law fiduciary duties through deference to fiduciaries, the range of actions that can be justified expands and more fiduciaries choose self-interested behavior.[16]

9 Id. at 443–45.

10 Id. at 435, 441–43.

11 See, e.g., Seth Davis, The False Promise of Fiduciary Government, 89 Notre Dame L. Rev. 1145, 1158 (2014) (politicians and bureaucrats); Ethan J. Leib & Stephen R. Galoob, Fiduciary Political Theory: A Critique, 125 Yale L.J. 1820, 1846 (2016) (international law).

12 Halabi, supra note 8, at 436 (citing, as an example, the idea that employers sponsoring ERISA plans are fiduciaries when administering those plans even though the rules that govern how they should behave are set forth in federal statutes and regulations).

13 Id. at 453–58.

14 Paul Weitzel, The Case against Officer Fiduciary Duties, 102 Neb. L. Rev. 344, 347 (2023).

15 Id. at 347–48.

16 See id. at 348–49 (explaining how fiduciary duties are likely to lead to more self-interested behavior instead of less when applied to corporate officers).

Fiduciary duties may be counter to broader policies or social goals. In the corporate world, fiduciary duties are "designed to align an officer's interests with those of the shareholders [instead of with society's]. . . .If the alignment is deep, it encourages executives to follow shareholder interests across ethical thresholds in pursuit of profit."[17] Similarly, the rules governing employer-sponsored insurance are designed to align the interests of providers and administrators with the employers' and insurers' – not with participants' and beneficiaries' interests.

3.2.2 *How to Play the Game*

Game theory is "a powerful tool to model and understand complex interactions."[18] In 1994, Douglas Baird, Robert Gertner, and Randal Picker published *Game Theory and the Law*.[19] Despite making a significant impact on other areas of the law, the application of game theory to health law has been limited.[20]

In game theory, a "player" employs a "strategy" each time she acts.[21] Assumptions about the player's motivations or the context in which the decisions are made must be clearly explained when discussing the game.

Games can be either "cooperative" or "noncooperative," with further subclassifications within each category. Cooperative games model behavior by a group of decision-makers, while noncooperative games model behavior of individual decision-makers who cannot consult each other.[22] The Prisoner's Dilemma is an example of a noncooperative game since the players are in different rooms and cannot cooperate. Much of game theory focuses on information asymmetries, signaling, and verification because a player's best strategy might differ depending on whether she knows the other player's best or likely strategy and whether she has complete or incomplete information.[23]

A payoff is defined as "[t]he utility a player derives under a particular combination of *strategies*. . . .What matters is not the amount of a payoff a player receives, but the

[17] Id. at 358.

[18] Aisha Farroqui & Muaz Niazi, Game Theory Models for Communication between Agents: A Review, 4(13) Complex Adaptive Sys. Model 2 (2016).

[19] Douglas Baird et al., Game Theory and the Law (1994).

[20] See, e.g., Peter Huang, Pandemic Emotions: The Good, the Bad, and the Unconscious – Implications for Public Health, Financial Economics, Law, and Leadership, 16 Nw. J.L. & Soc. Pol'y 81 (2021); Leslie M. Henry & Maxwell Stearns, Commerce Games and the Individual Mandate, 100 Geo. L.J. 1117 (2012); Russell Korobkin, The Efficiency of Managed Care "Patient Protection" Laws: Incomplete Contracts, Bounded Rationality, and Market Failure, 85 Cornell L. Rev. 1 (1999).

[21] Farroqui & Niazi, supra note 18, at 2 ("Strategy considers how agents act, what they prefer, how they make their decisions, and their behaviors etc.").

[22] Id.

[23] See Validimir Mazalov, Mathematical Game Theory and Applications (2014).

amount of that payoff relative to what the player would receive from choosing other *strategies*."[24]

Games can be "represented" in normal form (bimatrix), extensive form (decision tree), or beyond normal extensive form. For simplicity, I focus on normal-form games (without repeated interactions).[25]

Solution concepts predict how the game will be played by focusing on which strategy a rational player will use, given their goals.[26] A dominant strategy is "a best choice for a player for every possible choice by the other player."[27] Where a player has a dominant strategy, she will always use that strategy, and cooperation with the other player would not make a difference.

Game theory offers promise for health law because of its ability to move away from "basic assumptions: people act rationally, perfect information, zero transaction costs."[28] While extensive-form games allow opportunities to model repeated interactions with signaling or the development of reputations and information sharing, normal-form games still illustrate discrete points about how providers and payors work in health care. These discrete games are part of a larger game in which people are repeat players and make deals over time.[29]

3.3 PLAYING THE GAME WITHOUT FIDUCIARIES

3.3.1 *The Set Up*

3.3.1.1 Providers

Parties in the health care game face a problem. If there is a maximum for what can be charged for health care at a given time, then any additional profits earned by one player must decrease the profits earned by another player.

Assuming that this is a zero-sum game for individual health care providers ("Providers") and insurance companies and administrators ("Payors") is not fully accurate, however. Health care expenses increase at a rate much faster than inflation, and employers and participants tolerate it for reasons including a lack of political will to develop a strong public option for working Americans. Pressure by employers and patients/health plan participants ("Patients") also constrains the rate of annual increases.

24 Baird et al., supra note 19, at 311.
25 Farroqui & Niazi, supra note 18, at 5 (figure 1).
26 Id. at 2.
27 Baird et al., supra note 19, at 11.
28 Kenneth Dau-Schmidt et al., On Game Theory and the Law, 31 Law & Soc'y Rev. 613, 616 (1997) (noting, however, that "[g]ame theory is most useful in providing the framework for thinking about the issues rather than being able to predict exact outcomes").
29 See Baird et al., supra note 19, at 45.

This game does not rely on the assumption that Providers and Payors behave solely in their self-interest by attempting to maximize profits, which is the opposite of what is required by their fiduciary duties. Assuming Providers and Payors have some nonzero quantity of altruism, they will want to provide appropriate care for Patients and for Patients to pay less.[30] Given a range of options that meet the standard of care for Patients, however, they will prefer the choice that increases profits.[31] Assuming fiduciary duties constrain Providers at all, they should also be forced to select the strategy that prioritizes a higher payoff for Patients over a lower one – even if it lowers their own payoff. Providers need not care about the profits or costs to Payors and employers, to whom they owe no fiduciary duty or altruism, unless they are likely to be moved to an out-of-network position and lose Patients and money.

With this background, Providers should maximize their compensation by increasing reimbursement rates for patient care and keeping their costs down. Yet they know that Payors servicing health plans want to minimize, or at least reduce, Provider compensation to keep profits high, regardless of whether they pass along the savings through lower premiums.

Although employers may put pressure on Payors to reduce costs, they face issues of lack of transparency associated with increased costs and prices that are uniformly high across service providers. Employers can also pass the increased costs along to Patients through reduced wages or higher employee contributions. Finally, Patients want to reduce Provider reimbursement rates as long as they impact their cost-sharing obligations.

In this health care game, I assume the players must choose from the range of options within the standard of care. As such, there will be only two strategies: Self-Interest and Fiduciary. For Providers, this assumes that their desire to maximize profits and their desire to act in the best interests of Patients are mutually exclusive. In reality, of course, all Providers act in their own self-interest at times and put the best interests of Patients first at other times.

Nonetheless, for each decision, Providers must choose to act primarily in their own self-interest or in the best interests of a patient. The game examines that one choice and draws conclusions for the health care system.

Providers have a choice to earn higher compensation through some combination of:

[30] Providers are also subject to ethical practice standards that, like fiduciary duties, are designed to constrain self-interested behavior. I would argue, however, that where those standards are regularly stretched to include questionable behavior, providers are no longer constrained.

[31] Given that Providers have common interests and typically no individual control over their reimbursements, all games must assume that Providers have sufficient information to keep their rates billed and the number of tests and procedures ordered within a range acceptable for remaining in-network for the desired insurance plans (and not violate applicable laws or professional standards).

- increasing their reimbursement rates,
- spending less time with Patients, and
- ordering more visits, medications, tests, and procedures.[32]

Payors and Patients have imperfect information about the necessity of each of these options that make up the Self-Interest strategy.

The second strategy for Providers is to provide higher quality care and ensure Patients pay less but results in lower Provider compensation. Providers can achieve these goals through some combination of:

- decreasing their reimbursement rates,
- spending more time with Patients, and
- eliminating any unnecessary or questionable visits, medications, tests, and procedures.

This is the Fiduciary strategy, which models the type of behavior broad fiduciary duties are supposed to incentivize.

3.3.1.2 Payors

Like Providers, Payors have fiduciary duties, too. Therefore, even though they want to keep reimbursements to Providers low, they are obligated to prioritize the best interests of Patients. Given their imperfect information about what is medically necessary, Payors constrained by fiduciary duties should defer to Providers when they think Providers will play the Fiduciary strategy but defect (i.e., betray them and refuse to cooperate to share profits or work together in the best interests of Patients) when they think Providers will play the Self-Interest strategy. Otherwise, costs will increase for Payors with no resulting benefit for Patients.

In game theory, a player typically does not know which strategy another player will use during a particular interaction without signaling or cooperation. Instead, each player has to try to divine which strategy the other will play when making her own choice (e.g., by looking at the other player's optimal strategy).

Payors have a choice to earn higher profits through some combination of:

- decreasing their reimbursement rates to Providers;
- denying approval for visits, medications, tests, and procedures;
- incentivizing cheaper solutions (e.g., generic drugs); and
- promoting preventive care that reduces future expenses.

The first two options put them in direct conflict with Providers and test their compliance with their fiduciary duties, and these situations are the focus of this chapter and this game.

[32] I am ignoring, for the moment, the possibility of kickbacks, referral fees, and other potential financial conflicts for Providers.

Interestingly, the Self-Interest strategy allows Payors to claim that they are acting in the best interests of Patients because it eliminates at least some unnecessary care to Patients.

However, a Payor acting as a fiduciary would defer to the judgment of a Provider absent some sort of signal that the care requested would be harmful to a patient.

The second option for Payors is keeping their reimbursement rates high(er) so Patients receive all the care they need. They can achieve this goal through some combination of:

- updating standards relating to reimbursable medications, test, and procedures when technology changes and
- deferring to the judgment of Providers when it seems beneficial (the benefits outweigh the costs) to Patients.

This is the Fiduciary strategy, which models the type of behavior broad fiduciary duties are supposed to incentivize.

3.3.1.3 Patients

While Patients are the beneficiaries of the game (and all of the other parties owe them fiduciary duties), they are not actually playing the game. Although they pay an increasing share of their health care and insurance costs, the only strategies they have are to seek care or not to seek care.[33] Because of the information asymmetry between Patients and Providers, Patients cannot usually evaluate whether Providers are acting in their best interests and providing the best care (although they can seek a second opinion and play another round).

3.3.2 *The Game*

The game can then be represented as follows:

		Payor	
		Self-Interest	Fiduciary
Provider	Self-Interest	2, 2	5, −5
	Fiduciary	−5, 5	0, 0

The payoffs are listed in the order of the row player first and then the column player. As a reminder, the absolute value of the payoffs listed does not matter.

[33] Patients could possibly seek out more altruistic Providers, but most Providers will follow the professional norm, and identifying more altruistic Providers may not be practical. Additionally, Patients could lobby their employers for reduced cost-sharing obligations or lobby their state government or the federal government to change the rules of the game through a single-payor system, for example. This chapter's focus, however, on the impact of fiduciary duties to constrain the players assumes the system maintains its status quo.

Instead, what affects the game is the value of each payoff relative to the value of another potential payoff.[34] Here:

- Each player's payoff is the highest (5) when she plays the Self-Interest strategy and the other player plays the Fiduciary strategy because she maximizes her compensation while the other player does not try to take more of the limited health care dollars because she is focused on the best interests of the Patient.
- Conversely, each player's payoff is the lowest (−5) when she plays the Fiduciary strategy and the other player plays the Self-Interest strategy because she is not focused on maximizing compensation and the other player takes more of the pie. I use a negative payoff to reflect the fact that the Provider can lose money by expending time seeing a patient that is later not reimbursed.
- When both players play the Fiduciary strategy, neither experiences a maximum or minimum payoff, but payoffs are minimal (0) because the Patient gets less care than will maximize Provider's compensation as Provider minimizes questionable treatments and spends more time with Patient, but more care than will maximize Payor's compensation as she defers to Provider.
- When both players play the Self-Interest strategy, neither experiences a maximum or minimum payoff, but payoffs are higher than when they both play the Fiduciary Strategy (2) because Patient gets more care as Provider tries to maximize her compensation with questionable treatments and by spending less time with Patient, but less care as Payor tries to maximize her compensation by deferring less to Provider.

If Provider plays the Self-Interest strategy, then Payor's best response is Self-Interest because it will result in a payoff of 2 instead of −5. If Provider plays the Fiduciary strategy, then Payor's best response is still Self-Interest because it will result in a payoff of 5 instead of 0.

Without enforcement of fiduciary duties – a financial or criminal sanction for deviating – Payor will never play that strategy (absent altruism that outweighs self-interest). Because the payoffs are symmetric, the same is true for Provider; she will always play the Self-Interest strategy.

If there is coordination (i.e., interaction between the players where they agree to adopt a particular strategy), then Provider and Payor will still both play the Self-Interest strategy to minimize the risk of the worst possible payoff. Coordination then changes no one's strategy.

[34] See infra Section 3.2.2. While the absolute value of the numbers is not important, the numbers chosen emphasize how profitable unconstrained, self-interested behavior is in this game.

Assuming no penalty from playing the Self-Interest strategy (as our system currently provides, assuming care is within a broad range of acceptable behavior), no rational actor would play the Fiduciary strategy.

3.4 PROPOSALS

The physician–patient relationship has long been described as constrained by fiduciary duties. However, state and federal legislation has been far more important in constraining self-interested behavior by physicians than judicial enforcement of fiduciary law.[35] Among the interventions discussed by Halabi are the following federal statutes (and their state analogues): the Anti-Kickback Statute, which penalizes payments made to incentivize or reward referrals in health care paid for by federal programs; the Stark Law, which limits a physician's ability to recommend services to a patient provided by a company that the physician has a financial interest in; and the Physician Payments Sunshine Act, which requires producers of drugs and medical devices covered by Medicare, Medicaid, or Children's Health Insurance Program (CHIP) to report payments and other incentives to physicians and teaching hospitals.[36] The framework provided by this legislation has been more detailed and easier to enforce than fiduciary duties.

What all of these laws have in common, in terms of the game, is that they penalize self-interest by Providers and Payors to prevent the worst outcomes for Patients. In effect, they force Providers and Payors to use the Fiduciary strategy.

3.4.1 *Statutes Limiting Financial Conflicts*

To illustrate, I will first examine how laws that prevent Providers from referring Patients to service providers they have a financial interest in and laws that prohibit kickbacks for recommending particular services, drugs, or devices change the game. For example, the federal Anti-Kickback Statute could be applied to private health insurance instead of only federal health care programs.[37] The statute would provide that "[w]hoever knowingly and willfully solicits or receives any remuneration (including any kickback, bribe, or rebate) directly or indirectly, overtly or covertly, in cash or in kind . . . in return for the furnishing . . . of any item or service [payable under a private health insurance plan] . . . or . . . in return for purchasing, leasing, ordering . . . any good, facility, service, or item [payable under the plan] . . . shall be guilty of a felony," imprisoned for up to ten years, and/or fined up to US$100,000.[38]

[35] Halabi, supra note 8, at 444; see Tamar Frankel, Fiduciary Law 17 (2011).

[36] Halabi, supra note 8, at 462 et seq.

[37] See 42 U.S.C. § 1320a-7b.

[38] Id. Exceptions and safe harbors can be included in the statute and through the Health and Human Services Office of Inspector General as is currently done when enforcing the statute applied to federal health programs. See Halabi, supra note 8, at 463.

The original game can now be represented as follows, with the modified payoffs in bold:

		Payor	
		Self-Interest	Fiduciary
Provider	Self-Interest	**1, 3**	**3, −4**
	Fiduciary	−5, 5	0, 0

The payoffs in bold have changed because the law constrains Provider, preventing her from maximizing her compensation in situations where it may harm Patient and is prohibited by statute. As a result, when Provider plays the Self-Interest strategy, her payoff goes from 2 to 1 where Payor also plays the Self-Interest strategy and from 5 to 3 when Payor plays the Fiduciary strategy. The payoffs for Payor also change, increasing from 2 to 3 when she plays the Self-Interest strategy and from −5 to −4 when she plays the Fiduciary strategy. This assumes that Payor keeps her prices the same when her costs from Provider decrease – increasing her profits.

The best strategy is still for Provider to play the Self-Interest strategy (and for Payor to play Self-Interest), but now the payoff has been reduced for Provider from 2 to 1 and increased for Payor from 2 to 3 because Provider cannot profit as much from acting in her own self-interest. Payor will take advantage to keep the profits that Provider would usually have gotten from her financial conflicts (assuming the market will bear it).

Coordination again changes no one's strategy because Self-Interest is still the best strategy for each regardless of what the other player does. Even enacting similar statutory provisions to restrict financial conflicts for Payor would merely reduce her payout for playing Self-Interest but not change her optimal strategy.

3.4.2 *Paying for Improved Outcomes*

Increasing payoffs for Providers who achieve better patient outcomes and for Payors whose insureds achieve better outcomes at lower costs is a systemic change that could move both players from the Self-Interest strategy to the Fiduciary strategy (because the payoffs would increase). This concept is behind value-based reforms,[39] which attempted to improve the value and quality of care under Medicare when enacted through the Patient Protection and Affordable Care Act (ACA).[40]

[39] See Michael Porter & Elizabeth Olmstead Teisberg, Redefining Health Care: Creating Value-Based Competition on Results (2006).

[40] Eleanor Kinney, The Affordable Care Act and the Medicare Program: Linking Medicare Payment to Quality Performance, 68 N.Y.U. Ann. Surv. Am. L. 567 (2013).

However, the consensus has been that these reforms have largely failed to achieve their goals.[41]

Looking at the original game again with the new changes in bold shows why short-term value-based reforms have not been as successful as hoped.

		Payor	
		Self-Interest	Fiduciary
Provider	Self-Interest	2, 2	5, −5
	Fiduciary	−5, 5	**2, 2**

To get Provider and Payor to shift strategy, the incentives awarded for improved patient outcomes must be equal to the financial incentives received when Provider and Payor previously acted instead in their own self-interest. Assuming any sense of altruism or fiduciary responsibility, they may then coordinate and play the Fiduciary strategy; if there is no altruism or fiduciary responsibility, then incentives for improved outcomes will need to be greater than those previously received for acting in their own self-interest.

Why do they need to coordinate? Each player's best strategy to avoid the worst possible outcome of a −5 payoff is to play the Self-Interest strategy (which results in a payoff of either 2 or 5). Unless a player can ensure that the other side will play Fiduciary (and she will not suffer a −5 payoff), then she will always play the Self-Interest strategy.

Even if they both play Fiduciary here, though, this results in cost-savings for the system only if the legislative solutions previously discussed are first imposed to reduce the rewards for self-interested behavior by Provider and Payor. The new incentives awarded for improved outcomes do not need to be as high to motivate a shift in strategies because of these existing laws.

From a game strategy perspective, this means that state and federal legislatures should draft specific, targeted legislation designed to limit and disclose conflicts of interest held by health fiduciaries and then implement incentive payments based on patient outcomes. In this way, patient outcomes improve while health care spending decreases. Otherwise, the system will fail to achieve the desired savings, as seen after the ACA implementation.

3.5 CONCLUSION

There is no evidence that health fiduciary behavior is successfully constrained at a systematic level by fiduciary duties. Fiduciaries are already behaving in a rational way when they ignore their fiduciary duties in health. The time has come to engage in a rational response.

[41] See, e.g., Rachel Werner et al., The Future of Value-Based Payment: A Road Map to 2030, Penn Leonard Davis Inst. (2021), https://ldi.upenn.edu/our-work/research-updates/the-future-of-value-based-payment-a-road-map-to-2030/; Ashish Jha, Value-Based Purchasing: Time for Reboot or Time to Move On?, JAMA F. (Mar. 21, 2017), https://jamanetwork.com/journals/jama/article-abstract/2612603.

4

European Distinctions between Private and Public Law in Health Care and the Emerging Influence of Private Lobbies

Barry Solaiman

4.1 INTRODUCTION

Private law plays an important, if not always recognized, role in European health law. It governs relationships between patients, health care professionals, and medical institutions they rely on for their care. Private law creates lines of accountability between manufacturers of medical devices and the end user. However, the legal landscape, regulatory frameworks, and academic literature are primarily premised on notions of care being a public good that falls under public law.[1] Nevertheless, there are important distinctions between the United States (US) and Europe, which this chapter highlights. Grasping these distinctions requires taking a step back from the sharp end of the law to understand important structural differences between the health systems and the influence of private entities that exist but which might not be the obvious first port of call for research.

The sections that follow examine three aspects of private health in Europe. First, this chapter explores the structural distinction between the health systems in the US and Europe. Public health is the predominant form of care in Europe, but that headline ignores the complex reality of a shared structure between public and private entities and the diversity of how those arrangements manifest between different European countries. Second, the chapter examines the extent and role of private law as a mechanism for governing health care disputes in Europe. While tort law is a given for resolving disputes, this chapter queries the extent to which contract law is used, finding that empirical evidence is limited.

Third, there is an examination of the influence of health care lobbies and private interests and how they can permeate all levels of governmental decision-making concerning health care down to decisions about commissioning services on the

[1] Constanze Semmelmann, Theoretical Reflections on the Public-Private Distinction and Their Traces in European Union Law, 2(4) Oñati Socio-Legal Ser. 25, 30 (2012).

ground. Public health has primacy in Europe, but that does not mean lobbyists do not constantly seek avenues to shape the policy and lawmaking environments to create new opportunities for funneling public funds toward their private services.

By highlighting these distinctions, this chapter provides a point of contrast to the US in other chapters of this volume, where private influences and private law are far more pervasive and a known part of the landscape. At the same time, the role of private influences and private law are less understood in Europe, and this chapter seeks to highlight their importance.

4.2 EUROPE DISTINGUISHED: THE STRUCTURE OF HEALTH SERVICES

There are four key distinctions between the US and Europe concerning the structure of health services that implicate the public and private distinction in health care.

First, the most pertinent distinction is that universal health care is a given in nearly every European country. In contrast, the US heavily relies on private health care to ensure that care is provided. In general, health care services in Europe are designated as public goods.[2] The form of public health coverage in Europe varies, but the underlying principles focusing on public universal health care are similar. For example, the United Kingdom (UK) has the National Health Service (NHS), Spain; the Sistema Nacional de Salud (SNS), and Italy; the Servizio Sanitario Nazionale (SSN), among others.[3] Of course, these are not absolutes. In the US, there are public hospitals, but these do not provide services for free, which precludes access to care for some. There are also elements of private care in Europe, but that does not preclude access to health.

Second, the role of government in providing health services and employing the health care workforce highlights another distinction. The UK is an extreme example because of its highly centralized nature, but it helps elucidate the government's role compared to the US. In the UK, policy is determined by the Executive (specifically, the Treasury headed by the Chancellor of the Exchequer), which moves money downwards to the Department of Health and Social Care (DHSC) for capital projects such as investment in buildings and equipment, salaries, medicines, vaccinations, and other public health programs.[4] The remaining money is trickled

[2] Id.

[3] Nigel Edwards, Why Has the NHS Not Been Copied? (Spoiler) It Has, Nuffield Trust (July 11, 2018), https://www.nuffieldtrust.org.uk/news-item/why-has-the-nhs-not-been-copied-spoiler-it-has.

[4] How Funding Flows in the NHS, The King's Fund (Apr. 2020), https://www.kingsfund.org.uk/sites/default/files/2020-04/NHS_Funding_Flow_April_2020.pdf.

down to NHS England (an executive non-departmental public body sponsored by the DHSC), which distributes that money further to various services and providers.[5]

In this manner, the government controls the NHS and is, therefore, the main employer of the health workforce and main provider of health services, whereas the US Government is not primarily a provider of health care services.

Third, health insurance is another significant difference. In the US, Medicaid and Medicare are public programs limited to specific individuals (such as low-income individuals, retirees, and disabled individuals). However, the predominant basis for coverage is through expensive private health insurance. In Europe, coverage is mainly provided by the state and is governed by public law. In some cases, coverage is provided by mandatory health insurance, such as in Germany, and supplemental private insurance is common in other cases, such as Belgium, Holland, and Slovenia.[6] Public coverage generally ensures that most individuals pay no (or nominal fees) at the point of service.

Where private providers exist, the cost of their services is usually paid by the national health insurance system or regulated social insurance schemes that coordinate the purchasing of such services.[7] How this plays out depends on the country. For hospital care, four approaches are pertinent in Europe. In one group (Belgium, Netherlands, Germany, and Norway), private hospital bed numbers are similar to those in the public sector, and the difference in services between public and private hospitals is minimal, with consumers and social health insurance payers deeming both functionally equivalent.[8] In a second group (Austria, France, Italy, and Portugal), private entities have increasingly offered lower-risk outpatient services for profit, offering fewer beds than the public system.[9] In the third group (Czechia, Estonia, Finland, Hungary, Latvia, and Poland), private providers offer a narrower range of short-stay services in specialized areas.[10] In the final group (Iceland, Ireland, the UK, and Lithuania), private facilities are in the minority.[11] Areas where private care tends to dominate in Europe include dental care. In most countries, 80 to 100 percent of dentists are private practitioners.[12] Further, primary

5 Gov UK, NHS England, https://www.gov.uk/government/organisations/nhs-england#:~:text=NHS%20England%20is%20an%20executive,of%20Health%20and%20Social%20Care (last accessed Nov. 1, 2023).

6 Dominic Montagu, The Provision of Private Healthcare Services in European Countries: Recent Data and Lessons for Universal Health Coverage in Other Settings, 9 Front Pub. Health 1, 2 (2021).

7 Id. at 2.

8 Id. at 4.

9 Id.

10 Id.

11 Id. at 5.

12 Id.

care tends to be provided in private settings,[13] and most pharmacies are privately owned and operated (although the state primarily pays for the medications).[14]

Fourth, the final difference between the US and Europe is the legal framework and the types of disputes that arise. There are disputes concerning health insurance coverage in the US, which are rarer in Europe. Health care fraud and antitrust rules also feature more prominently in the US. Disputes in Europe center on administrative decisions, quality of care, and access to care.

These distinctions highlight that private entities and private care in Europe fall within a broader public care matrix. The next query is the extent to which private law plays a role in this matrix.

4.3 THE ROLE OF PRIVATE LAW

While public law is of primary importance in Europe for regulating the relations between citizens and public authorities, private law can also regulate the medical field and ensure access to health.[15] One central area of law providing redress in Europe is tort law.[16] Similar underlying principles concerning duty, breach, and causation apply when compared to the US, but the application of those principles will likely differ between EU states. For contract law, contractual agreements can exist between medical institutions and doctors, between doctors and patients, and between insurance companies and hospitals.[17] It has been noted that the increased expansion and sophistication of regulations in Europe, such as consumer protections and anti-discrimination law in contractual relations, "amounts to an instrumentalisation of private law for political purposes."[18] However, as a legislative matter, there is no "health care" law basis in legislation for managing relationships between doctors and patients (although they can be regulated "through different modes of market regulations").[19]

While European countries primarily deal with malpractice cases through tort or contract law,[20] the number of private contracts governing such relationships and any disputes arising from them is unclear. In the UK, at least from a patient perspective, there are no contracts between patients and the NHS, so breach of contract cannot

13 Id. at 6.

14 Id.

15 Anniek de Ruijter, EU Health Law & Policy: The Expansion of EU Power in Public Health and Health Care 52, 63 (2019).

16 For broader analyses of tort law in Europe, see Athanasios Panagiotou, Medical Liability in Europe at the Dawn of Cross-border Healthcare, 23(4) Eur. J. Health L. 350, 350–72 (2016); Cees van Dam, Europe, in European Tort Law 23–50 (Cees van Dam ed., 2013).

17 de Ruijter, supra note 15, at 63.

18 Semmelmann, supra note 1, at 32.

19 Id. (citing Tamara K. Hervey & Jean V. McHale, Health Law and the European Union (2004)).

20 Kenneth Watson & Rob Kottenhagen, Patients' Rights, Medical Error and Harmonization of Compensation Mechanisms in Europe, 25(1) Eur. J. Health L. 1, 13 (2018).

be relied upon to sue health care institutions.[21] This is true not only for matters of care but also for the disclosure of confidential information. While the court may find an implied contract in such cases, it is thought to be unlikely.[22] A breach of contract claim may be more successful by the employer against their employee where the employee clinician divulges confidential patient information (thereby breaching the terms of the employment contract).[23] Linked to the legal pathway pursued is the concern about creating a compensation culture like in the US. A fear is that the slightest opportunity will be taken to make a "fast buck," and the ability to sue for breach of contract could contribute to that culture.[24] However, it has been determined that this concern is a myth.[25] Overall, empirical evidence is needed to determine how prevalent contractual disputes between patients, doctors, and health care institutions are in other European countries.

Another area of note is private litigation concerning access to health for individuals in the EU on the grounds of free movement of persons.[26] With citizens moving across borders for work, demands arose for access to health in other member states.[27] The courts also addressed specific issues like abortion. In the early 1990s, the Court of Justice of the European Union (CJEU) determined that Irish citizens had the right to access abortion services in other member states, and they could not be prohibited from doing so.[28] A line of case law raised the issue of whether the EU operates as a free market for health, whereby citizens can travel from their country to another country to receive care and then be reimbursed by their home country. Those cases determined that citizens could travel and be reimbursed for their care (although the home state could impose restrictions on the extent of this).[29]

Cohen has examined the intricacies of this paradigm, including the related case law, regulations, treaty provisions, and directives.[30] One major question has been whether patients are required to seek prior authorization from their home state for reimbursement of care in another EU member state. Case law has determined that prior authorization may constitute a restriction on the freedom to provide services,

21 Jonathan Herring, Medical Law and Ethics 139 (9th ed. 2022).
22 Id. at 306.
23 Id. at 306 (citing X v. Y [1988] 2 All ER 649).
24 Id. at 139.
25 John Hyde, Compensation Culture Is 'Media-Created' Myth – Dyson, L. Soc'y Gazette (Mar. 25, 2013), https://www.lawgazette.co.uk/news/compensation-culture-is-media-created-myth-dyson/70091.article.
26 de Ruijter, supra note 15, at 79.
27 Id. at 80.
28 Id. at 80 (citing Society for the Protection of Unborn Children Ireland Ltd v. Grogan [1991] ECR I-4685; for a discussion, see Stéphanie Hennette Vauchez, The Society for the Protection of Unborn Children v. Grogan: Rereading the Case and Retelling the Story of Reproductive Rights in Europe, in EU Law Stories: Contextual and Critical Histories of European Jurisprudence 393–417 (Fernanda Nicola & Bill Davies eds., 2017)).
29 de Ruijter, supra note 15, at 82.
30 I. Glenn Cohen, Patients with Passports: Medical Tourism, Law, and Ethics (2014).

and that prior authorization requirements may not be justified for outpatient care.[31] Requirements for prior authorization may be justified where the patient has access to treatment without undue delay, otherwise the ability of the patient's home country to "fund and organize its internal health care system" may become threatened.[32] If a patient is entitled to reimbursement, the level of reimbursement will depend on whether treaty or regulatory provisions apply. In some cases, where the level of reimbursement in their home country is lower than the cost of care they are seeking in another member state, the patient is entitled to be reimbursed for the additional costs they incur. In other cases, the patient will be required to make up the financial difference themselves.

Directive 2011/24[33] is also important in this area. It states that "decisions of refusal to grant prior authorisation, shall be restricted to what is necessary and proportionate to the objective to be achieved, and may not constitute a means of arbitrary discrimination or an unjustified obstacle to the free movement of patients."[34] Matters falling under the "necessary and proportionate" criteria include the "financial balance of a social security system" and "planning requirements" for ensuring access to high-quality treatments.[35] A significant concern during the negotiations of the Directive involved the movement of expatriate pensioners. For example, Spain was concerned that expats living there would return home for medical care, which would be charged back to Spain. To combat this, several countries agreed that patients entitled to receive a pension from their country (even where they are no longer resident there) would pay for the treatment of those patients returning home for care, as opposed to the expat's country of residence.[36] This would not apply to countries not on the list, or where the patient seeks treatment in a third country – in which case, the expat's resident country would be required to pay.[37]

Aside from medical tourism-type cases, there has also been a plethora of case law brought before the European Court of Human Rights (ECtHR) by individuals and groups concerning the right to "private or family life."[38] The cases do not involve contract law issues but illustrate how individuals have brought a range of matters to the courts concerning their care.

These involve medically assisted procreation, surrogacy, abortion, prenatal testing, informed consent, and end-of-life situations. They also cover the health of

[31] Id. at 184.
[32] Id.
[33] Directive 2011/24/EU of the European Parliament and of the Council of 9 March 2011 on the application of patients' rights in cross-border healthcare, OJ L 88, 4.4.2011.
[34] Id. at art. 8(1).
[35] Id. at recital (43).
[36] Cohen, supra note 30, at 193.
[37] Id.
[38] Council of Europe/European Court of Human Rights, Health-Related Issues in the Case-Law of the European Court of Human Rights (June 2015), http://www.antoniocasella.eu/salute/ECHR_health_2015.pdf.

detainees, health and immigration, health and the environment, health and the workplace, and the protection of medical data.[39]

For example, in surrogacy cases, the courts have had to navigate a complex terrain between adhering to public law prohibitions on commercial surrogacy and permitting private contractual surrogacy arrangements. In the UK, the Surrogacy Arrangements Act 1985 was passed to discourage surrogacy following a case involving a British woman being employed as a surrogate mother for a Swedish couple via a US agency.[40] It is illegal to negotiate or arrange surrogacy on a commercial basis under the Act.[41] However, surrogacy is legally permitted when organized by an individual or non-commercial body, and there is no payment.[42] In one case in the UK Supreme Court in 2020, the court rejected an argument that surrogacy was contrary to public policy and noted that it was not unlawful to enter into commercial surrogacy abroad.[43] In most cases, the courts will promote the child's welfare by determining what is in their best interests.

The particular arrangements and payments to the surrogate will not likely stand in the way of the courts giving a parental order because it will be in the child's best interests. This was seen in one case where a British couple paid a Ukrainian surrogate 235 Euros per month and 25,000 Euros upon birth (which she used to pay the deposit on her flat). A parental order was still given, with the judge holding that:

> The difficulty is that it is almost impossible to imagine a set of circumstances in which by the time the case comes to court, the welfare of any child (particularly a foreign child) would not be gravely compromised (at the very least) by a refusal to make an order.[44]

Thus, despite the restrictions in public law, the reality is that commercial surrogacy exists, and the courts will likely only refuse a parental order in the clearest cases of fraud and bad faith because the best interests of the child will usually be served by granting the order.[45]

Another area that intersects with private law is competition law. Increased competition may be seen as a solution to support the sustainability of public health care systems that are under strain. Yet, the applicability and scope of competition law is determined on a case-by-case basis, resulting in an inconsistent application of competition law to health care providers by the courts and the European

[39] Id.
[40] Herring, supra note 21, at 485.
[41] Surrogacy Arrangements Act, 1985, c. 49, § 2(1) (UK).
[42] Herring, supra note 21, at 485.
[43] Id. (citing XX v. Whittington Hospital NHS Trust [2020] UKSC 14 (appeal taken from [2018] EWCA (Civ) 2832)).
[44] Re X and Y (Parental Order: Foreign Surrogacy) [2008] EWHC 3030 (Fam) (Eng.).
[45] Re P-M [2013] EWHC 2328 (Fam) (Eng.).

Commission.[46] EU states do not favor introducing elements of competition law into the health care system because those systems are highly regulated, and it would increase the risk of conflicts between state interventions and EU law.[47] Exempting EU law from these realms could be an easier option in theory, but states cannot exempt health systems and the provision of care from competition law.[48] Consequently, there is limited scope for competition law to be adapted to enable more competition in health care in Europe.

Finally, it is worth noting developments concerning data. A survey by a European consumer organization finds that while Europeans are comfortable sharing their health data with doctors, they are not happy sharing that data with technology or insurance companies.[49] There is a particular reluctance to share health habits, genetic data, and sexual and reproductive data.[50] Some have called for protections for consumers to protect such data. The proposed European Health Data Space is a health-specific ecosystem designed to give individuals control over their health data while providing a consistent framework for using health data for research, innovation, policy, and regulatory activities.[51] There are already queries about how this space will intersect with contract law matters, such as whether data can be transmitted for research purposes based on contracts.[52]

4.4 THE INFLUENCE OF PRIVATE LOBBIES ON PRIVATE AVENUES OF CARE

The last area of examination pertains to lobbying. There has been a gradual creep of private health providers in Europe. The reason for this creep is multifaceted and complex, but much of it is enabled at the policy formulation level of government and even before that. The health care lobby is one of the most powerful in Europe.[53] Officially reported spending figures in the EU transparency register for pharmaceutical companies alone is 36 million Euros annually, but the figure is likely far higher

46 Bruno Nikolić, Applicability of European Union Competition Law to Health Care Providers: The Dividing Line between Economic and Noneconomic Activities, 46(1) J. Health Pol. Pol'y & L. 49, 49 (2021).

47 Id. at 51.

48 Id. at 52.

49 Consumers Uneasy Sharing Their Health Data, Survey Shows, BEUC (May 2, 2023), https://www.beuc.eu/press-releases/consumers-uneasy-sharing-their-health-data-survey-shows.

50 Id.

51 European Comm., European Health Data Space, https://health.ec.europa.eu/ehealth-digital-health-and-care/european-health-data-space_en (last accessed Dec. 23, 2023).

52 Wenkai Li & Paul Quinn, The European Health Data Space: An Expanded Right to Data Portability?, 52 Comput. L. & Sec. Rev. 1, 4 (2024).

53 Pharma Industry's EU Lobbying, Corp. Europe Observatory (May 31, 2021), https://corporateeurope.org/en/2021/05/big-pharmas-lobbying-firepower-brussels-least-eu36-million-year-and-likely-far-more.

owing to the voluntary nature of the EU's transparency register.[54] Even from the reported figures, those companies far outspend civil society actors (at a rate of 15 to 1).[55] The aims of lobbyists are broad, but in general, they seek to influence the formulation of laws that are favorable to them, delay and eventually remove bills from the legislative agenda that may be harmful to their profits, and seek lucrative contracts for providing health services to the public health system. Despite these aims, the results of their efforts reveal a nuanced picture.

The UK provides an illustrative case study of how lobbyists operate in this space.[56] Various avenues exist for lobbyists and citizens to get involved in policy development.[57] The most obvious route is influencing decision-makers in Government (the Executive), Parliament, and political parties on health care bills, policies, or legislation.[58] For political parties, the aim is to influence their internal policies and their manifesto. While party members have some influence, the greatest power may lie with a few vested interests. Think tanks such as the Institute of Economic Affairs for the Conservatives and Demos for Labour have been quite influential in this manner.[59] In Parliament, Members of Parliament (MPs) will scrutinize Government bills, and extra scrutiny is undertaken for different aspects of NHS performance by parliamentary committees, including the Health and Social Care Committee, the Public Accounts Committee, and the Public Administration and Constitutional Affairs Committee. For example, in 2017, the Health Committee considered the potential impact of Brexit on health and social care in the UK.[60]

For the Government, the DHSC is the ministerial department tasked with supporting and advising ministers, setting direction, and acting as "guardian" for the health and care framework.[61] It is chaired by the Secretary of State for Health and Social Care, whose responsibilities to Parliament are outlined under the National Health Service Act 2006. In practice, power is shared between ministers and civil servants, which will vary considerably depending on the personality and strength of the minister in charge.[62] The balance also depends on the quality of

[54] Id.

[55] Id.

[56] See generally, Barry Solaiman, Lobbying in the UK: Towards Robust Regulation, 76(2) Parliamentary Affs. 270 (2021) https://doi.org/10.1093/pa/gsab051; see also, Barry Solaiman, Evaluating Lobbying in the United Kingdom: Moving from a Corruption Framework to "Institutional Diversion" (Thesis, University of Cambridge, 2017) https://doi.org/10.17863/CAM.15615.

[57] I.e., identifying problems, recognizing issues, policy formulation, policy implementation and evaluation. See, K. Buse et al., Making Health Policy 13–14 (2d ed. 2012).

[58] Also, civil servants.

[59] Peter Dorey, Policy Making in Britain 48, 53 (2d ed. 2014).

[60] House of Commons Health Comm., Brexit and Health and Social Care – People & Process, 2016-17, HC 640, at 41 (UK).

[61] About Us, DHSC (Dec. 20, 2023), https://www.gov.uk/government/organisations/department-of-health-and-social-care/about.

[62] Christopher Ham, Health Policy in Britain 152 (6th ed. 2009).

advice given by civil servants, the weight given to the departmental view on an issue, and the commitment of a minister to the relevant matter.[63] Numerous conflicts of interest have been detailed concerning relationships between decision-makers and the private health sector.

This can be seen with the Health and Social Care Act (HSCA) 2012, which was created to restructure the NHS and encourage more private-sector competition. One report argued that many people involved in policy formulation had personal interests in private health companies.[64] Individuals with links to private health companies and think tanks had previously held positions as health ministers, members of the Cabinet, or MPs who had voted for the Bill,[65] which led to accusations of large-scale conflicts of interest.[66] These concerns should be understood in the context of a historical revolving door problem of former ministers being employed by private health companies as advisers.[67]

Another report revealed how McKinsey & Company (a management consulting firm that drew up many of the proposals for the Bill) had paid for the head of NHS regulator, Monitor, to attend an event with a banquet, five-star hotel, and first-class flights, which raised conflict of interest and undue influence concerns.[68] Finally, during the Bill stages, the Government "paused" the progression of the Bill to undertake a "listening exercise" after the proposals were subject to much criticism. During that period, the Government was accused of having private discussions with proponents of more privatization following a leaked document revealing that their purpose was to ensure that competition remained a core part of the Bill following the listening exercise.[69]

Despite all these efforts, the ultimate results of these efforts by private lobbyists paint a nuanced picture. The King's Fund (a health and social care charity) argued that the HSCA 2012 extended market-based principles and introduced more competition into the NHS, resulting in more contracts awarded to private

63 Id.

64 Tamasin Cave, The Health Industry Lobbying Tour, Alliance for Lobbying Transparency, Mancha Productions (Jan. 18, 2011), https://youtu.be/zrb3rJoLu9g?si = EvNDuUeI1fRcRF3w.

65 Id.

66 Adrian O'Dowd, Fifth of Coalition MPs Have Links to Private Healthcare Firms, 349 Brit. Med. J. 1 (2014), https://www.bmj.com/content/349/bmj.g6982.

67 Cave, supra note 64; Hamid Sarwar, NHS Is Not Working 99–100 (2d ed. 2019).

68 David Rose, The Firm That Hijacked the NHS, Daily Mail (Feb. 12, 2012), http://www.dailymail.co.uk/news/article-2099940/NHS-health-reforms-Extent-McKinsey–Companys-role-Andrew-Lansleys-proposals.html.

69 Daniel Boffey, David Cameron Is Accused of a "Sham Listening Exercise" on NHS Reform after Links to Lobbyist Are Revealed, Observer (Nov. 25, 2012), http://www.theguardian.com/politics/2012/nov/25/sham-listening-exercise-nhs-reform; Unedited Document from NHS Private Healthcare Lobby Group Reveals Actions Taken to Ensure Competition Remained in Health Bill, Social Investigations (July 17, 2012), http://socialinvestigations.blogspot.co.uk/2012/07/unedited-document-from-nhs-private.html.

providers.[70] However, the overall proportion of the budget spent on private providers did not increase. The King's Fund also noted that the Health and Care Act 2022 removed the competition and market-based approaches introduced by the 2012 Act.[71] Other findings are far more critical. One study concluded that:

> The privatisation of the NHS in England, through the outsourcing of services to for-profit companies, consistently increased in 2013–20. Private sector outsourcing corresponded with significantly increased rates of treatable mortality, potentially as a result of a decline in the quality of health-care services.[72]

There was also criticism from the Deputy Chair of the British Medical Association (BMA), who argued that ministers were "throwing huge amounts of money at private firms rather than investing in rebuilding our health and care system."[73] However, other findings argue that the ability of private firms to make profit in this paradigm is limited by a top-down squeeze on prices, and the state's dominance of funding and provision.[74] Thus, while the result of private lobbying is contentious, the HSCA 2012 provides a useful case study for how private lobbyists can shape law and policy to encourage a shift toward greater marketization, creating more room for private entities to operate. Other European countries and the EU are not immune to the same influences.[75] Brussels is the world's second capital for lobbyists, followed by Washington, DC.[76] Following COVID-19, commentators highlighted a "frenzy"

[70] Charlotte Wickens, Health and Social Care in England: Tackling the Myths, The King's Fund (Mar. 15, 2023), https://www.kingsfund.org.uk/insight-and-analysis/long-reads/health-and-social-care-england-myths.

[71] Id.

[72] Benjamin Goodair & Aaron Reeves, Outsourcing Health-Care Services to the Private Sector and Treatable Mortality Rates in England, 2013–20: An Observational Study of NHS Privatisation, 7(7) Lancet Pub. Health e638–46 (2022).

[73] Andrew Gregory, NHS Privatisation Drive Linked to Rise in Avoidable Deaths, Study Suggests, The Guardian (June 19, 2022), https://www.theguardian.com/society/2022/jun/29/nhs-privatisation-drive-linked-to-rise-in-avoidable-deaths-study-suggests.

[74] Nick Krachler & Ian Greer, When Does Marketisation Lead to Privatisation? Profit-making in English Health Services after the 2012 Health and Social Care Act, 124 Soc. Sci. & Med. 215 (2015).

[75] For more detailed studies, see Scott L. Greer et al., Mobilizing Bias in Europe: Lobbies, Democracy and EU Health Policy-Making, 9 Eur. Union Pol. 403 (2008); Scott L. Greer, The Changing World of European Health Lobbies, in Lobbying the European Union: Institutions, Actors, and Issues 189–211 (David Coen & Jeremy Richardson eds., 2009); this phenomenon is also not limited to Europe and is likely a global problem. For example, on the influence of lobbyists in Africa, see Barry Solaiman, Lobbying in Tunisia: Developing a Transparency Regime to Tackle Perceptions of Corruption, in Deconstructing Corruption in Africa 104–27 (Inna Kubbe, Emmanuel Saffa Abdulai and Michael Johnston eds., 2024) https://doi.org/10.4324/9781003468608-8.

[76] Harry Cooper, Brussels Influence, Presented by EUI STG: EU-funded Fair Trade Campaign – Wealthy Lobbyists – Rise of the Robots, Politico (Feb. 2, 2018), https://www.politico.eu/newsletter/politico-eu-influence/politico-brussels-influence-presented-by-eui-stg-eu-funded-fair-trade-campaign-wealthy-lobbyists-rise-of-the-robots/.

of lobbying activity in the EU's health policy space.[77] In the future, systematic research concerning the actual health policies influenced by private entities in the EU would help delineate the extent to which laws are being shaped to benefit those interests.

4.5 CONCLUSION

While public law is predominant as a matter of legal governance for health care matters, the reality is somewhat more complex in Europe. This chapter has explored the topic from three lenses to provide points of contrast with the US. First, by examining the structure of health care services, we can see how private care fits into the overarching system of health care services.

Second, while contract law mechanisms exist to resolve disputes, there is little empirical evidence to analyze their implications where they exist. As the data regulation ecosystem develops, more avenues for private law may arise. Finally, the influence of private lobbyists in Europe highlights how laws and policies can be shaped to create new avenues for those entities to provide services.

77 Helen Collis et al., Health Is Where the Money Is in Brussels and Disease Groups Are Circling, Politico (Nov. 30, 2021), https://www.politico.eu/article/health-where-money-is-brussels-disease-lobby-groups-eu-budget/; see also the concern that decision-making powers of doctors and patients where artificial intelligence is used in patient care may be ceded to private entities, Barry Solaiman and Abeer Malik, Regulating Algorithmic Care in the European Union: Evolving Doctor-Patient Models through the Artificial Intelligence Act (AI-Act) and the Liability Directives, Med. L. Rev. 1–22 (2024); see also, Barry Solaiman, From AI to Law in Healthcare: The Proliferation of Global Guidelines in a Void of Legal Uncertainty, 42(2) Med. L. 391–406 (2023).

PART II

Tools of Private Law

Torts, Contracts, and Property as Vehicles of Health Policy Introduction

Wendy Netter Epstein

This part takes up the quintessential tools of private law – torts, contracts, and property – and considers their potential for fixing what ails our health care system. The list of problems in need of solutions is long. But at the top of that list are *cost* – we spend twice as much per person on health as peer nations – *quality* – we perform worse than peer nations in important quality metrics – and *access* – too many Americans are uninsured, underinsured, or otherwise lack equitable access to care.

The authors in the chapters that follow take a nuanced approach to a wide range of issues impacting health policy. They don't all agree on whether private law is the right tool to deploy, or whether we should instead be turning to public law, such as statutory or regulatory fixes. What emerges is a view that private law can be a useful tool, particularly when public law fixes are inadequate or unavailable, but that it cannot solve all problems.

The first two chapters consider the promise of tort law. Mark A. Hall, in Chapter 7 "Adaptation of Tort Law to Modern Health Care Delivery in the Restatement of Medical Malpractice," takes up the classic example of medical liability law. As a reporter for the American Law Institute's first project to restate medical liability law, he explores whether tort law is meeting the needs of a rapidly evolving health care system that bears little resemblance to its much simpler origins. Hall discusses three examples from the new Restatement: the formation of a treatment relationship, the scope of individual liability when professionals work in treatment teams, and the extent to which institutions may be liable for medical error. In a nuanced discussion, he concludes that tort law's dual features of inertia and adaptability make it capable of evolving as practice evolves but also make it not well suited to leading reform.

Alberto De Diego-Habel, Jill Horwitz, and Daniel Rodriguez also consider the promise of tort law – in their case, to both compensate for and deter pandemic harms. The harm that flowed from COVID-19 was immense, not just in the loss of over 1 million American lives but also in the health and economic consequences for many more. In their chapter (Chapter 8), "Pandemic Harms and Private Law's Limits: A Proposal for Tort Replacement," they argue that civil tort claims proved an inadequate legal tool and will continue to be ill-suited to address the harms of future pandemics. Difficulty proving causation largely stymied the usefulness of tort to COVID-19 victims. But it is also not clear that a better result would have been opening up the floodgates of liability to businesses already operating in a tenuous time. Instead, they argue that a publicly administered tort-replacement scheme – a form of compensation through social insurance – would be a better alternative in providing quicker, more efficient, more equitable compensation to those harmed, while also providing finality and certainty to businesses.

Two chapters then take on the promise and peril of using contract law as a vehicle of health policy.

In their chapter (Chapter 6), "States as Contractor: Attempts to Drive Health Care Cost Containment through State Purchasing Power," Christine H. Monahan, Maanasa Kona, and Madeline O'Brien describe how states, functioning as "de facto private actors," are using their contract powers to further public policy goals like cost containment. Some states use their gatekeeping power over their state-based ACA exchange to negotiate lower prices and better product offerings. States can extract concessions from insurers who seek access to state enrollees. Other states have contracted with private insurers to offer market-based public options, which advance cost containment goals without requiring a state to operate its own health insurance plan. State employee health plans also leverage their contracting power to contain costs, primarily by using their market power to negotiate lower reimbursement rates. In a world where regulatory price control might be the first-best option for cost containment but is politically infeasible, Monahan, Kona, and O'Brien see promise in state contractual approaches to control cost.

Craig Konnoth's chapter (Chapter 5), "Data Transparency, ERISA Preemption, and Freedom of Contract," similarly describes a complicated interplay between private actors, state law, and freedom of contract. Specifically, Konnoth takes on the recent proliferation of state laws aiming to improve transparency in health care, including regulation promoting All Payers' Claims Databases, requiring disclosure of pharmaceutical pricing methodology, and obligating plans and providers to disclose network status to guard against surprise medical bills. As a category, transparency laws serve a public regulatory function, but also support private market functioning, providing information to support consumers in making more informed choices. Courts have been finding state transparency laws to be preempted by ERISA. But Konnoth argues that courts may be more likely to reject ERISA preemption challenges if they consider the role transparency laws play in supporting contracting between private parties. Konnoth turns the original question on its head, addressing the extent to which public law or regulation should be used to improve the functioning of private markets.

Finally, in Chapter 9 "The Human Body Commons: A Private Law Contribution for the Advancement of the Right to Health," Enrique Santamaría Echeverría takes on the important problem of the privatization of research, which can hinder innovation to promote collective health. Echeverria acknowledges the difficulty of the problem. On the one hand, keeping scientific knowledge in the public domain has tremendous value for researchers who seek to build on each other's work. On the other hand, innovation is spurred along by a promise of profits, which incentivizes innovators to protect their work from the public domain. Recognizing both the importance of the profit motive and the benefits of open access to research, Echeverria explores how private law, including contracts and property rights, can promote both interests.

These chapters together suggest important, continuing roles for tort, contract, and property law to promote the health and welfare of society. But they also highlight the insufficiency of these tools standing alone. Policymakers and lawmakers will have to continue to wrestle with how private law can be used to bolster systemic goals, but also with which policy goals and reform efforts require statutory and regulatory intervention.

5

Data Transparency, ERISA Preemption, and Freedom of Contract

Craig Konnoth[*]

5.1 INTRODUCTION

In recent years, an increasingly libertarian judiciary has struck down a range of health care transparency regulation under the Employee Retirement and Income Security Act (ERISA). ERISA preempts state laws that "relate to" employee benefit plans.[1] This test is an indeterminate one,[2] and thus, lower courts bolster their analysis with policy considerations in striking down these laws.

Several scholars, including myself, have argued that invalidating these transparency laws is undesirable for various reasons.[3] I do not seek to reprise that debate here. Rather, this chapter focuses on rebutting a specific policy consideration that courts advance when invalidating transparency laws – namely, that such laws undermine freedom of contract by forcing plaintiffs to disclose information in violation of contracts to which they are parties. This chapter identifies a doctrinal thread in ERISA cases that rebuts such freedom of *contract* claims using freedom of *choice* arguments: indeed, as various cases hold, it is freedom of *choice* that truly vindicates freedom of contract values. Based on those cases, I argue that transparency laws advance both freedom of choice and contract by giving parties necessary information.

Advancing this argument is important. State defendants generally highlight the public regulatory interests that transparency laws serve. But many market-oriented

[*] This is a truncated version of the essay. A fuller version of the essay is on file with the author.

[1] 29 U.S.C. § 1144(a).

[2] Prudential Ins. Co. of Am. v. Nat'l Park Med. Ctr., Inc., 154 F.3d 812, 818 (8th Cir. 1998).

[3] Erin C. Fuse Brown & Jaime S. King, ERISA as a Barrier for State Health Care Transparency Efforts, in Transparency in Health and Health Care in the United States: Law and Ethics 304–05 (Holly Fernandez Lynch et al. eds., 2019); Craig Konnoth, Health Data Federalism, B.U. L. Rev. 2169, 2187–89 (2021); Craig Konnoth, Privatization's Preemptive Effects, 134 Harv. L. Rev. 1937, 1961, 2207 (2021).

judges are less attuned to the goals of public regulation. Advancing arguments that vindicate market- and contract-based values might prove more successful.

The chapter begins by describing how courts have invalidated significant amounts of state transparency regulation, including regulation pertaining to All Payers' Claims Databases (APCDs),[4] pharmacy data,[5] and surprise billing prohibitions.[6] Sections 5.3 and 5.4 then explain how, to justify ERISA preemption of state law, courts invoke policy arguments sounding in freedom of contract.

While such arguments have a powerful resonance, Section 5.5 traces a line of ERISA cases, namely those involving any willing provider (AWP) laws, in which state defendants neutralized freedom of contract claims by advancing freedom of choice arguments. It also looks to historical contract law cases, which juxtaposed freedom of choice and freedom of contract to hold that ultimately, freedom of choice helped vindicate true freedom of contract values.

Section 5.6 lays out the argument that transparency laws furthers freedom of choice, and, resultantly, of contract. States have generally offered arguments sounding in public regulatory interests, such as cost- and quality-control to defend these laws. I argue that presenting transparency rationales as ways to allow informed consumers to make choices to promote well-functioning markets may produce better outcomes before market-oriented judges. By forcing information availability, data transparency laws promote contracting in the private market as did AWP laws.

5.2 TRANSPARENCY LEGISLATION

"[H]ealth care price transparency initiatives are all the rage."[7] While the Affordable Care Act and subsequent federal legislation have taken significant steps to promote transparency, states have been at the forefront of the effort. Three initiatives have received significant commentary.

The first are laws that promote APCDs – databases containing information that providers send to insurance companies for reimbursement.[8] Many state laws require health insurance companies to submit this data to a state agency.[9] APCDs serve a dual purpose: first, giving states information to address public health crises like COVID-19 and opioid misuse, and, second, cross-checking health data accuracy, calculating reimbursement rates, and the like. The databases also promote price transparency as they supply information to consumers and health care providers.

4 Gobeille v. Liberty Mut. Ins. Co., 577 U.S. 312, 323–24 (2016).

5 Pharm. Care Mgmt. Ass'n v. Gerhart, 852 F.3d 722, 728–30 (8th Cir. 2017).

6 Brown & King, supra note 3, at 308.

7 Stephen Barlas, Health Care Price Transparency Initiatives Are All the Rage: But Burgeoning Efforts Suffer from Myriad Shortcomings, 43 P&T 744 (2018).

8 Konnoth, Health Data Federalism, supra note 3.

9 Id. at 2189–90, 2205–10.

Next, starting in 2016, numerous states have passed bills requiring pharmacy benefits managers (PBMs) to report pricing methodology to state insurance commissioners and, often, to the pharmacies with which they contract. Information includes "increases in list prices, . . . aggregated dollar amount of rebates, [and] fees or price concessions provided by manufacturers."[10]

A third category in which states have shown a pattern of promoting health transparency is in the context of surprise billing by out-of-network providers. Several states have enacted regulations requiring plans and providers to disclose information about network participation so that patients are not surprised by the higher costs incurred from going to out-of-network providers.[11] As of 2022, federal legislation also provides out-of-network coverage protection,[12] but some state laws go further.[13]

5.3 ERISA PREEMPTION CASES

ERISA preempts state laws that "relate to" employee benefit plans.[14] The inquiry has two prongs. First, a state law that makes "reference" to a plan is preempted. Next, laws that have a "connection to" ERISA plans are also invalid.[15] This chapter will not analyze this test in detail. Suffice it to say that a series of cases have invalidated state transparency laws under this test.

In *Gobeille v. Liberty Mutual*, the Supreme Court invalidated data collection mandates for self-insured employers in APCDs under the "connection to" prong of the preemption test. According to the Court, the APCD reporting law would "govern, or interfere with the uniformity of, plan administration and so ha[s] an impermissible connection with ERISA plans."[16] As a result of the ruling, 60 percent of all employers can ignore information mandates in their states.[17]

A year after *Gobeille*, in *Pharmaceutical Care Management Association v. Gerhart*, the Eighth Circuit targeted the second category of transparency regulation—PBM reporting, under both prongs of the preemption test. *Gerhart* held first that, because the state PBM statute explicitly *exempted* certain ERISA

[10] Colleen Becker, Digging into Prescription Drug Data: Affordability Boards and Transparency, Nat'l Conf. of State Legislatures (Oct. 26, 2022), https://www.ncsl.org/health/digging-into-prescription-drug-data-affordability-boards-and-transparency.

[11] Brown & King, supra note 3, at 303–04.

[12] No Surprises Act, 42 U.S.C. § 300gg-111(e) (effective Jan. 1, 2022).

[13] Jack Hoadley et al., No Surprises Act: A Federal-State Partnership to Protect Consumers from Surprise Medical Bills, The Commonwealth Fund (Oct. 20, 2022), https://www.commonwealthfund.org/publications/fund-reports/2022/oct/no-surprises-act-federal-state-partnership-protect-consumers.

[14] 29 U.S.C. § 1144(a).

[15] Pharm. Care Mgmt. Ass'n, supra note 5, at 729.

[16] Gobeille, supra note 4, at 320 (quotation marks omitted).

[17] Konnoth, Privatization's Preemptive Effects, supra note 3, at 2204.

plans from compliance, the statute therefore made explicit "*reference*" to the plans.[18] Then, for good measure, the court also relied on *Gobeille* to hold that the law failed under the "connection to" prong. PBMs act as third-party administrators of pharmacy benefits for ERISA plans, reasoned the court. Referencing *Gobeille*'s language that I quote above, the court held that a law that "compels PBMs as third-party administrators to report to the commissioner and to network pharmacies their [reimbursement] methodology" therefore "intrudes upon a matter central to plan administration and interferes with nationally uniform plan administration."[19]

Notwithstanding subsequent Supreme Court case law on PBM legislation, *Gerhart* remains – in part – good law. In 2020, the Supreme Court upheld a state law requiring PBMs to reimburse pharmacies at higher rates. The Court noted that the PBM regulation does not "refer" to an ERISA plan as it "does not act immediately and exclusively upon ERISA plans because it applies to PBMs whether or not they manage an ERISA plan."[20] *Gerhart*'s "reference to" analysis thus no longer survives. But *Gerhart*'s analysis under the "connection with" prong remains intact.[21]

5.4 THE FREEDOM OF CONTRACT BACKDROP

The cases above purport to rely on formalistic analysis, and scholars treat *Gobeille* in particular as a straightforward example of ERISA preemption.[22] But ERISA doctrinal analysis is indeterminate.[23] As a practical matter, courts invoke policy considerations such as uniformity of administration or burdens on administrators, and scholars have commented on these policy claims. But one policy justification that has received no attention is that concerning freedom of contract.

As I argue elsewhere, there was more to *Gobeille* than met the eye. The employer's ERISA plan argued in its briefing that preemption of state law was required because the state regulation displaced contracts between beneficiaries and the insurance company, which, it claimed, required keeping data confidential.[24] Significant text was devoted to this argument by the United States Solicitor

18 Id. Somewhat confusingly, the court held that ERISA also made "implicit" reference to ERISA by regulating PBMs, which provide services to ERISA plans.

19 Id. at 731.

20 Rutledge v. Pharm. Care Mgmt. Ass'n, 141 S. Ct. 474, 481 (2020).

21 *Rutledge*'s PBM regulation involved reimbursement standards and was therefore governed by N.Y. State Conf. Blue Cross & Blue Shield Plans v. Travelers Ins. Co., 514 U.S. 645 (1995), which had approved of such standards. Rutledge, supra note 20, at 480. But *Gerhart*'s regulation involved data transparency, and would be governed by *Gobeille*. Space limitations do not allow me to explain further.

22 Konnoth, Privatization's Preemptive Effects, supra note 3, at 2204.

23 See, e.g., N.Y. State Conf. Blue Cross & Blue Shield Plans v. Travelers Ins. Co., supra note 21, 655 ("[i]f 'relate to' were taken to extend to the furthest stretch of its indeterminacy, then for all practical purposes pre-emption would never run its course").

24 Id. at 2204–05; Konnoth, Privatization's Preemptive Effects, supra note 3; Harris v. BP Corp. N. Am. Inc., No. 15 C 10299, 2016 WL 8193539, at *7 (N.D. Ill. July 8, 2016).

General's Office before the ERISA plan even filed its brief.[25] This debate over the importance of respecting contracts was strange: While the Supreme Court in the nineteenth and early twentieth centuries was sympathetic to plaintiffs who challenged state laws that, they claimed, undermined freedom of contract under the Contract Clause, since the New Deal, this approach to the Contract Clause has been repudiated. State law has generally been understood to govern contract terms.[26]

Despite the demise of freedom of contract arguments in constitutional doctrine, they retained a strange afterlife in ERISA cases. The earliest ERISA preemption cases in the 1970s concerned pension benefits,[27] with plaintiffs complaining that ERISA undermined freedom of contract in pension arrangements. Courts replied that that was exactly what ERISA was *meant* to do. As an Alabama district court wrote in 1979, with ERISA, "freedom of contract was largely eliminated from the world of pension agreements."[28] That line of thinking filtered its way into courts of appeals.[29]

While freedom of contract arguments failed in the 1970s pension cases, in the 1980s, employers brought a new set of preemption cases, claiming that state laws regarding *health plans* were preempted. By this time academic, and then, judicial, attitudes to freedom of contract had changed, and courts took a different tack.[30] A decade after one Alabama district court opinion repudiated freedom of contract principles in pension plans, another Alabama district court held that those principles remained alive and well in welfare benefit plans: "Congress included welfare benefit plans within the scheme of ERISA, but did not provide an extensive array of mandatory provisions as it did for pension plans. The implication here is that parties retain a greater degree of freedom to contract between themselves as to what benefits will be provided under welfare plans."[31] This language became boilerplate in

[25] See Konnoth, Privatization's Preemptive Effects, supra note 3, at 2208. As Respondent, the ERISA plan filed its briefs only *after* the US brief was filed. Space constraints prevent a full treatment of the argument.

[26] See generally James W. Ely, Jr., Whatever Happened to the Contract Clause?, 4 Charleston L. Rev. 371 (2010).

[27] Patricia McDonnell et al., Self-Insured Health Plans, 8(2) Health Care Fin. Rev. 1–2 (Winter 1986).

[28] Thomas v. Marshall, 482 F. Supp. 160, 164 (S.D. Ala. 1979).

[29] For example, van Boxel v. Journal Co. Emps. Pension Tr., 836 F.2d 1048, 1052 (7th Cir. 1987); Williams v. Rohm & Haas Pension Plan, 497 F.3d 710, 714 (7th Cir. 2007); Esden v. Bank of Bos., 229 F.3d 154, 173 (2d Cir. 2000); all argued that in pension contexts, ERISA was meant to eliminate freedom of contract.

[30] See F. H. Buckley, Introduction, in The Fall and Rise of the Freedom of Contract 1–2 (F. H. Buckley ed., 1999) (noting how freedom of contract sentiments had returned to vogue since the 1970s).

[31] Carland v. Metro. Life Ins. Co., 727 F. Supp. 592, 597 (D. Kan. 1989), aff'd, 935 F.2d 1114 (10th Cir. 1991).

judicial opinions that emphasized the importance of freedom of contract in welfare benefit plans.[32]

While there were some asides in opinions that recognized the limitations of freedom of contract doctrine,[33] in a small but steady diet of cases since the 1980s through today, courts have infused the policy analysis that characteristically underlies ERISA preemption cases with freedom of contract claims. One district court linked the "'vital public interest' in health care cost containment … with the traditional freedom to contract as one pleases."[34] Another emphasized that "the public has an interest in protecting the freedom to contract by enforcing contractual rights and obligations."[35] And in 2017, a court held that "[r]equiring … compl [iance] with … plan[] procedures not only respects freedom of contract, but will also serve important purposes," relating to the ERISA dispute resolution process.[36] Every court to invoke freedom of contract has found that ERISA preempts the state statute. Even though freedom of contract is never the centerpiece of the holdings, its appearance is notable.

ERISA preemption cases involving transparency statutes also endorse contract principles (albeit not as explicitly as the ERISA preemption cases I describe above). The *Gobeille* Court began its application of ERISA doctrine by observing that "ERISA does not guarantee substantive benefits. The statute, instead, seeks to make *the benefits promised by an employer more secure* by mandating certain oversight systems and other standard procedures."[37] Similarly, the offense in *Gerhart* is described as "dictating the manner by which PBMs contract with pharmacies regarding … pricing."[38]

5.5 REBUTTING FREEDOM OF CONTRACT – THE AWP CASES

How might one address the freedom of contract anxiety that courts evince in striking down transparency statutes? One answer might lie in a line of cases that successfully defeated these arguments – those concerning AWP statutes.

These statutes require insurers or PBMs to contract with any provider willing to abide by their terms to prevent insurers from limiting costs by artificially throttling

32 Carland v. Metro. Life Ins. Co., 935 F.2d 1114 (10th Cir. 1991) (quoting cases with similar holdings).

33 Buce v. Allianz Life Ins. Co., 247 F.3d 1133, 1150 n.1 (11th Cir. 2001) (Barkett, J., concurring) (noting in a footnote "the limits the 'savings clause' imposes on an ERISA insurer's freedom to contract").

34 St. Francis Reg'l Med. Ctr. v. Blue Cross & Blue Shield of Kansas, Inc., 49 F.3d 1460, 1466–67 (10th Cir. 1995).

35 MBI Energy Servs. v. Hoch, No. 1:16-CV-329, 2016 WL 9307197, at *4 (D.N.D. Sept. 19, 2016).

36 In re UnitedHealth Grp. PBM Litig., No. 16-CV-3352, 2017 WL 6512222, at *14 (D. Minn. Dec. 19, 2017).

37 Gobeille, supra note 4, at 320–21 (emphasis added).

38 Pharm. Care Mgmt. Ass'n, supra note 5, at 728.

the ability of individuals to access care.[39] By 1986, eight states had passed these AWP statutes,[40] leading to some of the earliest ERISA preemption litigation. But outcomes conflicted. Two circuits held that ERISA preempted these laws; two circuits held the opposite.[41]

Those supporting the laws argued that even if these laws "relate[d] to" a plan, and therefore met ERISA's preemption test, they survived under a preemption exception which allowed states to "regulate[] insurance."[42] The Supreme Court, through Justice Scalia, sided with this view in *Kentucky Association of Health Plans v. Miller*.[43]

The doctrine surrounding the insurance savings clause, as the Court admits in *Miller* itself,[44] is far from clear.[45] Indeed, commentators have suggested that *Miller* was "self-contradictory" and probably unworkable.[46] Just as courts rely on policy arguments to determine whether state laws "relate to" an ERISA plan in the first place because of the term's indeterminacy, those parsing the insurance savings clause also invoke policy claims – including freedom of contract arguments.

The previous section notes that in ERISA health preemption cases, courts that mention freedom of contract arguments do so to hold that the state laws are invalid. The AWP cases are no exception. In *CIGNA Healthplan of Louisiana v. Ieyoub*, the first lawsuit that resulted in appellate invalidation of an AWP law,[47] the plaintiffs sought freedom of contract as an independent ground of relief. They argued both that "the Any Willing Provider Statute is preempted by ERISA" and, "[a]s an alternative claim, ... that the statute violates the Due Process Clause ... because it interferes with the plaintiffs' freedom to contract with health care providers of their choice."[48] In a ruling affirmed on appeal, the court held that ERISA preempted the AWP law. Similarly, in a lower court ruling in the Eighth Circuit (the other

39 The countervailing concern is that network providers would not be incented to provide discounts if out of network providers could force their way into the network.

40 Elizabeth Rolph et al., State Laws and Regulations Governing Preferred Provider Organizations 47–48 (1986).

41 Petition for a Writ of Certiorari at 11, Ky. Ass'n Health Plans v. Miller, 538 U.S. 329 (2003) (No. 00-1471). While courts that uphold AWP statutes tend to conflate mandated provider laws and AWP laws, see Cmty. Health Partners, Inc. v. Com. of Ky., 14 F. Supp. 2d 991, 1000 (W.D. Ky. 1998), there are meaningful differences between the laws, see Express Scripts, Inc. v. Wenzel, 102 F. Supp. 2d 1135, 1150 (W.D. Mo. 2000).

42 29 U.S.C. 1144(b)(2)(A).

43 Ky. Ass'n Health Plans v. Miller, 538 U.S. 329, 341–42 (2003).

44 Id.

45 Id. at 339–40.

46 Sara Rosenbaum et al., Law and the American Health Care System 403 (2d ed. 2012).

47 CIGNA Healthplan of La., Inc. v. State, ex rel. Ieyoub, 883 F. Supp. 94, 96 (M.D. La. 1995), aff'd sub nom., CIGNA Healthplan of La., Inc. v. State of La. ex rel. Ieyoub, 82 F.3d 642 (5th Cir. 1996). In a previous case, a Virginia district court had invalidated an AWP law only to be overturned on appeal. Stuart Circle Hosp. Corp. v. Aetna Health Mgmt., 995 F.2d 500 (4th Cir. 1993).

48 CIGNA Healthplan, supra note 47, 883 F. Supp. at 96.

jurisdiction to invalidate AWP laws) the court explained that the effect of AWP laws "on ERISA plans is to eliminate their freedom to contract with HMOs."[49] In the other AWP cases as well, petitioners advanced arguments that sounded in freedom of contract – ultimately, and unsuccessfully – at the Supreme Court.[50]

But two circuits, and later, the Supreme Court, upheld these laws and rejected ERISA preemption. In these cases, freedom of contract was never mentioned. Rather, courts emphasized a different concept – freedom of choice. As proponents of AWP statutes emphasized, the laws allowed consumers to choose providers they wanted. For instance, in *Stuart Circle v. Aetna*, the court explained that the state legislature had given "priority to an insured's freedom to choose doctors and hospitals over the possibility of reduced insurance premiums .... The wisdom of this decision is a concern of the legislature, not the judiciary."[51]

Five years later, faced with the challenge that would mature into *Miller*, the district court quoted extensively from *Stuart Circle*, and noted that "freedom to choose a treating physician is inextricable from the nature of the coverage provided."[52] On appeal, the Sixth Circuit plugged the same refrain with even greater vigor. It noted that the law would "increase benefits to the insureds by giving them greater freedom to choose health care providers,"[53] and noted that policyholders were concerned with "restriction on their freedom of choice in seeking medical treatment."[54] Indeed, the freedom of choice argument attracted the dissent's ire. After questioning whether the AWP law actually promoted "freedom of choice," the dissent curtly cautioned, "any concerns over freedom of choice are beside the point."[55] The Supreme Court affirmed the majority, though without mentioning freedom of choice.

The contrast is clear. Cases coming down in favor of ERISA preemption generally, and with respect to AWP laws in particular, raise freedom of contract as one of ERISA's aims. In the AWP context, however, courts that decided against ERISA preemption invoked freedom of choice arguments instead.

Critics might suggest that I am reading too much into these cases. After all, prominent literature that defends freedom of contract uses the terms "contract" and

49 Express Scripts, Inc. v. Wenzel, 102 F. Supp. 2d 1135, 1147 (W.D. Mo. 2000), aff'd, 262 F.3d 829 (8th Cir. 2001).

50 Petition for a Writ of Certiorari at 5 n.2, Miller, 538 U.S. 329, (No. 00-1471) ("restrictions on petitioners' freedom to contract with chiropractors"); Express Scripts, 102 F. Supp. 2d at 1147 (W.D. Mo. 2000) ("The alleged impact of H.B. 335 on ERISA plans is to eliminate their freedom to contract. . . .").

51 Stuart Circle, supra note 47, at 504–05.

52 Health Maint. Org. Ass'n of Ky. v. Nichols, No. CIV.A. 97-24, 1998 WL 34103663, at *7 (E.D. Ky. Aug. 6, 1998) (citation omitted).

53 Kentucky Ass'n of Health Plans, Inc. v. Nichols, 227 F.3d 352, 368 (6th Cir. 2000).

54 Id. at 370.

55 Id. at 380 (Kennedy, J., dissenting).

"choice" interchangeably,[56] as do widely cited judicial decisions,[57] and one appellate ERISA preemption case.[58] Yet, however the terms are used elsewhere, in the ERISA opinions I describe above, and in related party submissions, freedom of choice constitutes a term of art, referring to a certain subset of laws that allows patients to see providers that they prefer. And the courts in *these* cases, at least, do not use the term interchangeably but almost in contraposition to each other.

Indeed, we see even more explicit juxtaposition of freedom of contract and choice in other lines of cases. During the 1970s, when courts were least sympathetic to freedom of contract claims,[59] the need to ensure true freedom of choice was widely relied on as a reason to ignore formalistic adherence to contract. In an influential and widely quoted passage,[60] for example, the New Jersey Supreme Court in *Kugler v. Romain* defended unconscionability doctrine, by noting, "[t]he intent of the clause is not to erase the doctrine of freedom of contract, but to make realistic the assumption of the law that the agreement has resulted from real bargaining between parties who had freedom of choice and understanding and ability to negotiate in a meaningful fashion."[61] Thus, held *Kugler*, "freedom to contract survives," but is dependent on whether there is actual freedom of choice.[62]

At the same time, these courts reasoned, it is a mistake to paint freedom of choice as a completely separate concept from 'true' freedom of contract. Indeed, many courts that relied on freedom of choice to counter freedom of contract arguments ultimately concluded that freedom of choice as they saw it enabled true freedom of contract. As the Puerto Rico Supreme Court explained in another highly cited opinion that drew limits around noncompete agreements: excessively stringent contracts "not only ... violate contractual good faith but also public policy, by excessively and unjustifiably restricting the employee's freedom of contract and the general public's freedom of choice."[63] As another court explained in the early years of freedom of contract's decline, "[l]iberty of contract does not mean the right to make any kind of contract with any body but merely the right to make contracts with competent persons on a plane of relative parity or freedom of choice."[64]

56 Robin Kar, Contract as Empowerment, 83 U. Chi. L. Rev. 759, 807 (2016); Gregory S. Alexander, Freedom, Coercion, and the Law of Servitudes, 73 Cornell L. Rev. 883, 903 (1988).

57 Barnes v. New Hampshire Karting Ass'n, Inc., 509 A.2d 151, 153 (1986) (exculpatory agreements) ("freedom of choice [means that] parties should be able to contract freely"); Essling v. Markman, 335 N.W.2d 237, 239 (Minn. 1983) (referring to "freedom of choice or contract").

58 St. Francis Reg'l Med. Ctr., supra note 34, at 1464. ("Congress has chosen not to interfere with the parties' own freedom of contract on this matter, so must we insist that the states not interfere with the parties' freedom of choice.")

59 See Ely, supra note 26.

60 See, e.g., 8 Richard A. Lord, Williston on Contracts § 18:8 (4th ed. May 2023).

61 Kugler v. Romain, 279 A.2d 640, 652 (N.J. 1971).

62 Id.

63 Arthur Young & Co. v. Vega III, 136 P.R. Dec. 157 (1994) (cited by PACIV, Inc. v. Perez Rivera, 159 P.R. Dec. 523, 2003 TSPR 84 (2003); TLS Mgmt. & Mktg. Servs., LLC v. Rodriguez-Toledo, 966 F.3d 46, 60 (1st Cir. 2020)).

64 McGrew v. Indus. Comm'n, 85 P.2d 608, 613 (Utah 1938).

Thus, "freedom of choice" considerations may undermine freedom of contract as a formal matter but ultimately advance its true goals. Such an approach to freedom of contract – which relies on whether parties have freedom of choice – has implications for the ERISA transparency cases.

5.6 TRANSPARENCY LAWS FURTHER FREEDOM OF CHOICE

It is hard to assess the extent to which freedom of contract arguments play a role in ERISA preemption. Yet, it would appear that increasingly market-oriented courts see freedom of contract as an important value, and view ERISA preemption as a means to vindicate it. These courts might be unsympathetic to counterarguments that draw on public regulatory goals, such as price-setting. But advancing freedom of choice arguments – which, ultimately, can be reframed as helping achieve true freedom of contract, might prove more successful.

Transparency laws in general serve dual purposes as Section 5.2 explains. For example, APCD laws serve public regulatory goals such as price setting, but also private purposes, such as providing data transparency to allow consumers and other stakeholders to negotiate with insurers. This is true of other transparency initiatives including those involving PBMs. State litigants, however, have tended to emphasize the regulatory importance of these laws.

Consider the *Gerhart* litigation. The state's brief did not raise concerns about inequitable bargaining power even once. It rather emphasized the public, regulatory goals of the PBM statute. The AWP law "*regulates* a PBM's reimbursement of pharmacies. It *regulates* the pharmacy side of PBMs' business."[65] Rather than explaining how the law helps pharmacies negotiate with PBMs, it emphasized how the law regulates the negotiation.

By contrast, amici heavily emphasized how the transparency laws promoted private bargaining between parties. They point to the bargaining inequity between parties: "independent pharmacies cannot simply refuse to do business with PBMs, much less insist upon fair contractual terms ... as PBMs manage drug benefits for 95 percent of all Americans with prescription-drug benefits .... Thus, PBMs are able to impose take-it-or-leave-it contracts on pharmacies." Notably, "even large pharmacies, like those managed by CVS, Walgreens, and Kmart, have struggled to secure fair treatment from PBMs."[66] The legislation addresses these concerns because – in part – it "requires PBMs to disclose how they calculate their reimbursement amounts in any contracts with Iowa pharmacies and gives contracting pharmacies a chance to contest the reimbursement amount."[67] In this way, their

[65] Brief of Defendants/Appellees at 31, Gerhart, 852 F.3d 722 (No. 15-3292) (emphasis added).

[66] Brief of the National Community Pharmacists Association at 3, Gerhart, 852 F.3d 722 (No. 15-3292).

[67] Id. at 4.

reasoning evoked the contract analysis of the courts in the AWP cases described above, who sought to promote freedom of choice.

The *Gobeille* briefing presented the same problem. Some – including government entities – did mention the importance of the data for private bargaining, though none of them foregrounded it as a purpose of the legislation. Thus, only after explaining how states used APCD data to address costs in their regulatory capacity did the brief of the AARP (formerly the American Association of Retired Persons) and others explain: "patients usually do not know the price of health care ... [and] need information to make informed choices about ... health care services, before they purchase these services – just as they would to make any other major purchase. They ... need to know ... whether they are getting the best value for their dollar."[68] The American Hospital Association with the American Association of Medical Colleges first emphasized the public health regulation that APCDs achieve at length, before, in a brief paragraph, noting that the "[p]atients – especially those who personally bear a significant share of their health care costs – need reliable sources of information for determining how to spend their health care dollars," and noting that Colorado had a website to promote this goal.[69] Other prominent briefs did the same, emphasizing a range of other significant public goals.[70] Few of these briefs mentioned, much less explained, the powerlessness that patient–consumers experience. None of them used the language of freedom of choice, which figured so prominently in the AWP cases, to defend the laws.[71]

And most of the briefs – including individual briefs filed by other states and by the American Medical Association[72] – did not even mention how data transparency furthered consumer choice. Most notably, the brief of the Petitioner, the state of Vermont, lists the uses of the data as follows: "improve the delivery of medical care to its citizens and guide health care regulation and policy."[73] Its Reply brief even mentions the federal uses to which the data is put.[74] Consumer and market participant needs were not mentioned.

Yet, there is a strong argument that transparency laws support freedom of choice. Colorado, New Hampshire, and Maine have each "used its APCD data to create a public website that enables its residents to compare the cost of health care services

68 Brief Amici Curiae of AARP et al., at 13–14, Gobeille, 577 U.S. 312 (No. 14-181).

69 Brief of Amici Curiae American Hospital Association, at 14, Gobeille, 577 U.S. 312 (No. 14-181).

70 Brief for the United States at 16, Gobeille, 577 U.S. 312 (No. 14-181); Brief for the States of New York et al. at 10–17, Gobeille, 577 U.S. 312 (No. 14-181) (hereinafter New York brief).

71 The closest was the US Department of Justice, which mentions it in passing. Brief for the United States at 19, Gobeille, 577 U.S. 312 (No. 14-181) ("over a dozen States have determined that such informational efforts can improve their citizens' healthcare, lower costs, and enhance consumer choice").

72 Brief of Amicus Curiae Connecticut Health Insurance Exchange at 2, Gobeille, 577 U.S. 312 (No. 14-181); Brief of Amici Curiae American Hospital Association, supra note 69.

73 Brief for Petitioner at 12, Gobeille, 577 U.S. 312 (No. 14-181).

74 Reply Brief for Petitioner at 23, Gobeille, 577 U.S. 312 (No. 14-181).

across providers within the State," while others intend to do so. Patients can "compare costs by selecting a particular kind of health care service [say, a hip replacement], a geographical area [say, within 25 miles from Denver], and the kind of insurance to be billed .... The website would then display the median price." The Maine website gives consumers and providers transparent information on provider performance, cost, and reimbursement.[75]

Arguing that data transparency supports freedom of choice for those who would otherwise lack it may prove to be important in advancing data transparency claims in other contexts. To be sure, the Supreme Court is unlikely to revisit APCDs. But other important data transparency efforts remain ongoing, as Section 5.2 describes. Further, the Department of Labor has drafted policies that would require self-funded plans to report APCD data federally – but only on a voluntary basis, likely fearing opposition to the policies.[76] Freedom of choice arguments might prove important in those policy contexts as well – while they are used in judicial decisions, they are policy arguments to begin with.

5.7 CONCLUSION

Freedom of choice is not the only, or arguably, even the most important, argument for data transparency. The public values – including those emphasized and foregrounded in the *Gobeille* briefing – are probably more vital than providing data to consumers to enable bargaining. Even with data, consumers will lack market power.[77] Data can also prove hard to parse and analyze for consumers, especially those experiencing serious medical conditions.[78] Yet, freedom of choice arguments allow promoters of transparency laws to meet those who promote freedom of contract on their own turf and can prove to be of strategic value in advancing the cause of data transparency before market-oriented courts. Rather than emphasizing public regulatory goals, then, state defendants and policymakers should create a record that emphasizes how these databases support contracting between private parties in order to withstand ERISA preemption challenges.

[75] New York brief, supra note 70, at 18–19.

[76] State All Payer Claims Databases Advisory Committee (SAPCDAC), U.S. Dep't of Labor, https://www.dol.gov/agencies/ebsa/about-ebsa/about-us/state-all-payer-claims-databases-advisory-committee.

[77] Michael K. Gusmano et al., Patient-Centered Care, Yes; Patients as Consumers, No, 38 Health Affs. 368, 370 (2019).

[78] Id.

6

States as Contractor

Attempts to Drive Health Care Cost Containment through State Purchasing Power

Christine H. Monahan, Maanasa Kona, and Madeline O'Brien[*]

6.1 INTRODUCTION

US health care costs are spiraling upwards, largely because of the high and rising prices set by hospitals and other health care providers. Commercial insurers and large employers mostly pass along these high prices to consumers in the form of increased premiums and cost-sharing, leaving many Americans financially unstable. Yet political and practical barriers block reforms that seek to limit provider prices via regulation. To circumvent these barriers, several states are leveraging their role as contracting entities and players in the private health care market to further public policy goals, such as controlling health care costs.

These government engagements in the private market fall somewhere along the porous border between private and public law. In the types of contracting relationships we discuss here, we posit that the state functions as a de facto private actor. While some might argue that the state can never function as a private actor, given its outsized power and the complex body of government contracting laws set up to protect its rights, we find that the similarities between the state as a private actor and large, fully privately owned, corporations are greater than the differences between them. Large corporations similarly bring their significant, sometimes monopolistic, power to bear in negotiating their contracts, and leverage centuries-old commercial laws to enforce those contracts. Both types of entities use their market position and legally provided protections to work toward their ultimate goals, which in the case of privately owned entities is profit, and in the case of state actors is the advancement of public policy goals such as saving taxpayer dollars or making health care affordable.

[*] Authors wish to thank Rachel Schwab and Kevin Lucia for their helpful edits and suggestions, as well as other faculty and staff at the Center on Health Insurance Reforms for their insights and inspiration.

In this chapter, we explore three examples of states turning to different types of typically private roles to try to lower commercial health care costs. First, we discuss how states can leverage their role as marketplace operators, like Amazon or Apple (vis a vis the "App" Store), to serve as a conduit between sellers and purchasers of insurance. This role allows states to engage in selective contracting practices with insurer-sellers to drive down premiums and drive up the value of the products offered on the marketplace. This is a tactic many envisioned as a best practice for marketplaces created under the Affordable Care Act (ACA). Second, we will turn to recent efforts by states like Washington to newly enter the private health insurance market by enacting public health insurance options in partnership with private health insurers. These efforts are also intended to bring to the market more high-value, low-cost insurance products to consumers. Third, we will examine how some states leverage their long-standing role as purchasers of health insurance to achieve cost containment. States, like most large, private employers, provide health insurance to their workers, retirees, and their dependents through employee health plans, and in any given state, the state employee health plan (SEHP) is one of the largest, if not the largest, purchasers of health benefit services from commercial insurers, who act as third-party administrators.

States have seen varying degrees of success and encountered different barriers, when engaging with the health insurance market in these three different roles. Other analyses of states engaging in the private market often focus on the merits of privatizing public programs and functions to reduce the size and scope of government and how these efforts risk the watering down of legal rights, remedies, and other protections for beneficiaries.[1] By contrast, our examples allow "agencies [to] extend their influence to matters and actors that they could not otherwise lawfully reach" and shape the market to achieve public interest goals.[2] Despite their promise, however, we find that market-driven reforms can only do so much when the marketplace is already as broken as the US health care system is. Nonetheless, they can still serve as intermediate steps on the way to a better-functioning health care market pending broader reforms to our health care delivery and payment systems.

6.2 ROADBLOCKS TO CONTAINING HEALTH CARE COSTS

The United States spends about twice as much as other high-income countries on health care, while performing relatively poorly on population health outcomes.[3]

1 See, e.g., David A. Super, Privatization, Policy Paralysis, and the Poor, 96 Calif. L. Rev. 393 (2008); Gillian E. Metzger, Privatization as Delegation, 103 Colum. L. Rev. 1367, 1376–400 (2003); Jody Freeman, The Contracting State, 28 Fla. St. U. L. Rev. 155, 176–88 (2000).

2 Jody Freeman, The Private Role in Public Governance, 75 N.Y.U. L. Rev. 543, 671 (2000).

3 Irene Papanicolas et al., Health Care Spending in the United States and Other High-Income Countries, 319 JAMA 1024, 1024 (2018).

These high costs are not driven by US patients using more services or the United States providing particularly high-quality care. Instead, they largely stem from the prices commercial insurers pay for hospital and physician services.[4]

Commercial insurers and group health plans in the United States pay for the health care of about 177 million people, and they pay significantly more than public insurers like Medicare and Medicaid for the same services.[5] In response to rising health care prices, these payers have shifted more of the cost burden to plan enrollees through higher premiums and out-of-pocket costs.[6] Given their ability to shift costs and market pressures to maintain good relationships with health care providers, commercial insurers have little incentive to negotiate lower prices with providers, and may in fact have an incentive to inflate spending because their profits are tied to a percentage of premiums collected (in the fully insured markets, due to federal medical loss ratio requirements) or claims paid (in self-insured markets, where insurers are administering plans funded by employers and employees).[7]

Insurers' insufficient incentive to negotiate lower prices, combined with rapid provider market consolidation, has given health care providers outsized leverage when contracting with insurers, and made it unlikely for the existing commercial insurance market to achieve meaningful cost containment absent government intervention. In response, experts and policymakers have debated a range of regulatory strategies to try and contain costs in the commercial sector and have largely reached the same conclusion: "the only solution that may be effective in a concentrated provider market is regulation of health care prices."[8] Yet few states currently regulate commercial health care prices and, with the exception of Maryland, efforts that have been made have generally been indirect (e.g., setting cost growth benchmarks) or narrowly focused (e.g., preventing "surprise" billing by out-of-network providers).[9] In the 1970s and 1980s, many more states directly regulated prices, but

4 Gerard F. Anderson et al., It's Still the Prices, Stupid: Why the US Spends So Much on Health Care, and a Tribute to Uwe Reinhardt, 38 Health Affs. 87, 93 (2019).

5 Cong. Budget Off., Policy Approaches to Reduce What Commercial Insurers Pay for Hospitals' and Physicians' Services 1 (2022), https://www.cbo.gov/publication/58222.

6 Gary Claxton et al., Employer Health Benefits: 2023 Annual Survey, Kaiser Family Found. 90–91, 111–14, 132–34 (2023), https://files.kff.org/attachment/Employer-Health-Benefits-Survey-2023-Annual-Survey.pdf.

7 Inside Big Health Insurers' Side Hustle, Tradeoffs (Sept. 23, 2021), https://tradeoffs.org/2021/09/23/inside-big-health-insurers-side-hustle/; Marshall Allen, Why Your Health Insurer Doesn't Care about Your Big Bills, Nat'l Pub. Radio (May 25, 2018, 5:00 AM), https://www.npr.org/sections/health-shots/2018/05/25/613685732/why-your-health-insurer-doesnt-care-about-your-big-bills.

8 Erin C. Fuse Brown, Resurrecting Health Care Rate Regulation, 67 Hastings L.J. 85, 128–29 (2015).

9 Provider Rate Regulation, The Source on HealthCare Price and Competition (May 2023), https://sourceonhealthcare.org/provider-rate-regulation/; Linda J. Blumberg et al., Can Employer-Sponsored Insurance Be Saved? A Review of Policy Options: Price Regulation, CHIRblog (Jan. 18, 2023), https://chirblog.org/can-esi-be-saved-review-of-policy-options-price-regulation/.

this fell out of favor for many interconnected reasons, including the general philosophical and political shift toward market-based mechanisms in the 1990s and the advent of managed care organizations promising to control costs via internal mechanisms.[10]

Renewed efforts to meaningfully regulate health care costs have failed largely due to political barriers.[11] The hospital industry holds significant political power and strongly opposes price regulation.[12] Because the insurance industry also profits from higher health spending, their interests are aligned.[13] Many policymakers also prefer a lighter regulatory touch, pushing back against government actions that can be seen as unduly affecting market dynamics.[14] When implemented, even narrow regulatory reforms face legal challenges and obstruction from industry.[15]

Given these obstacles, policymakers are turning to reforms that make use of government purchasing power and contracting tools, as more politically attractive and easier to implement. We explore three examples of states leveraging their contracting authority and purchasing power, rather than their regulatory authority, to lower health care costs in the private health insurance market. Although the reach of these reforms is narrower than traditional regulatory reforms, we explore the extent to which states can use them to effect incremental change while waiting for political winds to return in favor of price regulation.

6.3 WIELDING A LIGHTER TOUCH: CAN STATES CONTRACT TO LOWER HEALTH CARE PRICES?

6.3.1 *Health Insurance Marketplaces*

A health insurance exchange or marketplace is a state-operated one-stop shop where consumers or businesses can compare and enroll in health insurance products. The marketplace serves as the key connection point between insurance plans and consumer purchasers, similar to how Apple's iTunes store connects artists looking to sell their music with fans looking to purchase it. And, just as Apple separately

[10] Provider Rate Regulation, supra note 9; Len M. Nichols et al., Are Market Forces Strong Enough to Deliver Efficient Health Care Systems? Confidence Is Waning, 23(2) Health Affs. 8 (2004); Gail B. Agrawal & Howard R. Veit, Back to the Future: The Managed Care Revolution, 65(4) Law & Contemp. Probs. 11 (2002).

[11] Fuse Brown, supra note 8, at 138.

[12] Rachel Cohrs, The Health Care Issue Democrats Can't Solve: Hospital Reform, STAT News (Oct. 26, 2023), https://www.statnews.com/2023/10/26/the-health-care-issue-democrats-cant-solve-hospital-reform.

[13] See Allen, supra note 7; Katie Keith, Insurer Accountability in the Next Generation of Health Reform, 15 St. Louis U. J. Health L. & Pol'y 331, 339–40 (2022).

[14] See, e.g., Joseph Antos & James C. Capretta, The Road Not Taken, in The Trillion Dollar Revolution 66, 71–72 (Ezekiel J. Emanuel & Abbe R. Gluck eds., 2020).

[15] See generally Timothy Stoltzfus Jost & Katie Keith, ACA Litigation: Politics Pursued through Other Means, 45 J. Health Pol., Pol'y, & Law 485 (2020).

contracts with music artists before they can sell music on iTunes, the state enters into contracts with private health insurers seeking to sell their plans through the state-run exchanges. Experts envisioned that states would engage in a practice known as "active purchasing," and negotiate with several insurers to extract better insurance products and lower rates for the products that eventually end up on the marketplace.[16] States and employers can achieve this by employing selective contracting practices, such as competitive bidding and negotiation processes, to advance goals like cost containment. By requiring private insurers to compete against each other to earn the ability to participate in the marketplace, these practices harness traditional forces of market competition to nudge private actors to provide a more robust product. If the marketplace is not attractive to insurers, however, they can opt out and offer their plans to consumers off-marketplace.

The first successful active-purchasing marketplace was established by the Massachusetts Connector Authority in 2006. The Authority created a system of two separate marketplaces: Commonwealth Care for low-income individuals who qualify for state-funded subsidies, and Commonwealth Choice for non-state-subsidized individuals and small businesses. By making Commonwealth Care the sole source of state subsidies, Massachusetts could create a "captive" market, with all subsidy-eligible consumers incentivized to participate in Commonwealth Care rather than shopping elsewhere and paying full price.[17] This captive market encouraged insurer participation. As a result, the state had enough insurers wanting to participate that it was able to selectively contract with insurers. The Connector authority also structured marketplace rules to encourage lower bids from insurers: for example, automatically enrolling participants who signed up but failed to choose a plan in the lowest-cost option, and administering risk-sharing to protect plans against the risks of enrolling disproportionally expensive enrollees.[18] These decisions resulted in annual premium increases with half the growth rate of private insurance.[19]

Massachusetts served as a model for federal lawmakers designing the ACA, but ten years into implementation of the ACA marketplaces, California is the only other state to take similarly aggressive measures. Marketplace officials report that they "extract[] concessions on price and product design as a condition for having access to the largest pool of new enrollees in the state" and have "excluded plans that have

[16] Sabrina Corlette & JoAnn Volk, Active Purchasing for Health Insurance Exchange: An Analysis of Options, Nat'l Acad. Soc. Ins. 4 (June 2011), https://www.nasi.org/wp-content/uploads/2011/06/Active_Purchasing_for_Health_Insurance_Exchanges.pdf (quoting Alain C. Enthoven, The History and Principles of Managed Competition, 12 Health Affs. 24, 29 (Supp. 1993)).

[17] Id. at 7.

[18] Sabrina Corlette et al., The Massachusetts and Utah Health Exchanges: Lessons Learned, Georgetown Univ. Health Pol'y Inst. Ctr. for Children and Families (Mar. 2011), https://ccf.georgetown.edu/wp-content/uploads/2012/03/Health-reform_exchanges.pdf.

[19] Id.

not demonstrated the administrative capability, prices, networks, or product designs that improve consumer value."[20] Additionally, the marketplace "jawbones down premiums to the extent it can, leveraging its private information on risk mix, competitor rates, and the price elasticity of demand."[21] Studies suggest that these reforms have had a positive effect on the individual market. California's premiums have grown more slowly than national averages, marketplace enrollment is one of the highest in the country, and statewide average risk scores have been in the bottom 10 percent of states each year for both on-and-off marketplace plans.[22]

Some other state marketplaces and the federal marketplace have taken more cautious approaches, primarily focused on improving the quality and adequacy of coverage by requiring insurers to agree to certain minimum standards as a condition of marketplace participation. But these marketplaces have been reluctant to push for lower premiums using the best tool available to them – selective contracting with those insurers offering the most competitive rates or engaging in California-style "jawbone" negotiations.

There are several explanations for this hesitancy. In some states, proponents of limited government object to states employing these contracting tactics because they perceive it as the state controlling insurer access to the marketplace – Colorado explicitly prohibits their marketplace from "solicit[ing] bids or engag[ing] in the active purchasing of insurance."[23] Some experts also have argued that states cannot justify the expenditure of resources required to engage in active purchasing, since they do not foot the cost of premiums.[24] Market dynamics, including increasing insurer consolidation, likely play the biggest role, however.

Few insurers participated in the individual and small group markets served by ACA marketplaces, when the law was passed. To encourage greater insurer participation while simultaneously increasing the minimum standards insurers must meet to serve these markets, the ACA provided federal financial assistance only to consumers who purchase coverage through the marketplaces and established risk adjustment and reinsurance programs to minimize adverse selection. Despite these efforts, individual and small group markets continue to be largely dominated by a small number of insurers. This leaves most marketplaces with little leverage to

[20] James C. Robinson et al., Whither Health Insurance Exchanges under the Affordable Care Act? Active Purchasing versus Passive Marketplaces, Health Affs. Forefront (Oct. 2, 2015), https://www.healthaffairs.org/content/forefront/whither-health-insurance-exchanges-under-affordable-care-act-active-purchasing-versus.

[21] Id.

[22] Al Bingham et al., National vs. California Comparison: Detailed Data Help Explain the Risk Differences Which Drive Covered California's Success, Health Affs. Forefront (July 11, 2018), https://www.healthaffairs.org/do/10.1377/forefront.20180710.459445/full/.

[23] Colo. Rev. Stat. § 10-22-104.

[24] See, e.g., William Kramer, Why Aren't State Exchanges Embracing Prudent Purchasing Strategies?, Health Affs. Forefront (Mar. 19, 2012), https://www.healthaffairs.org/content/forefront/why-aren-t-state-exchanges-embracing-prudent-purchasing-strategies. This rationale, however, does not apply to states funding subsidies that supplement federal financial assistance.

threaten to exclude one or more insurers in a bidding or negotiation process. Even in states with relatively unconsolidated insurer markets, marketplaces can be hesitant to restrict consumer choice – "the bedrock of the American economy and, increasingly, of the American health economy"[25] – in the name of cost containment. A marketplace with just one or two insurers may struggle to compete with less-regulated and cheaper plans offered outside the marketplace to attract consumers, especially those who do not qualify for significant marketplace subsidies.

In order for states to be able to follow Massachusetts' and California's leads to fully exert the powers of private law and extract lower premiums, they must (1) remove any barriers preventing marketplaces from using the full arsenal of contractual tools available to them and (2) push against the forces of consolidation that are throttling the performance of the health insurance market. One such mechanism is our next example of states increasing competition in the private market in nontraditional ways: by establishing a new state public health insurance option to compete against private insurers' products.

6.3.2 *Market-Based Public Options*

Traditionally, a public option is a publicly insured health plan that competes against private insurers. With these plans, the state is engaging in the private market itself and subject to the same rules as a private insurer. However, because the government controls provider reimbursement rates and lacks a profit motive, public option plans can be a tool to lower health care costs and expand coverage, while expanding consumer choice.

No such plan exists today, albeit not for lack of trying; these proposals have faced steep practical barriers. Establishing and financing a new health insurance plan is no small endeavor, particularly for budget-strapped state governments. Like other cost containment reforms, public option proposals garner significant opposition from industry groups seeking to preserve the status quo, and activists and legislators hoping to minimize government involvement in health care. Nonetheless, two states – Washington and Nevada – have enacted laws authorizing the state to contract with private insurers to offer new "Market-Based Public Options" (MBPOs), advancing state cost containment and other policy goals without the government directly taking on the financial and administrative burden of operating a health insurance plan.[26]

25 Robinson et al., supra note 20.

26 See Jaime S. King et al., Are State Public Option Health Plans Worth It, 59 Harv. J. on Legis. 145, 150–51, 166–68, 174–77 (Winter 2022); Christine Monahan et al., State Public Option-Style Laws: What Policymakers Need to Know, Commonwealth Fund (July 23, 2021), https://www.commonwealthfund.org/blog/2021/state-public-option-style-laws-what-policymakers-need-know. Colorado also has implemented a quasi-public option law, but it legally requires all insurers to offer "Colorado Option plans" that meet statutory premium reduction targets, and, if

To effectuate these MBPOs, states must get the insurers and providers that vehemently opposed enactment of these programs to participate. And because these plans are starting with no covered lives, states cannot woo insurers or providers with the promise of a large volume of enrollees. Although states could use their regulatory power to simply mandate participation, both Washington and Nevada have instead sought to leverage their purchasing power to encourage insurers and providers to participate, more akin to how a private company may engage with suppliers. Of the two, Washington warrants the closest consideration; its program has been in operation for three years while Nevada's remains in the planning stages.

Washington's initial approach to both insurer and provider participation was purely voluntary: The state imposed no explicit incentives or disincentives for insurers to offer MBPOs or providers to join MBPO networks. Although several insurers (including two new entrants to the marketplace) successfully bid to contract with the state, providers largely declined to join MBPO networks, resulting in limited MBPO availability. This was most likely because MBPOs cap aggregate provider payments at no more than 160 percent of Medicare reimbursement rates as its primary method of containing costs, while imposing no explicit cost reduction obligations on insurers.

To improve provider participation in subsequent years, Washington leveraged its market power and required providers that (voluntarily) participate in other state health insurance programs, including Medicaid, to join at least one MBPO network. While lawmakers were told this would have the same effect as a mandate, the legal and political optics may have been more palatable, as providers ultimately maintained a choice of whether or not to participate in state-aligned programs.[27] Indeed, this tactic is akin to how many private actors engage in health care markets (albeit subject to criticism as anticompetitive). For example, large health systems commonly negotiate all-or-nothing contracts with insurers, where the insurer must contract with all providers within the system or none at all. Washington's tying requirement helped expand MBPO plan availability and enticed more insurers to bid to offer MBPO plans. The increased competition even allowed Washington to selectively contract with just a subset of insurers that offered the best mix of geographic reach and lower premiums.

Washington's MBPOs are increasingly becoming the lowest premium options in the marketplace, but they still have not been able to achieve significant premium

these targets are not met, authorizes the state to administratively order health care providers to participate in Colorado Option plan networks at state-imposed reimbursement rates. See Monahan et al.

[27] Off. of Fin. Mgmt. (Wash. State), Multiple Agency Fiscal Note Summary: 5377SB, 3 (2021), https://fnspublic.ofm.wa.gov/FNSPublicSearch/GetPDF?packageID=62340. An earlier version of the bill amending Washington's public option law would have required certain hospitals systems to contract with at least one MBPO. See S. Rep. SB 5377, at 5–6 (Wash. Feb. 22, 2021), https://lawfilesext.leg.wa.gov/biennium/2021-22/Pdf/Bill%20Reports/Senate/5377%20SBR%20WM%20OC%2021.pdf?q=20211031060456.

reductions and enrollment remains low. Looking ahead, market dynamics – and the political choices that shape them – will continue to affect how well Washington's public option program will be able to reduce costs. The biggest test may be whether the MBPOs can attract consumers in substantial numbers while keeping prices in check. As with marketplaces, the American preference for choice may limit how much costs can be constrained with private market tools alone: Current MBPO plan networks are narrower than their competition, which has allowed insurers to negotiate lower reimbursement rates by promising greater volume to the limited number of in-network providers. But consumers may prefer to maintain their choice of provider or hospital even if it means paying more. Washington and other states implementing or considering MBPOs have to tread carefully and find the right balance between making the products competitive in the market and achieving cost containment.

6.3.3 *State Employee Health Plans*

State Employee Health Plans present one of the biggest opportunities for states to contain health care costs by engaging with, rather than regulating, the market. State employee health plans have significant purchasing power: State and local governments are frequently the biggest employer in a given state and administer an employee benefit program. State employee health plans also have a direct interest in reducing spending on employees' health care services – amplified by the frequent threat of state budget cuts. But unlike other employer health plans, SEHPs often cannot achieve cost savings by shifting costs to their employees, due to legal and practical constraints.

State employee health plans contract with private insurers – either as a third-party administrator (TPA) or insurer – and these private insurers, in turn, negotiate rates with health care providers. The dynamics between these parties affect the success of any cost-containment initiative. Some SEHPs have leveraged their purchasing power in negotiations with both providers and TPAs to promote cost containment. For example, in 2016, Montana SEHP administrators used their purchasing power to cap what they would pay for hospital services at 234 percent of Medicare rates,[28] which saved the state about US$47.8 million over three years.[29] Additionally, at least fourteen states have leveraged their vendor procurement process to "extract[] performance guarantees and hold[] TPAs accountable to cost

[28] Julie Appleby, "Holy Cow" Moment Changes How Montana's State Health Plan Does Business, Kaiser Health News (June 20, 2018), https://khn.org/news/holy-cow-moment-changes-how-montanas-state-health-plan-does-business/.

[29] Adney Rakotoniaina, Overview of States' Hospital Reference-Based Pricing to Medicare Initiative, Nat'l Acad. for State Health Pol'y (Oct. 19, 2021), https://nashp.org/overview-of-states-hospital-reference-based-pricing-to-medicare-initiatives/.

containment goals."[30] For example, one study reports that a state implemented a "reverse auction" strategy when soliciting bids from their TPAs, sharing information about bids received with all competing vendors to encourage better offers in subsequent bidding rounds. The study finds that this state succeeded in lowering prices and increasing cost transparency.[31] These reforms have been possible because SEHPs' captive enrollee population draws both providers and insurers to the negotiating table.

Cost-containment efforts by state administrators have been rare, however. In many cases, SEHPs are limited by their need for state legislative approval to pursue these types of cost-containment strategies, opening the door to industry opposition that can kill reform efforts or create loopholes.[32] For example, the New Jersey SEHP has legislative authority to use the above-mentioned "reverse auctioning" procurement strategy to get concessions from its pharmacy benefit managers, but not its TPAs.[33]

Even when legislative authority is not a barrier, SEHPs still face an uphill battle when implementing reforms. State employee health plans are entrenched in decades-old traditions and policies, making it difficult for policymakers and many SEHP administrators to see SEHP agencies as agents of reform. State employee health plan administrators have limited resources at their disposal compared to other large private purchasers. Developing cost containment initiatives can be resource intensive: states that have tried to develop innovative provider payment models, like episode-based or bundled payments, have described it as "a ton of work."[34] Third-party administrators have also made it difficult for SEHPs to access and use their own claims data, a prerequisite for developing new cost-containment initiatives. Even when the data is available, many SEHPs lack the staffing and funding to adequately analyze it.

And, as with our other examples, market consolidation and consumer preferences also significantly limit SEHPs' negotiating power. Public employees expect generous benefit packages with broad provider networks and eye efforts to contain costs with skepticism, viewing money saved as a benefit that accrues to the state, not to them directly. Provider consolidation exacerbates this problem, as employees do not want to lose access to a dominant health system, tying the plan's hands when negotiating rates with providers. Similarly, states with a dominant insurer cannot

[30] Sabrina Corlette et al., Unleashing the Giant: Opportunities for State Employee Health Plans to Drive Improvements in Affordability, Ctr. on Health Ins. Reforms 22 (June 2021), https://sehpcostcontainment.chir.georgetown.edu/documents/SEHP-report-final.pdf.

[31] Id. at 23.

[32] See, e.g., Adney Rakotoniaina, How Oregon Is Limiting Hospital Payments and Cost Growth for State Employee Health Plans, Nat'l Acad. for State Health Pol'y (Aug. 30, 2021), https://nashp.org/how-oregon-is-limiting-hospital-payments-and-cost-growth-for-state-employee-health-plans/.

[33] Corlette et al., supra note 30, at 23.

[34] Id. at 15.

afford to lose access to their current TPA, making it difficult to fully leverage the state procurement process to reduce costs. Dominant providers and TPAs can also wield considerable political influence and financial resources. For example, North Carolina's SEHP recently conducted a transparent and thorough process requesting proposals for a TPA, and selected Aetna instead of Blue Cross and Blue Shield of North Carolina (Blue Cross NC), which had been the TPA for over forty years.[35] Blue Cross NC is now directing significant resources toward trying to get this decision overturned.[36]

Despite the barriers, given their captive market and relative size, SEHPs remain an opportunity for states looking to experiment with cost-containment initiatives without generating the political opposition inherent in the legislative process.

6.4 STATE CONTRACTING AS A STOPGAP: HOLDING THE LINE FOR BROADER REFORMS

Implementing effective cost-containment reforms is an immense challenge. Above, we have shared examples of how a handful of states have leveraged their role as private actors and contracting entities to advance this goal. While regulatory efforts to control prices largely remain politically infeasible, these examples offer a potential path forward. However, these state contractual approaches are not a panacea.

Despite working within a private law framework governed by market forces, state contractual and market-based approaches to cost containment can be seen as being closely intertwined with exercises of legislative and regulatory authority. Indeed, state actors frequently require legislative authorization to use their market power, and this opens the door to opposition. Even though these strategies mirror those private actors commonly use, proponents of "free market principles" or small government may reject these efforts as a proxy for government regulation or fail to adequately fund state agencies to effectively implement them. Perhaps even more detrimentally, these efforts face opposition from well-funded industry actors who no more wish to feel meaningful competitive or market pressure from the government than regulation.

Nonetheless, experience to date suggests contractual approaches carry a much lower risk of legal challenge and obstruction than direct price regulation, and SEHP reforms appear to have particular support from conservative policymakers.[37]

35 Theresa Opeka, Appeals from BCBSNC & UMR, Inc. Rejected by NC State Health Plan, Carolina J. (Jan. 20, 2023), https://www.carolinajournal.com/appeals-from-bcbsnc-umr-inc-rejected-by-nc-state-health-plan/.

36 C. J. Staff, Blue Cross NC Takes State Health Plan Decision to Court, Carolina J. (Feb. 16, 2023), https://www.carolinajournal.com/blue-cross-nc-takes-state-health-plan-decision-to-court/.

37 See Brian C. Blase, Demonstrate Leadership: Reform the State Employee Health Plan, in Don't Wait for Washington: How States Can Reform Health Care Today 9–20 (Brian C. Blase ed., 2021).

The more profound limitations on contractual approaches to cost containment is consolidation in US health care markets combined, perhaps ironically, with an intense desire to preserve consumer choice. Often the government does not have meaningful bargaining power because there are only one or two dominant insurers and/or health systems in the market. The consolidation in the health care market is resulting in a market failure, where prices and premiums keep increasing, and anticompetitive practices are rampant. Even when the market is not heavily consolidated, policymakers remain hesitant to leverage their negotiating power and exclude higher-cost options and thereby limit consumer choice. That a "faith in ... consumer choice"[38] can hijack cost containment efforts is only made more questionable by the fact that consumers, universally, struggle to make informed, rational health care decisions.

This conclusion brings us back to where many economists and policy experts started: If consumer choice and market power cannot achieve meaningful price controls, then comprehensive rate regulation may be in order. But if the opportunity arises, states may want to try the mechanisms discussed, here, while Congress debates broader federal reforms. US health care reform has tended to be a story of incrementalism, and experiences like selective contracting by the Massachusetts and California health insurance marketplaces, introduction of a market-based public health insurance option by Washington, and Montana's experimentation with capping provider reimbursement can serve as precursors to more significant changes. Under the right circumstances, these policies benefit enrollees and can even have modest spillover effects. In acting now with the tools available, states can not only benefit themselves but lay the groundwork and show support for Congress to tackle health care costs nationally.

[38] Martha Minow, Public and Private Partnerships: Accounting for the New Religion, 116 Harv. L. Rev. 1229, 1230 (2003).

7

Adaptation of Tort Law to Modern Health Care Delivery in the Restatement of Medical Malpractice

Mark A. Hall[*]

7.1 INTRODUCTION

Prior to the mid-1960s, with the advent of Medicare and Medicaid, health law looked predominantly to various sources of private law – principally branches of common law – to address major issues at the time. Naturally, that legal landscape has changed a great deal, but common law still undergirds many of the classic components of the field. This chapter explores the extent to which common law remains capable of adjusting itself to evolving structures and dynamics in health care finance and delivery. It does so in the particular context of medical liability.

As we begin the inquiry, it helps to recognize that common law has two core but conflicting, features: stability and adaptability. Stability arises through stare decisis. Adaptability is inherent in the judge-made quality of common law doctrine. As the landscape changes that gives rise to common law, so too can the judicial outlook that applies the law's principles, generating not only different rulings under established principles but also revision of governing principles at both second-order and higher levels of conceptualization.[1] Such doctrinal evolution or revolution can be slow and fitful, but many successful examples can be given of this innate adaptability.[2] At the same time, the common law's precedential inertia can create impatience among scholars, regulators, and reformers eager to modernize hidebound legal principles.

[*] I serve as a Reporter for this Restatement project along with Nora Freeman Engstrom and Michael D. Green.

[1] Countless discussions of these themes can be found, but each owes its intellectual debt to the classic work of Oliver Wendell Holmes Jr., The Common Law (1881).

[2] My co-reporters, for instance, canvass a number of such examples in their review of a companion Restatement project called Torts: Miscellaneous Provisions. See Nora F. Engstrom & Michael D. Green, Tort Theory and Restatements: Of Immanence and Lizard Lips, 14 J. Tort Law 333 (2021).

The American Law Institute's (ALI or Institute) first-ever project to restate medical liability law provides a fitting occasion to explore these tensions and themes in the context of tort law's application to medical care delivery. Tort law has been a principal focus of the ALI from its beginning a century ago.[3] This medical liability project arose at the concluding phase of the Institute's quarter-century work to issue its third Restatement of Torts law. Previous Restatements addressed medical malpractice only briefly, as a leading example of a more general concept of professional liability, discussed in just a single section.[4] In solipsistic contrast, the Restatement of the Law Governing Lawyers devotes eleven sections to legal malpractice.

A review of various provisions reveals that judicially determined common law is capable, to some extent, of evolving with the health policy times; however, there are significant points of inertia that may be hindering useful health policy developments. Surveying this landscape may help lawmakers and public policy officials identify where regulatory nudges or overt overrides can be helpful in freeing up precedential logjams.

Medical malpractice law arose in the nineteenth century, at a time when medical care could be described in its best light as primitive.[5] Importantly, treatment relationships then were almost entirely dyadic (with just a single provider) and episodic, addressing primarily acute issues. Also, patients paid entirely out-of-pocket and providers delivered care mostly in noninstitutional settings, either at home or in the doctor's office. As common law is expected to do, it reflected, and thus was premised on, these essential features. As I have written elsewhere, the private law features of health law in particular are especially adept at recognizing and responding to the essential features of illness, vulnerability, trust, professionalism, and other core attributes of health care delivery and finance.[6]

Obviously, it greatly understates things to say that much has changed in medicine over the past 200 years. Thus, we might expect that critical doctrinal elements and principles have shifted dramatically over time. However, many or most of the core essentials of the medical enterprise – the ontological assault of illness, the vulnerability a treatment relationship entails, the complexity and unpredictability medical practice, the fundamental existential stakes of the enterprise – inhere in the human condition and thus remain true today. But, for essential features that are more contingent, the common law's precedential inertia might stunt doctrinal evolution. The emerging Restatement of Medical Liability provides an opportunity to learn the

3 John C. P. Goldberg, Torts in the American Law Institute, in The American Law Institute: A Centennial History (Andrew S. Gold & Robert W. Gordon eds., 2023).

4 Restatement (Second) of Torts § 299A (Am. Law Inst. 1969).

5 For historical accounts, see, e.g., Kenneth A. DeVille, Medical Malpractice in Nineteenth-Century America (1990); Iain Hay, Money, Medicine, and Malpractice in American Society (1992); James C. Mohr, American Medical Malpractice Litigation in Historical Perspective, 283 JAMA 1731 (2000).

6 Mark Hall, The History and Future of Health Care Law: An Essentialist View, 41 Wake Forest L. Rev. 347 (2006).

extent to which these competing features of private law affect the Institute's ability to bring coherence to the common law of medical liability.[7]

7.2 THE TREATMENT RELATIONSHIP

When does a physician or other care provider enter the realm of medical professional responsibility? According to tort law, this occurs when the provider forms a treatment relationship, that is, begins to undertake the care of a patient. Undertaking care is the critical point at which a provider leaves the zone of generic negligence law, which holds actors responsible only for risks they create judged by a general reasonableness standard and assumes the more affirmative responsibilities defined by professional standards.

A treatment relationship's timeline – its beginning and ending – is defined largely by contractual principles. Sometimes overt agreements to start or end a treatment relationship can be identified, but often they cannot. A physician simply starts to engage with a patient and then stops engaging, or they engage in ways that can be ambiguous as to the nature and scope of the engagement. Thus, the Restatement of Medical Malpractice begins by addressing the foundational contours of a treatment relationship.[8]

At the threshold, one visible indication of common law adaptation is the modernizing of the rules around formation of the treatment relationship. Historically, courts have tended to apply what might be called a "hair trigger" test for relationship formation, by finding that contractual elements are met with only a slight indication of potential intent by the provider to assume responsibility. Thus, in various circumstances, courts have found that a treatment relationship formed when a patient made an appointment, or when a provider discussed the patient's situation and needs only briefly, or only with a colleague.

The quick trigger approach stands in sharp contrast to lawyers undertaking client representation. Lawyers commonly consult with a potential client before launching representation, and that launch rarely occurs without an explicit understanding about its basic scope and terms.

When patients are sick and in need of immediate attention, there are obvious reasons to dispense with formalities. Recognition, however, that greater complexities and subtleties can legitimately arise in the modern setting, coupled with the emergence of a more overtly "consumerist" ethos in medicine, led the Restatement to endorse a moderating stance. Based on limited, but sufficient, case

[7] This analysis is based on the current version of the project's drafting, which is not yet completed.

[8] As with other Restatements, this one addresses only the common law, and not statutory law. Many states, however, have statutes that codify medical liability essentials. In doing so, statutory law embraces common law concepts and thus decisions interpreting and applying these statutes often employ common law reasoning.

law, the Restatement advises that, "in appropriate nonemergency circumstances, medical providers should have leeway, similar to that in legal representation, to first assess a patient's condition and to discuss potential courses of treatment and costs before initiating a patient-care relationship."[9] That passing sentence is a small but instructive example of common law adaptation.

The unhelpful aspect of inertia in the common law can be seen, however, in its episodic conception of treatment relationships. Following well-established case law, the Restatement declares that a treatment relationship ceases "once the particular condition or conditions that gave rise to treatment no longer need attention, unless the patient has reason to believe that the provider intends to continue the relationship." As it notes, this "captures what is sometimes referred to as a 'spell of illness' demarcation of treatment relationships."[10] The Comment acknowledges, however, that "patients as well as providers often think of themselves as having an established and ongoing relationship that bridges episodes of illness."

Here, the Restatement urges courts to better adapt the law to modern practice. The Comment instructs that medical liability law should attempt "to shape itself to the actual contours of patient-provider interactions and understandings." Further, it notes that "several modern developments support, in appropriate circumstances, embracing a more continuous rather than episodic conception of patient-care relationships." An obvious example is chronic illness with episodic flare-ups. Another, which is more institutionally contingent, is the contemporary emergence of primary-care "medical home" arrangements, "in which a primary-care provider is paid to manage a patient's needs on an ongoing basis across a range of providers and conditions." The Comment prompts courts to recognize that these (or similar) arrangements "can form an ongoing patient-care relationship that transcends spells of illness."[11]

This type of small-bore, stepwise evolution is a hallmark of the common law and thus is comfortably within the bounds of the Institute's guidelines and practices for how Restatements justifiably may guide further legal development.[12] The Restatement embraces a similarly less transactional and more relational view in its section on informed consent. There, it keys the informed consent duty to a "course of treatment" rather than to a specific intervention, recognizing (again without much explicit precedent) that "it is typical, and permissible, to obtain informed

9 § 2 cmt. k. Unless otherwise noted, section numbers refer to the current version of the Restatement (Third) of Torts: Medical Malpractice.

10 § 2 cmt. n. As an example, the Reporters' Note mentions the classic decision in Hurley v. Eddingfield, 59 N.E. 1058, 1058 (Ind. 1901), which absolved a general practitioner from refusing to aid a former patient who ended up dying during childbirth. Although the court noted that the doctor "had been decedent's family physician," the court (without discussion) treated this as a refusal to initiate, rather than to continue, a treatment relationship.

11 § 2 cmt. n.

12 See Goldberg, supra note 3 for additional discussion.

consent in a manner that bundles a variety of discrete items of treatment."[13] In these several respects, we see a somewhat successful, but still limited, ability of common law to adapt to basic changes in treatment relationships.

7.3 SHARING RESPONSIBILITY AMONG MEDICAL PROFESSIONALS

Common law has been somewhat less successful, however, in adapting to changes in how medicine is practiced. Tort law has frequently had to determine the scope of an individual provider's professional responsibility in the context of multiple professionals working together as part of a treatment team.[14] This first arose in the surgical operating arena. Cases a century ago asked whether a surgeon is responsible for errors that surgical assistants make, such as nurses charged with counting sponges to ensure none are left behind. As surgical techniques advanced, subsequent courts were asked to determine a lead surgeon's responsibility for another physician's error in, for instance, administering anesthesia.[15]

Initially, courts adopted a strong version of vicarious liability known as the "captain of the ship" doctrine, which held the lead surgeon responsible as a matter of law for any negligence under their "command," regardless of the surgeon's actual control over the team member.[16] One rationale at the time for this small-scale form of enterprise liability was that, with respect to nurses, if the surgeon were not liable then there would be no adequately sized pocket from which to seek recovery, given that almost all hospitals at the time were immune from liability, either as charitable or governmental institutions.

In many cases, modern courts have appropriately backed away from this literal-absolutist application of the captain-of-the-ship metaphor, in favor of a more fact-based inquiry, now referred to as the borrowed "employee" doctrine.[17] This modern version appropriately adapted to changing circumstances in the profession and applies more conventional vicarious liability principles to inquire whether a surgeon, in a particular situation, controls, or has the right to control, "the manner and means" by which a colleague performs their work. Recognizing that in modern practice, the training and oversight of nurses is typically the hospital's responsibility, this more

[13] § 12 cmt. k.

[14] In addition to the examples discussed in text, also relevant is the long-standing doctrine that, in applying *res ipsa loquitor* to mishaps in surgical settings, courts rule that it is sufficient if anyone on the surgical team was probably at fault, rather than requiring the plaintiff to identify which particular actor was most likely responsible. § 7 cmt. b. In essence, this variation in the doctrine holds the entire team responsible for any member's mistake, unless evidence emerges about which particular team member was at fault.

[15] See Stephen H. Price, The Sinking of the "Captain of the Ship": Reexamining the Vicarious Liability of an Operating Surgeon for the Negligence of Assisting Hospital Personnel, 10 J. Leg. Med. 323 (1989).

[16] See §15 reporters' note cmt. e.

[17] § 15 cmt. g.

nuanced doctrine nevertheless allows a finding based on the facts of a particular case that a surgeon assumed temporary control of a team member's action.

But the story isn't all a positive one. Variability remains in how these principles play out in recurring scenarios, including the original scenario of sponges, clamps, or other foreign objects accidentally left behind during surgery.[18] Some courts look to how providers themselves allocate responsibility, recognizing that "operating room personnel have specialized tasks to perform during surgery, . . . [and] that it [may] not [be] practical for [surgeons] to exercise control of the nurses in their sponge-counting task."[19] Other courts, however, continue to hold surgeons responsible as a matter of law.[20] They do so without resuscitating an explicit and free-ranging captain-of-the-ship notion; instead, they embrace the more limited common-sense notion that when a surgeon inserts a foreign object, the surgeon remains responsible for ensuring its proper removal. That line of thinking is more appropriately considered to be a straightforward recognition of a nondelegable duty.[21]

These established strands of doctrine have not matured, however, into more general principles of shared professional liability when errors occur in team-based care settings. The Reporters' Note to the Comment on borrowed employees explains that, "[a]lthough such team-care arrangements are increasingly common, courts continue to resist viewing them as a basis for vicarious liability among individual medical professionals, as long as none of the providers actively supervises or controls his or her counterpart. Instead, courts apply a highly compartmentalized view of shared physician responsibility." The Note continues in an editorial vein to say:

> This highly compartmentalized view is subject to the criticism that it fails to reflect the increasing emphasis in modern medicine on caring for patients through coordinated teams, as seen, for instance, in the rise of "accountable care organizations" and "care coordination teams" based with multidisciplinary primary care medical homes that monitor and coordinate care patients receive from a range of providers.[22]

[18] As summarized by Restatement (Third) of Agency § 7.03 cmt. d(2) (Am. Law Inst. 2006), owing to the highly fact-intensive nature of the inquiry, "[e]ven within the same jurisdiction, it may be difficult to predict whether a given set of indicia will demonstrate that a special employer has assumed the right of control." The associated Reporter's Note points in particular to "examples drawn from medical-malpractice cases [to] illustrate the fact-specificity of borrowed-servant cases [and hence their unpredictable outcomes], regardless of the doctrinal formulation a court applies."

[19] Holger v. Irish, 851 P.2d 1122, 1127–28 (Or. 1993).

[20] § 15 reporters' note cmt. e.

[21] As another example, under-informed consent law courts hold the principal physician solely responsible for making necessary disclosures even though physicians, following institutional policies, often delegate such tasks to subordinates employed and supervised by hospitals. § 15, cmt. e. See also note infra.

[22] Similarly, the § 1 Reporters' Note to comment g observes that the Restatement only partially and thus inadequately accounts for the fact that "many bad outcomes result from poor system design or multiple reinforcing mistakes rather than primarily from individual error" and that, accordingly, "it is widely accepted that a systems approach is needed to improve medical quality and reduce medical error."

These sentiments are those only of the Reporters, however, and do not speak for the Institute. The ALI's official position is expressed in Comments recognizing that "much of this Restatement addresses a simple one-on-one relationship between provider and patient, even though much medical care, especially in hospital settings, is in fact provided by teams that share and assign responsibilities in complex ways," and noting that the "Restatement only partially accounts for this complexity."

Here, then, we see a glaring example of the limits of common law tort principles, rooted in an anachronistic framing of medical care delivery. Despite dramatic changes in how modern medicine structures care delivery, tort law can struggle to fully adapt to modern conditions.

Partly accounting for this doctrinal rigidity, however, is that medical professionals themselves hold on to a bounded view of their own responsibilities. Thus, when providers collaborate across disciplines or fulfill supervisory roles, they form explicit understandings about the nature of limits of their separate but dovetailing responsibilities.[23] In honoring these understandings, tort law is not so much stubborn to change, as it is compliant with professional norms. Thus, the common law is more subject to the criticism of declining to push for overarching structures of responsibility, than of failing to recognize professional and institutional realities.[24]

7.4 INSTITUTIONAL RESPONSIBILITY

Common law's rigidity can be seen in the failure of institutional liability to fully adapt to modern circumstances. A few years before work began on the Third Restatement of Torts, the Institute commissioned a project, led by a group of eminent torts scholars, to restate institutional responsibility for personal injury. The group's work proved too scholarly and lacked grounding in existing case law. The Institute therefore downgraded what was originally intended as a Restatement to simply a "Reporters' Study,"[25] meaning that it spoke only for the reporters and not the Institute.[26] For similar reasons, this Restatement attempts no bold move toward sweeping enterprise liability for medical institutions.[27] That move would require

[23] Various examples the Restatement gives and documents include medical examinations for purposes of employer or insurance, physicians who supervise nurse practitioners or physician assistants, consulting and on-call arrangements. See also Mark A. Hall et al., Liability Implications of Physician-Directed Care Coordination, 3 Ann. Fam. Med. 115, 115–20 (2005) (discussing the limited legal exposure of physicians who coordinate care in managed care settings).

[24] Possibly, this reluctance to push harder is informed by a concern that doing so may deter professionals from assuming new responsibilities that, if they were not professionally controllable, would carry unknown liability risks.

[25] Am. Law Inst., Reporters' Study on Enterprise Responsibility for Personal Injury (1991).

[26] Recounting this history, see Engstrom & Green, supra note 2, at 341; Goldberg, supra note 3, at nn. 104–17.

[27] Indeed, that term purposefully does not appear in the official Comments, but only in the § 15 Reporters' Note to comment f. For further discussion of potential enterprise liability for

fairly dramatic legislation action. Short of that, however, this Restatement recognizes a number of doctrinal advancements that, potentially, form building blocks for more sweeping enterprise liability.

First, the Restatement's institutional liability ambit is substantially broader than just hospitals and nursing homes. The institutions subject to some form of medical liability are "entities that arrange for or furnish medical care through the services of medical professionals," including: "medical facilities that treat patients, such as hospitals, clinics, and nursing homes; entities, such as managed care insurance plans, that arrange medical care for their customers; and newly emerging arrangements such as 'accountable care organizations.'"[28] This Section is explicit, however, that all such institutions do not have the same set of duties. Instead, different duties apply according to whether the institution directly delivers care or instead merely helps to arrange for care.

Ample precedent exists to articulate the basic duties owed by institutions engaged in direct medical care. Precedent is limited, though, for other forms of institutions – those that merely arrange for or influence patient care rather than act as a provider. Managed care insurers are the primary example, but, owing to preemption by the Employee Retirement Income Security Act (ERISA), relevant precedents are scarce.

Despite this absence of precedent, the Section is able to state based on general principles that any such medical institution owes a "duty of reasonable care" to the extent that it "select[s] and retain[s] the medical professionals who furnish care under its auspices," or that it "make[s] or actively review[s] medical decisions."[29] Comments explain that this structure and wording does not require institutions to engage in such activities unless they actually deliver care; if not, the Section tailors medical duties to the functions that particular institutions choose to undertake.[30] These principles provide appropriate room for flexible development both of different types of medical institutions and different attendant duties, rather than embracing a "one size fits all" rule.

The Institute is especially careful to avoid insisting that medical institutions actively supervise medical professionals in a manner that requires institutions to regularly inject themselves directly into medical decision-making as it occurs (rather than reviewing decisions more retrospectively). If institutions choose to do so,

hospitals or managed care insurers, see generally Kenneth Abraham & Paul Weiler, Enterprise Liability and the Evolution of the American Health Care System, 108 Harv. L. Rev. 381 (1994); Kenneth Abraham & Paul Weiler, Enterprise Medical Liability and the Choice of the Responsible Enterprise, 20 Am. J.L. & Med. 29 (1994); Clark C. Havighurst, Making Health Plans Accountable for the Quality of Care, 31 Ga. L. Rev. 587 (1997); Philip G. Peters, Resuscitating Hospital Enterprise Liability, 73 Mo. L. Rev. 369, 369–97 (2008); William Sage, Enterprise Liability and the Emerging Managed Care Health Care System, 60 Law & Contemp. Probs. 159 (Spring 1997).

28 § 14 cmt. a.

29 § 13(a), (c).

30 See, e.g., §13 cmts. a, i, & j.

naturally they assume a more exacting duty of care, but requiring institutions to take on this responsibility would contravene public policies that seek to minimize untoward institutional influence in professional judgment. In these ways, the Section aims to set a doctrinal stage for the ongoing development of a wide variety of different types and forms of medical institutions.

The Restatement also addresses institutional liability through vicarious liability doctrine. In particular, the Restatement discusses the substantial body of case law that has developed under the "apparent (or ostensible) agency" doctrine.[31] In developing and applying this and other aspects of vicarious liability, the Comments emphasize that courts are especially attentive to public policy consideration, such as:

> (1) patients' reasonable understandings about who is responsible for their care; (2) medical professionals' and institutions' reasonable understandings about how roles and responsibilities are assigned, shared, and allocated; and (3) society's broader interest in promoting safe, efficient, and high-quality care.[32]

Because these policies can point in different directions or can be given differing weights, there is notable variability in the extent to which different courts, sometimes from the same jurisdiction, assess whether an adequate manifestation of authority exists to invoke institutional vicarious liability.

Nevertheless, the Restatement is explicit that doctrinal articulation and application of vicarious liability should change in response to changes in health care delivery and finance. Thus, Comments note that the classic model – of independent physicians on a hospital medical staff having no other contractual relationship with the hospital – no longer predominates. Instead, physicians who treat hospital patients increasingly either work for the hospital or are part of a group that contracts, or is affiliated, with the hospital or a parent organization. Legal precedents from the pure independent-practice era may not necessarily be a good fit with these more complex "integrated delivery systems."[33]

Institutional liability for hospital-based specialists that a hospital does not employ is the leading example of doctrinal evolution that reflects several of these public policy considerations. Conventionally, when a professional (or other actor) is not an actual employee or agent of an institution, the institution assumes no vicarious liability unless the injured party (here, a patient) detrimentally relies on the institution representing that the professional is acting on its behalf as its agent.[34] Courts increasingly have relaxed these doctrinal demands of actual reliance and overt representation. They have held, for instance, that patients need not show reliance in the form that a different understanding about agency would have caused them to

31 § 15(2) & cmt. i.
32 § 15 cmt. a.
33 Id. cmt. c.
34 Restatement (Third) of Agency § 7.03, supra note 18.

seek care elsewhere. Instead, patients need only show simply that they assumed the doctor was working for the hospital. Moreover, in many jurisdictions, patients need not point to a specific holding out or representation of agency; instead, it suffices that the patient's assumption was reasonable in the circumstances.

The Restatement makes ample room for these doctrinal liberalizations but does not insist on their adoption, recognizing that doing so appropriately requires taking account of factual circumstances. Noting the variability that remains among decisions, as well as the fact-sensitivity of these standards, the relevant Comment sets an outer limit of apparent agency only at the point where "a patient establishes a relationship with an independent physician prior to hospital treatment."[35] Then, "the patient cannot convincingly claim that the independent physician is the hospital's apparent agent, simply because the physician is on the hospital's medical staff or is entitled to work on the hospital's premises." Otherwise, for hospital-based specialists, "various circumstances can give rise to a patient's reasonable belief that the physician is acting and has authority to act on behalf of the hospital when, in fact, the physician is an independent contractor."[36]

Beyond this expansion of apparent agency, tort law has not gone much further toward possible full-scale enterprise liability for hospitals or other medical institutions, nor does this Restatement encourage doing so, recognizing that Restatements are not an overt law-reform initiative.[37] In this respect, basic institutional liability remains much as it was a half-century ago. It remains to be seen whether dramatic innovations such as artificial intelligence – allowing much more detailed real-time interaction with professional decision-making – will push institutional roles and legal doctrine to a tipping point of more encompassing liability.

In the meantime, this Restatement does contain limited doctrine that may become seeds for future development of more encompassing enterprise liability. It notes that, in emergency room settings, where public policy considerations loom especially large, more courts are willing to curtail or dispense with the factual issues that might complicate a finding of apparent institutional agency. These courts, for instance, tend to adopt a presumption of reasonable impression of agency status, and they decline for obvious reasons to honor disclaimers of agency contained in form paperwork presented to emergency patients.

35 § 15 cmt. i.

36 Id.

37 Indeed, it endorses one particularly retrograde position that, based on substantial case law, absolves hospitals from responsibility for ensuring that patients' informed consent is obtained for physician treatment – despite the fact that hospitals routinely take measures to ensure that physicians comply with their informed consent obligations. § 12 reporters' note cmt. e. The reason courts give for abnormally limiting institutional responsibility is in order to keep the central focus of responsibility for informed consent on the treating physician. Although scholars find this reason unconvincing, case law currently is too consistent for the Restatement to reject it outright. See id.

The relevant Comment takes an important further step, pointing courts to the availability of a more straightforward, but still limited, embrace of nondelegability as a matter of law. Building from decisions that presume apparent agency, the Comment notes that, "for certain core hospital functions, such as nursing care, it may be unacceptable as a matter of law to permit a medical institution to disavow vicarious liability for the negligence of independent contractors – even if it furnishes patients clear and timely notice of the contractors' independent (nonemployee) status."[38]

The extent to which courts take up this invitation remains to be seen. But, even with some uptake, wholescale enterprise liability for independent physicians remains inconceivable in the short or medium term. More likely, continuing integration among facilities and professionals will diminish the practical importance of any major doctrinal reform regarding independent physicians.

7.5 CONCLUSION

This chapter presents several examples of tort law's ability to thoughtfully adapt to changes in health care delivery at a measured pace – a pace that does not attempt to anticipate changes before they become widespread but also does not lag too terribly far behind important changes. The new Restatement of Medical Malpractice dutifully reflects where such changes have already taken hold and points to other changes that are primed to occur or to become more mature. Considering how rapidly health care delivery has changed, tort law appears by this assessment to be performing acceptably well on the adaptability score.

In some respects, however, this assessment highlights challenges to tort law governing and shaping modern health care delivery. Because the DNA of tort law adapts to practices, structures, and norms as they are, it is not well suited to leading or pushing for reform. Because a Restatement is, at its core, a synthesis of existing doctrine rather than a law-reform enterprise, Restatements have very limited ability to force tort law to improve or modernize. Nevertheless, embedded in the Restatement are a number of key passages that point in potentially constructive directions that future evolution of tort doctrine might take. Other points of doctrinal rigidity, however, might require more overt law-reform efforts to overcome.

38 § 15 cmt. i.

8

Pandemic Harms and Private Law's Limits

A Proposal for Tort Replacement

Jill R. Horwitz, Alberto De Diego-Habel, and Daniel B. Rodriguez

8.1 INTRODUCTION

In the early days of the COVID-19 pandemic, many people predicted a flood of tort litigation against commercial businesses by individuals alleging negligent exposure to the virus.[1] Although negligently caused injuries almost certainly occurred, the flood of litigation never materialized.[2] In part, the small number of claims can be explained by many states' efforts to avert economic disaster by immunizing businesses.[3] But the private law of tort itself also proved a formidable barrier, particularly given the difficulty of establishing causation in this context. This absence of tort claims may well have helped businesses ranging from residential health care providers to restaurants, as well as the economy and social life more generally. But the dearth of claims almost certainly left a great number of negligently injured parties without recourse or compensation to address their devastating harms.

The case of the pandemic suggests that traditional private law tools ordinarily available to address negligently caused harms – civil tort claims that leave it to private parties to litigate over whether the victim or the wrongdoer will bear the financial burden of wrongdoing – were poor legal tools for the job. An obvious response would be to adjust tort law standards to ease the path toward recovery under a private system, but this approach to addressing the need for compensation would risk the flood of litigation that observers were worried about in the first place.

We propose that a publicly administered tort-replacement scheme could have done a better job. Most obviously, it would have done a better job compensating

[1] Justine Coleman, Cruz Predicts "Tidal Wave" of Lawsuits against Reopening Small Businesses without Legislation, The Hill (May 6, 2020), https://thehill.com/homenews/senate/496351-cruz-predicts-tidal-wave-of-lawsuits-against-reopening-small-businesses.

[2] See Elaine S. Povich, States Braced for a Wave of COVID-19 Lawsuits. It Never Arrived, Stateline.org (July 21, 2021), https://perma.cc/BX29-FXW7/.

[3] See generally 50-State Update on COVID-19 Business Liability Protections, Husch Blackwell (Feb. 22, 2021; updated Mar. 18, 2021), https://perma.cc/A6LV-W4C2.

negligently injured victims who otherwise received no compensation. Moreover, a carefully designed system of tort replacement might have provided such compensation without sacrificing (much of) the deterrence that tort law, albeit imperfectly, often provides. In other words, with appropriate regulation, tort replacement can address the twin goals so commonly associated with private law tort: compensation and deterrence.

In fact, as we explain below, the government has historically replaced the private law of tort with a publicly administered system to address analogous problems to those raised by the COVID-19 pandemic. Recognizing that this pandemic will neither be the last crisis nor even the last pandemic that will raise the need for unmet financial burdens to negligently injured victims, we can learn from this history.

Section 8.2 explores the limits of applying private tort law to the COVID-19 transmission context, limits we suggest could apply to pandemics and other emergencies more generally. Section 8.3 reviews past examples of the government replacing private tort law with a publicly administered compensation system. Section 8.3.1 highlights two instances in which tort replacement was used primarily to facilitate access to compensation, whereas Section 8.3.2 highlights instances in which tort replacement was used to prevent a flood of litigation. Taken together, these examples suggest that replacing tort (rather than loosening doctrinal barriers to recovery in court or erecting new ones in the form of liability shields) is the right solution in this context. In Section 8.4 we set out a brief discussion of how public law can be used to supplement, or even supplant, private law to fill the needs left by private law to set out the substantive claim. Section 8.5 considers objections, and Section 8.6 concludes.

8.2 THE PANDEMIC LIABILITY DILEMMA: INDIVIDUAL COMPENSATION VERSUS ECONOMIC AND SOCIAL DISRUPTION

The COVID-19 pandemic harmed people around the world. In the United States alone, nearly 1.2 million people died because of the virus, and many more suffered serious, often permanent injuries.[4] The economic loss has been massive as well, with some estimates at US$14 trillion by the end of 2023.[5] Some of the spread of the disease was caused by individual negligence; some was caused by businesses,

4 Number of COVID-19 deaths reported to WHO (cumulative total), United States of America, World Health Org., https://perma.cc/M767-DQVF (last accessed Sept. 25, 2024); Effects of COVID-19 Pandemic on Workplace Injuries and Illnesses, Compensation, Occupational Requirements, and Work Stoppages Statistics, U.S. Bureau of Lab. Stat., https://perma.cc/AVH4-BFAL (last accessed Sept. 25, 2024).

5 COVID-19's Total Cost to the U.S. Economy Will Reach $14 Trillion by End of 2023, USC Schaeffer (May 16, 2023), https://perma.cc/93EQ-ACAB.

including health care businesses, such as nursing homes, that failed to take appropriate precautions to reduce the risks of spreading disease.

Although many victims of COVID-19 had health insurance or other forms of insurance to cover some of the financial costs of their injuries, many did not. Private insurance, as others have pointed out,[6] has proved inadequate to handle most business- and health-related losses. For those who became infected in the workplace, workers' compensation was not available for the spread of disease in many jurisdictions. Many victims of negligently transmitted COVID-19 who were otherwise uncompensated needed immediate relief to pay for ongoing medical care, time off work, and other harms.

In theory, private tort law could provide that relief. Consider a hypothetical case of COVID-19 transmission vis-à-vis the elements of a conventional tort: (1) Injuries in the form of death, disability, treatment costs, and lost wages are all obvious consequences of COVID-19 transmission; (2) businesses owe duties to employees, customers, patients, and others to whom they could cause harm by failing to adopt reasonable precautions to prevent the spread of COVID-19; (3) businesses might breach these duties by failing to adopt such reasonable (even statutorily required) precautions; and (4) both actual and proximate cause could theoretically be established, such as where an employer knew or should have known that an employee was likely infected yet required her to come to work. Some combination of these circumstances could establish a case for damages.

In practice, however, COVID-19's characteristics pose roadblocks to the prima facie case, particularly the element of causation. Contact with any person – while shopping, filling a car with gasoline, interacting with a neighbor, or even visiting outside – raises the possibility of exposure. Thus, unless the facts line up just so or reliable DNA sequencing is applied to trace transmission – both of which are unlikely – it is nearly impossible to establish causation by a preponderance of the evidence. Tort law thus proves an ineffective mechanism for compensating injured individuals in this context. And given the nature of infectious diseases more generally, this is likely to be true in the context of future pandemics as well.

One answer to address all this uncompensated suffering is to conceive of it as an accident and allow loss to "lie where it falls."[7] But to the extent that such losses were caused by negligent behavior, it would seem unfair to leave victims without recourse for this but not other wrongs, particularly given the extent of the suffering. Moreover, there are strong policy reasons for extending coverage via tort replacement to those victims who are not eligible for other forms of relief. As we have seen

[6] Qihao He et al., The Possibilities and Limits of Insurance as Governance in Insuring Pandemics, Nat'l Libr. of Med. (2023), https://www.ncbi.nlm.nih.gov/pmc/articles/PMC10028328/; Steven Ross Johnson, Millions at High Risk of Severe COVID-19 Outcomes Lack Coverage to Cover Costs, Modern Healthcare (June 10, 2020), https://perma.cc/38AT-LDFK.

[7] Oliver Wendell Holmes, Jr., The Common Law 49 (1881).

through this and earlier pandemics, the more serious and sustained the human suffering, the greater the threat to our economy and social life. Indeed, we can recall in the early months of the COVID-19 pandemic the profoundly unsettling tableaux of empty streets, unattended funerals and religious gatherings, and the sudden paucity of normal human connection that accompanied the draconian steps to stop the spread of the virus.

Yet even if the causation problem could have been solved by better tracing, it is not obvious that widespread tort liability for negligent COVID-19 transmission would have been any more desirable than tort replacement during the pandemic or that it would be during the next pandemic. After all, even if plaintiffs could overcome these proof challenges (as well as other challenges such as liability shields and workers' compensation restrictions), the enormous costs for businesses (especially small ones given what would be untenably high insurance costs), the economy, and the judicial system might not be worth the benefits to victims.

Similarly, the potential negative effects of tort on social life, such as more widespread quarantines and shutdowns, might be catastrophic. A public tort-replacement system may provide an answer.

8.3 LESSONS FROM PRIOR EXAMPLES OF TORT REPLACEMENT

Unlike COVID-19, the liability dilemma posed by the virus is not novel. In the past, legislatures have adopted administrative compensation schemes to (1) meet the needs of potential plaintiffs who face substantial obstacles to recovery under the conventional tort system and (2) avoid excessive costs to defendant businesses, industries, the economy, and social order that could result from reforming tort to allow mass recoveries.

8.3.1 *Meeting the Unmet Needs of Potential Plaintiffs*

Here, we consider two examples of administrative solutions that legislatures have offered in the past that provide a useful analogy to COVID-19:

8.3.1.1 The Federal Black Lung Compensation Scheme

Following a deadly explosion at a mine in West Virginia in 1968, Congress passed the Federal Coal Mine Health and Safety Act, including Title IV, the Black Lung Benefits Program.[8] Congress designed the program to compensate coal miners

[8] Federal Coal Mine Health and Safety Act, Pub. L. No. 91-173, 83 Stat. 798 (codified as amended at 30 U.S.C. § 901 et seq.).

suffering from black lung disease and address the lack of benefits for inactive miners and their survivors.[9]

As in the COVID-19 context, injured miners had difficulty establishing a tort claim, and workers' compensation was not generally viable. State administrative programs tended to exclude occupational disease,[10] and injuries often emerged from symptomless exposure, taking the form of long-term and unpredictable respiratory disorders that were hard to identify within the statutes of limitations.[11]

Congress' first attempt to aid miners faltered. Despite Congress creating two rebuttable presumptions to assist claimants – that (1) the disease "arose out of the [ir] employment" and (2) the death was a direct result of the disease[12] – claimants continued to struggle with the statute's causation requirements for reasons similar to why they struggled to establish causation under tort law, namely the amount of time between exposure and illness and the unpredictable nature of the disease. In 1972, Congress loosened the tort-like requirements to expand eligibility for benefits, such as by allowing surviving spouses to demonstrate only that at death the miner "was totally disabled due to black lung disease," rather than that the miner's death was the result of the disease.[13] The Act provides a useful example of a legislative solution when potential plaintiffs are unable to establish causation or access workers' compensation benefits.

8.3.1.2 The Federal Nuclear Worker Compensation Program

In 2000, President Clinton issued an executive order recognizing the thousands of Americans exposed to nuclear radiation who developed "disabling or fatal illnesses" while building America's nuclear defense.[14] Like black lung victims, these potential plaintiffs faced significant evidentiary hurdles in recovering under tort particularly with respect to causation "because of long latency periods, the uniqueness of the hazards to which they were exposed, and inadequate exposure data."[15]

In 2000, Congress passed the Energy Employees Occupational Illness Compensation Program Act (EEOICPA), which confers on the Department of Labor the primary responsibility of administering the compensation program[16] and provides cash compensation for medical expenses to workers and survivors "who

9 30 U.S.C. § 901(a).
10 Robert L. Rabin, The Renaissance of Accident Law Plans Revisited, 64 Md. L. Rev. 699, 704 (2005).
11 Peter S. Barth, The Tragedy of Black Lung: Federal Compensation for Occupational Disease 169–71 (1987).
12 30 U.S.C. § 921.
13 Id.
14 Exec. Order No. 13179, Providing Compensation to America's Nuclear Weapons Workers (Dec. 7, 2000).
15 Id.
16 42 U.S.C. § 7384 et seq.

contracted certain diseases as a result of exposure to beryllium, silica, or radiation while working for [the Department of Energy], its contractors, or subcontractors in the nuclear weapons industry."[17] Although EEOICPA presents a different reason for tort replacement than the pandemic scenario – the government employed the injured workers and, therefore, stood in the role of the tortfeasor, whereas in the COVID-19 case the government would provide relief to victims harmed by others – the example remains relevant insofar as the government stepped in to compensate injured parties who needed relief but were unable to show causation or access workers compensation. Some level of deterrence may have been preserved during the shift from private tort law to administrative tort replacement, given the dual role of the government as both the administrative payer and the tortfeasor.

8.3.2 *Harms to Industry, the Economy, and Society*

One way to meet the needs of frustrated, would-be tort plaintiffs would be to loosen the causal requirements of tort law so that those plaintiffs can bring claims. Such a reconfiguration of tort law, however, would introduce the problem that so many worried about at the start of the pandemic: The costs of defending all claims and satisfying judgments in successful claims would harm certain industries and the economy more generally. As with the compensation problem discussed above, tort replacement has been employed to solve the problem of expected harms being too widespread and the costs imposed on defendants being too high. Here we review two examples of tort-replacement schemes established to protect the public interest by shoring up an industry or service – those for 9/11 victims and for neurologically impaired infants. We then briefly consider workers' compensation, the most salient example of tort replacement.

8.3.2.1 The 9/11 Victims Compensation Fund

Congress enacted the Air Transportation Safety and System Stabilization Act both to compensate 9/11 victims via the US$7.375 billion Victims' Compensation Fund and to prevent devastation to the airline industry and its insurers from flight stoppages, decreased demand, and tort litigation.[18] Although the former purpose is more well-known, the preamble to the Act describes it as "[a]n act to preserve the continued viability of the United States air transportation system."[19] The Act provided air

[17] The Act/EEOICPA, Part B, Ctrs. for Disease Control and Prevention, https://perma.cc/3Y2B-E45W.

[18] 49 U.S.C. § 40101. See also Raymond L. Mariani, The September 11th Victim Compensation Fund of 2001 and the Protection of the Airline Industry: A Bill for the American People, 67 J. Air L. & Com. 141, 142 (2002).

[19] Preamble Public Law No: 107-42 (Sept. 22, 2001).

carriers with US$5 billion in direct grants for losses incurred due to the attacks,[20] up to US$10 billion in loan guarantees,[21] and, as amended, precluded compensated victims from filing claims,[22] capped damages in cases against airlines by plaintiffs not eligible for or otherwise participating in the Fund,[23] and capped liability for other types of industry participants such as aircraft manufacturers, airport owners, and governmental entities.[24]

Potential 9/11 and COVID-19 plaintiffs faced some similar challenges; namely, identifying the tortfeasor (the negligent COVID-19 transmitter or the terrorist organization) was difficult if not impossible. And the airlines – like many businesses in the COVID-19 context, particularly smaller ones – faced potential damages amounts far exceeding insurance funds.[25]

8.3.2.2 No-Fault Medical Malpractice: Neurologically Impaired Infant Programs

The American medical malpractice system has long been criticized as imprecise and unjust, largely ineffective at addressing the high rate of medical errors in the medical system.[26] In brief, "only a small fraction of those injured by medical negligence ever bring a claim; those who do sue may face years of litigation before they recover; and much of the money spent on malpractice litigation goes to cover its costs rather than to compensate the victims of malpractice."[27] And what these deficiencies reveal, apropos of the larger dialogue of the book of which this chapter is a part, is the often intrinsic difficulties of using classic tort law remedies to accomplish wider social aims, be they deterring bad behavior while maintaining an optimal level of social activity or, returning to our central focus, providing adequate compensation to redress harm.

No-fault malpractice – a system under which an administrative body awards compensation for medical injuries based on a predetermined, standardized

[20] 49 U.S.C. § 40101, sec. 101(a)(2).

[21] Id. at sec. 101(a)(1).

[22] Id. at sec. 405(c)(3)(B)(i).

[23] Id. at sec. 408.

[24] Id. at sec. 201(b)(2).

[25] Kenneth S. Abraham & K. D. Logue, The Genie and the Bottle: Collateral Sources and the 9/11 Victim Compensation Fund, 53 DePaul L. Rev. 591, 595 (2003).

[26] See, e.g., Troyen A. Brennan et al., Incidence of Adverse Events and Negligence in Hospitalized Patients – Results of the Harvard Medical Practice Study I, 324 N. Engl. J. Med. 370 (1991); Lucian Leape et al., The Nature of Adverse Events in Hospitalized Patients: Results of the Harvard Medical Malpractice Study II, 324 N. Engl. J. Med 377 (1991); David M. Studdert et al., Claims, Errors, and Compensation Payments in Medical Malpractice Litigation, 354 N. Engl. J. Med. 2024 (2006); Allen B. Kachalia et al., Beyond Negligence: Availability and Medical Injury Compensation, 66 Soc. Sci. Med. 387 (2008); Eric J. Thomas et al., Incidence and Types of Preventable Adverse Events in Elderly Patients: Population Based Review of Medical Records, 38 Med. Care. 261 (2000).

[27] Catherine Struve, Improving the Medical Malpractice Litigation Process, 23(4) Health Affs. 33, 34 (2004).

schedule – garnered considerable attention in the 1990s and early 2000s.[28] For example, in 2002, before becoming Administrator of the Centers for Medicare and Medicaid Services, Don Berwick wrote: "We badly need at least one courageous, time-limited experiment on a no-fault tort system at a statewide or regional level with enterprise-level responsibility for compensating victims of medical injury."[29] Two states subsequently adopted (quite narrow) no-fault medical malpractice programs.

In response to insurers canceling obstetricians' malpractice coverage and obstetricians' subsequent threats of quitting, Florida and Virginia implemented tort-replacement programs for the families of severely injured newborns, the cases constituting the largest percentage and highest-cost obstetrical claims.[30] These programs provide compensation in the form of medical, rehabilitation, nursing care, and other expenses for categories of newborns who suffer particular iatrogenic harms, regardless of whether the cause of the harm was negligent.[31] The programs were primarily designed to prevent an exodus of medical providers,[32] and they largely worked. Hospitals and physicians participate in extraordinary numbers.[33] Whereas previously, obstetricians increasingly could not obtain medical malpractice liability insurance due to untenable cost, the programs took the most expensive cases out of the malpractice system, spread costs beyond obstetricians, and ultimately resolved the crisis.

8.3.2.3 Workers' Compensation

Perhaps no administrative tort-replacement scheme is as well-known and long-standing as workers' compensation. Until the mid-nineteenth century, the common law provided workers effectively no recourse to recover against their employers

[28] See, e.g., David M. Studdert & Troyen A. Brennan, No-Fault Compensation for Medical Injuries: The Prospect for Error Prevention, 286(2) JAMA 217–23 (2001); Marie Bismark & Ron Patterson, No-Fault Compensation in New Zealand: Harmonizing Injury Compensation, Provider Accountability, and Patient Safety, 25(1) Health Affs. 278, 278–83 (2006); Randall R. Bovbjerg & Frank Sloan, No Fault for Medical Injury: Theory and Evidence, 67 U. Cincinnati L. Rev. 53 (1998).

[29] Don Berwick, A User's Manual for the IOM's "Quality Chasm" Report, 21(3) Health Affs. 89 (2002).

[30] James A. Henderson, The Virginia Birth-Related Injury Compensation Act: Limited No-Fault Statutes as Solutions to the "Medical Malpractice Crisis," in Medical Professional Liability and Delivery of Obstetrical Care: Volume II: An Interdisciplinary Review 194 (Victoria P. Rostow & Roger J. Bulger eds., 1989).

[31] Jill Horwitz & Troyen A. Brennan, No-Fault Compensation for Medical Injury: A Case Study, 14(4) Health Affs. 164 (1995).

[32] Id. See also Cynthia L. Gallup, Can No-Fault Compensation of Impaired Infants Alleviate the Malpractice Crisis in Obstetrics?, 14(4) J. Health Pol. Pol'y L. 691 (1989), https://read.dukeupress.edu/jhppl/article/14/4/691/74327/Can-No-Fault-Compensation-of-Impaired-Infants.

[33] Gil Siegal et al., Adjudicating Severe Birth Injury Claims in Florida and Virginia: The Experience of a Landmark Experiment in Personal Injury Compensation, 34 Am. J.L. & Med. 489 (2008).

under tort for injuries suffered on the job.[34] The lack of recourse was grounded in an outdated notion that "an employee should be grateful for the opportunity for gainful employment … any special legal protection on top of his good fortune was quite unthinkable."[35] As the law developed and workers began to win some tort claims, concerns about employer liability costs grew.[36]

Based on the Prussian system of workers' compensation,[37] which offered benefits and compensation for "job-related injuries and medical care and rehabilitation…" and precluded employees from suing their employers, states began adopting comprehensive workers' compensation laws in the 1920s.[38] By 1948, every state had adopted some form of this no-fault insurance, a move that was largely motivated by the need to mitigate a broad threat to the economy, one similar to the economic paralysis that has often accompanied pandemics in the past and present.

8.4 A BRIEF PROPOSAL AND POLICY IMPERATIVES

Wrongs between private parties – whether in health care or outside – are typically adjudicated under private law. Yet, however coherent a system for deciding where the costs of accidents should fall generally, sometimes private law fails to realize either its own goals (e.g., compensation and aligning incentives) or important social goals. In such cases public law can supplement, or even supplant, private law to fill the needs left by private law.

Offering a full proposal is far beyond the scope of this short chapter. Instead, we have focused on two more modest aims. First, we suggest that tort replacement in the form of a social insurance-like compensation scheme might have solved some of the problems that private tort law failed to address during the pandemic and offers a policy solution for next time. Second, we offer multiple examples of effective use of tort replacement to solve compensation problems or, in the alternative, to forestall crushing litigation.

Importantly, we do not envision complete replacement but, instead, propose to supplement tort. For example, conventional tort should be available for cases involving any breach more culpable than negligent behavior, including grossly negligent, reckless, willful and wanton, and intentional behavior that causes harm. Moreover, we recognize the need to protect against the risk that tort replacement would effectively provide social insurance for all relevant harms, such as all COVID-19 transmission, and, thereby, lead to unsustainable costs. We, therefore, envision

34 Richard A. Epstein, The Historical Origins and Economic Structure of Workers' Compensation Law, 16 Ga. L. Rev. 775, 777–78 (1982).

35 Id.

36 Gregory P. Guyton, A Brief History of Workers' Compensation, 19 Iowa Orthopaedic J. 106 (1999), https://perma.cc/M7CU-EGRE.

37 Id. at 107.

38 Id. at 108.

limiting the program in various ways, such as through subrogation rules that would only cover damages not otherwise covered through existing health insurance, unemployment coverage, business insurance, or other programs.

Tort replacement is worth considering in the pandemic or similar contexts for at least the following four overlapping policy reasons:

First, it would provide compensation more quickly and efficiently than tort law can likely do during the time of a pandemic. COVID-19 victims, for example, have faced great obstacles in maintaining a successful tort suit. To wit, they are not likely to establish causation, and even if they could, many defendant tortfeasors (namely, small businesses) would be effectively judgment-proof. With a replacement regime, these would-be plaintiffs could promptly receive the compensation they need to take care of health and other pressing expenses.

Second, equity and fairness favor tort replacement in these circumstances. More than in other mass tort settings, the facts often differ by case – the manner of exposure varies tremendously across and within industries. Consider the differences in congregate care settings, nursing homes, and college dorm rooms. With such different underlying facts, opportunities for class actions or other consolidated litigation are limited. Compensation schemes are likely to reach more potential plaintiffs and be more equitable across a range of plaintiffs and defendants than conventional tort law.

Third, a sensible administrative mechanism would provide greater certainty and finality for potential plaintiffs. It would also lead to less business disruption because businesses could plan for the fees they would need to pay to benefit from a replacement system, and they would not need to adjust business to avoid a potential and uncertain spate of claims, which happened not to arrive during this pandemic. Of course, the cost of this system would be deterrence. We would address this in two ways. As discussed above, we would maintain the tort system for cases that involve breaches based on more culpable behavior than ordinary negligence. And we would rely on accompanying regulation that required compliance with safety standards for a business defendant to benefit from the replacement system. Other regulations, potentially at all levels of government, might penalize defendants who did not adhere to specific standards of behavior. Establishing workable criteria for business conduct consistent with current scientific expertise would be both more effective and less turbulent than the behavior required as revealed through aggregated tort judgments.

Fourth, the vast majority of states immunized businesses from tort liability to encourage them to stay or reopen in the face of various uncertainties relating to insurance, liability, and other factors beyond their control. The impact on certain segments of the economy, such as restaurants and concert venues, has been massive, and it likely would have been worse without such immunity. However, the benefits of immunity in terms of maintaining and restoring commerce and social life came at a great cost. Tort replacement would have allowed victims to have some recourse. In terms of potential defendants, linking participation in a replacement system with adhering to safety standards, as some immunity statutes did, might have avoided some harm.

8.5 POTENTIAL OBJECTIONS

A tort-replacement system raises a host of practical and theoretical considerations as well as federalism issues. We briefly consider some of the most salient objections to tort replacement in this context.

First, and perhaps the biggest objection, is that a compensation scheme might fail to motivate individuals and businesses to take adequate precautions to reduce risk. As we explained above, although no-fault might impede certain corrective actions, we believe a system can be developed to incentivize good behavior and deter bad behavior. Moreover, one should not overstate the deterrent effects of conventional tort law; since most claims predictably have little chance of success, they are unlikely to deter bad behavior.

The second is that replacing tort might undermine a morally centered conception of tort law and liability recovery. To over-simplify, scholars have argued that tort is fundamentally about addressing a wrong committed by a particular party against a particular party, and so it is important that the tortfeasor, not an anonymous fund, compensate the victim. Under the contrary view – where tort consists of a simple economic calculation based only on deterrence and compensation – it doesn't matter that a victim is compensated by the responsible tortfeasor, as long as potential tortfeasors are deterred by the threat of penalty and victims are compensated.[39]

Although this objection is theoretically important, the practical counterfactual matters. The moral case for tort law assumes that businesses' misconduct will be redressed through litigation between parties. But as we've discussed, litigation in this context has been stymied. Moreover, insofar as it is very difficult to identify misconduct in the infectious disease context, unless we make the untenable assumption that the very fact of operating a business and not knowing the health status of customers or employees is negligent behavior requiring redress, these pandemic cases are not viewed well through the lens of morally condemnable action.

The third objection is that this short chapter has not grappled with important practical questions, perhaps chiefly funding needs, which could be very large.

[39] Horwitz thanks Professor Don Herzog for this insight.

Importantly, we are not suggesting the establishment of a new entitlement but only a supplement to existing insurance systems. Applying subrogation rules and the like, we propose tort replacement only for individuals and small businesses that do not have adequate means through insurance or other resources to deal with the serious harms that COVID-19 or some future pandemic disease may cause. In evaluating schemes, and especially in doing the cost/benefit analysis integral to making sound regulatory choices, policymakers should consider the economic (and other) effects of not dealing effectively with the matter of damage and compensation.[40] So viewed, it is by no means clear that a scheme of the sort we describe is much more costly than doing nothing of the sort.

Finally, this chapter cannot adequately analyze the enormous and enduring issues of federalism and comparative institutional competence that tort replacement raises. On the one hand, as tort is traditionally state law, it may make good sense to pursue compensation reform at the state level. On the other hand, the characteristics of COVID-19-related injuries, beginning with the ineluctability of borders in controlling transmission and the national impact on public health and the economy, suggest that an effective compensation scheme might require national action. In any event, our suggestion to consider tort replacement does not depend on whether a scheme is enacted by Congress or the states, and any constitutional problems can and should be addressed in the structure of proposed legislation.

8.6 CONCLUSION

Rather than reforming private tort law to address the great needs caused by pandemics such as COVID-19, we have considered replacing it with a public system. Precedents for such replacement were motivated by issues we saw in this latest pandemic, namely (1) the unmet needs of potential plaintiffs and (2) the significant harms to social life and the economy that would result from reforming tort by relaxing the requirement to connect the injury with the commission of a wrong. These programs have been generally successful at addressing both issues and serve as models for the type of compensation scheme legislatures should consider adopting in the COVID-19 context and in the face of pandemics to come.

40 Innovative financing would be necessary to support what would be an expensive program. Because protecting businesses, especially small businesses, from ruinous lawsuits partly motivates the proposal, legislatures might contemplate a special tax on businesses to generate a fund. Although such a tax might become complex in implementation (e.g., are lawyers involved? Are punitive damages available?), not to mention politically difficult, the issues are not insurmountable, as the creation of enduring or sinking funds is a budget device familiar to Congress and state legislatures.

9

The Human Body Commons

A Private Law Contribution for the Advancement of the Right to Health

Enrique Santamaría Echeverría

9.1 INTRODUCTION

For much of history, research results and scientific knowledge were considered a part of the public domain. Basic research, carried out by academic and other nonprofit institutions, was heavily financed by public funds and agencies, which generally required data deposit into public repositories.[1] However, around the 1980s, a push for privatization of research[2] led to what has been termed the "enclosure of the mind"[3] and a resultant profit-driven culture around scientific research.[4]

Biomedical research has been particularly affected by this process of privatization. Broadly speaking, biomedical research is a field of science that aims to develop tools (e.g., medicines, tests, vaccines, medical devices) that prevent and treat diseases. This type of research relies heavily on three different but connected types of resources: human biological materials (HBM), health data, and previous scientific knowledge.

In biomedical research, the epistemological shift, from a public domain-oriented conception of science and knowledge to a profit-driven research culture, has limited the advancement of knowledge and, consequently, the human right to health.

Historically, private law – through patents, licenses, other intellectual property mechanisms, contracts, and property rights – has been instrumental to privatization

[1] See Sheldon Krimsky, The Profit of Scientific Discovery and Its Normative Implications, 75(1) Chi.-Kent L. Rev. 15, 17 (1999). ("(I)n the mid-1950s, the federal government provided about fifty-five percent of the support for university research, industrial firm supplied eight percent of the funds and the remaining thirty-seven percent came from foundations and state governments. By the late 1960's, the government share expanded to more than seventy rising budget deficits and the leveling of science funding in the 1980s.")

[2] Jerome H. Reichman & Paul F. Uhlir, A Contractually Reconstructed Research Commons for Scientific Data in a Highly Protectionist Intellectual Property Environment, 66 L. & Contemp. Probs. 315 (2003).

[3] James Boyle, The Public Domain: Enclosing the Commons of the Mind (2008).

[4] Krimsky, supra note 1.

and commodification. However, a political and legal struggle to subvert the privatization of resources in biomedical research has emerged, based largely on the argument that bringing back scientific knowledge to the public domain may cause positive spillovers (e.g., innovation, economic value, and protection of human rights). The "idea of the commons" plays a pivotal role in this argument.

Private law and the commons in biomedical research are typically regarded as opposing concepts. While the traditional understanding of private law elicits notions of ownership, patents, and privatization, the imagery of the commons in biomedical research evokes opposing notions of open access to HBM, data, information, and knowledge.

However, these two approaches are not always mutually exclusive. Scientific practice has demonstrated how private law rules can enhance and protect the commons, while at the same time, encouraging innovation. This chapter therefore explores how private law, via the establishment of property rights, intellectual property, licenses, and other contracts, can serve to advance the right to health by reinforcing biomedical research anchored in the commons. In particular, it explores how the interplay between private law and the commons is instrumental in protecting and promoting individual and collective human rights, with particular emphasis on the right to health and health care and the right to enjoy the benefits of science and scientific progress. More specifically, it explores whether the traditional functions of private law's institutional arrangements can be modeled, and if necessary, subverted, to develop commons on (health) data, HBM, and scientific knowledge (together "human body commons").

9.2 HUMAN BODY COMMONS ENTANGLED: UNRAVELING GENEALOGIES AND TYPOLOGIES

The terms "commons" or "communing" elicit different meanings and are used differently by different bodies of literature and disciplines.[5] While the terminology may be similar, the normative foundations and objectives behind these strands of scholarship differ significantly. This difference has led to considerable confusion and misunderstanding of the concept of the commons. A clear disambiguation is therefore essential to understand the potential application of this concept to health data, HBM, and scientific knowledge.

This chapter focuses on two distinct, but intertwined, bodies of literature that have developed clear theories on the commons: (1) theories on open commons (OC) and the public domain;[6] and (2) the works on the Institutional Analysis and

5 Tine de Moor, What Do We Have in Common? A Comparative Framework for Old and New Literature on the Commons 57(2) Int'l Rev. Soc. Hist. 269, 272 (2012).

6 See, e.g., Carol Rose, The Comedy of the Commons: Custom, Commerce, and Inherently Public Property, 53(3) Univ. Chi. L. Rev. 711 (1986), https://www.jstor.org/stable/1599583?seq=1&cid=pdf-; James Boyle, The Public Domain: Enclosing the Commons of the Mind

Development (IAD) framework for the governance of common pool resources (CPR),[7] as proposed by Elinor Ostrom and further developed and adapted to account for different types of commons and institutions for collective action.[8]

The OC envisions an open commons with a symmetric freedom to operate. Nobody from an unidentified class of users can rely on the power of the State to restrict access to the resource (usually non-rival or partially congestible). In this sense, OC is conceptually located outside the property regime.[9] Common pool resources are bottom-up arrangements with clear rules of membership and access to a resource (characterized by high rivalry and low excludability).[10] From this perspective, CPR are commons inside, but property outside, as members can rely on the power of the State to prevent nonmembers from accessing the resources.

Despite their differences, both types of commons (OC and CPR) share the underlying assumption that state or market solutions for the governance of resources are not always sufficient, nor necessary.[11] Nonetheless, these two theories on the commons can offer a compelling normative underpinning for the de-privatized governance of science and knowledge.

Two related problems at the intersection of both types of commons make the case: (1) the problem of sharing and circulating the managed resources and (2) the problem of freeriding, reseeding the commons, and distributing its benefits.

These problems are particularly complex for the governance of the different resources within the human body commons. First, individual rights on informed consent, privacy, and data protection tend to limit the circulation and the repurposing (secondary uses) of data and HBM. This makes personal data and HBM highly excludable (i.e., the use of these resources by others without consent is very

(2008); Yochai Benkler, The Wealth of Networks: How Social Production Transforms Markets and Freedom (2006); Yochai Benkler, Between Spanish Huertas and the Open Road, in Governing Knowledge Commons 69–98 (Brett Frischmann et al. eds., 2014); Yochai Benkler, The Political Economy of Commons, IV(3) Upgrade Eur. J. Informatics Pro. 6, 6–9 (2003); Yochai Benkler, Open Access and Information Commons, in 2 The Oxford Handbook of Law and Economics: Private and Commercial Law 256, 256 (Francesco Parisi ed., 2017); Lawrence Lessig, Code and the Commons, Keynote Address at Fordham L. Sch. Conference on Media Convergence (Feb. 9, 1999), https://dash.harvard.edu/bitstream/handle/1/12942294/COMMONS?sequence = 1; Brett M. Frischmann, Infrastructure: The Social Value of Shared Resources (2012).

7 Elinor Ostrom, Governing the Commons: The Evolution of Institutions for Collective Action (1990); Elinor Ostrom, Background on the Institutional Analysis and Development Framework, 39(1) Pol'y Stud. J. 7 (2011).

8 Tine de Moor, From Common Pastures to Global Commons: A Historical Perspective on Interdisciplinary Approaches to Commons, 19(4) Natures Sci. Societes 422, 422–31 (2011); De Moor, supra note 5.

9 Even if one may formally find different underlying titles of property, it is the case of some types of infrastructure falling under the public property regime.

10 Charlotte Hess & Elinor Ostrom, Understanding Knowledge as a Commons: From Theory to Practice 5 (2007); De Moor, supra note 5, at 426.

11 David Bollier, The Growth of the Commons Paradigm, in Hess & Ostrom, supra note 10, at 27.

limited).[12] Second, HBM, (health) data, and scientific knowledge are different types of resources: While scientific knowledge and data are, in principle, non-rival intangible resources (i.e., many can use the same resource at the same time) provisioned in market, public, or social processes, HBM are naturally provisioned tangible rival resources (i.e., the use of HBM prevents simultaneous consumption by others).

Third, the material dimension of HBM makes them perishable, consumable, and prone to contamination. Human biological samples are often consumed after they have been analyzed and, if not, it is difficult to guarantee that the samples have not been altered after the first analysis, which would make them unsuitable for research. Fourth, these resources are circularly connected – HBM are necessary for the extraction of data, which in turn, together with other types of health and medical data, are the raw materials for the creation of scientific knowledge. The latter is an input for further innovation and a source of positive societal spillovers. The obvious consequence of this interdependence is that the enclosure and privatization of one of these resources negatively affects the existence of the other two, while opening them contributes to the growth of the value of the others.[13]

Against this backdrop, the question is: How can OC and CPR be applied to the governance of the human body commons? Several specific theories have been put forward to make use of these overarching frameworks to govern the resources included under the umbrella term "human body commons": knowledge, data, and HBM. These theories include medical knowledge commons,[14] genome or genomic commons,[15] and medical information commons.[16]

[12] The European Data Protection Regulation (GDPR), for example, prohibits as a rule the processing data without the consent of the data subject. However, the GDPR also established a series of exceptions, among which the use of sensitive data for scientific research. See Enrique Santamaría, Governing Health Data for Research, Development and Innovation: The Missteps of the European Health Data Space Proposal, Bill of Health (Mar. 23, 2023), https://blog.petrieflom.law.harvard.edu/2023/03/23/governing-health-data-for-research-development-and-innovation-the-missteps-of-the-european-health-data-space-proposal/ (with further references).

[13] Bollier, supra note 11, at 34.

[14] Governing Medical Knowledge Commons (Katherine J. Strandburg et al. eds., 2017).

[15] Jorge L. Contreas & Bartha M. Knoppers, The Genomic Commons, 19 Ann. Rev. Genomics Hum. Genetics 429 (2018); Jorge L. Contreras, Constructing the Genome Commons, 99 Governing Knowledge Commons 112, 112–13 (Brett M. Frichmann et al. eds., 2014). Similar proposals for commons on the results on genetic tests have also been advanced, see, e.g., Barbara J. Evans, Genomic Data Commons, in Governing Medical Knowledge Commons 74, 74–101 (Katherine J. Strandburg et al. eds., 2017).

[16] Robert Cook-Deegan & Amy L. McGuire, Moving beyond Bermuda: Sharing Data to Build a Medical Information Commons, 27(6) Genome Rsch. 897 (2017); Robert Cook-Deegan et al., Sharing Data to Build a Medical Information Commons: From Bermuda to the Global Alliance, 18 Ann. Rev. Genomics Hum. Genetics 389, 389–415 (2017); Patricia A. Deverka et al., Creating a Data Resource: What Will It Take to Build a Medical Information Commons?, 9(1) Genome Med. 1 (2017).

Although these theories reach different conclusions,[17] their importance lies in their theorization of knowledge (and data) as a resource: (1) The fact that knowledge is cumulative makes sharing and creation inextricably related processes; (2) the intellectual products of the past are inputs for future products; (3) the non-rivalry and non-excludability of knowledge in abstracto lead its boundaries to be either artificially built (e.g., through patents) or derived from the embodiment of the knowledge resource (e.g., HBM containing data); and (4) the creation of knowledge depends on rivalrous inputs (e.g., time and money).

Through the analysis of commons-based initiatives of different scales and purposes, the next section examines how private law, by accounting for the aforementioned characteristics, can contribute to the further construction of the human body commons.

9.3 PRIVATE LAW AND HUMAN BODY COMMONS: BETWEEN OPEN COMMONS AND CPR

Commons may be the result of a top-down regulatory approach or, on the contrary, may arise as a response to a legal system establishing a proprietary regime for the governance of a given resource. In the latter case, the commons are carved out of the background law, by using or subverting the legal tools disposed by that very same legal regime.

Contract law and contracts constitute a relevant legal tool for the construction of human body commons. Jerome Reichman and Paul Uhlir were perhaps the first ones to explore the idea of a contractually reconstructed scientific commons.[18] Their advancement constitutes, yet again, a response to the phenomenon of privatization of science and data taking place in the last two decades of the twentieth century in the United States. Precisely because of the cumulative and circular nature of knowledge, their analysis focused primarily on the deposit of data in publicly accessible databases. However, it did not include the sharing of HBM.

But building on their work, a combination of theory and practice may show how contracts can contribute to the construction of commons on HBM. Material transfer agreements, the Structural Genomics Consortium Open Trust Agreement, and data cooperatives serve as examples.

[17] The point of departure of these theories is either: (1) Hess and Ostrom's variation of IAD framework for data and information which – together with other intelligible ideas and scientific knowledge – are covered under the umbrella term "knowledge commons," and/or (2) the Governing Knowledge Commons framework (GKC) developed by Katherine J. Strandburg, Brett M. Frischmann, and Michael J. Madison. See, e.g., Hess & Ostrom, supra note 10, at 7; Governing Knowledge Commons (Brett M. Frischmann et al. eds., 2014).

[18] See Reichman & Uhlir, supra note 2 (providing information on contractual models for scientific data commons); Arti Rai & James Boyle, Synthetic Biology: Caught between Property Rights, the Public Domain, and the Commons, 5(3) PLOS Biology 389 (2007) (providing a specific analysis in the field of synthetic biology).

A material transfer agreement (MTA)[19] is a contract in which a provider and a recipient agree to the transfer of tangible research materials, including HBM, for the recipient's use.[20] Beyond their importance in determining the intellectual property rights for provider and recipient, MTAs are also central to one of the core institutions in the collection, processing, and sharing of HBM: the biobank. Despite the many differences in types and purposes, from population to disease-specific, a biobank is essentially an organized collection of human biological samples and associated data for the purposes of present and future research.[21] Biobanks may rely on tailor-made MTAs or can adopt a standardized MTA to share the samples in their collection to researchers and institutions. However, depending on the type of MTA, the recipient of the materials may not be allowed to further share original or derived materials.

For this reason, several standardized MTA models have been developed to facilitate the transfer and sharing of biological materials beyond the first recipient. These models include the Uniform Biological MTA (hereafter UBMTA),[22] the Science Commons MTA,[23] and the Open MTA.[24]

The first of these models, the UBMTA, was developed in the United States by the National Institutes of Health (NIH) in collaboration with other repositories.[25] Although it facilitated sharing materials by eliminating the need for lengthy or impractical negotiations between institutions, it was also limited to academic or nonprofit institutions and precluded both commercial uses and the further distribution of materials and derivatives.[26]

[19] See Victor Rodriguez, Material Transfer Agreements: Open Science vs. Proprietary Claims, 23 (4) Nature Biotech. 489, 489–91 (2005) (an overview of the notion of material transfer agreement and the debate around open science on human materials).

[20] Int'l Soc'y for Biological and Env't Repositories (ISBER), Best Practices for Repositories: Collection, Storage, Retrieval and Distribution of Biological Materials for Research 88 (3rd ed. 2001).

[21] Lisa Dive et al., Public Trust and Global Biobank Networks, 21 BMC Med. Ethics 1 (2020).

[22] Uniform Biological Material Transfer Agreement, dated March 8, 1995, for the Transfer of Materials between Non-Profit Institutions and an Implementing Letter for the Transfer of Biological Material, World Intell. Prop. Org. (1995) https://www.wipo.int/tk/en/databases/contracts/texts/ubmta.html.

[23] Thinh Kguyen, Science Commons: Material Transfer Agreement Project, 3(2) Innovations Tech., Governance, Globalization 137, 137–43 (2007).

[24] Linda Kahl et al., Opening Options for Material Transfer, 36(10) Nature Biotech. 923, 923–27 (2018).

[25] Kguyen, supra note 23, at 140.

[26] More than 300 institutions have become signatories of the UBMTA. See UMBTA Signatories, Ass'n of Univ. Tech. Managers, https://autm.net/surveys-and-tools/agreements/material-transfer-agreements/mta-toolkit/uniform-biological-material-transfer-agreement/ubmta-signatories (last accessed May 8, 2023). Addgene, one of the biggest repositories of plasmids in the world, is an example of successful implementation of the UBMTA. Addgene, acting as an intermediary, continues to use the UBMTA for sharing plasmids deposited in its repository. See MTA: UBMTA, Addgene, https://www.addgene.org/agreement/1/ (last accessed May 8, 2023).

To remedy this situation, the Science Commons MTA permitted, under certain circumstances, the commercial use of materials, but continued to prohibit their further distribution. To overcome this limitation, the Open MTA was designed. The Open MTA not only allows its use to for-profit and nonprofit entities alike but also permits the use for commercial purposes and the further distribution of materials and derivatives (including tissue samples). Its design was based on the principles of nondiscrimination, access, attribution, redistribution, and reuse.[27] Despite their differences, these standardized MTAs constitute essential tools to guarantee and facilitate redistribution of biological materials.

Moreover, because standard MTAs can be easily adopted, they also enable biobanks to integrate in wider biobank networks,[28] participating in that way as nods in an open and growing network of human body commons.[29]

Although the use of MTAs to facilitate the construction of human body commons is not completely new, their use has highlighted some of the advantages of using private law to facilitate the commons. But there are also disadvantages to consider. First, if MTAs do not include clauses on how research results would return to the commons (the problem of reseeding the commons described above), MTAs may in fact contribute to the privatization of research instead of advancing its opening. Second, the limits of MTAs stem from their contractual nature: as contracts are, as a general rule, not enforceable against third parties,[30] it would be difficult for the original provider of the materials to start an action against a third party who received the materials from the recipient side of the MTA. In other words, MTAs are not very useful in enabling the circulation of materials and data under the same set of rules and limitations.

Perhaps because of this very reason, private law has also relied – beyond contract – on property law for the circulation of research materials and the promotion of open science. The case of the Structural Genomics Consortium (SGC) Open Science Trust Agreement (OSTA) provides an important example.

SGC is a charity registered in the United Kingdom, the mission of which is to accelerate research in new areas of human biology and drug discovery.[31]

[27] The Open MTA was developed as a collaborative effort led by the Biobricks Foundation and the OpenPlant Synthetic Biology Research Centre. See Frequently Asked Questions, BioBricks Found., https://biobricks.org/openmta-faq/ (last accessed May 8, 2023); The Open Material Transfer Agreement, BioBricks Found., https://biobricks.org/open-material-transfer-agreement/ (last accessed May 8, 2023).

[28] Darren Shickle et al., Inter- and Intra-biobank Networks: Classification of Biobanks, 77(4) Pathobiology 181, 181–90 (2010).

[29] See Andrea Boggio, Population Biobanks' Governance: A Case Study of Knowledge Commons, in Governing Medical Knowledge Commons 102–20 (2017) (a parallel between population biobanks and knowledge commons).

[30] Niva Elkin-Koren, What Contracts Cannot Do: The Limits of Private Ordering in Facilitating a Creative Commons, 74 Fordham L. Rev. 375 (2005).

[31] For information on the Structural Genomics Consortium and the Open Science Trust Agreement, see Frequently Asked Questions – SGC Open Science Trust Agreement,

Unlike MTAs, in which a bilateral agreement is concluded between provider and recipient, the SGC OSTA is an agreement in which the recipient of the materials agrees to become a trustee of the research material.

According to the SGC's website:

> A trust such as the OSTA is a legal mechanism under which an appointed trustee takes legal possession of property but assumes a duty to use or manage that property to benefit certain beneficiaries, which can be third parties and/or the public. With the OSTA, unlike under an MTA, by becoming a trustee of SGC-provided research material, a recipient is undertaking a specific duty to benefit the public through open science.[32]

Some of the obligations of the trustee include (1) not seeking or enforcing intellectual property rights covering the material, which could deter or prevent others in the research community from using the material to further the public good, and (2) placing the research findings and data resulting from their work with the material into the public domain, which helps to accelerate discovery.

Furthermore, the trustee is permitted to disseminate "the material to other researchers who likewise agree to become trustees, thus expanding the community of researchers committed to open science for the public good."[33]

According to the SGC, the rationale behind such an agreement, instead of an MTA, for example, is that treating the materials, not as a proprietary good, but as a public one to be shared broadly, accelerates discoveries stemming from the use of the material. Although initially mandated (i.e., the investigator requesting the materials must become a trustee), further transfers to new trustees must happen on a voluntary basis.

While the OSTA was not specifically designed to share HBM,[34] one can envision ways to modify it and include the possibility of sharing materials of human origin.[35] More specifically, it would be possible at the point of collection of the materials, for example, via broad consent mechanisms, to enable circulation of materials that otherwise could not circulate freely. An alternative to consent mechanisms for the circulation of materials of human origin would be to devise a specific set of

Structural Genomics Consortium, https://www.thesgc.org/sgc-open-science-trust-agreements (last accessed May 8, 2023).

32 Id.

33 Id.

34 Aled Edwards et al., A Trust Approach for Sharing Research Reagents, 9(392) Sci. Translational Med. 1, 1–3 (2017). The idea of putting highly commercially valuable reagents and data in the public domain is not new. See, e.g., Declan Butler, GlaxoSmithKline Goes Public with Malaria Data, Nature (Jan. 20, 2010), https://www.nature.com/articles/news.2010.20 (Glaxo's released 13,500 structures of possible drugs against Malaria into the public domain).

35 Here, the question on the existence of property rights on HBM is of paramount importance. However, it is beyond the scope of this chapter to dwell in this litigious issue.

principles for which research on HBM without consent would be legally and ethically permissible.

In addition to contracts and property law, other private law instruments allow for the creation of institutions of collective action for the construction of the human body commons. Cooperative-based initiatives for the governance of health data are particularly interesting.

Health data cooperatives are associations of individuals under a cooperative structure for the collective governance of their individual health data for mutual benefit.[36]

According to some cooperative models for the use of health data, when data are controlled by citizens themselves, potential value of data can be maximized, while at the same time guaranteeing the protection of the data subjects' rights. Thus, one could think of models in which the storage and secure handling of data is overseen by a trusted entity: the cooperative (co-op). Users could purchase a membership certificate for an amount of money and use the co-op as a trusted repository.

Although the cooperative model was initially intended for genomic data, nothing prevents people from depositing all kinds of personal or health data, regardless of their origin (e.g., applications, wellness devices, and medical devices). In this way, the members of the cooperative would have the right to vote on decisions related to the benefits derived from the exploitation of their data by third parties.

Under this model, a pharmaceutical or medical technology company, for example, would pay a sum of money for the right to exploit the data that the members of the cooperative have decided to share, and could also, depending on the agreements adopted, deliver the results of the research to the accounts of the associates or to the cooperative. The economic benefits of the information that the cooperative obtains from the exploitation of the data could be reinvested in research programs or other types of projects of public interest.

Data cooperatives are a perfect example of a CPR that integrates different sorts of data and data sources for biomedical research.

MIDATA *Genossenschaft* (MIDATA), a Swiss health data cooperative, serves as a case in point. According to its articles of association,[37] MIDATA operates a secure IT platform for the processing and sharing of personal data, and in particular, health data. The cooperative makes the platform available to natural persons so they can use it to store and share their data as self-determining agents with the aim of supporting research purposes.

[36] See generally E. Hafen et al., Health Data Cooperatives – Citizen Empowerment, 53(2) Methods Info. Med. 82 (2014); Alessandro Blasimme et al., Democratizing Health Research through Data Cooperatives, 31(3) Phil. Tech. 473, 473–79 (2018); Van Ilse Roessel et al., Potentials and Challenges of the Health Data Cooperative Model, 20(6) Pub. Health Genomics 321 (2018).

[37] Articles of Association, MIDATA Genossenschaft (2019), https://www.midata.coop/wp-content/uploads/2019/08/MIDATA_Statuten_20190626_EN.pdf.

MIDATA promotes the collective interests of account holders by enabling the shared use of their personal data. Individual account holders can consent to data analysis and secondary use by third parties in return for economic compensation.[38]

At this point, it becomes evident how data cooperatives, as a form of CPR, can successfully manage genomic and other types of health data, while at the same time reseeding the commons with the profits and research results arising from the use of pooled data.

MIDATA is also relevant from the point of view of managing privacy in the human body commons.[39] Although in this case, explicit informed consent is necessary for the processing and sharing of health data, it is possible to find other legal pathways to govern health data sharing and access for secondary uses. Moreover, although data cooperatives have not yet proliferated, it is very likely that an increase in their number will follow their legal recognition by the EU Data Governance Act.

9.4 CONCLUSION

From the analysis of theories on the human body commons and private law examples from biomedical practices, several conclusions can be derived: (1) It is necessary to integrate different types and sources of data, facilitating interoperability and data sharing; (2) due to the circular nature of knowledge and data commons, to build a human body commons, it is necessary to strike an equilibrium between the positive societal data sharing spillovers and data protection and other individual human rights; (3) HBM, and not only knowledge and data, must be integrated in the analysis; and (4) it is paramount to establish clear rules for the reseeding of the human body commons in such a way that the intellectual products of the past become the input for future knowledge.

Furthermore, because human body commons integrate different types of resources (i.e., HBM, health data, and scientific knowledge), a combination of different types of commons is necessary for its further construction and development: top-down Open Commons and carved-out Common Pool Resources commons. By way of explanation, public ordering solutions open the scope of the public domain for the creation of open human body commons, while private ordering solution create common property regimes.

New theories on data, which facilitate the repurposing and reuse of health data, would change the status of personal health data from highly excludable to non-

[38] Id. at 2 (Article 2(h)).

[39] For a detailed analysis of privacy and MIDATA, see Felix Gille and Effy Vayena, How Private Individuals Maintain Privacy and Govern Their Own Health Data Cooperative: MIDATA in Switzerland, in Governing Privacy in Knowledge Commons 53–69 (Madelyn R. Sanfilippo et al. eds., 2021). On privacy in the commons, see generally Madelyn R. Sanfilippo et al., Governing Privacy in Knowledge Commons (2021).

excludable. In this sense, a jump from a CPR to an OC can be envisioned with the help of regulatory instruments, which allow to bypass consent for the use of data for the "common good."

For HBM, the embodied resource of the human body commons, it seems difficult to imagine a fully open commons. However, private law has proven useful for the circulation and sharing of materials and associated data. Here, commons on HBM can be organized as multiple nodes (e.g., biobanks) of CPR connected to a wider mixed network of health data OC and CPR.

For scientific knowledge, it is necessary to guarantee that the developments and innovation derived from the use of OC and CPR in HBM and health data, return and reseed the commons in the forms of knowledge, benefit sharing, and money. This could be enabled by top-down regulation or by forms of collective action and negotiation (e.g., health data cooperatives) with data users and industry.

This chapter demonstrated how contracts, property, and other private law mechanisms may be used as vehicles for the governance of health research resources and health policy.

Such policy must develop a framework to avoid freeriding from actors using the commons, as well as a normative framework well-grounded in the promotion and protections of human dignity and human rights,[40] with specific reference to the right to health and the right to enjoy the benefits of science may be a good starting point.

[40] Roberto Andorno, Human Dignity and Human Rights as a Common Ground for a Global Bioethics, 34(3) J. Med. Phil. 223 (2009); Roberto Andorno, Principles of International Biolaw: Seeking Common Ground at the Intersection of Bioethics and Human Rights (2013); Eric M. Meslin & Ibrahim Garba, Biobanking and Public Health: Is a Human Rights Approach the Tie that Binds?, 130(3) Hum. Genetics 451 (2011); Bartha M. Knoppers et al., A Human Rights Approach to an International Code of Conduct for Genomic and Clinical Data Sharing, 133(7) Hum. Genetics, 895 (2014).

PART III

Russian Dolls, Reproduction, and Private Law

Introduction

I. Glenn Cohen

The famous Russian dolls, *matryoshka* as they are called in Russia, are nesting dolls one inside the other, often depicting stylized women with the smallest doll as a baby. As Yelena Titova, director of the All-Russian Museum of Decorative, Applied and Folk Art in Moscow, noted, they are also a potent symbol of fertility: "For all Russians the matryoshka is obviously Matryona, the embodiment of woman's health, fertility, a wonderful female disposition and a symbol of the family."[1] The chapters in this part reveal a similar nesting structure of public and private law in the *law* of reproduction and fertility. Private law is often called on to fill some gaps in public law, which sometimes causes the public law to itself change either to foster or negate that gap-filling and so on and so forth. But this project is heavily dynamic; it is as though the matryoshka dolls are not only dancing alongside one another but growing and shrinking and reconfiguring their order as we see changes in high-level public law – such as the 2022 decision in *Dobbs v. Jackson Women's Health Organization* that effectively ended federal constitutional protection for abortion.[2] But while some of this re-ordering and gap-filling is possible, as the chapters in this part show the result is far from a perfect whole – some dolls don't fit, some dolls end up empty, and rarely does it resemble the matryoshka we had before the public law changed.

Valarie K. Blake and Elizabeth Y. McCuskey's chapter (Chapter 10), "Employer-Sponsored Abortion Coverage: Private Law's Role in Reproductive Freedom,"

[1] Elena Kostomárova, More Than Just a Pretty Face: The Secrets of the Russian Matryoshka, Russia Beyond (Aug. 8, 2015), https://www.rbth.com/arts/2015/08/08/the_secrets_of_the_russian_matryoshka_48375.html.

[2] 597 U.S. 215 (2022).

shows how in the wake of *Dobbs* the underappreciated reality is that private employers have ended up as some of the chief policymakers on abortion access in America through their coverage decisions as part of employer-sponsored health insurance. They trace a complicated matryoshka structure – within the public law question of abortion as a constitutional right nests the public law question of whether state insurance mandates require the coverage of abortion; but within *that* "doll," because of the operation of another piece of public law (the Employee Retirement Income Security Act of 1974 [ERISA]), we get the preemption of state insurance mandates such that decisions on abortion coverage are now devolved back to employers and to private law. The end result is that "[t]hat private law grants employers nearly total discretion on abortion coverage," but this "illustrates the limitations on private law's efficacy in this role," and indeed the "agency costs involved in employers' power over employee reproduction ultimately exacerbate existing power differentials and inequities, without assurances that employers will act in their employees' interests."

Myrisha Lewis' chapter (Chapter 11), "Reproductive Innovation and Reproductive Exceptionalism: How Private Health Insurance Coverage of Fertility Treatment Complements Hostile Governmental Action and Expands Access to Assisted Reproduction in the United States," continues the consideration of health insurance but shifts the focus from abortion to family formation through reproductive technologies. She catalogs an uneven mix of public law and private choice across the United States: Some states have passed insurance mandates requiring the coverage of reproductive technologics to some extent but many have not, and even those that have done so, due to ERISA preemption, end up with self-insured employers not governed by the insurance mandates. She notes that "[a]mongst companies with over 500 employees, as of 2020, 27% of those employers offer IVF coverage, up from 24% in 2015 and 11% offer egg freezing, an increase from 2015, when only 5% of those companies covered egg freezing." But finding the right employers remains a challenge for many employees, who rely not only on lists created by fertility patients but also Reddit threads and even TikTok videos! She also explores how leaving the decision whether and to what extent to cover these services to employers produces job lock and also puts patients facing layoffs in a precarious position, given that services like IVF often stretch over many years.

In her chapter (Chapter 12), "Business Responses to *Dobbs*: The Return to a 'Reproductive Rights' Approach, and Suspicions around Corporate Care," Asees Bhasin applies a critical reproductive justice lens to the way in which corporate decisions have filled in gaps post-*Dobbs*. She tracks corporate social responsibility type responses, such as donations to reproductive rights organizations, travel stipends or reimbursement for travel to get an abortion out of state, bail funds for persons arrested protesting anti-abortion measures, but also notes that private law has left us in a place where these "initiatives lack enforceability and teeth and are left to be shaped by the corporation itself." While such moves by corporations are desirable, she also emphasizes "that the vision of the [Reproductive Justice] movement is at odds with the profit-maximization-centered approach of corporations" and calls out the neoliberal worldview as relying on "institutional supports and business-friendly measures taken by the state, while simultaneously promoting the idea that government should be restrained in almost all other ways, including in the provision of welfare and social services." In arguing that private law has allowed corporations to fail to live up to objectives of the reproductive justice movement, she points to the wide discretion in designing employer-sponsored health insurance packages, the failure to give paid parental leave or adequately support working parents, and the decision to schedule work hours or classify workers as independent contractors rather than employees and thus deprive them of much-needed benefits. Far from filling the gap left by *Dobbs*, Bhasin sees private law as *the problem* in many such instances.

Finally, Thomas W. Williams' chapter (Chapter 13), "Privatizing the Creation of Equity in Women's Health," looks at the gaps and opportunities that private law (especially corporate law) has made for Femtech, technologies aimed at promoting women's health with a special focus on the reproductive needs of women. Williams argues that "FemTech companies extract value from gaps in existing markets serving women's health needs," and that these "gaps are often in part due to policy choices of government and policy makers," such as the failure to prioritize funding research into women's health – he gives the example of research into menopause, and research connecting the fallopian tube to ovarian cancer. But Femtech companies face the challenge of balancing two (or in some instances) more purposes: "(i) bettering the overall picture of women's health and, (ii) ensuring that the company itself remains a fiscally viable going concern." The chapter explores the way corporate actors use contract law to help adjust existing corporate structures to this reality. At the same time, it acknowledges the imperfect way that private law and private ordering solve for the dual-purposes; in particular, how the entry of private equity and venture capital into the Femtech space may upset the apple cart.

After reading these chapters, one is left with two competing visions as to the legal matryoshka. The first is a system running as intended, where private law interventions act as a sort of shock absorber to changes or gaps in the public law and enable innovation and entrepreneurship and a hundred flowers blooming. The second is a system, perhaps also running as intended (depending on one's cynicism), where public law has passed the buck as to abortion, fertility, and other reproductive needs. In this later vision, family formation and women's health now operate under the logic of the market such that those pushing for change need to do so in a way that centers what market actors care about. While these chapters are mixed in their view, overall I read them as leaning toward the second vision and yearning for more not less public law intervention.

10

Employer-Sponsored Abortion Coverage

Private Law's Role in Reproductive Freedom

Valarie K. Blake and Elizabeth Y. McCuskey

10.1 INTRODUCTION

Access to abortion care depends largely on public law, with federal and state governments controlling the legality and regulation of services and providers, and courts articulating individual reproductive rights. *Dobbs v. Jackson Women's Health Organization*[1] upended the right to abortion, casting public-law governance of abortion rights into turmoil. This chapter explores one context in which private law plays a limited but remarkable role in access to abortion care: employer-sponsored insurance (ESI). Employers provide health insurance for over half of reproductive-aged Americans, controlling the financial access to abortion care for many. The private laws of insurance regulation grant capacious discretion to employers to offer or not offer abortion coverage, regardless of what public law prohibits or requires.

Employers' own interests in when and whether their employees reproduce inform how they exercise this discretion granted by private law. As we explain below, by covering abortion employers can avoid some of the much greater health plan and workforce costs of pregnancy and birth. But employers may instead prioritize their own religious objections to abortion and refuse coverage. Either way, the employer acts on its own interest. We turn to concepts of agency to assess what duties employers may owe in their conflicted role. In the regular course of business, employers act as principals and their employees as agents. But as arrangers of health benefits, the roles reverse: Employers act on their employees' behalf, and so ought to serve their employees' interests in accessing health care. If guided by agency principles, employers *should* include coverage for abortion services in their health plans, to the extent the law allows.

[1] Dobbs v. Jackson Women's Health Organization, 597 U.S. 215 (2022).

If public law continues to erode access to abortion care, ESI creates a space for private law to support access, especially if employers take seriously their responsibilities as health care funders for their employees. That private law grants employers nearly total discretion on abortion coverage, however, illustrates the limitations on private law's efficacy in this role. And the agency costs involved in employers' power over employee reproduction ultimately exacerbate existing power differentials and inequities, without assurances that employers will act in their employees' interests.

10.2 PRIVATE LAW GRANTS EMPLOYERS DISCRETION OVER ABORTION BENEFITS

Even in states where abortion remains legal after *Dobbs*, the cost of the procedure poses a significant obstacle to access. In 2022, around 11 percent of Americans lacked cash, savings, credit card balances, or other finances to pay a US$400 bill.[2] The average price for abortion services surpasses this at US$500–US$2,000,[3] and after *Dobbs*, travel time required for abortion care has quadrupled,[4] adding expenses for travel, lodging, and lost wages to the cost of the procedure.

Few can afford these costs without insurance.

Health insurance coverage practically determines people's access to abortion care, like other health care services.[5] For the majority of Americans who have commercial insurance, a dense mix of state insurance law, the Affordable Care Act (ACA), and antidiscrimination laws guide the coverage decisions and administration of their plans.[6] Most reproductive-age Americans rely on ESI for coverage.[7] This effectively gives employers a gatekeeping role in determining what health care services will receive funding.[8]

ESIs are regulated primarily by the ACA and the Employee Retirement Income Security Act of 1974 (ERISA). But ERISA more de-regulates, through sweeping

2 Economic Well-Being of U.S. Households, Bd. of Gov. Fed. Reserve Sys. (May 2022), https://www.federalreserve.gov/publications/2022-economic-well-being-of-us-households-in-2021-dealing-with-unexpected-expenses.htm.

3 Allison McCann, What It Costs to Get an Abortion Now, N.Y. Times (Sept. 28, 2022), https://www.nytimes.com/interactive/2022/09/28/us/abortion-costs-funds.html.

4 Benjamin Rader et al., Estimated Travel Time and Spatial Access to Abortion Facilities in the US before and after the Dobbs v. Jackson Women's Health Decision, 328 JAMA 241 (2022), https://jamanetwork.com/journals/jama/article-abstract/2798215.

5 See Lunna Lopes et al., Americans' Challenges with Health Care Costs, Kaiser Fam. Found. (Dec. 21, 2023), https://www.kff.org/health-costs/issue-brief/americans-challenges-with-health-care-costs/.

6 See generally Elizabeth Y. McCuskey, Agency Imprimatur & Health Reform Preemption, 78 Ohio St. L. J. 1099, 1125 (2017).

7 Gary Claxton et al., 2022 Employer Health Benefits Survey, Summary of Findings, Kaiser Fam. Found. (Oct. 27, 2022), https://files.kff.org/attachment/Report-Employer-Health-Benefits-2022-Annual-Survey.pdf.

8 See generally Valarie K. Blake & Elizabeth Y. McCuskey, Employer-Sponsored Reproduction, 124 Colum. L. Rev. 273 (2024).

preemption of state law, and comparatively sparse federal requirements for what ESI must cover.[9] Similarly, the ACA incentivizes large employers to offer health benefits by taxing their choice not to and imposes comparatively lighter coverage requirements for ESI plans than on individual insurance.[10]

Employers have designed plans that exclude certain services from coverage to save money. State (and occasionally federal) legislators have enacted piecemeal mandates for insurance coverage of certain services. Insurance companies must comply with state mandates, but ERISA preemption exempts employers who structure their health plans as "self-funded" plans from compliance.[11] ERISA itself imposes few coverage requirements. ERISA does not require employers to cover maternity or hospitalization; it merely requires that *if* an employer plan chooses to cover those two services, *then* it must cover hospitalization for up to forty-eight hours after vaginal delivery.[12]

ERISA does not require that employer plans cover maternity care at all. That requirement comes from the Pregnancy Discrimination Act (PDA) of 1978, which applies only to employers with fifteen or more employees,[13] while also allowing employers with fifty or more employees to exclude labor and delivery coverage for employees' dependents.[14]

Even as the ACA, ERISA, and other laws add bits and pieces to employer plan requirements, the forces of abortion exceptionalism leave employers with nearly unfettered discretion on whether to include abortion in the coverage of their employee benefit plans.[15] ERISA and the ACA expressly preserve employer plans' discretion to exclude abortion from coverage.[16] The PDA explicitly states that employers are not required to offer coverage for abortions.[17]

State laws vary, with some requiring that health insurance cover abortion, and others prohibiting it.[18] ERISA's preemption loophole for self-funded plans, however, preserves employers' discretion to cover or refuse to cover abortion despite state

9 Cong. Rsch. Serv., Summary of the Employee Retirement Income Security Act (ERISA) (May 19, 2009), https://crsreports.congress.gov/product/pdf/RL/RL34443/6.

10 See Abbe R. Gluck et al., ERISA: A Bipartisan Problem for the ACA and the AHCA, Health Affs. Forefront (June 2, 2017), https://www.healthaffairs.org/do/10.1377/forefront.20170602.060391/.

11 See McCuskey, supra note 6.

12 E.g., Newborns' and Mothers' Health Protection Act of 1996, 29 U.S.C. § 1185.

13 42 U.S.C. § 2000e(k).

14 See FAQs: Health Insurance Marketplace and the ACA – Women's Health, Kaiser Fam. Found. (2024), https://perma.cc/T8P2-VQES.

15 See, e.g., Maya Manian, The Consequences of Abortion Restrictions for Women's Healthcare, 71 Wash. & Lee L. Rev. 1317, 1318–20 (2014); Gillian E. Metzger, Abortion, Equality, and Administrative Regulation, 56 Emory L. J. 865, 898 (2007).

16 See Lisa C. Ikemoto, Abortion, Contraception and the ACA: The Realignment of Women's Health, 55 How. L.J. 731, 757–64 (2012).

17 42 U.S.C. § 2000e(k).

18 Michelle Long et al., Exclusion of Abortion Coverage from Employer-Sponsored Health Plans, Kaiser Fam. Found. (May 12, 2020), https://www.kff.org/womens-health-policy/issue-brief/exclu

law.[19] In states with abortion insurance mandates or prohibitions, employers may purchase policies from insurers who must comply with these rules, or employers may choose to self-fund their plans and avoid these rules. Thus, ERISA preempts states from enforcing antiabortion laws against those self-funded plans that cover abortion and related travel expenses in the wake of *Dobbs*.[20]

The private law of abortion coverage is more flexible than its public law counterparts, and somewhat less exceptionalized. Public insurance programs have long operated under the Hyde Amendment's prohibition on the use of federal funds to cover abortion services except when necessary to save the pregnant person's life,[21] restricting coverage options in Medicare and Title X. State Medicaid programs may choose to cover abortion in more circumstances but must do so solely with state funds.[22] Similarly, the federal government as an employer is subject to the Hyde Amendment restrictions in its employee benefit plans.[23] State governments as employers have the option of covering abortion, or not.

The ACA, PDA, and ERISA operate to give employers ultimate flexibility in deciding whether to cover abortion.

10.3 PRIVATE LAW'S EFFECTS ON ACCESS TO ABORTION

Abortion rights are largely viewed through the lens of public law, specifically the extent to which the Constitution permits *government* intrusion into individual reproductive choices. Yet finance – a critical facet of access to abortion, and most other health care – falls largely to employers and the promises they make to their employees, guided by private law.[24]

The reliance on private law to govern the major source of funding for abortion has some advantages to leverage and pitfalls to avoid if the goal is to secure safe and affordable abortions for those who most need it in an era of eroding constitutional rights to abortion.

sion-of-abortion-coverage-from-employer-sponsored-health-plans/ (eleven states prohibit coverage for abortion, five states require insurers to cover it).

19 See Elizabeth Y. McCuskey, State Cost-Control Reforms and ERISA Preemption, Commonwealth Fund (May 16, 2022), https://www.commonwealthfund.org/publications/issue-briefs/2022/may/state-cost-control-reforms-erisa-preemption.

20 Id.

21 See Alina Salganicoff et al., The Hyde Amendment and Coverage for Abortion Services, Kaiser Fam. Found. (Mar. 5, 2021), https://www.kff.org/womens-health-policy/issue-brief/the-hyde-amendment-and-coverage-for-abortion-services/.

22 See Cong. Rsch. Serv., The Hyde Amendment: An Overview (June 20, 2022), https://crsreports.congress.gov/product/pdf/IF/IF12167.

23 See Pub. L. No. 98-151, § 101(f), 97 Stat. 964, 973 (1983).

24 Cf. Abbe R. Gluck, Why Health Lawyers Must Be Public-Law Lawyers: Health Law in the Age of the Modern Regulatory State, 18 J. Health Care L. & Pol'y 323, 332 (2015).

10.3.1 *Benefits and Limitations of Relying on Private Law*

After *Dobbs*, many states limited, banned, or criminalized abortions.[25] Other states passed laws expanding protections for abortion access. In the chaos that *Dobbs* engendered, the reactions of employers through their employee health plans illustrate the main benefits and limitations of private law as bulwark against the erosion of reproductive rights.

Employers who covered abortion services were forced to examine impacts of *Dobbs* and state legislation on the benefits offered for their current plan year. In states that outlawed or further curtailed abortion after *Dobbs*, some employers who fund abortions may have been tempted to shift course. Private law offers temporary protections here in the form of the contractual commitments employers make to their employees for the given benefit year.

Employers who already elected to cover some form of abortion for employees searched for ways to reconcile these benefit promises with the post-*Dobbs* waves of restrictive state legislation.[26] Many employers found providers out-of-state willing to perform services for their employees for no additional cost-sharing.

Many employers, especially large private sector ones, included provisions for travel coverage and other expenses to offset additional costs patients face to access abortions.[27] Some government employers followed suit.[28] Most companies are reimbursing travel under their employer health plans, much as they reimburse travel for specialty health services like cancer treatments that are only available from some specialty sites.[29] After international law firm Sidley Austin promised reimbursement for out-of-state abortion travel costs to employees of its Dallas and Houston offices, Texas legislators accused the firm of violating state laws prohibiting the "aiding and abetting" of abortions.[30]

25 An Overview of Abortion Laws, Guttmacher Inst. (Aug. 31, 2023), https://www.guttmacher.org/state-policy/explore/overview-abortion-laws?gad=1&gclid=Cj0KCQjwpPKiBhDvARIsACn-gzAZ-UcuVKhXtl3tRr5ejSStw7L1svc7Us7PTby1tsqLR55iYec7WWoaArSREALw_wcB (a repository of state laws developing post-Dobbs).

26 Employer plans are not obliged to enforce provisions of their benefits that are or have become unlawful, and ERISA permits plans to make a "material reduction in covered services or benefits." 29 C.F.R. § 2520.104b-3.

27 Emma Goldberg, These Companies Will Cover Travel Expenses for Employee Abortions, N.Y. Times (Aug. 19, 2022), https://www.nytimes.com/article/abortion-companies-travel-expenses.html.

28 Memorandum for Senior Pentagon Leadership Re: Ensuring Access to Reproductive Health Care, Sec'y of Def. (Oct. 20, 2022), https://media.defense.gov/2022/Oct/20/2003099747/-1/-1/1/MEMORANDUM-ENSURING-ACCESS-TO-REPRODUCTIVE-HEALTH-CARE.PDF.

29 Goldberg, supra note 27.

30 Letter from Texas Freedom Caucus, to Yvette Ostolaza, Chair of the Mgmt. Comm. at Sidley Austin LLP (July 7, 2022), https://www.freedomfortexas.com/uploads/blog/3b118c262155759454e423f6600e2196709787a8.pdf.

Private law also protects employers who wish to cover abortion care going forward. ERISA enables self-funded employer benefit plans to help people access abortion, even across state lines.[31] Employers with the will can design their plans to cover abortion services received out-of-state, and to safeguard employee information from states where the act of receiving abortion care in or beyond the state border is illegal. Given the national reach of many large employers, and the number of people they cover through health plans, employers have a powerful tool to secure access to abortion for large numbers of people.

For lawmakers who wish to limit access to abortion, the private law of ESI requires them to do battle on an entirely different legal terrain, with powerful corporations and the entrenched decades-old behemoth that is ERISA. Many public laws treat abortion exceptionally, but ERISA is abortion-blind. Its safeguards apply equally to employers funding abortions as any other employer health benefit, forcing legislatures to attack a law with broad general applicability. In an era of eroding abortion rights, the private law supporting employer benefits has become an unanticipated safe haven.

Still, there are significant limits to this privatized model of coverage, from the perspective of advancing reproductive rights, access, and justice. The private funding model of ESI does not construct a durable or widespread protection for abortion funding, and it excludes many of the people most in need of financial assistance.

The very same forces of private law that can protect abortion benefits so too can be used to undermine and evade state laws that protect abortion access and mandate coverage. For self-funded plans, ERISA preempts the enforcement of a state mandate for abortion coverage in the same way that it preempts the enforcement of a prohibition for such coverage. Ten percent of employees work for employers whose plans expressly exclude abortion coverage in some (6 percent) or all (4 percent) circumstances.[32] Large companies, and self-funded plans and private nonprofits (often religiously affiliated organizations) are all more likely to exclude or limit abortions.[33] Even for workers with plans that do not expressly exclude abortions, many face limits on access with respect to gestational age, method, and caps on covered services per employee.[34]

Similarly, private law does nothing for the 20 million federal workers, veterans, and active-duty military and their dependents who do not receive abortion coverage under their employer plans owing to the Hyde Amendment.[35]

[31] Brendan S. Maher, Pro-Choice Plans, 91 Geo. Wash. L. Rev. 446 (2023).

[32] Long et al., supra note 18.

[33] Id.

[34] Id.

[35] Id.

Private law also does little for low-income women and women of color who are most likely to seek abortions,[36] more likely to be on Medicaid, and less likely to receive insurance through their work.[37] Medicaid is a workhorse for funding reproductive care generally in this country, paying for more than four in ten births nationwide and a majority of all births in some states.[38] Yet thirty-three states have enacted their own Hyde-style amendments barring Medicaid coverage for abortions.[39] Many of those states have higher than average maternal morbidity and mortality rates, with Black women bearing the greatest burden.[40] Those most in need of help accessing abortion care are left to the public funding programs that most frequently refuse to cover abortion.[41]

The abortion-access gains via ESI thus are not equitably distributed. Nor are they durable. Employers decide on their plans annually and can change any aspect from year to year. A firm that considers abortion coverage to be in its political and/or financial self-interest one year may act differently the next.

10.3.2 *Employers as Agents for Reproductive Choice*

As the dust settles on *Dobbs*, employers will face external pressures from various groups to fund or not to fund abortions. How should employers weigh these many competing interests as they craft benefit plans and abortion coverage going forward?

Health law and policy scholars have proposed the principal–agent relationship as a theoretical framework to explore the inherent obligations and conflicts within the employer–employee relationship and the acquisition of health benefits and, moreover, when these relationships demand that public law step in.[42] In employment law, the principal–agency relationship views employees as agents of the principal employer, serving the employer's best interests. In health benefits, this is reversed. The employee engages her employer "to perform the service of purchasing and administering a health insurance plan on [her] behalf."[28]

36 Medicaid Coverage of Abortion, Guttmacher Inst. (Feb. 12, 2021), https://www.guttmacher.org/evidence-you-can-use/medicaid-coverage-abortion.

37 See generally Clark C. Havighurst & Barak D. Richman, Distributive Injustice(s) in American Health Care, 69 Law & Contemp. Probs. 7 (2006).

38 Usha Ranji et al., Medicaid Coverage of Pregnancy-Related Services: Findings from a 2021 State Survey, Kaiser Fam. Found. (May, 19, 2022), https://www.kff.org/report-section/medicaid-coverage-of-pregnancy-related-services-findings-from-a-2021-state-survey-report/.

39 Salganicoff et al., supra note 21.

40 Brief for Reproductive Justice Scholars as Amicus Curiae at 31–35, Dobbs v. Jackson's Women's Health Org., 597 U.S. 215 (2022).

41 Likewise, the federal Title X Family Planning Program excludes abortion from its funding. 42 U.S.C. § 300a-6.

42 John Bronsteen et al., ERISA, Agency Costs, and the Future of Health Care in the United States, 76 Fordham L. Rev. 2297, 2304–05 n.24 (2008); Dayna Bowen Matthew, Controlling the Reverse Agency Costs of Employment-Based Health Insurance: Of Markets, Courts, and a Regulatory Quagmire, 31 Wake Forest L. Rev. 1037, 1040–41 (1996).

The principal–agent concept holds as a broad construct, though the employee benefits relationship does not capture all elements of traditional agency law.[43] Employees do not necessarily have control over their employer-agent in the health benefits scenario, as employers have already negotiated and secured their benefit plans before they hire new employees.[44] Most privately employed people likewise have little say in or even knowledge of their employers' benefit plan negotiations until after the plans are set. *Dobbs*' massive disruption may sharpen individuals' awareness of the degree to which their current plans cover reproductive services, including abortion.

The principal–agent concept applied to employer health benefits reveals many agency costs, or times when the agent employer's interests conflict with the principal employees. Most obviously, employers are financially incentivized to offer the least generous health benefits possible to their employees.[45] These agency costs have been used to explain the shortcomings of the ESI model from health policy perspectives.[46] Agency costs sometimes make employer benefits models unworkable, demanding public law stand in for the failures of private law.[47] ERISA, the Consolidated Omnibus Budget Reconciliation Act (COBRA), the Americans with Disabilities Act, and finally the ACA all can be understood as times where public law was deployed to patch failings of private law. This piecemeal patching faces an uphill battle correcting the fundamental design flaw that social policy relies on employers to secure access to care for working Americans and their dependents, but employers primarily serve their own business interests.[48]

What does the principal–agent concept instruct for employers as keepers of abortion benefits in an increasingly fraught era of reproductive justice? Counter-intuitively, private law may impose a higher duty on employers than the government imposes on state actors when it comes to rights to abortion. Governmental actors who forbid or require abortion coverage through public law owe no formal duties to the constituents impacted by their decisions, apart from democratic accountability. *Roe*'s framework recognized a "compelling governmental interest" in fetal protection, even when in tension with protecting the pregnant person,[49] and *Dobbs* only minimized the level of scrutiny applied to government restrictions on abortion.

But private employers' negotiation of health care benefits implicates duties owed directly to the beneficiaries, including persons who are or may become pregnant. If employers are to act as agents in the best interests of their principal employees in designing their health plans, they *ought* to cover abortion fully and to the greatest

43 Bronsteen et al., supra note 42.
44 Id. at n.24.
45 Id.
46 Id.
47 Matthew, supra note 42.
48 Id.
49 See Planned Parenthood v. Casey, 505 U.S. 833 (1992).

extent permitted by law, including offering abortion benefits out-of-state and with travel support where needed. Reproductive justice demands that principals (employees and other plan beneficiaries) have control over their reproductive potential, including the right not to have a child,[50] and concepts of bodily autonomy and informed consent further underscore this interest.[51] Full access to abortion coverage furthers the individual's health interests, as well as the social, personal, and economic consequences that flow from pregnancy, birth, and child-rearing.

The principal–agent concept also reminds employers that their fiduciary obligations flow to employees and dependents when it comes to health benefits. In this role, employers' duties are *not* to the public, state or federal lawmakers, their customers, or their shareholders. Nor are they duties owed to fetuses as potential future plan beneficiaries, distinguishing employers' role from state actors regulating abortion. Courts since *Roe* have recognized a compelling governmental interest in protecting potential life if the government chooses to deploy public law for this purpose. But the private principal–agent relationship is a fiduciary one, whose formation typically assumes some amount of agreement and commitment between already-existing parties.[52] Stretching the concept of principal–agent in health benefits to encompass the hypothetical future unborn would have implications for abortion, as well as infertility care and fetal therapies, and would likely strain the doctrine in ways that are beyond the scope of this chapter.

Employers do need to serve all their employees in their benefits design, as well as nonemployee beneficiaries. This has been a central challenge for employers in navigating this agency relationship in the past, as employees may each be owed a fiduciary duty but may want very different things from their health benefits.[53] While some may argue that abortion coverage would serve some employees but not others, this neglects to consider fully the importance of reproductive freedom as an individual right to decide for oneself. With that in mind, no single employee or employee interest group ought to be able to block access to this care simply because it is not in their own interests. The fiduciary interest is owed to all beneficiaries. This necessitates that beneficiaries individually have the right to choose for themselves, and so the benefit of abortion must be available to all, even if some do not want it or do not want it covered for others.

50 For instance, see Zakiya Luna & Kristin Luker, Reproductive Justice, 9 Ann. Rev. L. & Soc. Sci. 327 (2013), outlining three prongs to reproductive justice: the freedom from having a child, the freedom to have a child, and the right to parent a child with dignity.

51 Maya Manian, The Irrational Woman: Informed Consent and Abortion Decision-Making, 16 Duke J. Gender L. & Pol'y 223 (2010); B. Jessie Hill, Reproductive Rights as Health Care Rights, 18 Colum. J. Gender & L. 1 (2009).

52 Although plan fiduciaries do owe some duties to "potential beneficiaries" under ERISA, this concept has never been extended beyond the current legal confines of existing people to potential future children.

53 See Matthew, supra note 42.

While the many regulatory laws governing employer benefit plans suggest broad discretion of employers with respect to abortion, the principal–agent framework directs employers to do what is in the interests of their employees. The concept of employer as agent of its employees suggests a potential limitation on employers' discretion to *exclude* abortion coverage and perhaps even a duty to *include* abortion coverage.

10.4 EMPLOYER BENEFITS AND REPRODUCTIVE AUTONOMY: AN UNCOMFORTABLE MARRIAGE

Private law enables employers to fund abortions and arguably imposes duties to do so, even in states where that decision will be met with increasing hostility. Yet, there are reasons to temper the enthusiasm for private law in this role. Employer control over reproduction is historically and existentially fraught[54] and does not square with a larger aim of reproductive autonomy. While the principal–agent framework directs employers to act in their employees' interests, in reality the ESI model places decisions about access to reproductive care in the hands of employers, privileging their interests over employees', fundamentally undermining the concept of reproductive autonomy.

"[A]t their core, reproductive rights cases are just as much about what is being safeguarded and why, as who the rights are being safeguarded from. They consistently describe, up until *Dobbs*, a universe in which private and intimate decisions around reproduction are left to the individual alone, in counsel with health care professionals."[55] In *Roe v. Wade*, for instance, the right to abortion was safeguarded in part because of pregnancy's potentially harmful effects on physical and mental health, financial well-being, and the experience of stigma against unwed mothers.[56] *Planned Parenthood v. Casey* characterized reproduction as a defining life choice "central to personal dignity and autonomy."[57] Contraception cases have emphasized the repulsive nature of intrusion into the sensitive and personal decisions about reproduction.[58] Even *Dobbs*, while overturning the federal constitutional right, does not challenge the idea that abortion care is deeply personal.

Employers do not exert control over abortion access to the level that state bans and criminalization do. Indeed, employers are statutorily prohibited from discriminating against employees who seek, obtain, or forego abortions.[59] But if reproductive

54 See generally Dorothy Roberts, Killing the Black Body: Race, Reproduction, and the Meaning of Liberty (1997).

55 Blake & McCuskey, supra note 8.

56 Roe v. Wade, 410 U.S. 113, 153 (1973).

57 Planned Parenthood v. Casey, supra note 49, at 851.

58 Griswold v. Connecticut, 381 U.S. 479, 485–86 (1965); see also Eisenstadt v. Baird, 405 U.S. 438, 453 (1972).

59 42 U.S.C. § 2000e(k); see U.S. Dep't of Lab., Equal Employ. Opportunity Comm'n, Enforcement Guidance on Pregnancy Discrimination and Related Issues (June 25, 2016),

autonomy demands the choice reside with individuals, then ESI and its level of employer control over abortion care represent a practical and existential challenge to the fulfillment of many Americans' reproductive autonomy.

Employers have their own economic, actuarial, moral, and other interests that may conflict with employees' interests, compromising employers' ability to be trusted fiduciaries of rights as important as reproduction.[60]

Employers may act on economic concerns, sometimes viewing pregnant workers as "economic liabilities."[61] Employers may discourage pregnancy because of the costs of accommodating parental leave and job modifications,[62] concerns about organizational fairness to other employees who must pick up extra work,[63] and desire to meet the sensibilities and preferences of customers.[64] These interests largely instruct that employers should fully fund abortion and contraceptive services, as a way to avoid some of these more onerous expenses.

Employees also sit as actuaries because they at least partially fund their employee health plan. Employers who self-insure see the direct cost of employee health consumption, while employers who pay insurers see consumption indirectly in the cost of employer contribution to the premiums. Pregnancy is costly to health plans. Labor and delivery costs can exceed US$20,000[65] and constitute one of the most frequent causes of hospitalization of the non-elderly. Abortions are a cost-saving mechanism for a health plan, with one study reporting that unintended pregnancies account for a full 1 percent of the employer's health benefits spending per year.[66]

But not all employer incentives flow from economic self-interest or point toward abortion coverage. Employers' moral or religious beliefs may influence their funding of reproductive services. Hobby Lobby, the nationwide craft chain, famously challenged the contraception mandate of the ACA, winning the right of some

https://www.eeoc.gov/laws/guidance/enforcement-guidance-pregnancy-discrimination-and-related-issues; Questions and Answers on the Pregnancy Discrimination Act, 29 C.F.R. pt. 1604 (1979).

60 Blake & McCuskey, supra note 8.

61 Reginald A. Byron, Discrimination, Complexity, and the Public/Private Sector Question, 37 Work & Occupations 435, 460 (2010).

62 Joanna Grossman, Pregnancy, Work, and the Promise of Equal Citizenship, 98 Geo. L.J. 567, 595 (2010).

63 Id.; see Byron, supra note 61.

64 Reginald A. Byron & Vincent J. Roscigno, Relational Power, Legitimation, and Pregnancy Discrimination, 28 Gender & Soc'y 13 (2014).

65 Matthew Rae et al., Health Costs Associated with Pregnancy, Childbirth, and Postpartum Care, Peterson-KFF: Health Sys. Tracker (July 13, 2022), https://www.healthsystemtracker.org/brief/health-costs-associated-with-pregnancy-childbirth-and-postpartum-care/#Average%20additional%20health%20spending%20associated%20with%20pregnancy,%20relative%20to%20women%20of%20the%20same%20age%20who%20do%20not%20give%20birth,%20among%20people%20with%20large%20employer%20coverage,%202018%20-%202020.

66 Gabriela Dieguez et al., The Cost of Unintended Pregnancies for Employer-Sponsored Health Insurance Plans, 8 Am. Health Drug Benefits 83 (Apr. 2015), https://www.ncbi.nlm.nih.gov/pmc/articles/PMC4437481/.

nonreligious entities to refuse to cover certain health services in employer plans on the basis of their religious objection.[67] Employers also court public opinion, which may direct them in favor of covering abortion services or against it at any moment or location. For example, in the aftermath of *Dobbs*, companies driven by socially conscious branding may capitalize on popular opinion, given that a majority of Americans oppose *Dobbs* and believe abortion should be legal in all or many circumstances.[68]

Employers thus have varied self-interests implicated in their decision whether to offer their employees coverage for abortion. Some interests argue for coverage; some argue against. This is not truly the point. Fundamentally, the very idea of a fiduciary of reproductive care funding is troubling to the goals of reproductive justice, which demand that individuals be supported in decisions to reproduce or not, as well as in safely raising their children.[69] A fiduciary inserts third-party control over the individual, whereas reproductive freedom demands the individual have control over their own reproductive future without interference from others (barring limited interests of the state). Employers' own economic interests might drive them to cover abortion care to avoid the costs of employees' reproduction, in convergence with one dimension of reproductive justice. Relying on this interest convergence, however, can thwart the other dimensions of reproductive justice. Consider that the same combination of economic interest and coverage discretion drives most employers to refuse coverage of assisted reproduction services unless mandated, as Myrisha Lewis illuminates in her chapter.[70]

When employers' interests conflict too powerfully with the interests of their employees, it imposes agency cost: "the cost arising from a system that gives an agent the incentive to act contrary to the interests of its principal" specifically "by providing inadequate health care to their employees" for the firms' financial gain.[71]

When agency cost is too great, this justifies the need for public governance. Consider the case of abortion benefits after *Dobbs*. In states that criminalized or banned abortion, employers will face enormous political pressures to discontinue abortion benefits. They will also face rising financial and other burdens in meaningfully supporting access to abortion, if it means networking to include out-of-state providers, and then covering the costs of out-of-state procedures and travel expenses.

This may be a time where agency cost is too great, and outside regulation of the employer–employee benefit regime is needed to ensure employers act in their

67 Burwell v. Hobby Lobby, 573 U.S. 682 (2014).

68 Majority of Public Disapproves of Supreme Court's Decision to Overturn Roe v. Wade, Pew Rsch. Ctr. (July 6, 2022), https://www.pewresearch.org/politics/2022/07/06/majority-of-public-disapproves-of-supreme-courts-decision-to-overturn-roe-v-wade/.

69 Dorothy Roberts, Reproductive Justice, Not Just Rights, Dissent (Fall 2015), https://www.dissentmagazine.org/article/reproductive-justice-not-just-rights.

70 Chapter 11 in this volume.

71 Bronsteen et al., supra note 42, at 2299; accord Matthew, supra note 42.

employees' best interests. Yet, employers are only involved in paying for abortions because federal and state governments have refused public funding through the Hyde Amendment. No governmental help is likely coming to secure the abortion-access interests of employees, especially not in the states where the greatest pressures to defund abortion will be. Any efforts by the government to expand health benefits and to align employer interests with increased health coverage will very likely continue to make abortion the exception, as has been the case in prior decades of health reform and regulation.[72]

10.5 CONCLUSION

Dobbs fully empowered public law to deny access to abortion. To the extent that ESI beats back against the tide of abortion bans that *Dobbs* enabled, advocates for reproductive autonomy have reasons to be thankful that private law plays this role. Despite their limited reach, these private law ramparts for ESI coverage present opportunities to expand abortion access in a new era of extreme restriction. Yet, theoretical examination of the employer-sponsored benefit model instructs caution. Employers have long privileged their own economic interests over the health needs of their employees. Employers may face external pressures to discontinue abortion coverage, absent legal requirements to do so. And, ultimately, employer control over abortion benefits, even if it sometimes means access, can be undermining to the very notions of reproductive autonomy. Ultimately, public and private law both prop up a system of employer choice, rather than individual autonomy.

[72] Blake & McCuskey, supra note 8.

11

Reproductive Innovation and Reproductive Exceptionalism

How Private Health Insurance Coverage of Fertility Treatment Complements Hostile Governmental Action and Expands Access to Assisted Reproduction in the United States

Myrisha S. Lewis

11.1 INTRODUCTION

The use of fertility treatment and assisted reproductive technology (ART) in the United States and globally is increasing over time.[1] As of April 2023, the World Health Organization estimates that approximately one in six individuals have faced infertility globally.[2] Fertility treatment includes the use of drugs to stimulate egg production, *in vitro* fertilization (IVF), and, for some, the use of gestational surrogacy to aid in childbirth.[3] Debates have abounded and continue to abound in federal legislatures, state legislatures, and society more broadly about the morality of abortion, contraception, and assisted reproduction, as well as whether governments, public insurers, and private insurers should facilitate access to these medical treatments.[4] This chapter explains how private health insurance, like public health insurance, can be a catalyst for innovation and societal acceptance. Insurance coverage can be an indication of medically accepted procedures and products, as well as a proxy for ethical views, social views, and employer views on appropriate health care. This is particularly the case in the realm of reproduction, especially in relation to assisted reproduction and abortion.

Fertility treatment is becoming an increasingly routine benefit offered by private employers to their employees through contracts with health insurance providers and

[1] IVF (In Vitro Fertilization), Cleveland Clinic (Mar. 2, 2022), https://my.clevelandclinic.org/health/treatments/22457-ivf.

[2] World Health Organization, Infertility Prevalence Estimates, 1990–2021 13 (2023).

[3] John A. Robertson, Gay and Lesbian Access to Assisted Reproductive Technology, 55 Case W. Rsrv. L. Rev. 323, 324–25 (2004).

[4] See, e.g., Greer Donley & Jill Wieber Lens, Abortion, Pregnancy Loss, & Subjective Fetal Personhood, 75 Vand. L. Rev. 1649, 1652–53 (2022); Dobbs v. Jackson Women's Health Organization, 597 U.S. 215 (2022); Social and Moral Considerations on Abortion, Pew Rsch. Ctr. (May 6, 2022), https://www.pewresearch.org/religion/2022/05/06/social-and-moral-considerations-on-abortion/; Burwell v. Hobby Lobby, 573 U.S. 682 (2014).

fertility benefit providers. Often, the provision of fertility insurance benefits stems from private law, not public law, even when the insurance contracts are entered into and implemented in states with fertility insurance mandates as those state insurance mandates are often preempted by federal law. The chapter proceeds as follows. Section 11.2 will address ART in the United States and the limitations of the few existing state health insurance mandates related to ART. Next, the chapter discusses employer-provided coverage of egg freezing and fertility treatment and the ways in which private law significantly impacts individuals' decisions related to assisted reproduction. The chapter concludes by considering the relationship between public and private health insurance and the means through which the two may influence each other in ways that lead to expanded insurance coverage of fertility products and procedures.

11.2 HEALTH INSURANCE AND FERTILITY EXCEPTIONALISM

The definition of ART has changed over the years, but this chapter focuses on IVF (the combination of eggs and sperm in the laboratory to create an embryo for implantation), egg freezing or oocyte cryopreservation, and the use of fertility drugs to increase the likelihood of pregnancy or to maximize the availability of eggs.[5] The World Health Organization, American Society for Reproductive Medicine, and American Medical Association consider infertility a disease.[6] Yet in the United States, infertility is not treated as a routine matter whose treatment is covered by insurance plans in the same way as other medical occurrences like high cholesterol, heart attacks, organ transplantation, pregnancy, or broken bones. Part of this aversion to the insurance coverage of fertility treatments stems from the same opposition that accompanies IVF, abortion, and contraception: extensive, often conservative hostility to these treatments based on moral or political views.

Insurance coverage is critical to accessing health care in the United States.[7] The Patient Protection and Affordable Care Act (PPACA) expanded access to health care through reforms such as precluding insurance companies from refusing to cover or requiring higher premiums for individuals with preexisting health conditions, requiring certain employers to provide health insurance coverage meeting minimum essential coverage requirements for their full-time employees or face an "assessable payment," and the requirement that individuals purchase health

5 What Is Assisted Reproductive Technology?, Ctrs. for Disease Control & Prevention (Oct. 8, 2019), http://www.cdc.gov/art/whatis.html; Fertility Medications, Am. Pregnancy Ass'n (2024), https://americanpregnancy.org/getting-pregnant/fertility-medications/.

6 Sara Berg, AMA Backs Global Health Experts in Calling Infertility a Disease, Am. Pregnancy Ass'n (June 13, 2017), https://www.ama-assn.org/delivering-care/public-health/ama-backs-global-health-experts-calling-infertility-disease.

7 Inst. of Med., Care Without Coverage: Too Little, Too Late 1–3 (2002); Health Insurance and Access to Care, Nat'l Ctr. for Health Statistics (Feb. 2017), https://www.cdc.gov/nchs/data/factsheets/factsheet_hiac.pdf.

insurance or face tax penalties.[8] The "minimum essential health benefits" that insurance plans must cover under the PPACA do not include ART services.[9] Today, private, employer-provided health benefits, which are significantly governed by private law, cover nearly 159 million people in the United States.[10]

As a preliminary matter, insurance coverage usually does not occur until a technique is recognized as "established" instead of "experimental."[11] Often, this recognition is top-down as private insurance companies often follow the coverage and reimbursement decisions of public insurance programs, namely Medicare.[12] In 2018, the American Society for Reproductive Medicine (ASRM) announced that "egg freezing," the colloquial term for "advance oocyte cryopreservation," was no longer an "experimental" treatment.[13] Even though the ASRM no longer considers egg freezing as "experimental," most health insurance programs do not include egg freezing as a covered treatment. While egg freezing is no longer considered "experimental," its success rates are lower than many individuals likely expect.[14] Even though it may be covered in certain instances of medically induced infertility such as when individuals become infertile after treatments for various forms of cancer or leukemia, fertility preservation as one waits for a preferred partner or better time in life is often not deemed a covered health insurance procedure in the same way preventive care is.[15]

The Cleveland Clinic characterizes IVF as "one of the most effective assisted reproductive technologies (ARTs) available."[16] Since the birth of Louise Brown, the first child in the world born as a result of IVF, on July 27, 1978, over 8 million babies

8 26 U.S.C. § 4980H (2022); Nat'l Fed'n of Indep. Bus. v. Sebelius, 567 U.S. 519, 530 (2012).

9 See, e.g., Inst. of Med., Clinical Preventive Services for Women: Closing the Gaps 109–10 (2011); Women's Preventive Services Guidelines, Health Res. & Servs. Admin., https://www.hrsa.gov/womens-guidelines.

10 Gary Claxton et al., Employer Health Benefits: 2022 Annual Survey 156 (Kaiser Fam. Found. ed., 2022), https://files.kff.org/attachment/Report-Employer-Health-Benefits-2022-Annual-Survey.pdf.

11 Tips to Help You Appeal an Experimental or Investigational Service Denial by Your Insurance Company, Va. State Corp. Comm'n, https://scc.virginia.gov/getattachment/a13ac2b5-efb6-4d1a-a1b5-a76bfbaa4a86/exptips.pdf.

12 See, e.g., Jeffrey Clemens & Joshua D. Gottlieb, In the Shadow of a Giant: Medicare's Influence on Private Physician Payments, 125 J. Polit. Econ. 1, 31–32 (2017); 45 C.F.R. § 156.122 (2023); Tom Murphy, Insurers Won't Cover New Alzheimer's Treatment for Some Customers, ABC News (Aug. 11, 2023, 10:11 AM), https://abcnews.go.com/Health/wireStory/insurers-cover-new-alzheimers-treatment-customers-102197604.

13 Ethics Comm. of the Am. Soc'y for Reprod. Med., Planned Oocyte Cryopreservation for Women Seeking to Preserve Future Reproductive Potential: An Ethics Committee Opinion, 110 Fertility and Sterility 1022 (2018).

14 Age and Fertility, Am. Soc. for Reprod. Med. 4 (2012), https://www.asrm.org/globalassets/rf/news-and-publications/bookletsfact-sheets/english-fact-sheets-and-info-booklets/Age_and_Fertility.pdf.

15 See, e.g., 27 R.I. Gen. Laws § 27-18-30; 27 R.I. Gen. Laws § 27-20-20 (coverage for infertility).

16 Cleveland Clinic, supra note 1.

have been born as a result of IVF.[17] Insurance coverage of fertility treatment is not routine, despite a lengthy effort over the past several decades by many patients, activists, and legislators to normalize medical coverage of fertility treatment.[18] As of May 2023, the following states have mandated some form of infertility coverage: Arizona, California, Colorado, Connecticut, Delaware, Hawaii, Illinois, Maryland, Massachusetts, New Hampshire, New Jersey, New York, Ohio, Rhode Island, Texas, and West Virginia.[19] Maine was added to this list on January 1, 2024.[20] Yet, coverage mandates vary extensively among states.[21] For example, West Virginia was the first state to include "infertility services" in its list of "basic health services" in 1977, but the statute does not define what "infertility services" that health maintenance organizations (HMOs) are required to cover.[22] In addition to the lack of statutory definition of "infertility services," West Virginia enacted its statutory mandate before the birth of Louise Brown.[23] As a result, it is likely that the drafters of the statute did not anticipate IVF or egg freezing. Montana's statute mandating insurance coverage also fails to define what "infertility services" are.[24] After advocacy by various groups, including RESOLVE: The National Infertility Association (RESOLVE) and the Colorado Fertility Advocates, the Colorado Building Families Act went into effect on January 1, 2022 (with a subsequent amendment effective January 1, 2023

17 Id.

18 Insurance Coverage by State, RESOLVE: The Nat'l Infertility Assoc. (June 2023), https://resolve.org/learn/financial-resources-for-family-building/insurance-coverage/insurance-coverage-by-state/.

19 Id. (Louisiana's statute, for example, specifically mentions ART but does not require insurers to cover ART. La. Stat. § 22:1036. Prohibited exclusion of coverage of correctable medical conditions on basis of infertility); see also Pavel Zagadailov et al., Do State Insurance Mandates Alter ICSI Utilization?, 18 Reprod. Biol. & Endocrinology 33 (2020), https://www.ncbi.nlm.nih.gov/pmc/articles/PMC7183130/.

20 An Act to Provide Access to Fertility Care, 2022 Me. Laws ch. 692 (codified at 24-A.M.R.S.A. § 4320-S), http://www.mainelegislature.org/legis/bills/getPDF.asp?paper=HP1144&item=5&snum=130.

21 See, e.g., I. Glenn Cohen & Daniel Chen, Trading-Off Reproductive Technology and Adoption: Does Subsidizing IVF Decrease Adoption Rates and Should It Matter?, 95 Minn. L. Rev. 485, 503–09 (2010).

22 Benjamin J. Peipert et al., Impact of In Vitro Fertilization State Mandates for Third Party Insurance Coverage in the United States: A Review and Critical Assessment, 20(1) Reprod. Biology & Endocrinology, no. 111 (2022), at 1–2; W. Va. Code § 33-25A-2 (defining "basic health services" as including "infertility services" but providing no definition of "infertility services"); RESOLVE: The Nat'l Infertility Assoc., supra note 18; see, e.g., Del. Code Ann. tit. 18 § 3556(i)(6); Tex. Ins. Code Ann. § 1366.006.

23 Press Release, The Nobel Prize, The Nobel Prize in Physiology or Medicine 2010 to Robert G. Edwards (Oct. 4, 2010), https://www.nobelprize.org/prizes/medicine/2010/press-release/; Louise Brown, Louise Brown on 40 Years of IVF: I Was the World's First IVF Baby, This Is My Story, The Independent (July 25, 2018), https://www.independent.co.uk/life-style/health-and-families/ivf-baby-louise-brown-story-test-tube-world-first-40th-anniversary-a8455956.html.

24 See, e.g., Mont. Code Ann. § 33-31-102.

"clarifying" the scope of the bill).[25] The Colorado Building Families Act requires certain insurance plans to cover egg retrieval and embryo transfers, and the Act specifically mentions "using single embryo transfer when recommended and medically appropriate."[26] On May 2, 2022, the Governor of Maine approved H.P. 1144 – L.D. 1539 "An Act To Provide Access to Fertility Care."[27] Per the Act, effective January 1, 2024, "the Act applies to all policies, contracts and certificates executed, delivered, issued for delivery, continued or renewed in [Maine] on or after January 1, 2024."[28]

Moreover, many exceptions exist even when fertility coverage is mandated by state statute. For example, the Colorado Building Families Act has a specific exclusion from coverage for certain religious organizations.[29] Similar exclusions exist in other states' statutes.[30] Furthermore, the scope of fertility coverage is limited. While some states' "fertility coverage" mandates include IVF (and the cryopreservation often combined with IVF), others simply include diagnosis of infertility and, in many instances, appear to cover contraception or medical sterilization as opposed to fertility drugs or procedures that aim to result in childbirth.[31] Maine's forthcoming Act allows health plans to enact "reasonable limitations" on their coverage.[32] Some state health insurance mandates specifically exempt "experimental procedures" from the health benefits that an insurance plan must cover.[33] Moreover, state insurance mandates often leave out same-sex couples or single individuals.[34] For example, three states' statutes cover IVF but require that women's eggs be fertilized with their husband's sperm.[35] Also, "infertility" is sometimes defined in a manner that requires the individual to have tried to naturally conceive unsuccessfully for a

[25] Colorado Insurance Law, RESOLVE: The Natl' Infertility Assoc., https://resolve.org/learn/financial-resources-for-family-building/insurance-coverage/colorado-insurance-law/; Good News for Coloradans in Need of Fertility Treatment, Yahoo News (Nov. 17, 2022), https://www.yahoo.com/now/good-news-coloradans-fertility-treatment-200000874.html.

[26] Colo. Rev. Stat. § 10-16-104(b).

[27] 2022 Me. Laws ch. 692, supra note 20.

[28] Me. Stat. tit. 24A, § 4320-U (2024), https://legislature.maine.gov/statutes/24-A/title24-Asec4320-U.html.

[29] Colo. Rev. Stat. § 10-16-104(e) ("A religious employer may request and a carrier subject to this subsection (23) shall grant an exclusion from the coverage required under this subsection (23) in a health benefit plan if the required coverage conflicts with the religious organization's bona fide religious beliefs and practices").

[30] Cal. Health & Safety Code § 1374.55(e); 18 Del. C. § 3556 (i)(5); N.J. Stat. Ann. § 17:48-6x.

[31] See generally RESOLVE: The Nat'l Infertility Assoc., supra note 18.

[32] 2022 Me. Laws ch. 692, supra note 20.

[33] Ohio Rev. Code § 1751.01 (West) ("'Basic health care services' does not include experimental procedures"); §4320-U, supra note 28 (noting that a carrier is not required to provide coverage for "any experimental fertility procedure").

[34] The Ethics Comm. of the Am. Soc'y for Reprod. Med., Disparities in Access to Effective Treatment for Infertility in the United States: An Ethics Committee Opinion, 116 Fertility and Sterility 52, 57 (2021).

[35] See Peipert et al., supra note 22, at 3 (citing the fertility coverage mandates in Arkansas, Hawaii, and Texas).

specified period of time.[36] LGBTQ couples and single individuals are thus often left out of state insurance mandates or individual health insurance policies.[37]

Opponents of insurance coverage of fertility treatments also often emphasize how costly they can be, which could in turn increase insurance premiums.[38] While surveys have limitations, a survey commissioned by RESOLVE, and carried out by Mercer, a consulting company, revealed that 97 percent of surveyed companies said "that adding infertility coverage did not result in a significant increase in medical plan cost."[39] Because of costs, various polities like Ontario and Québec have reconsidered the provision of fertility benefits or limited its availability.[40] Actuarial costs have also motivated insurance companies to reduce costs, which is why insurance companies have incentivized single embryo transfers, for example, so as to minimize the likelihood and significant costs of non-singleton pregnancies and multiple births, which are costlier than singleton pregnancies.[41] Generally, insurance coverage does not subsidize unfettered access to fertility treatments, so insurance-covered or publicly provided ART often comes with limitations on access to maximize success rates and minimize costs, including age restrictions, restrictions on the number of covered cycles, restrictions on the number of embryos that can be transferred in a single IVF cycle, and restrictions on the marital status of those who may access the treatments.[42] The restrictions that exist in state insurance mandates as

36 See, e.g., Daniel Basco et al., Insuring against Infertility: Expanding State Infertility Mandates to Include Fertility Preservation Technology for Cancer Patients, 38 J.L. Med. & Ethics 832 (2010).

37 Peipert et al., supra note 22, at 3; see also Gabriela Weigel et al., Coverage and Use of Fertility Services in the U.S., Kaiser Fam. Found. (Sept. 15, 2020), https://www.kff.org/womens-health-policy/issue-brief/coverage-and-use-of-fertility-services-in-the-u-s/; The Ethics Comm. of the Am. Soc'y for Reprod. Med., supra note 34.

38 Me. Bureau of Ins., Concerning LD 1539: An Act to Provide Access to Fertility Care to the Committee on Health Coverage, Insurance, and Financial Services, 131st Legis. (Jan. 2023), https://legislature.maine.gov/doc/9670#:~:text=L.D; The Ethics Comm. of the Am. Soc'y for Reprod. Med., supra note 34.

39 2021 Survey on Fertility Benefits, Mercer (Jan. 2021), https://resolve.org/wp-content/uploads/2022/01/2021-Fertility-Survey-Report-Final.pdf.

40 Alana Cattapan, Medical Necessity and the Public Funding of In Vitro Fertilization in Ontario, 53 Can. J. Pol. Science 61, 61–62, 68–71 (2020); Free In-Vitro Fertilization Treatment Is Back in Quebec, But There Are Restrictions, Can. Broadcasting Corp. News (Nov. 10, 2021, 2:17 PM), https://www.cbc.ca/news/canada/montreal/in-vitro-fertilization-funded-public-1.6244008. But see B.C. Could Save $78 Million by Funding In Vitro Fertilization, Can. NewsWire (Feb. 4, 2013, 8:45 AM), https://www.newswire.ca/news-releases/bc-could-save-78-million-by-funding-in-vitro-fertilization-511915581.html.

41 See, e.g., Peipert et al., supra note 22, at 2, 4; Georgina M. Chambers et al., Funding and Public Reporting Strategies for Reducing Multiple Pregnancy from Fertility Treatments, 114 Fertility and Sterility 715 (2020); Public Funding for IVF Will Save Alberta Health Care System Millions, Can. NewsWire (May 22, 2012), https://www.newswire.ca/news-releases/public-funding-for-ivf-will-save-alberta-health-care-system-millions-510263821.html.

42 See, e.g., Dep't of Health, Minister for Health Announces Full Funding for Assisted Human Reproduction Treatment from September, Gov. of Ir., https://www.gov.ie/en/press-release/c2e96-minister-for-health-announces-full-funding-for-assisted-human-reproduction-treatment-

well as insurance policies' contractual restrictions on access can reduce the costs of ART to health insurance plans.[43]

Many state insurance mandates only apply to employer-sponsored health insurance plans, and grandfathered health plans may be specifically exempted.[44] Beyond these statutory exemptions, as Professors Blake and McCuskey note in this volume, "[the Employee Retirement Income Security Act of 1974] preemption exempts employers who structure their health plans as 'self-funded' plans from compliance."[45] Approximately 65 percent of covered workers were in a self-funded health plan in 2022, and 64 percent in 2021.[46] Due to these coverage exclusions, state insurance mandates for fertility coverage may only apply to 40 to 58 percent of health insurance plans in a state, assuming the state even has a fertility coverage mandate.[47] Yet, in spite of these statutory exceptions and some public opposition to the provision of fertility benefits, many private employers still opt to provide these benefits through health insurance contracts or contracts with fertility benefit providers.[48]

11.3 EMPLOYER-SPONSORED PRIVATE COVERAGE OF FERTILITY TREATMENT

There is a significant body of literature that focuses on the disparities that exist in access to fertility treatments.[49] These disparities in access to ART include a lack of

from-september/ (last accessed July 27, 2023); *in-vitro* Fertilization Will Once Again Be Free for Quebec Couples, but Only for One Cycle, Can. Broadcasting Corp. News (Nov. 11, 2020, 1:21 PM), https://www.cbc.ca/news/canada/montreal/quebec-public-ivf-1.5798240. On the other hand, fertility coverage can be expansive in terms of eligible groups. See Cattapan, supra note 40; see also Peipert et al., supra note 22.

43 See, e.g., Private Health Insurance Premiums and Federal Policy, Congressional Budget Off. 6–7 (Feb. 2016), https://www.cbo.gov/sites/default/files/114th-congress-2015-2016/reports/51130-Health_Insurance_Premiums.pdf.

44 N.Y. Comp. Codes R. & Regs. tit. 11, § 52.71; see generally State and Territory Infertility Insurance Laws, Am. Soc'y Reprod. Med., https://www.reproductivefacts.org/resources/state-infertility-insurance-laws/ (last accessed Apr. 23, 2023).

45 See Chapter 10 in this volume.

46 Claxton et al., supra note 10, at 156.

47 Mercer, supra note 39; Health Insurance Coverage of the Total Population, Multiple Sources of Coverage, Kaiser Fam. Found. (2021), https://www.kff.org/other/state-indicator/health-insurance-coverage-of-the-total-population-multiple-sources-ofcoverage/?currentTimeframe=0&sortModel=%7B%22colId%22:%22Location%22,%22sort%22:%22asc%22%7D.

48 Megan Cerullo, The Latest Employee Benefit? Helping Workers Have Babies, CBS News (Feb. 21, 2022, 6:00 AM), https://www.cbsnews.com/news/fertility-reproductive-benefits-important-for-recruitment-inclusion/; Megan Carnegie, More Companies Offer Fertility Benefits. It's Only the Beginning, Wired (Dec. 1, 2021), https://www.wired.com/story/fertility-benefits-work/; Kate Beioley, Law Firms Cooley and Clifford Chance Offer UK Staff Fertility Benefits for First Time, Fin. Times (June 13, 2021), https://www.ft.com/content/d0efaee1-8848-4971-894e-e5db44881c9c.

49 See, e.g., The Ethics Comm. of the Am. Soc'y for Reprod. Med., supra note 34, at 56; Ada C. Dieke et al., Disparities in Assisted Reproductive Technology Utilization by Race and

access to ART and use of it based on race, income, and geographic location.[50] Lack of insurance coverage for fertility treatments exacerbates these disparities. While targeted toward infertile couples, ART has become more appealing to varied groups including those who are not medically infertile, but who use it to reproduce and create families. While there have been a few programs to aid low-income individuals without insurance coverage who are experiencing infertility, assisted reproduction generally requires hefty out-of-pocket spending in the absence of subsidies.[51] This renders the actions of individual employers, who decide what nonessential health benefits like fertility coverage will be available to their employees through private health insurance contracts, especially significant to ART accessibility in the United States. Where employer-provided coverage of fertility treatment exists, even in the absence of mandated coverage, disparities still exist.[52]

Competition among employers to attract the most attractive employees can lead to expanded benefits packages for employees as can state insurance mandates.[53] There are significant disparities in what is covered by employee plans. For example, 24 to 42 percent of surveyed large employers cover IVF, and 23 to 38 percent of the largest employers cover intrauterine insemination.[54] Yet, those plans did not always cover egg freezing, which the technology sector has been a leader in covering for its employees.[55] Among companies with over 500 employees, as of 2020, 27 percent of those employers offer IVF coverage, up from 24 percent in 2015, and 11 percent offer egg freezing, an increase from 2015, when only 5 percent of those companies covered egg freezing.[56] Moreover, fertility providers sometimes provide lists on their

Ethnicity, United States, 2014: A Commentary, 26(6) J. Women's Health (Larchmt) 605 (June 2017), https://www.ncbi.nlm.nih.gov/pmc/articles/PMC5548290/pdf/nihms886177.pdf.

50 The Ethics Comm. of the Am. Soc'y for Reprod. Med., supra note 34, at 56 ("... even in states with comprehensive infertility mandates, infertility care still is used disproportionately by non-Hispanic white women of high socioeconomic and educational status").

51 Kara W. Swanson, Adultery by Doctor: Artificial Insemination, 1890–1945, 87 Chi.-Kent L. Rev. 591, 614 (2012) (citing instances where lower-income individuals received artificial insemination services through "the public Sterility Clinic of the New York Hospital" and a physician in Brookline, Massachusetts) (citations omitted).

52 See, e.g., Isabel Galic et al., Disparities in Access to Fertility Care: Who's In and Who's Out, 2 F&S Reps. 2666 (2021); Tarun Jain & Mark D. Hornstein, Disparities in Access to Infertility Services in a State with Mandated Insurance Coverage, 84 Fertility and Sterility 221, 222 (2005); Eve C. Feinberg et al., Economics May Not Explain Hispanic Underutilization of Assisted Reproductive Technology Services, 88 Fertility and Sterility 1439, 1440 (2007).

53 See, e.g., Julia La Roche, Goldman Sachs to Give All New Parents 20 Weeks Paid Leave, Yahoo News (Nov. 4, 2019), https://finance.yahoo.com/news/goldman-sachs-to-give-all-new-parents-20-weeks-paid-leave-152722590.html.

54 Mercer, supra note 39, at 6.

55 See, e.g., Ali L. Nicolette, Empty Benefits: Employer-Sponsored Oocyte Cryopreservation and Potential for Employment Discrimination, 27 Hastings Women's L.J. 341 (2016).

56 Karen Gilchrist, Egg Freezing, IVF and Surrogacy: Fertility Benefits Have Evolved to Become the Ultimate Workplace Perk, CNBC (Mar. 14, 2022, 2:43 AM EDT, updated Oct. 4, 2022, 9:38 PM EDT), https://www.cnbc.com/2022/03/14/egg-freezing-ivf-surrogacy-fertility-benefits-are-the-new-work-perk.html.

websites of local companies providing fertility coverage in their employee benefits packages.[57] These provider lists are in addition to many "crowdsourced" methods, of identifying employers who provide fertility insurance benefits, like Reddit threads and TikTok videos.[58]

Some are critical of employer subsidization of egg freezing by noting that it implies that women are expected to delay childbirth and increase labor productivity.[59] Yet, there is no requirement that individuals avail themselves of these employee benefits. Moreover, as those who study the coupling of health insurance and employment note, individuals often move from employer to employer.[60] Therefore, one could take advantage of one employer's health benefits and move to another employer. Additionally, providing fertility benefits could be beneficial to employers from the perspective of employee retention. A FertilityIQ survey found that "61% of employees who received fertility coverage from an employer said they felt more loyal and committed to the company ... [and] 88% of women who had IVF treatment fully paid for by their employer chose to return to that employer after maternity leave, compared to around 50% of the regular population without fertility benefits."[61] Similarly, 62 percent of surveyed companies found that offering infertility coverage aided them in "staying competitive and attracting and retaining talent."[62]

Employer-provided fertility benefits offer a subsidy to those who otherwise may not have the funds on hand to finance assisted reproduction. Thus, employer-sponsored reproduction can save these individuals from the fates of many others who pursue assisted reproduction, which includes depleting their savings, taking out loans, or having no means to pay at all.[63] For example, a cycle of IVF without fertility drugs is estimated to cost between US$12,000 and US$17,000; the cost with fertility drugs raises

57 See, e.g., The Growing List of Companies Offering Fertility Benefits, RADfertility, https://radfertility.com/does-my-company-provide-ivf-coverage/.

58 Leticia Miranda & Louise Matsakis, Some Starbucks Workers Forgo Paychecks to Access IVF Treatments, NBC News (Mar. 27, 2022, 6:00 AM EDT, updated Mar. 28, 2022, 6:26 AM EDT), https://www.nbcnews.com/business/starbucks-workers-forgo-paychecks-access-ivf-treatments-rcna16381#; Luz Pena, Bay Area Woman Travels to Spain to Freeze Eggs, ABC News (July 20, 2019), https://abc7news.com/ovally-fertility-spain-bay-area-travel/5407303; Cara Hutto, 57 Companies That Offer Awesome Fertility Benefits, InHerSight (Sept. 24, 2021, updated Sept. 23, 2022), https://www.inhersight.com/blog/parenting/companies-with-fertility-benefits; see, e.g., Reddit, Anyone Have a Copy of the FertilityIQ Workplace Index?!, https://www.reddit.com/r/stilltrying/comments/quogma/anyone_have_a_copy_of_the_fertilityiq_workplace/; Reddit, Infertility, Pregnancy Loss, and Trouble Conceiving Community, https://www.reddit.com/r/infertility/.

59 Gilchrist, supra note 56.

60 June Carbone & Naomi Cahn, Uncoupling, 53 Ariz. St. L. J. 1, 33 (2021).

61 Gilchrist, supra note 56; Ann Carrns, Tech Companies Get High Marks for Covering Infertility Treatments, N.Y. Times (Nov. 15, 2017), https://www.nytimes.com/2017/11/15/your-money/infertility-treatment-coverage.html.

62 Mercer, supra note 39, at 7.

63 Melissa B. Jacoby, The Debt Financing of Parenthood, 72 L. and Contemp. Probs. 147, 147–48, 150–51, 157–58 (2009).

the estimated cost to US$25,000.[64] Egg retrieval and freezing is estimated to cost between US$15,000 and US$25,000.[65] Storing frozen eggs can cost up to US$800 per year, and storing banked sperm costs between US$100 and US$500 per year.[66]

In the wake of health care reform, economic downturns, and social change, the disadvantages of having health insurance and other leave inextricably connected to employment and marriage have become more apparent.[67] Subsidized access to fertility treatments is often provided through a third-party provider, as opposed to the standard employee health insurance plan.[68] For example, shortly after Elon Musk's purchase of Twitter, news coverage focused on how Twitter's layoffs stymied employee access to Carrot, a fertility benefits provider.[69] One individual who was fired from Twitter stated that "... she would have left the company [a year earlier] if it weren't for the fertility treatment benefit, and she was promised health benefits would continue a year after any takeover. In the end, she had one week."[70] Thus, the disadvantages of employer-sponsored health insurance coverage may also accompany employer-sponsored fertility benefits.

The focus of this volume is on private law, but there is a relationship between private health coverage and public health coverage. Lessons and practices are often exchanged between private and public health insurance companies. Private health insurance drug formularies generally cover, at a minimum, for example, drugs covered by public health insurance programs. There are many entities in the federal government that provide health care and health insurance, including Medicare, the Federal Employees Health Insurance Benefit Plan, TRICARE, the Indian Health Service, and the US Department of Veterans Affairs. While private law may not aid those individuals directly, the innovations of private health insurance can directly influence public health programs. For example, while Utah does not have a fertility insurance mandate, the Centers for Medicare and Medicaid Services approved Utah's 2020 application for a waiver to permit the state to "provide *in vitro*

64 Amy Klein, I.V.F. Is Expensive. Here's How to Bring Down the Cost, N.Y. Times (Apr. 18, 2020), https://www.nytimes.com/article/ivf-treatment-costs-guide.html (citing Nat'l Conf. State Legislatures, State Laws Related to Insurance Coverage for Infertility Treatment (Mar. 12, 2021), https://www.ncsl.org/research/health/insurance-coverage-for-infertility-laws.aspx).

65 Pena, supra note 58.

66 Alyssa Jeong Perry & Audrey Nguyen, How to Decide If Freezing Your Eggs Is Right for You – And Where to Get Started, NPR (Dec. 21, 2022, 1:31 PM ET), https://www.npr.org/2021/11/18/1056834875/egg-freezing-process-how-much-does-it-cost; Amin Sedaghat Herati, Sperm Banking, Hopkins Med., https://www.hopkinsmedicine.org/health/treatment-tests-and-therapies/sperm-banking.

67 See, e.g., Carbone & Cahn, supra note 60; Emma Goldberg & Tripp Mickle, When Having a Baby and Losing Your Job Collide, N.Y. Times (Feb. 9, 2023), https://www.nytimes.com/2023/02/09/business/layoffs-parental-leave.html.

68 Carnegie, supra note 48.

69 Chris Stokel-Walker, They Wanted a Baby Then Twitter Fired Them, WIRED (Nov. 25, 2022, 7:00 AM), https://www.wired.com/story/twitter-layoffs-health-benefits-ivf/; Carrot, Home Page, https://www.get-carrot.com.

70 Stokel-Walker, supra note 69.

fertilization services and genetic testing for Medicaid eligible individuals who have one of the following conditions: Cystic fibrosis, spinal muscular atrophy, Morquio syndrome, myotonic dystrophy, or sickle cell anemia."[71] A subsequent five-year waiver renewal application was approved until June 30, 2027.[72]

Despite the lack of a federal mandate for health insurance reform to include fertility preservation, there is a notable federal exception: certain wounded servicemembers. Despite years of debate about whether Congress should mandate coverage of fertility treatment for federal civilian employees, specifically, and the public, more broadly, in 2016, Congress authorized the Department of Defense to expand coverage of or directly provide ART services to certain categories of veterans and enlisted personnel, namely those with service-related injuries.[73] Some veterans with service-related conditions that have resulted in infertility are eligible for ART services, yet those ART services do not cover donor gametes, gestational surrogacy, or unmarried individuals.[74] Former Secretary of Defense, Ashton Carter, was "inspired during visits to Silicon Valley" to create Initiative #35, "Egg and Sperm Cryopreservation," that would permit deploying service members to freeze their gametes before deploying although ultimately Initiative #35 was never funded.[75] In the meantime, members of Congress continue to introduce legislation to expand access to ART for servicemembers although the provisions are routinely curtailed by conservative opposition.[76] Additionally, military family advocate groups use their own money to subsidize ART access for active-duty Special Forces

[71] See Letter from Emma Chacon to Seema Verma (Dec. 30, 2020), https://medicaid.utah.gov/Documents/pdfs/1115AmendmentInVitro.pdf (Utah 1115 Primary Care Network Demonstration Waiver Amendment Request In Vitro Fertilization and Genetic Testing for Qualified Conditions, Demonstration Project Nos. 11-W-00145/8 and 21-W-00054/8); see also Utah Code § 26-18-420.

[72] Letter from Spencer J. Cox to Javier Becerra (June 30, 2021), https://medicaid.utah.gov/Documents/pdfs/Utah%201115%20Waiver%20Renewal-combined%20draft.pdf; Letter from Jennifer Strohecker to Chiquita Brooks-LaSure (July 7, 2022), https://www.medicaid.gov/sites/default/files/2022-07/ut-pcn-state-accept-ltr-07112022_0.pdf.

[73] See, e.g., Associated Press, Abortion Arguments at Play in Limiting Veterans' IVF Benefit, NBC News (July 8, 2019), https://www.nbcnews.com/health/health-care/abortion-arguments-play-limiting-veterans-ivf-benefit-n1027461; Congress Passes Bill to Help Wounded Veterans Start Families, PR Newswire (Sept. 29, 2016, 10:52 ET), https://www.prnewswire.com/news-releases/congress-passes-bill-to-help-wounded-veterans-start-families-300336557.html; Community Care: In Vitro Fertilization Treatment, U.S. Dep't of Veterans Affs., https://www.va.gov/COMMUNITYCARE/programs/veterans/ivf.asp (last accessed Sept. 29, 2023).

[74] U.S. Dep't of Veterans Affs., supra note 73.

[75] Patricia Kime, Military's New Fertility Benefit Will Let Troops Freeze Their Sperm and Eggs, Military Times (Jan. 29, 2016), https://www.militarytimes.com/pay-benefits/military-benefits/health-care/2016/01/29/military-s-new-fertility-benefit-will-let-troops-freeze-their-sperm-and-eggs/; Report to Congressional Armed Services Committees on Force of the Future Pilot Program on Cryopreservation of Gametes, Dep't of Defense 2 (Feb. 2, 2018).

[76] See, e.g., Press Release, U.S. Senator Tammy Duckworth, Duckworth, Murray, Larsen, Jacobs Reintroduce Legislation to Expand Fertility Treatments, Help Veterans Start Families (Sept. 15, 2023), https://www.duckworth.senate.gov/news/press-releases/duckworth-murray-larsen-jacobs-reintroduce-legislation-to-expand-fertility-treatments-help-veterans-start-families; Patricia Kime, Nonprofits Are Filling a Void of Fertility Help for Service Members, But Hope Congress Steps

personnel.[77] In the summer of 2023, two lawsuits were filed against the Department of Defense and Department of Veterans Affairs on behalf of current and retired servicemembers who were excluded from ART coverage based on the agencies' restrictive policies.[78] In January 2024, Judge Caproni issued a 90-day stay of some of the claims in the New York case in order to give the Department of Defense and Department of Veterans Affairs time to finalize changes to their IVF health insurance coverage policies.[79] These policy changes are expected to increase the number of individuals who could access covered IVF treatments by modifying the requirement that those accessing covered IVF services be in an opposite-sex marriage as well as permitting the use of donor gametes in certain instances. Private health insurance programs can influence public health insurance programs and mitigate conservative political views in a way that expands access to fertility treatments.

11.4 CONCLUSION

Insurance coverage can have a substantial role in normalizing a treatment, especially in the realm of reproductive innovation. Moreover, views about "necessity" can change. The routine health insurance coverage of childbirth expenses is something that started and evolved over approximately the past thirty years.[80] Similarly, in October 2023, the American Society of Reproductive Medicine issued a "new, more inclusive" definition of infertility that specifically includes individuals "regardless of relationship status or sexual orientation." It is possible that the new definition of infertility may be incorporated into future legislation or private insurance contracts.[81] Private health insurance or other subsidized coverage can constitute significant action, especially when legislators are actively avoiding a topic by failing to introduce or consider legislation or policies that could further it. Private coverage of fertility treatment aids in the normalization of ART in the United States, which may ultimately overcome moral and political opposition to the use of and funding of assisted reproduction more broadly in the United States.

Up, Military.com Network (June 29, 2022), https://www.military.com/daily-news/2022/06/29/nonprofits-are-filling-void-of-fertility-help-service-members-hope-congress-steps.html.

77 Kime, supra note 76.

78 Complaint, Nat'l Org. for Women-New York City v. U.S. Dep't of Defense et al., Case 1:23-cv-06750 (S.D.N.Y. 2023); Complaint, Ashley Sheffield v. U.S. Dep't of Veterans Affairs, Civil Case No. 23-11757 (D. Mass. 2023).

79 Memo Endorsement, Nat'l Org. for Women-New York City v. U.S. Dep't of Defense et al., Case 1:23-cv-06750 (S.D.N.Y. Jan. 2, 2024).

80 See Elissa Strauss, 40 Years Later, Why Is IVF Still Not Covered by Insurance? Economics, Ignorance, and Sexism, CNN (July 25, 2018), https://www.cnn.com/2018/07/25/health/ivf-insurance-parenting-strauss/index.html; 29 U.S.C. § 1185.

81 ASRM Publishes a New, More Inclusive Definition of "Infertility", Am. Soc. for Reprod. Med. (Oct. 15, 2023), https://asrmcongress.org/asrm-publishes-a-new-more-inclusive-definition-of-infertility/.

12

Business Responses to *Dobbs*

The Return to a "Reproductive Rights" Approach, and Suspicions around Corporate Care

Asees Bhasin

12.1 INTRODUCTION

On June 24, 2022, *Roe v. Wade* was officially overturned by the Supreme Court of the United States, causing abortion care, an already inaccessible and stigmatized health care option, to become further out-of-reach for people. The decision in *Dobbs* received widespread resistance, including in the form of protests, civil society activism, advocacy, and legislative and administrative action. Several corporations doing business in the United States also condemned this ruling and took action to signal their commitment to reproductive rights.

This chapter engages with the hypothesis that while private action undertaken by corporations may in some cases enhance individuals' access to reproductive rights and supports, a general reliance on corporations to meet reproductive needs and demands of people and communities may be ill-advised. Section 12.2 of this chapter asks the question of *how* corporations responded in support of reproductive rights in the aftermath of *Dobbs*. Section 12.3 of this chapter asks *why* they were motivated to do so. Section 12.4 unpacks the broader societal impacts of these responses in juxtaposition to demands made by the Reproductive Justice (RJ) movement. Section 12.5 sets out a research agenda that, if undertaken, will allow us to get clearer answers about the overall desirability for reliance on private law to provide reproductive health care.

12.2 THE CORPORATE RESPONSES TO *DOBBS*

There is a broad literature documenting the evolution of corporate form and purpose.[1]

[1] See Elizabeth Pollman, Reconceiving Corporate Personhood, Penn L.: Legal Scholarship Repository (2011), https://scholarship.law.upenn.edu/faculty_scholarship/2563/; Milton Friedman, The Social Responsibility of Business Is to Increase Its Profits, N.Y. Times

Debates about corporate purpose touch on important ethical questions about the involvement of corporations in social, political, and economic spheres. In the recent past, Corporate Social Responsibility (CSR) has gained traction as a corporate practice, with businesses considering the social, economic, political, and environmental impacts of their actions, and engaging in philanthropy or volunteering as a result. According to a poll conducted in 2019, 41 percent of Fortune 500 CEOs viewed "solving social problems" as part of their strategy to conduct business.[2] A separate but related framework, the Environmental, Social, and Governance (ESG) framework, is also gaining popularity, accompanied by an increase in rating agencies quantifying corporate performance in these areas and measuring how sustainable a corporation is.

Due to these shifts in the conceptualizations of corporate purpose (from a shareholder wealth maximization approach to a more progressive stakeholder theory), there has been a rapid increase in corporations publicly engaging with social and political issues. As per a survey of at least 274 US corporations, a relatively significant number of corporations had taken public stances on issues of racial equality (61 percent), LGBTQ+ rights (44 percent), and gender equality (39 percent).[3] These engagements influence social policy on many fronts, including health policy.

All social issues do not receive equal attention. A study found that only 10 percent of corporations had responded or planned to respond to the *Dobbs* decision with public statements.[4] Additionally, only about 51 percent of corporations had addressed or planned to address the issue of reproductive rights in the aftermath of *Dobbs*.[5] Given the importance of the moment and its implications for people of reproductive age, this response seemed very muted. The following paragraphs will briefly describe some of the ways corporations publicly and internally addressed the implications of *Dobbs*.

Publicly, some corporations made statements denouncing the Supreme Court's decision.

Corporations such as Johnson & Johnson used this opportunity to emphasize how decisions about reproductive care must be left to individuals and their healthcare providers.[6] Corporate statements, such as that of Reddit, also framed reproductive rights as an issue concerning the health and safety of their own employees. Importantly, some corporations such as Levi Strauss & Co. implored other business

(Sept. 13, 1970), at SM17, https://www.nytimes.com/1970/09/13/archives/a-friedman-doctrine-the-social-responsibility-of-business-is-to.html; See generally Andrew Keay, Stakeholder Theory in Corporate Law: Has It Got What It Takes?, 9 Rich. J. Global L. & Bus. 249 (2010).

2 Alan Murray, America's CEOs Seek a New Purpose for the Corporation, Fortune (Aug. 19, 2019), https://fortune.com/longform/business-roundtable-ceos-corporations-purpose/.

3 The U.S. Corporate Response to Recent Supreme Court Decisions, The Conf. Bd. (2022), https://www.conference-board.org/pdfdownload.cfm?masterProductID=39648.

4 Id.

5 Id.

6 Emma Goldberg et al., Here Are the Companies That Will Cover Travel Expenses for Employee Abortions, N.Y. Times (June 24, 2022), https://www.nytimes.com/2022/06/24/business/abortion-companies-travel-expenses.html.

leaders to make their voices heard, given that the protection of reproductive rights "is a critical business issue impacting [the] workforce, []economy, and progress towards racial and gender equity."[7]

In addition to making public statements, some corporations also pledged donations to reproductive rights organizations including the Planned Parenthood Federation of America and the Center for Reproductive Rights. While some organizations donated to the National Network of Abortion Funds, it seems that most corporate donations went toward national-level reproductive rights and advocacy organizations instead of state or local organizations or those working specifically on issues of RJ – organizations that often require resources due to being underfunded.[8]

Many corporations responded to the abortion ruling internally. This included making announcements around travel stipends or reimbursements for expenditures related to travel undertaken to receive reproductive care out of state. Internal policies differed by the amount reimbursable, travel miles required to be able to take advantage of the policy, and the provision of other travel benefits such as the cost of lodging, childcare, and taking a support person. Some corporations also made changes to employer health plans to include the provision of reproductive health care services.[9]

Companies responded by adopting other policies as well.[10] For instance, some companies announced that they would cover legal costs that may arise under new abortion state laws. An example of this is the costs related to transporting individuals to abortion clinics by Lyft and Uber drivers.[11] Patagonia, on the other hand, announced the creation of a bail fund for employees who were protesting antiabortion measures.[12] Some corporations, such as Google, also announced the option for employees to relocate without justification to states where abortion is legal.[13]

There is literature on whether and how there should be legal enforcement of CSR, and whether CSR codes are binding depends on several factors – which makes

[7] Id.

[8] Narciso Novogratz, 9 Reproductive Justice Organizations You Can Support, Latina (2022), https://latina.com/9-reproductive-justice-organizations-you-can-support/.

[9] See Haleluya Hadero, Walmart Expands Abortion Coverage for Employees, PBS (Aug. 19, 2022), https://www.pbs.org/newshour/economy/walmart-expands-abortion-coverage-for-employees; Chapter 10 in this volume.

[10] See generally #WhatAreYourReproBenefits, Rhia Ventures, https://rhiaventures.org/corporate-engagement/whatareyourreprobenefits/; Abortion Care Benefits at Tech Companies, Leopard.fyi, https://leopard.fyi/abortion-care-database/.

[11] Shannon Bond, Lyft and Uber Will Pay Drivers' Legal Fees If They're Sued under Texas Abortion Law, NPR (Sept. 3, 2021), https://www.npr.org/2021/09/03/1034140480/lyft-and-uber-will-pay-drivers-legal-fees-if-theyre-sued-under-texas-abortion-la.

[12] Kim Bhasin, Patagonia Will Bail Out Employees Arrested in Abortion Protests, Bloomberg (June 24, 2022), https://www.bloomberg.com/news/articles/2022-06-24/patagonia-to-bail-out-employees-arrested-in-abortion-protests.

[13] Igor Bonifacic, Google Tells Workers They Can Relocate "Without Justification" Following Supreme Court Decision, Engadget (June 25, 2022), https://www.engadget.com/google-tells-employees-they-can-relocate-following-supreme-court-abortion-ruiling-181926101.html.

it hard to discuss whether they are enforceable in general.[14] Professor Anna Beckers importantly discusses the "self-regulating" nature of CSR, and how "private law, exemplified with the contract law regarding CSR self-regulation, currently adopts a predominantly facilitative approach towards CSR self-regulation in the sense that it allows for its adoption and interprets its legal consequences in the light of the intention of the company having adopted it."[15] Consequently, the way in which private law operates, in status quo, has upheld a system where CSR and ESG initiatives lack enforceability and teeth and are left to be shaped by the corporation itself.

Regardless of whether CSR initiatives are enforceable, private law and action impact social policy, and there is a more important question about whether corporate action on certain subjects is desirable, and more beneficial than harmful to social movements.

12.3 ANALYZING CORPORATE MOTIVATION

The following paragraphs seek to dive into the different reasons that drove corporations to signal their support for reproductive rights. There are two reasons why such an analysis may be important. First, it may weaken claims that corporations participating in proabortion politics are doing so purely altruistically and show how their participation is self-interested. Second, they may help us identify strategies and pressure points when thinking about ways to influence corporate behavior or facilitate private law interventions.

Evidence has shown that CSR initiatives lead to improved bottom lines for corporations by gaining competitive advantages and developing reputational capital.[16] For starters, providing reproductive supports and taking pro-choice stances internally and externally may be an important strategy to attract and retain employees. Studies have shown that women in states with better access to contraception have higher rates of labor force participation and more frequently pursue full-time employment.[17] People in the workforce themselves have expressed a preference to work in states where abortion is legal. A study has also shown that 63 percent of college-educated workers would not apply for a job in a state that has recently

[14] Jan M. Smits, Enforcing Corporate Social Responsibility Codes under Private Law: On the Disciplining Power of Legal Doctrine, 24 Ind. J. Global Legal Stud. 99 (2017).

[15] Anna Beckers, Towards a Regulatory Private Law Approach for CSR Self-Regulation? The Effect of Private Law on Corporate CSR Strategies (Tilburg Priv. Law, Working Paper No. 3, 2019), https://papers.ssrn.com/sol3/papers.cfm?abstract_id=3369596.

[16] Matteo Tonello, The Business Case for Corporate Social Responsibility, Harvard L. School F. on Corp. Governance (June 26, 2011), https://corpgov.law.harvard.edu/2011/06/26/the-business-case-for-corporate-social-responsibility/.

[17] Kate Bahn et al., Linking Reproductive Health Care Access to Labor Market Opportunities for Women, Ctr. for Am. Progress (Nov. 21, 2017), https://www.americanprogress.org/article/linking-reproductive-health-care-access-labor-market-opportunities-women/.

banned abortion.[18] Not only do corporations need fresh talent, but they also are obliged to meet their gender and racial diversity commitments.

A new study by Adrjan et al. utilized data on job satisfaction, job search behavior, and wages from Glassdoor and Indeed to analyze how companies that offered abortion-related benefits in the wake of *Dobbs* fared compared to companies that did not provide those benefits.[19] This has been among the first and only studies that have documented the causal impact of the announcements of such benefits. Their research found that from July 2022 (the month after the *Dobbs* decision) through January 2023, job seekers explicitly included abortion or related words in their search criteria 147 percent more often relative to job seekers in January 2019. In relation to this, they also observed two other phenomena: (1) that the increase in clicks on the job postings of announcing firms is particularly pronounced in female-dominated job postings – particularly, among high-wage women in trigger states; and (2) smaller firms enjoyed the largest increase in job seeker clicks, and while they may typically struggle to stand out and compete for labor, the announcement of abortion benefits may have helped them to attract job seekers.

In addition to the issues of attracting and retaining talent, companies face a lot of pressure to adopt certain policies from their investors and stakeholders. For instance, in 2019, in an initiative organized by Rhia Ventures, a cohort of forty institutional investors, signed a letter to over thirty corporations to inquire about reproductive health-related insurance policies and benefits, as well as about public policy and political positions that would impact reproductive rights.[20]

Chapter 20 in this volume describes how shareholder proposals serve as a vehicle for participation in corporate governance, and as a tool for raising existential questions about corporate purpose.[21] Post-*Dobbs*, several shareholder proposals were introduced where shareholders actively put pressure on companies to issue public reports on the impact of the abortion ruling on their employees. For instance, a shareholder proposal introduced by shareholders at TJX asked for the public report to "evaluate any risks and costs to the company associated with new laws and legislation severely restricting reproductive health care" and "include any effects on employee hiring, retention, and productivity, and decisions regarding closure or

[18] How "Top Talent" Views Politics and Social Issues in Their Workplace: Findings from a National Survey, Perry Undem Rsch. & Commc'n (Oct. 4, 2022), https://perryundem.com/wp-content/uploads/2022/03/PerryUndem-Tara-Health-Report.pdf.

[19] Pawel Adrjan et al., We've Got You Covered: Employer and Employee Responses to Dobbs v. Jackson SSRN (2023), https://papers.ssrn.com/sol3/papers.cfm?abstract_id=4531372&isid=hiringlab_us&ikw=hiringlab_us_2023%2F08%2F09%2Fjobs-after-dobbs%2F_textlink_https%3A%2F%2Fpapers.ssrn.com%2Fsol3%2Fpapers.cfm%3Fabstract_id%3D4531372.

[20] Hidden Value: The Business Case for Reproductive Health, Rhia Ventures (June 2022), https://rhiaventures.org/wp-content/uploads/2022/08/Hidden-Value-The-Business-Case-for-Reproductive-Health-2022.pdf.

[21] Chapter 20 in this volume.

expansion of operations in states proposing or enacting restrictive laws."[22] While the Board of Directors unanimously voted against this proposal and other proposals similar to this one, they mark the arrival of abortion as a new ESG frontier, and similar reproductive health-related proposals are expected in the upcoming proxy seasons.[23]

Finally, in addition to pressure from investors, corporations are susceptible to pressure from their employees and consumers. A notable example of this pressure can be seen in Wayfair's decision to enter into a contract with an immigrant detention center, leading to widespread employee protests and walk-outs, which eventually led to their share price falling by more than 10 percent.[24] While understanding that the pressure from various stakeholders described above is offered to explain why corporations have acted in support of reproductive rights, it is important to note that such phenomena are not limited to social issues associated only with left-leaning politics. For example, Target received considerable opposition from Conservatives for their Pride Month-related merchandise, causing Target to remove some of the items it was selling.[25]

12.4 ANALYZING CORPORATE POWER THROUGH A REPRODUCTIVE JUSTICE LENS

Having discussed how and why corporations weighed in during the aftermath of *Dobbs*, this section will now discuss the impact of private law as it engages in reproductive rights politics. To analyze this question, this chapter will look at the goals and visions of the RJ movement and look at how corporate action falls within this framework.

The RJ movement was conceptualized by Black women activists who met before the International Conference on Population and Development in 1994. The framework considers how individuals negotiate intersecting identities including race, class, gender, and sexuality, and how those, in turn, impact their reproductive decisions. The RJ framework has three foundational principles – the right *not* to

[22] Proposal 7: Shareholder Proposal, Report on Risk Due to Restrictions on Reproductive Rights, TJX Companies (2022), https://www.sec.gov/Archives/edgar/data/109198/000010919822000024/a2022proxystatement.htm#ibd1d957d8d0d47d598341251f8d5d525_1099511628918.

[23] Michelle N. Diamond et al., Shareholder Focus on Reproductive Rights Post-Dobbs, WilmerHale (Oct. 4, 2022), https://www.wilmerhale.com/en/insights/blogs/esg-epicenter/20221003-shareholder-focus-on-reproductive-rights-post-dobbs.

[24] Abha Bhattarai, Wayfair Is Supplying Beds to Texas Detention Centers for Children – and Its Employees Are Protesting, Wash. Post (June 25, 2019), https://www.washingtonpost.com/business/2019/06/25/wayfair-is-supplying-beds-texas-detention-centers-children-its-employees-are-protesting/.

[25] Emily Stewart, Target Giving in to Conservative Pressure on Pride Is Not a Great Sign, Vox (May 25, 2023), https://www.vox.com/politics/2023/5/25/23737338/target-abprallen-pride-boycott-bud-light-trans-controversy-stock-price.

have a child; the right to have a child, and the right to parent children with dignity in a safe and healthy environment.[26]

The following sections will build on the foundation of this tension between corporate reproductive politics and RJ visions and discuss the impacts of adopting the former framework on different stakeholders.

12.4.1 "*Choice as a Marketplace Concept*"

It is important to preface that the vision of the RJ movement is at odds with the profit-maximization-centered approach of corporations. The RJ framework roots the rights it advocates for in a human rights framework – one that posits that any interference with the rights and dignity of reproducing persons is a "blow against their humanity."[27] For this reason, it also champions the existence of positive rights – focused on the government's obligation to create conditions so that people can enjoy their freedoms.

On the other hand, the neoliberal worldview, championed by corporations and businesses, "inscribes on politics and culture the needs of a global capitalism that sustains itself on the free flow of capital, goods, disembedded labor, and market-friendly state policies."[28] It relies on institutional supports and business-friendly measures taken by the state, while simultaneously promoting the idea that government should be restrained in almost all other ways, including in the provision of welfare and social services. Neoliberal policy initiatives, championed by some of these corporations acting in the wake of *Dobbs*, can be traced to the dilution of worker protections, the expansion of the carceral state, and the sync between money and political campaigns.[29] A manifestation of the tension between neoliberalism and RJ, and an example of the shortcomings of private law in providing reproductive care, can be seen starkly as we observe how several corporations that have taken pro-abortion stances in the wake of *Dobbs* have been making significant political donations to antiabortion policymakers in the hope that they can gain influence over their agendas and receive other advantages that often entail deregulatory aims.[30]

Some may argue that a neoliberal approach is baked into our jurisprudence around reproduction. The constitutional right to abortion was recognized in *Roe v. Wade* and was rooted in the right to privacy, giving women the "right to choose"

[26] Loretta J. Ross & Rickie Solinger, Reproductive Justice: An Introduction 9 (1st ed. 2017).

[27] Id. at 10.

[28] Daniel Rodgers, The Uses and Abuses of "Neoliberalism," Dissent Mag. (2018), https://www.dissentmagazine.org/article/uses-and-abuses-neoliberalism-debate.

[29] Id. at 101.

[30] See Jedd Legum & Rebecca Crosby. These 13 Corporations Have Spent $15 Million Supporting Anti-Abortion Politicians since 2016, Popular Info. (May 4, 2022), https://popular.info/p/these-13-corporations-have-spent.

whether they wish to continue their pregnancy or not. The "choice" framing has been criticized as it does not consider the other barriers, including financial, social, religious, and geographical factors that impact an individual's ability to make choices. Instead, it implies (by design) that every woman can enter the marketplace of options and pay for whatever option she chooses – a neoliberal approach that prioritizes private relationships and is contingent on the possession of resources. The blind spots of the choice framework are evident in *Harris v. McRae*, where the Supreme Court of the United States held that the Hyde Amendment, which blocked the use of Medicaid funding for abortions in most circumstances, was constitutional because it did not impinge on choice, given that it was poverty, not state action, that impeded a woman from having an abortion.[31] This case had devastating effects and led to the denial of abortion care for scores of individuals who were left to the devices of private law – particularly those who are low-income people, young people, and racial and ethnic minorities.[32]

Due to the embrace of a pro-choice paradigm leaving individuals to fend for themselves, and in the absence of public law stepping in to protect reproductive rights, the reliance on private law and corporations to provide abortion care has increased. About 48.5 percent of Americans are covered by employer health plans,[33] and therefore rely on their employers for their health care, including access to reproductive health care. In their chapter in this volume, Chapter 10, *Employer-Sponsored Abortion Coverage: Private Law's Role in Reproductive Freedom*, Valarie K. Blake and Elizabeth Y. McCuskey analyze how a regime that fosters reliance on private relationships, particularly with one's employers, to provide reproductive health care continues to exclude those who are most in need of financial assistance, including those who do not receive health care coverage through their jobs, and those who are on Medicare, Medicaid, or are federal workers. This chapter also discusses how, for employees who may receive health care coverage from their employers, claiming that they have the right to "choice" is a falsity.

Data has shown that about 75 percent of employers only offer one health plan to their employees.[34] Moreover, what is covered within those plans is also left up to the

31 See Harris v. McRae, 448 U.S. 297, 316 (1980) ("The financial constraints that restrict an indigent woman's ability to enjoy the full range of constitutionally protected freedom of choice are the product not of governmental restrictions on access to abortions, but rather of her indigency").

32 Alina Salganicoff et al., The Hyde Amendment and Coverage for Abortion Services, Kaiser Fam. Found. (Mar. 5, 2021), https://www.kff.org/womens-health-policy/issue-brief/the-hyde-amendment-and-coverage-for-abortion-services/.

33 Health Insurance Coverage of the Total Population, Kaiser Fam. Found. (2021), https://www.kff.org/other/state-indicator/total-population/?currentTimeframe=0&selectedRows=%7B%22wrapups%22:%7B%22united-states%22:%7B%7D%7D%7D&sortModel=%7B%22colId%22:%22Location%22,%22sort%22:%22asc%22%7D.

34 2022 Employer Health Benefits Survey, Kaiser Fam. Found. (Oct. 27, 2022), https://www.kff.org/report-section/ehbs-2022-section-4-types-of-plans-offered/.

discretion of corporations.[35] Using the specific example of abortion, employers have near total discretion in their decision to cover abortion care or not, resulting in about 10 percent of all employees being covered by plans that exclude abortion care.[36] Corporations may also design plans with restrictions on service providers and impose cost-sharing arrangements that may impinge on an individual's choice-making. While some may argue that individuals "choose" to work at the firms and corporations they are at, most people may have no option but to accept the terms of coverage they are being provided.

12.4.2 *Hyper-Focus on Abortion and Disregard for the Right to Parent and Raise Children in Safe Environments*

One major critique of the mainstream movement for reproductive rights was that it did not address or grapple with the concept of "stratified reproduction" or the idea that reproductive labor is differently valued and rewarded based on where they fall in intersecting hierarchies of race, class, gender, and so forth.[37] Consequently, this movement ignored the demands of people who desired to become parents but faced significant barriers to doing so from the state.

This ignorance of the *right to parent* and the *right to raise one's children in safe and healthy environments* is mirrored by corporations. While they continue to signal their support for reproductive rights, their supports are inadequate for parents and parenthood. This is not shocking, given the anti-pregnancy environment in the United States, which is among the only developed nations not to mandate paid parental leave. Despite legislation such as the Pregnancy Discrimination Act, pregnancy discrimination is rampant, particularly in corporations. Research has shown that 23 percent of parents reported that they "considered leaving a job because of discrimination or lack of reasonable accommodations during a pregnancy."[38] In addition to being perpetrators of this type of discrimination, businesses have also lobbied against federal paid parental leave, and when they have supported it, they "have advocated for preemption from state and local standards by organizations that meet a minimum floor of coverage."[39]

[35] Chapter 10 in this volume.

[36] Michelle Long et al., Exclusion of Abortion Coverage from Employer-Sponsored Health Plans, Kaiser Fam. Found. (May 12, 2020), https://www.kff.org/womens-health-policy/issue-brief/exclusion-of-abortion-coverage-from-employer-sponsored-health-plans/.

[37] See Shellee Colen, "Like a Mother to Them": Stratified Reproduction and West Indian Childcare Workers and Employers in New York, in Conceiving the New World Order: The Global Politics of Reproduction 78 (Faye D. Ginsburg & Rayna Rapp eds., 1995).

[38] Voter Opinions on the Pregnant Workers Fairness Act, Nat'l Women's L. Ctr. (Oct. 2022), https://nwlc.org/wp-content/uploads/2022/10/NWLC-Pregnant-Workers-Fairness-Act-Morning-Consult-PPT-10.21.pdf.

[39] See Valarie Blake & Elizabeth McCuskey, Employer-Sponsored Reproduction, 124 Colum. L. Rev. 273, 323(2024) (quoting Letter from The ERISA Indus. Comm. to Deputy Director Joan Harrigan-Farrelly, the Letter from IBM to Deputy Dir. Joan Harrigan-Farrelly, and the

There are reports of corporations cutting parental leave, in response to inflationary pressures, while at the same time responding to *Dobbs* by creating new abortion benefits.[40] A survey by the Society for Human Resource Management (SHRM) found that organizations that had increased parental leave during the pandemic were now scaling back – and the number of organizations offering paid maternity leave dropped to 35 percent in 2022, from 53 percent in 2020.[41] During the same period, the number of corporations granting paid paternity dropped as well – from 44 percent to 27 percent.[42] These rates indicate a return to pre-pandemic levels, showing that gains, in terms of progressive parental leave policies that were achieved during the pandemic, were short-lived and not consolidated. Additionally, it shows that corporations may be expanding abortion provisions in response to the political moment but may scale these back in a few years when attention on this subject reduces.

All of these examples of such seemingly inconsistent behavior show just how, in the absence of public law providing adequate reproductive supports to parents and children, corporations are left to fill the gaps and are afforded a wide amount of flexibility and discretion in their approaches.

12.4.3 *Accounting for Intersectional Harms*

The RJ movement was conceptualized by Black women activists in 1994 and broadened in scope by women of color coalitions. Women of color groups, who were originally seen as objects of reproductive control, demonstrated the power in their collective organizing work that was rooted in the needs of their communities. The RJ movement's strengths lie in its understanding that "the impacts of race, class, gender, and sexual identity oppressions are not additive but integrative. For each individual and each community, the effects of these impacts will be different, but they share some of the basic characteristics of intersectionality: universality, simultaneity, and interdependence."[43] In this way, it does not only address women of color but also looks at how issues intersect with one another, thereby impacting the reproductive lives of people.

In the aftermath of *Dobbs*, any assessment of corporate reproductive politics failed to focus on groups of individuals or workers who were situated at the intersections of

Letter from HR Pol'y Ass'n to Deputy Dir. Joan Harrigan-Farrelly), https://ssrn.com/abstract=4388974.

40 Brit Morse, Women to Pay the Price as Companies Cut Parental Leave Benefits and Abortion Trigger Bans Take Effect, Inc. (Sept. 9, 2022), https://www.inc.com/brit-morse/abortion-trigger-bans-parental-leave-benefits.html.

41 Simon Read, Employers in the US Are Cutting Back on Parental Leave, Survey Shows, World Econ. F. (Oct. 3, 2022), https://www.weforum.org/agenda/2022/10/maternity-paternity-parental-leave-employers/#:~:text=The%20number%20of%20organizations%20offering,foster%20is%20also%20becoming%20rarer.

42 Id.

43 Ross & Solinger, supra note 26, at 75.

different identities and were sidelined or excluded by "reproductive rights" politics. In other words, some of the most vulnerable people did not receive priority or protection from corporations. An example of this can be seen in the case of independent contractors.

Several corporations such as Uber and Lyft have been at the forefront of a battle to classify their workers (particularly workers for rideshare companies, delivery service, etc.) as independent contractors instead of employees. This dualism has been powerfully critiqued as creating precarious working conditions in terms of pay and working conditions, as well as disrupting worker collectivities.[44] In the aftermath of *Dobbs*, various corporations held that independent contractors were excluded from receiving abortion benefits by corporations. While these policies implicate a larger issue of worker misclassification, in the short run, it may lead to denying individuals crucial reproductive supports they may need.

For instance, Amazon's US$4,000 reimbursement for travel expenses only applies to those US employees who are enrolled in employer-sponsored health plans, thereby excluding about 115,000 delivery drivers. This also excludes Amazon's 2.9 million gig workers who work on the Amazon Flex app and thousands of Amazon warehouse employees who work under twenty hours a week, on a so-called flex schedule, or receive Medicaid as their health insurance.[45] In corporations such as Amazon, Uber, and Doordash, independent contractors are often the most vulnerable workers. For instance, the average income of Amazon delivery workers is about US$43,207 per year or about US$21 per hour.[46] The average cost of an in-clinic first-trimester abortion before *Dobbs* was estimated to be about US$800,[47] which in itself (if paid out of pocket) would amount to the wages earned in a full week by an independent contractor – not counting the travel costs, costs of lodging, child care, and other related costs. This cost may be prohibitively high and have dire consequences for individuals, particularly those who may also have caregivers and breadwinners. The corporate decision to leave out gig workers earning minimum wage may put abortion out of bounds for many individuals, with Hispanic and Black people being disproportionately impacted.[48]

[44] See Veena Dubal, Wage Slave or Entrepreneur?: Contesting the Dualism of Legal Worker Identities, 105 Cal. L. Rev. 101 (2017).

[45] Lauren K. Gurley, Amazon's Abortion Travel Benefit Doesn't Include Its Most Vulnerable Workers, Motherboard (May 3, 2022), https://www.vice.com/en/article/7kbnpd/amazons-abortion-travel-benefit-doesnt-include-its-most-vulnerable-workers.

[46] Clare Mulroy, How Much Do Amazon Delivery Drivers Make? Annual and Hourly Wage Breakdown, USA Today (Nov. 3, 2022), https://www.usatoday.com/story/money/careers/2022/10/24/how-much-do-amazon-drivers-make/10350464002/.

[47] See Attia, How Much Does an Abortion Cost?, Planned Parenthood (Apr. 29, 2022), https://www.plannedparenthood.org/blog/how-much-does-an-abortion-cost.

[48] Risa Gelles-Watnick & Monica Anderson, Racial and Ethnic Differences Stand Out in the U.S. Gig workforce, Pew Rsch. Ctr. (Dec. 15, 2021), https://www.pewresearch.org/short-reads/2021/12/15/racial-and-ethnic-differences-stand-out-in-the-u-s-gig-workforce/.

As seen above, some corporations seemingly ignored the needs of their most vulnerable workers. A similar example can be seen in the context of unionizing employees who have received threats that their reproductive benefits would be lost for union organizing.[49] This selective approach was possible due to the existing lack of public law protections and regulations in support of these workers, thereby allowing for conditions of precarity to prevail.

12.5 RESEARCH AGENDA

This chapter has shown how and why pro-choice corporations have participated in reproductive politics in the aftermath of *Dobbs* and has analyzed the shortcomings of private law in providing important reproductive health care services, in the absence of adequate state-funded supports. That said, there are several gaps in the literature on corporate involvement in reproductive politics which, if filled, may help us adequately assess the value of private law specifically in achieving the goals set out by the RJ movement.

Some open questions that may be explored in potential research are explored below.

12.5.1 *Corporate Action on Reproductive Rights*

At the outset, there is a lack of data at the national level that analyzes how corporations are responding to issues of RJ in the post-*Dobbs* landscape. Researchers can conduct a comprehensive analysis of how corporations responded to the ruling in *Dobbs*, and where they stand on reproductive rights and RJ issues. This analysis could include examining factors that may have influenced corporate decision-making in this realm. Some important factors to consider include whether the corporation is public or private, the size of the corporation taking the action, the state in which the corporation is headquartered, the gender and racial makeup of the Board of Directors, and if the corporation provides campaign finance to antiabortion policymakers.

Additional research is also required to assess the impact of these political stances on different stakeholders, including employees, shareholders, investors, and consumers. For instance, Adrjan et al. found that job satisfaction appeared to have declined among workers at firms announcing abortion benefits, especially for workers in male-dominated jobs.[50] This study leaned toward accepting a finding that this may be caused due to a newfound political misalignment, and there could

[49] Alisha Humphrey, Starbucks's Abortion Promises for Workers Are PR Stunts. We Want a Union Contract, Jacobin (Aug. 11, 2022), https://jacobin.com/2022/08/starbucks-abortion-transgender-health-care-promises-pr-stunt-union-contract.

[50] See Adrjan et al., supra note 19.

be a vocal minority of workers who are angered by these announcements while the "silent majority" of existing employees do not change their opinions. Despite the reason behind the decline in job satisfaction, it might be interesting to study how corporations respond to such a dip in job satisfaction or other variables such as worker productivity.

More broadly, this research may help us compare the approaches taken by different corporations and better understand motivations underlying private action and corporate decision-making.

12.5.2 *Legal Risks and Liabilities*

Private action is also subject to the law and is significantly shaped by the laws of the state it is conducted in. In light of the fact that abortion is not legal in several states, private action by corporations is under scrutiny. For starters, corporations were warned of criminal and civil liabilities for providing benefits such as travel stipends for employees in states that banned abortion.[51] The provision of these benefits is also accompanied by privacy risks for employers under state and federal law. Recently, there were reports that a Republican Commissioner of the Equal Employment Opportunity Commission (EEOC) opened up at least three discrimination probes into companies providing abortion-related travel benefits, alleging that they were discriminating against pregnant and disabled workers by providing different treatment to those seeking reproductive care.[52] As these risks play out, it would be valuable to have a state-by-state analysis of lawsuits and corporate responses to liability, lawsuits, and the strategies they adopt to protect themselves and their employees. It would also be important to keep an eye out for how corporations deal with stakeholders they consider "disposable." For instance, would corporations protect certain classes of workers more than others if they were implicated in lawsuits arising out of *Dobbs*? It would also be interesting to study whether there is an increase or decrease in corporate action in the reproductive rights space in response to activity in the legal realm.

12.5.3 *Normative Involvement of Corporations in Reproductive Politics*

The truth is that regardless of one's assessment of the harms and benefits of corporate participation in reproductive politics, it is likely to continue, motivated by the

[51] Daniel Wiessner, Legal Clashes Await U.S. Companies Covering Workers' Abortion Costs, Reuters (June 27, 2022), https://www.reuters.com/world/us/legal-clashes-await-us-companies-covering-workers-abortion-costs-2022-06-26/.

[52] Ari Blaff, Equal Employment Opportunity Commissioner Opens Discrimination Probes into Companies That Fund Abortion Travel, Nat'l. Rev. (Nov. 14, 2023), https://www.nationalreview.com/news/equal-employment-opportunity-commissioner-opens-discrimination-probes-into-companies-that-fund-abortion-travel/.

reasons outlined in Section 12.2 of this chapter. One important question for RJ advocates and scholars is regarding the normative involvement of corporations in reproductive politics. How can private law step in to offset the harms created in states where there are legislative and administrative barriers to accessing reproductive health care? Is it sufficient for corporations to merely increase attention on social issues by taking public stances, and implementing internal policies? If not, what does an expanded vision look like?

Movement actors must also weigh in on the type of economic support that is desirable from corporations. What type of economic involvement should corporations have, and what are acceptable conditions attached to providing such support? At the same time, what are the harms of allowing corporations to co-opt progressive politics?

Finally, researchers could assess the long-term impact of corporations' involvement in reproductive politics on public perception, corporate reputation, and social change, and examine the sustainability of corporations' commitments to RJ over time and their alignment with broader corporate practices.

13

Privatizing the Creation of Equity in Women's Health

Thomas W. Williams

13.1 INTRODUCTION

Examining the role of private law in health care systems and delivery requires some consideration of the corporation and private ordering's impact on US health affairs.[1] Corporate law's structure allows individuals with shared interests to pool resources and share governance through formal agreements recognized by the state.[2] The individuals forming entities can further negotiate internal contractual relationships through bylaws, shareholder agreements, indemnifications, and other instruments. Entities can also enter into contractual relationships with individuals and other organizations – creating networks of physicians, integrating health care systems, or forming binding relationships with pharmaceutical companies through contract. In recent years, corporate form has provided the foundation for the creation of a wide range of companies focused on tech-based health care interventions.

Ida Tin, a serial entrepreneur, coined the term "FemTech" in 2016.[3] Since then, the market has grown at a staggering clip, and it appears that it will continue to at a similar rate.[4] Tin used FemTech to refer to a wide range of products and

[1] Inst. of Med., Committee on Implications of For-Profit Enterprise in Health Care, For-Profit Enterprise in Health Care (Bradford H. Gray ed., 1986).

[2] Asaf Raz, Why Corporate Law Is Private Law, 25 U. Pa. J. Bus. L. 981 (2023) (arguing that despite reliance on statutes for formation, corporate law belongs squarely under the umbrella of private law).

[3] Hannah Ward-Glenton, Meet the Woman Who Invented a Whole New Subsection of Tech Set to Be Worth $1 Trillion Dollars, CNBC (Mar. 6, 2023), https://www.cnbc.com/2023/03/06/meet-the-woman-who-invented-a-whole-new-subsection-of-tech-set-to-be-worth-1-trillion.html#:~:text=Ida%20Tin%20created%20the%20term%20%E2%80%9CFemTech%E2%80%9D%20in%202016.&text=Clue-,Ida%20Tin%20wanted%20to%20study%20art%20at%20college%20when%20she,worth%20more%20than%20%241%20trillion.

[4] Emma Kemble et al., The Dawn of the FemTech Revolution, McKinsey & Co. (Feb. 2021), https://www.mckinsey.com/industries/healthcare/our-insights/the-dawn-of-the-femtech-revolution (estimating a market size of FemTech at over one trillion dollars by 2030).

technologies "designed to support and advance women's health care."[5] Under this umbrella, she includes "fertility solutions, period and fertility tracking apps, reproductive system health care, women's sexual wellness products, pregnancy and nursing care [products], period care goods, as well as at-home fertility monitoring devices and general healthcare [products]."[6] When she coined the term, she was founder and CEO of Clue, a Berlin-based start-up. Creating the term was strategic; it was an effort to focus investors on this private market aimed at correcting for the lack of consumer goods and services devoted to women's health needs.

FemTech is a form of tech-enabled private enterprise that is centered on private entities' ability to create innovative solutions to problems. The market has led to broad expansion of private funding and research in women's health through entities focused on the overlooked needs of women.[7] Most FemTech firms are focused on the reproductive health needs of women during their prime reproductive years. Products and services include period tracking apps, such as Clue,[8] fertility apps, and focused telehealth solutions.[9] Opportunities for the expansion of the FemTech market include products focused on menopause and nonreproductive health care needs of these consumers.

This essay proceeds in three parts. Section 13.2 will focus on the rationale behind the creation of FemTech as a market and its intersection with limited investment in women's health care research. Section 13.3 will consider the difficulties associated with the multiple-purpose private entities. Section 13.4 will discuss the limitations private ordering faces as a response to health care inequities with a focus on (Section 13.4.1) how funding impacts private ordering and (Section 13.4.2) how the value of consumer data and, in some cases, state laws undermine privacy goals, and the ways both can dilute private law efforts to remedy health care resource gaps.

13.2 FEMTECH RATIONALE

In women's health, FemTech has emerged as a private ordering-based solution for women's unmet health needs. The term "FemTech" refers to a subset of companies focused on "technology-enabled, consumer-centric products and solutions."[10] Like other markets, FemTech companies rely on basic corporate law as the foundation for introducing market-based solutions to consumers. The consumers they target

5 About Clue, Clue, https://helloclue.com/about-clue (last accessed 2023).

6 Id.

7 Kemble et al., supra note 4.

8 Tin founded Clue; their Period Tracking Plus product provides services including broad menstrual tracking and analysis. Clue Period Tracking Plus Explained, Clue, helloclue.com/articles/how-to-use-clue/clue-period-tracking-plus-explained (last accessed 2023).

9 According to its website, Maven claims to provide "[o]ne inclusive integrated benefit platform supporting every path to parenthood." Get a Personalized Demo, Maven Clinic, https://www.mavenclinic.com/contact/us-for-a-personalized-demo (last accessed 2023).

10 Kemble et al., supra note 4.

have been seeking reliable health-related products traditional markets have overlooked or devalued for decades.[11] Because of this FemTech is unique. A large number of FemTech firms attempt to balance goals that are generally considered in tension with one another – maximizing profits and returns for investors while at the same time creating and/or maximizing social good.[12] Despite developments in corporate law that attempt to ease these tensions, they remain in play for many FemTech companies. Relatively recent adoption of new corporate forms[13] and emerging legal scholarship[14] are pushing toward structures that ensure firms' ability to maintain multiple purposes. But FemTech firms must look to private law more generally to ensure firms balance profit and corporate social responsibility goals.

Private markets rely on public law and related public policy decisions. In their work, Private Actors in Public Markets, Robert Hockett and Saule Omarova explore the link between private markets and public law noting that "… states and markets are not 'separate but equal' – they are inseparable and deeply interconnected parts of the nation's economic organism."[15] FemTech companies extract value from gaps in existing markets serving women's health needs.[16] These gaps are often in part due to policy choices made by government and policymakers. Examples include funding and research priorities.[17] Public law and public health's concern with disparate allocation of limited health care resources initially focused on racial inequities.[18] A focus on similar inequities related to sex and gender followed soon after.[19]

The long-standing failure to prioritize research into basic questions related to women's health has left our understanding of it decades behind that of men's health.[20] Basic questions overlooked in women's health include areas in which differentials in diagnostics and outcomes continue. Reproductive health is one area

[11] Chloe E. Bird, Underfunding of Research in Women's Health Issues Is the Biggest Missed Opportunity in Health Care, RAND Corp. (Feb. 11, 2022), https://www.rand.org/pubs/commentary/2022/02/underfunding-of-research-in-womens-health-issues-is.html.

[12] Min Yan, Corporate Social Responsibility versus Shareholder Value Maximization: Through the Lens of Hard and Soft Law, 40 Nw. J. Int'l. L. & Bus. 47 (2019).

[13] Del. General Corporation Law Title 8, Ch. 1 § 362.

[14] Emilie Aguirre, Beyond Profit, 54 U.C. Davis L. Rev. 2077 (2021) (making the claim that for dual-purpose entities further constriction on profit maximization is required at the point of incorporation to allow them to retain that dual purpose over the long term).

[15] Robert C. Hockett & Saule T. Omarova, Public Actors in Private Markets: Toward a Developmental Finance State, 93 Wash. U. L. Rev. 103 (2015).

[16] See Michael Silverstein & Kate Sayre, The Female Economy, Harv. Bus. Rev. (Sept. 2009), hbr.org/2009/09/the-female-economy.

[17] Bird, supra note 11.

[18] About the Office of Minority Health, Off. of Minority Health (2022), minorityhealth.hhs.gov/about-office-minority-health.

[19] The Office of Research on Women's Health: A History of Fostering Diversity and Inclusion in Biomedical Research, Office of Research on Women's Health, Nat'l Inst. of Health (Dec. 5, 2023), orwh.od.nih.gov/about/mission-history/office-research-womens-health-history-fostering-diversity-and-inclusion.

[20] Paula A. Johnson et al., Sex-Specific Medical Research: Why Women's Health Can't Wait: A Report of the Mary Horrigan Connors Center for Women's Health & Gender Biology at

in which there have been relatively few attempts to understand medical science as it applies to women. Health research institutions tasked, at least in part, with ensuring Americans' health and disseminating information to the public too often avoided research involving women in order to avoid the complexity presented by hormonal cycles[21] and to avoid research in women of childbearing age. Public health education campaigns then used the results of research excluding women, further entrenching problems for female patients.

To better understand where we need private ordering to fill gaps created by public law, look to those areas in which disparate investment in health care research and communication continues to impact women. Cardiac events are the number one cause of death for men and women in the United States. Cardiac arrest, however, presents differently in the two sexes.[22] While both men and women are likely to experience chest pain during events, women also commonly experience symptoms that occur less frequently in men. Had such symptomatology been (1) understood and (2) its indications been more widely disseminated, physicians and women would have been better equipped to recognize and treat those symptoms early, mitigating deaths attributable to cardiac arrest. Notable gender disparities exist across a number of other nonreproductive ailments, including Alzheimer's, lung cancer, and depression.[23]

Within reproductive health, similar trends are present. Only recently have medical recommendations acknowledged the role the fallopian tubes likely play in the development of advanced ovarian cancers.[24] Gaps in understanding the function and character of the placenta are also attributable to this lack of focus on research related to women's health.[25] Public understanding and dissemination of information

Brigham and Women's Hospital, Brigham and Women's Hosp. (2014), https://www.brighamandwomens.org/assets/bwh/womens-health/pdfs/connorsreportfinal.pdf.

21 Deborah Netburn, Researchers Avoid "Messy" Hormonal Female Mice. And That Hurts Women, L.A. Times (May 30, 2019), https://www.latimes.com/science/la-sci-emotional-stereotypes-about-women-20190530-story.html#:~:text=Scientists%20justified%20this%20exclusion%20by,women%2C%20like%20depression%20and%20PTSD.

22 Johnson et al., supra note 20. But see Lori Mosca et al., Sex/Gender Differences in Cardiovascular Disease Prevention; What a Difference a Decade Makes, Circulation (Nov. 2019), https://pubmed.ncbi.nlm.nih.gov/22064958/ (detailing positive developments in rates of death from cardiovascular disease).

23 Johnson et al., supra note 20.

24 Zeina Mohammed, More Physicians Are Calling for Fallopian Tube Removal to Prevent Ovarian Cancer, Bos. Globe (Feb. 23, 2023), https://www.statnews.com/2023/02/23/ovarian-cancer-tube-removal/. See also Nat'l Cancer Inst., Many Ovarian Cancers May Start in Fallopian Tubes, Study Finds, Cancer Current Blogs (Nov. 15, 2017), hwww.cancer.gov/news-events/cancer-currents-blog/2017/ovarian-cancer-fallopian-tube-origins.

25 Jocelyn Kaiser, NIH Sets Aside More Than $40 Million for Study of Human Placenta, Sci. Insider (Feb. 27, 2015), https://www.science.org/content/article/nih-sets-aside-more-40-million-study-human-placenta (documenting the funding that eventually provided for the Human Placenta Project).

related to menopause is another.[26] This is but a partial list; when considered in totality, it represents a hollowed-out middle in the collective women's health knowledge.

Such gender-based gaps in research and public understanding of women's health have received more attention in the past several decades. Despite this attention, those gaps remain frustratingly salient.[27] Identifying and correcting for gaps in women's health require women's participation as research subjects and placing women at the center of male-dominated scientific institutions. When women are engaged in these ways within science, research that can change diagnosis and treatment emerges.

13.3 THE MULTIPLE PURPOSE CORPORATE CONUNDRUM

Elevating engagement with problems in women's health should not be limited to machinations of public law and health policy. Private law enabled through corporate structure creates a nimble infrastructure through which to understand and respond to the health needs of groups marginalized by medical research and existing health care infrastructures, including women.

Many FemTech companies seek to achieve dual, or more, purposes.[28] Those purposes include (1) bettering the overall picture of women's health and (2) ensuring that the company itself remains a fiscally viable going concern. In the post-*Dobbs* era of women's health care, many FemTech companies have also made a public commitment to ensuring that women they serve in the United States are assured that the confidentiality of sensitive reproductive health data of consumers is protected.[29] Tin and the company she founded have noted the necessity of privacy as being central to the creation of the market.[30]

[26] Susan Dominus, Women Have Been Misled about Menopause, N.Y. Times (Feb. 1, 2023), www.nytimes.com/2023/02/01/magazine/menopause-hot-flashes-hormone-therapy.html (highlighting the broad misunderstanding of menopause among women).

[27] Cat Bohannon, Eve: How the Female Body Drove 200 Million Years of Human Evolution (2023) (providing a general analysis of the ways in which medical science has failed to center the female body in research).

[28] William Bratton, Framing a Purpose for Corporate Law, 39 J. Corp L. 713 (2014) (explaining the idea of dual purpose and going on to examine the tensions between social welfare and shareholder maximization).

[29] Despite assurances, a 2022 review of popular period tracking apps found that "18 out of 25 reproductive health apps and wearable devices that Mozilla investigated for privacy and security practices received a *Privacy Not Included warning label. These findings raise concerns in the post-Roe landscape that data could be used by authorities to determine if users are pregnant, seeking abortion information or services, or crossing state lines to obtain an abortion." Post Roe v. Wade Era, Mozilla Labels 18 of 25 Popular Period and Pregnancy Tracking Tech with *Privacy Not Included Warning, Mozilla (Aug. 17, 2022), https://foundation.mozilla.org/en/blog/in-post-roe-v-wade-era-mozilla-labels-18-of-25-popular-period-and-pregnancy-tracking-tech-with-privacy-not-included-warning/.

[30] Clue, supra note 5.

Private ordering uses public law foundations to create stable relationships among groups of individuals with a shared purpose through various organizational forms. Following an organization's creation, private law paradigms begin to govern the relationships between owners of organizations and/or those in control of decision-making, such as boards or managing members. For example, corporate actors use contract law to create governance structures through documents that are often outside the purview of the general public. Stockholder agreements, LLC membership agreements, and similar documents often limit the ability and power of individual owners to sell their ownership interests through binding agreements, often including a right of first refusal. Controlling the ownership structure through these contractual agreements ensures owners are committed to the same goals. Firms also use contract law to mitigate risks associated with tort liability, limit or ensure employee rights, and protect trade secrets and other valuable information from disclosure. Tort liability also informs corporate governance, employee training and oversight, and entry into new markets.

Despite the ways in which private ordering allows individuals with shared interests to coalesce around a unifying idea or mission, commitment to that mission may evolve over time. Often, changes emerge from concerns regarding liquidity and capital access. In the context of entrepreneurship, access to sufficient capital is critical to success.[31] The recent collapse of Silicon Valley Bank laid bare how much small tech firms rely on ongoing capital access.[32] Capital access is also entangled with questions of governance, implicating organizational leadership's ability to adhere to multiple purposes. This can result in tension with additional purposes companies espouse, such as access to tools and services that better enable health equity, data privacy, or public benefit. Capital access also raises higher-level questions implicating race, gender, and class, notable among FemTech firms, given the large number that are female-owned.[33]

Aside from some well-capitalized FemTech firms like Clue, FemTech founders face substantial challenges to raising capital.[34] When companies are able to raise capital and scale, growth may further challenge a firm's ability to focus on non-monetary purposes such as protecting consumer privacy. Commentators and legal

[31] Access to Capital, U.S. Senate Comm. on Small Bus. & Entrepreneurship, www.sbc.senate.gov/public/index.cfm/accesstocapital (last accessed 2023).

[32] Rohan Goswami & Ari Levy, Silicon Valley Bank's Struggles Spell Further Trouble for Beleaguered Tech Startup Market, CNBC (Mar. 9, 2023), www.cnbc.com/2023/03/09/silicon-valley-banks-struggles-signal-more-trouble-for-tech-startups.html.

[33] Robert W. Fairlie & Alicia M. Robb, Disparities in Capital Access between Minority and Non-Minority-Owned Businesses: The Troubling Reality of Capital Limitations Faced by MBEs, Minority Bus. Dev. Agency (Jan. 2010), www.mbda.gov/sites/default/files/migrated/files-attachments/DisparitiesinCapitalAccessReport.pdf.

[34] Melissa Houston, The Challenges of Raising Capital for Business Owners in the FemTech Industry, Forbes Mag. (Sept. 29, 2021), https://www.forbes.com/sites/melissahouston/2021/09/29/the-challenges-of-raising-capital-for-business-owners-in-the-femtech-industry/.

scholars have already made the argument that women using FemTech applications' privacy interests have been fundamentally undermined. Two scholars have gone so far as to argue that we are at the origin point of a FemTech-enabled dystopia.[35]

13.4 THE LIMITS OF PRIVATE ORDERING SOLUTIONS

Questions related to the long-term durability of multiple purposes within organizations challenge the notion that FemTech, and other forms of private ordering, are an appropriate response to health care inequity.[36] This essay argues that FemTech steps in to mitigate a lack of attention to women's health in the public sphere. To do this, FemTech companies use public law to create privately ordered entities that can devote resources to such problems.[37] Asserting a reliance on private ordering to correct for a public law failure, however, also requires consideration of the risks it presents.

One risk, alluded to previously, relates to FemTech companies' for-profit status, despite more not-for-profit entities like Euki appearing on the market. Even when for-profit FemTech entities are dual purpose, focus on shareholder primacy and profit maximization may lead to the neglect of other named purposes. Scholars can point to many examples of multipurpose companies that lost their way, becoming solely or primarily interested in short-term return on investment as they grew.[38] For decades, these concerns have been raised as especially concerning within health care. Those concerns are becoming more urgent with private equity's increased investment in many areas of health care.[39] In segments of the industry where consumers face limited choices, which include women's health care, the concerns are arguably more pressing due to those limited choices.

When entrepreneurs secure funding, they often become beholden to the interests of investors or funders. Those interests almost always impact their governance structures. Funders' interests will sometimes be in tension with organizational values and principles, including those of FemTech companies that acknowledge multiple purposes.[40] At the same time, reasonable profits are important to ensuring a company's

35 Leah Fowler & Michael Ulrich,FemTech Dystopia, 75 Stan. L. Rev. 1233 (2023).

36 Jan-Willem Scheijgrond, How Can the Private Sector Help Advance Health Equity?, World Econ. F. (May 2, 2023), www.weforum.org/agenda/2023/05/how-can-the-private-sector-help-advance-health-equity/ (noting the need for health tech companies to play a role in the transformation of health care).

37 Kemble et al., supra note 4.

38 Aguirre, supra note 14.

39 Erin Fuse Brown & Mark Hall, Private Equity and the Corporatization of Health Care, 76 Stan L. Rev. 527 (2024).

40 Use of creative funding mechanisms that allow small firms to pick and choose investors can limit this impact. In spring 2023, Clue raised seven million euros through a call for community investment. About Clue, Clue Launches First-Ever Community Investment Round, Clue (Apr. 4, 2023), helloclue.com/articles/about-clue/clue-launches-first-ever-community-investment-round.

future and in FemTech, broader progress in women's health, even within a dual-purpose structure. Profits can be reinvested in research and other avenues that increase the value of the products and create broader benefits in the field.

Most funders' primary aim is either to recoup their investment or turn a profit. Banks seek to ensure that debt and interest are repaid, often securing their interests under UCC Article 9, which allows them to seize appropriately collateralized assets when a company's failure to pay principal and/or interest results in default. As a general rule, banks do not seek equity, but debt itself can impact governance.[41] Venture capital firms, individual shareholders, and other equity investors exert more direct pressure on a company, often in an effort to maximize returns on their investments. It would be normal to expect these players to seek to limit costs and increase revenue in an effort to maximize their individual financial returns. This will not always be the case; in recent years more shareholder and management activity has focused on questions of corporate social responsibility which remains a focus in corporate law discourse.[42]

Financial and governance obligations limit the choices of organizational leadership. These limits impact FemTech firms' ability to focus on non-fiscal purposes. Even firms primarily focused on social good require capital to meet basic needs. Capital is further required to scale activities of companies whose work creates a positive social impact. With respect to debt, obligations associated with funding are usually limited to liabilities that must be accounted for in cash flows and financial projections. Where investors are concerned, agreements create obligations that include equity ownership and/or creation of special classes of equity, which can redefine firm governance. Agreements often provide investors with Board seats, or other powers, which can impact organizational priorities. Ensuring liquidity and access to capital requires companies to meet those obligations as consideration for the capital provided.[43] These provisions give investors the opportunity to force the hands of cash-hungry entrepreneurs in ways that can contradict purposes of health equity-focused, dual-purpose organizations, including values important, if not critical, to many FemTech entrepreneurs and their companies and consumers.

13.4.1 *Privacy Concerns*

Another concern related to the tensions between financial interests and governance is tech-based entities' frequent reliance on unmitigated collection of consumer data

[41] Tomer S. Stein, Debt as Corporate Governance, 74 Hastings L.J. 1281 (2023).

[42] VC Funding: What to Expect, Silicon Valley Bank, https://www.svb.com/startup-insights/ready-to-raise/VC-funding-things-you-lose/#:~:text= Key%20Takeaways,your%20say%20in%20key%20decisions (last accessed 2023).

[43] Y Combinator, a well-known start-up accelerator provides for a five hundred-thousand-dollar investment in exchange for a 7 percent equity stake in the founders' company with incremental increases in equity stakes as the company raises additional money. Kristy Nathoo, The Y Combinator Deal, Y Combinator, https://www.ycombinator.com/deal (last accessed 2023).

to augment corporate value. As author Shoshana Zuboff notes in her 2018 book, a new paradigm has emerged in which consumer data has become the end product for major companies, including Google and Facebook.[44] Similar concerns also exist within FemTech – there is enormous money to be made in selling consumer data. As these companies grow, they will need more capital, and their ability to sell consumer data to access it can become central to those efforts.

More concerning than general data collection is the nascent industry's collection of reproductive health data of women of childbearing age. In FemTech Dystopia, authors Leah R. Fowler and Michael R. Ulrich extend Zuboff's thesis about economic concerns of such data collection to encompass fears of state action based on such data in the post-*Dobbs* era. The authors raise concerns regarding state use of reproductive health care data stored by FemTech companies in abortion-related prosecutions. Similar questions around seizure of individual data by state actors have previously been raised. At one time, whether Homeland Security had the ability to require individuals to unlock their phones to allow the agency to search their contents upon entry to the country was such a question. The answer – Homeland Security has the power to do so.[45]

The concerns of Fowler and Ulrich are of critical import, but there are reasonable questions to raise in response to them. In recent cases brought in state court by prosecutors where abortion bans have been issued, they have used data from non-FemTech online platforms to prosecute women for obtaining abortions and those who assist them. In July 2023, a Nebraska court sentenced a forty-two-year-old woman guilty of "tampering with human remains, false reporting and providing an abortion after at least 20 weeks of gestation" under the state's abortion statute.[46] The prosecutions' case, however, relied not on data pulled from a period tracker or other FemTech-related consumer data but on messages the parties exchanged on the social media application Facebook Messenger. This is likely in part because it is easier to isolate cases for investigation where there is direct communication related to prohibited conduct. Information indicative of pregnancy status can also be sourced by the state through data seemingly unrelated to reproductive health, but that nonetheless provides highly predictive indicators of pregnancy status.[47]

[44] Soshana Zuboff, The Age of Surveillance Capitalism: The Fight for a Human Future at the New Frontier of Power (2019).

[45] Tatum Hunter, How to Prevent Customs Agents from Copying Your Phone's Content, Wash. Post (Sept. 18, 2022), www.washingtonpost.com/technology/2022/09/18/phone-data-privacy-customs/.

[46] Margery A. Beck, Nebraska Mother Sentenced to 2 Years in Prison for Giving Abortion Pills to Pregnant Daughter, Associated Press (Sept. 22, 2023), https://apnews.com/article/abortion-charges-nebraska-sentence.

[47] Manuela López Restrepo, Does Your Rewards Card Know If You're Pregnant? Privacy Experts Sound the Alarm, NPR (Aug. 13, 2022), www.npr.org/2022/08/13/1115414467/consumer-data-abortion-roe-wade-pregnancy-test-rewards-card-target-walgreens.

Utilization of entire FemTech consumer data sets to seek out parties for prosecution would be more onerous than using explicit Facebook messages. Doing so would require the state to analyze enormous amounts of data held by companies, and, prior to being able to do so, access that data. In the future, quantum computing and advanced algorithmic programs will make analysis of such large data sets much easier. In the near term, however, it is easier to imagine FemTech tracked data's use in cases where individualized data is sought through court order and used to convince juries of intent to commit a crime, especially where questions of whether a woman knew she was pregnant exist. Many FemTech companies claim they already have strong data privacy protections in place, though those claims have been questioned.[48] Other companies, in response to privacy concerns, have taken measures they claim will better protect user data. One example of such measures involves US companies moving their operations to Europe, in an attempt to subject them to the more robust data privacy standards required under the General Data Protection Regulation, or the GDPR. The GDPR, however, fails to protect user data from subpoenas and other attempts to access records by US courts and law enforcement personnel, which is at the root of post-*Dobbs* concerns.[49]

At the end of the day, companies control the ways in which they engage with consumer data – holding it, selling it to third parties, or using it internally to create better products. In the current era, companies do not enter into contractual agreements with consumers that require them to protect consumer data from unconsented releases, whether to law enforcement or third parties. Instead, companies request users to acknowledge privacy policies. Companies can be more aggressive in placing formal obligations on their organizations; they can create legally binding and enforceable contractual terms which serve consumers whose data they access and store for research and other purposes. At the same time, these companies can mitigate the risk of financial harms and reputational damage that might result in the event of a breach of their promises to keep user data confidential. Firms that want to put their money where their corporate purpose is can seek insurance and utilize internal policies and compliance mechanisms to mitigate the risks associated with adoption of such contractual obligations.

Consumers are increasingly concerned with questions of data security. In response, Apple has begun to bend its operations toward ensuring consumer data is protected, and they have paid special attention to health-related data. As is the case in many other areas, while there are minimal protections for consumers under state and federal law, companies can use contract law to legally constrain the ways in which they collect and use sensitive consumer data.

48 Angela Petkovic, The FemTech Problem: How Dobbs Shifted the Data Privacy Landscape for Period-Tracking Apps, JTIP Blog (Apr. 19, 2023), jtip.law.northwestern.edu/2023/04/19/the-femtech-problem-how-dobbs-shifted-the-data-privacy-landscape-for-period-tracking-apps/.

49 Id.

There is an obvious tension between FemTech firms' data collection practices and claims that they will ensure data privacy. A more nuanced tension exists between data privacy concerns and the necessity of large data sets to better understand many areas of women's health. Data is an essential element in elevating the science in the field. These intersecting tensions between data collection, privacy, and research are likely to leave mindful consumers and the FemTech companies seeking to serve them at an impasse. Providing an individual's data can, in addition to being a goldmine for companies, collectively advance our understanding of women's health.

There is a case to be made that the women most vulnerable, marginalized, and likely to be surveilled by law enforcement are also the most likely to need insights that existing research and health systems fail to provide. These individuals would seem to have no reasonable alternative to advance their health other than subjecting themselves to greater surveillance through FemTech usage in an effort to create better health outcomes for the whole until public law does a better job of ensuring that for them.

13.4.2 *Reconsidering Private Law Tools for FemTech Governance*

Until states begin adopting binding statutory structures to ensure entities fulfill multiple purpose obligations in perpetuity, private law provides viable routes to create long-term obligations that outlive founders and protect the interests of consumers. These private law tools can also be used to devise mechanisms that leave room for internal reordering through private law structures and internal organization to entrench dual and multiple-purpose regimes for women's health firms.

Shadow governance may provide an innovative means to ensure commitment to multiple purposes without further public law intervention. In their article Shadow Governance, authors Yaron Nili and Cathy Hwang define shadow governance as "non-charter, non-bylaw governance documents [that] express a corporation's commitment to and process on issues."[50] The shadow governance docket includes committee charters, governance guidelines, and codes of conduct. These more innovative and less tested mechanisms should be utilized by emerging FemTech firms to ensure a long-term commitment to their indicated corporate purposes. That being said, these types of assurances of purpose may be easily unwound after changes in Board and/or voting structure following investment. They do not require the same votes to nullify or change bylaws or other organizational governance documents, which can better entrench purpose.

Firms can also use basic contract law to entrench their multiple corporate purposes across their contracting activity and in their internal affairs. For example, companies can require Board members to agree to be bound by contractual terms at

[50] Yaron Nili & Cathy Hwang, Shadow Governance, 108 Cal. L. Rev. 1097 (2020).

the start of their terms that require coinsideration of all purposes of the company in decision-making. One challenge with this approach is drafting language concretely defining something as amorphous as a "value." Values shift with time, much like language, reflecting culture and other normative elements. Even explicit terms like data privacy will shift with time and public expectation. Establishing a contractual framework that aligns the concerns of FemTech companies with their obligations to consumers and third parties, and also provides some flexibility to meet the requirements of lenders and investors, is critical to cementing multiple purposes of emerging entities in the absence of statutory mechanisms. Where possible, these companies should be selective in choosing funding sources, with an eye toward ensuring alignment between corporate purposes and funder interests. Legally binding contractual agreements with funders can further entrench such alignment. In the absence of changes to public corporate law, FemTech entities must look to private law to both appropriately protect consumers and further women's health.

FemTech is by no means a panacea. It will not correct all of the problems in women's health. What FemTech has done, however, is to acknowledge the role private law and, by extension, private markets may need to play in correcting for extensive histories of government inaction to address the problems women face with respect to health care.

Acknowledging the limitations facing FemTech entities is a necessary step toward challenging public law and private markets to fill those gaps to create greater gender equity in accessing appropriate health care resources.

PART IV

How Private law Can and Cannot Control Costs

Introduction

Christopher Robertson

Perhaps more than in any other domain of US health policy, private law is central to who pays for health care at what prices. Remarkably, almost the entire structure is built around the privity of contract. With some narrow exceptions, physicians are generally free to choose whether to provide care to any given patient, and thus free to set the terms of those agreements. This means that physicians can choose whether to join any particular insurer's network, agreeing to their contracts.

State and federal governments provide health insurance coverage for 36 percent of the population directly, and they also pay indirectly for other care through tax subsidies.[1] But the coverage is often incomplete, leaving individual patients bearing substantial cost exposures, in the form of copays, deductibles, and coinsurance, where any obligation to pay (at the point of service, or later as debt) is also governed by contract. And of course, about 11 percent of Americans remain uninsured, leaving them seeking care in *quid pro quo* settings, if at all.

It is important to approach these questions not just at the level of the contract, but with a view for the competitiveness of the entire market, which will set the terms of any contract. The federal government is an important bulk purchaser of health care. This market power allows it to secure lower prices than the private payors, and also to set reimbursement rates in ways that spill over to the private market. In building their networks of providers, private payors tend to haggle over the multiplier over the federal reimbursement rates for particular procedures. We have private law in the shadow of a public giant.

In Chapter 14, "Federalism, Private Law, and Medical Debt," Erin C. Fuse Brown explores the issue of medical debt in the United States, focusing on the interplay between federal and state laws in addressing this problem. Medical debt is a significant burden for millions of Americans, impacting their financial well-being

[1] K. Keisler-Starkey et al., Health Insurance Coverage in the United States: 2022, U.S. Census Bureau (Sept. 12, 2023), https://www.census.gov/library/publications/2023/demo/p60-281.html.

and health outcomes, and it worsens racial and ethnic disparities as well. Federal laws like the Dodd-Frank Act and Affordable Care Act aim to protect consumers from medical debt through the Consumer Financial Protection Bureau (CFPB) and IRS regulations. Yet, these measures are limited in scope and enforcement, leaving gaps in protections for individuals. States have enacted various laws to address medical debt, including setting standards for financial assistance, limiting collection practices, and empowering individuals to sue for violations. Fuse Brown encourages more private enforcement mechanisms like Unfair and Deceptive Acts or Practices (UDAP) laws to increased accountability for health care providers, debt collectors, and government agencies.

In Chapter 15, "Paying for Health Care and Private Law's Internal Point of View," James Toomey explicates the internal logic of legal obligations to pay for health care where the prices are not prespecified, and Toomey uses this as a case study for a larger argument against the idea that legal reasoning is merely a mask for policy-making. Toomey advocates for taking the language and concepts of private law seriously, arguing that it's possible and beneficial to reason about them to address novel situations like opaque health care pricing. Traditional contract law enforces agreed-upon prices, but in cases where no price was agreed upon, courts can determine a "reasonable" price. Toomey argues for a certain conceptual unity behind the various domains of private law, here suggesting that contract law can draw from tort law, which uses "reasonableness" to determine damages. Toomey suggests this approach aligns with the core principles of contract law (enforcing agreements) and promotes consistency with tort law's treatment of reasonableness. It also avoids policy-driven rules that might conflict with basic legal concepts.

Jackson Williams also picks up the theme of litigating health care costs but from a practical rather than conceptual approach. His chapter title reveals the challenge: "Health Law's Sheathed Sword: Why Hasn't Civil Litigation Dented Health Care Costs?" (Chapter 16). Not all excessive prices are legally actionable (since again, they are typically based on freely agreed contracts), but some clear cases exist, like antitrust violations, upcoding, and excessive billed charges.

While some payer-initiated cost containment litigation does happen, it has not been systematic. The payors – private health insurance companies – would be an obvious candidate to pursue this litigation against providers, but they face collective action problems – it's hard for them to coordinate and share the costs of litigation. Williams identifies tools that may help, including class actions, involvement of state attorneys general, and patron-sponsored litigation (e.g., foundations funding lawsuits). In the search for the right champion to wield this "sword," unions and other employee-based groups may have better-aligned interests.

Jamie S. King's Chapter 17 is titled "The Canary in the Coal Mine: Private Antitrust Law and New Dynamics in Health Care Markets." She argues that antitrust enforcement in health care has not kept pace with market changes, leading to insufficient competition and high prices. Public enforcers struggle to address new consolidation strategies like vertical, cross-market, and cross-industry mergers. Private actors could bring cases challenging restrictive employment contracts or anticompetitive contract terms. Such private cases can illuminate complex market dynamics and gaps in public enforcement, leading to improved guidelines and interventions. For example, in a case involving Sutter Health, private plaintiffs challenged anticompetitive contracting practices, leading to a landmark settlement and influencing public enforcement. Likewise, in a case involving Envision Healthcare, the challenges to restrictive physician contracts brought attention to private equity's role in market consolidation.

Finally, Jessica Mantel's Chapter 18 explains, "Health Care Finance Law's Relational Bias." One classic challenge for contracting generally, and especially health care contracting in particular, is to align incentives of the provider and the payor (who at least theoretically represents the interests of the patient). A simple fee-for-service system may generate more services and more expensive services than patients need. Various payment reforms have been implemented, but Mantel identifies a particular challenge in the fragmentation of our health care system: If one insurer implements a payment reform, but other insurers implement different or no payment reforms, the providers receive mixed signals and may not change their behavior accordingly. Multi-Payer Alignment Initiatives (MPAIs) encourage voluntary coordination but are limited by low participation. Mantel argues for a public law framework to improve health care delivery, which could take the form of a mandatory cooperative scheme or single-payer system.

Altogether, these chapters evince the challenges of making a private law framework achieve its potential as applied in the real world of the US health care system. Whether examined in the pristine conceptual clarity of a 1:1 contract for services, or at the system-level perspective assessing the market power of providers and payors, the issues cannot be ignored.

14

Federalism, Private Law, and Medical Debt

Erin C. Fuse Brown[*]

14.1 INTRODUCTION

Medical debt is the largest form of consumer debt in collections, with US$88 billion recorded on credit reports, affecting roughly one in five US households.[1] Medical debt pushes millions into financial distress and is exacerbated by harsh collection practices to garnish wages, seize assets, place liens on homes, and reduce credit-worthiness. Concerned federal and state policymakers have pursued policies to protect consumers from medical debt.

Medical debt is a creature of private law, resulting from the contractual obligation by patients to pay for items and services provided by health care providers that are not covered by the patient's health insurance plan.[2] According to one account, public law is best suited to addressing diffuse problems where the costs are borne by a broad and undifferentiated public, while private law is better used to regulate concentrated costs borne by specific identifiable persons.[3] Public law's response is to tax, fine, and penalize conduct, whereas private law assigns liability for wrongful injuries to affected individuals.[4] Private law remedies can be the product of common law (torts, contracts, property) or legislation (statutory standards and remedies for private individuals).[5]

[*] Professor Fuse Brown acknowledges the excellent research assistance of Abayomi Jones MD, JD (GSU 2024).

[1] CFPB Estimates $88 Billion in Medical Bills on Credit Report, Consumer Fin. Prot. Bureau (Mar. 1, 2022), https://www.consumerfinance.gov/about-us/newsroom/cfpb-estimates-88-billion-in-medical-bills-on-credit-reports/.

[2] Wendy Netter Epstein, Price Transparency and Incomplete Contracts in Health Care, 67 Emory L. J. 1, 35 (2017).

[3] Aditi Bagchi, Other People's Contracts, 32 Yale J. on Regul. 211, 231 (2015).

[4] Id. at 236.

[5] Hanoch Dagan & Avihay Dorfman, Postscript to Just Relationships: Reply to Gardner, West, and Zipursky, 117 Colum. L. Rev. Online 261, 267 (2017) (describing fields such as employment

Consumer protection law writ large is best conceived of as a mixture of public and private laws. Most federal medical debt policies are forms of public law – namely administrative requirements imposed by government on health care and consumer finance entities. Nevertheless, significant gaps in the federal public law of medical debt persist, leaving an important role for states, particularly in the creation of private enforcement actions for violations of state consumer protections against medical debt. States have created both public law and private law protections that alter the patient's contractual obligation to pay medical debts, including prescribing standards for financial assistance, limiting the amounts providers may charge patients, barring certain collection actions, and empowering individuals to seek private remedies for violations.

The problem of medical debt is best addressed through combining federal and state, as well as public and private law approaches. Stronger national, public law standards to guard against medical debt are critical, but federal policy should retain a vital role for what states do well – policy innovation and filling the gaps in federal underenforcement through private remedies. Preserving a meaningful role for states and private law in consumer protection policy enhances separation of powers and serves as a check against federal regulatory failure.

14.2 THE PROBLEM OF MEDICAL DEBT AND ITS RACIAL INEQUITIES

The US burden of medical debt is extensive. Approximately 41 percent of adults, about 100 million individuals, currently carry medical debt totaling an estimated US$195 billion.[6] Medical debt has driven millions of people into financial distress through drained households' savings, garnished wages or liens on homes, damaged creditworthiness, delayed college or homebuying, or bankruptcy. Medical debt also worsens health as debtors forego essential health care and necessities, ration medications, or are denied care due to unpaid bills, ultimately leading to worse health outcomes.

The medical debt problem in the United States stems from two issues: unaffordable health care prices and aggressive debt collection practices. Uninsured patients are often charged prices that are significantly higher than the rates charged to government and commercial payers. Even individuals with health coverage are

law, consumer protection, and landlord-tenant law as private law despite that their doctrines are the product of statute and not common law).

6 Lunna Lopes et al., Health Care Debt in the U.S.: The Broad Consequences of Medical and Dental Bills, Kaiser Fam. Found. (June 16, 2022), https://www.kff.org/health-costs/report/kff-health-care-debt-survey/; Noam Levey, 100 Million People in America Are Saddled with Health Care Debt, Kaiser Fam. Found. Health News (June 16, 2022), https://kffhealthnews.org/news/article/diagnosis-debt-investigation-100-million-americans-hidden-medical-debt/.

not protected, as many are "underinsured" and unable to pay for their growing share of their health care costs through cost-sharing and deductibles.[7]

Harsh debt collection practices further exacerbate the problem of unmanageable medical bills. These practices include selling debts to collection agencies, suing patients, seeking foreclosure or liens on patients' homes, garnishing wages, seizing bank accounts and property, charging high interest rates, requiring up-front payment before providing additional care, and even seeking arrest for failing to appear in court for a debt collection hearing. Medical debt collection imposes significant financial, emotional, and health-related hardship for patients.

Unmanageable medical debt is associated with higher levels of stress, anxiety, and poorer health – often called the "financial toxicity" of unaffordable health care.[8]

Consumers who lack legal representation may find themselves ill-equipped to fight debt collection actions, which fill the dockets of state civil courts. According to one report, more than 70 percent of debt collection cases end in default judgment against the debtor, usually because the debtor did not respond to the action or show up in court.[9] Once a judgment is entered, the debt balloons from added court fees and accrued interest.

Medical debt disproportionately affects Black and Hispanic families, who historically have lower levels of wealth and health insurance coverage.[10] Medical debt is also more prevalent in Southern states that did not expand Medicaid, where nearly 60 percent of those who fall into the coverage gap are people of color.[11] Kaiser Family Foundation reports that 56 percent of Black adults and 50 percent of Hispanic adults have medical debt, compared with 37 percent of White adults.[12] One study found that Black adults were 2.6 times more likely to carry medical debt than their White counterparts, where differential incomes and insurance status

7 Sara R. Collins et al., State of U.S. Health Insurance in 2022, Commonwealth Fund (Sept. 29, 2022), https://www.commonwealthfund.org/publications/issue-briefs/2022/sep/state-us-health-insurance-2022-biennial-survey; Christopher T. Robertson, Exposed: Why Our Health Insurance Is Incomplete and What Can Be Done about It (2019).

8 Peter A. Ubel et al., Full Disclosure – Out-of-Pocket Costs as Side Effects, 369 New Engl. J. Med. 1484 (2014).

9 Pew Charitable Trs., How Debt Collectors Are Transforming the Business of State Courts (May 6, 2020), https://www.pewtrusts.org/en/research-and-analysis/reports/2020/05/how-debt-collectors-are-transforming-the-business-of-state-courts.

10 Berneta L. Haynes, The Racial Health and Wealth Gap: Impact of Medical Debt on Black Families, Nat'l Consumer L. Ctr. (Mar. 2022), https://www.nclc.org/images/pdf/medical-debt/RacialHealth-Rpt-2022.pdf.

11 Raymond Kluender et al., Medical Debt in the U.S., 2009–2020, 326 JAMA 250 (2021); Robin Rudowitz et al., How Many Uninsured Are in the Coverage Gap and How Many Could Be Eligible if All States Adopted the Medicaid Expansion?, Kaiser Fam. Found. (Mar. 31, 2023), https://www.kff.org/medicaid/issue-brief/how-many-uninsured-are-in-the-coverage-gap-and-how-many-could-be-eligible-if-all-states-adopted-the-medicaid-expansion/.

12 Lopes et al., supra note 6.

explained nearly one-fifth of the gap.[13] Blacks were more likely than Whites to be contacted by a collection agency or borrow money to pay off medical debt.[14] Debt collection suits are more prevalent in Black communities, with 40 percent more judgments than in mostly White neighborhoods.[15] The racial inequities in medical debt create a vicious cycle: Historically marginalized communities carry more debt, avoid care, skip medications, and become sicker as their chronic conditions are poorly managed, which results in higher costs, more debt, and worse health outcomes.[16]

The United States is experiencing a growing medical debt crisis. As a result, many Americans have come to fear medical bills more than the illness itself.[17] Federal and state policymakers' efforts to create consumer financial protections against medical debt have been unable to stem the problem.

14.3 FEDERAL AND STATE PROTECTIONS AGAINST MEDICAL DEBT

14.3.1 *Federal Law and Policy Protecting Consumers from Medical Debt*

In 2010, the Dodd-Frank Act (Dodd-Frank) and the Affordable Care Act (ACA) marked a historic inflection point in federal policies to address the problem of medical debt in the United States, through the creation of the Consumer Financial Protection Bureau (CFPB) and new Internal Revenue Service (IRS) requirements for tax-exempt hospitals' billing and collections policies.[18] Federal medical debt policies largely take the form of public law. The CFPB can impose administrative requirements on credit reporters and debt collectors to ameliorate the negative impacts of medical debt on US consumers, and the IRS regulates the financial assistance and collection policies of tax-exempt hospitals. Yet the federal public law of medical debt is inadequate in scope and enforcement, leaving consumers without remedies when faced with medical debt or collection actions that violate federal standards.

[13] Jacqueline C. Wiltshire et al., Medical Debt and Related Financial Consequences among Older African American and White Adults, 106(6) Am. J. Pub. Health 1086, 1086–91 (2016).

[14] Id.

[15] Jessica LaVoice & Domokos F. Varmossy, Racial Disparities in Debt Collection, SSRN (Oct. 2019), https://ssrn.com/abstract=3465203.

[16] Lopes et al., supra note 6; Haynes, supra note 10, at 5–7 (describing medical debt as a consequence and driver of the racial health gap).

[17] NORC at the University of Chicago, Issue Brief: Americans' Views of Healthcare Costs, Coverage, and Policy (Mar. 26, 2018), https://www.norc.org/Research/Projects/Pages/americans-views-of-healthcare-costs-coverage-and-policy.aspx.

[18] Dodd-Frank Wall Street Reform and Consumer Protection Act, Pub. L. No. 111-203, 124 Stat. 1376 (2010); Patient Protection and Affordable Care Act (PPACA), Pub. L. No. 111-148, 124 Stat. 119 (2010, as amended by Health Care Education and Reconciliation Act, Pub. L. No. 111-152, 124 Stat. 1029 (2010)).

14.3.1.1 Consumer Financial Protection Bureau Action on Medical Debt

The CFPB oversees consumer financial products and services, including debt collection and credit reporting. Dodd-Frank authorized the CFPB to regulate credit reporting and collection of medical debts under the Fair Debt Collection Practices Act (FDCPA) and Fair Credit Reporting Act (FCRA), but the CFPB lacks authority under the FDCPA to regulate collection activities by health care providers themselves, only those by third-party collection agents.[19]

To date, CFPB's actions have largely taken the form of studies, reports, and nonbinding guidance to credit reporting agencies on the treatment of medical debt under its FCRA authority.[20] Driven by these reports and public pressure, credit reporting agencies and industry actors have voluntarily adopted changes to the treatment of medical debt on credit reports. First, the three major credit reporting agencies agreed to remove paid medical debts and those under US$500 from credit reports and to delay reporting of medical debts for one year.[21] Second, credit-scoring organizations agreed to reduce the weight assigned to medical debts compared to nonmedical debts when calculating credit scores (in the case of Fair Isaac Corporation [FICO]) or exclude medical debts from credit scores altogether (in the case of VantageScore).[22] Nevertheless, larger and older unpaid medical debts still remain on credit reports, which could be used by employers, mortgage lenders, or landlords to discriminate against consumers with high health costs from chronic conditions or a disability. Moreover, the industry's voluntary measures are nonbinding, reversible, and virtually unenforceable. Despite CFPB's regulatory authority, its policy actions on medical debt can hardly be characterized as "law."

19 Medical Debt Burden in the United States, Consumer Fin. Prot. Bureau 42–43 (Mar. 1, 2022), https://www.consumerfinance.gov/data-research/research-reports/medical-debt-burden-in-the-united-states/.

20 See, for example, CFPB Data Point: Medical Debt and Credit Scores, Consumer Fin. Prot. Bureau (2014), https://www.consumerfinance.gov/data-research/research-reports/medical-debt-and-credit-scores/; Data Point: Recent Changes in Medical Collections on Consumer Credit Records, Consumer Fin. Prot. Bureau (Apr. 29, 2024), https://www.consumerfinance.gov/data-research/research-reports/recent-changes-in-medical-collections-on-consumer-credit-records/; Medical Debt Burden in the U.S., Consumer Fin. Prot. Bureau (Feb. 2022), https://files.consumerfinance.gov/f/documents/cfpb_medical-debt-burden-in-the-united-states_report_2022–03.pdf; Compliance Bulletin and Policy Guidance, Medical Debt Collection and Consumer Reporting Requirements in Connection with the No Surprises Act, Consumer Fin. Prot. Bureau (Jan. 13, 2022), https://www.consumerfinance.gov/compliance/supervisory-guidance/cfpb-bulletin-2022-01-medical-debt-collection-consumer-reporting-requirements-in-connection-with-no-surprises-act/.

21 National Credit Bureaus Support Consumers with Changes to Medical Debt Collection Debt Reporting, Consumer Data Indus. Ass'n (Mar. 18, 2022), https://www.cdiaonline.org/news/2022/03/18/equifax-experian-and-transunion-support-u-s-consumers-with-changes-to-medical-collection-debt-reporting/.

22 Fair Isaac Corp., FICO Score 9 (July 13, 2015), https://www.fico.com/blogs/impact-medical-debt-collections-ficor-scores; Medical Debt and the Changes to VantageScore, VantageScore (Aug. 10, 2022), https://vantagescore.com/medical-debt-and-the-changes-to-vantagescore/.

Consumer advocacy organizations have urged the CFPB to pass rules to codify and expand protections by eliminating medical debts from credit reports and to increase enforcement against medical debt collectors who use unfair practices, such as failing to ensure patients are screened for financial assistance eligibility before pursuing collection.[23] It would take an act of Congress to expand the scope of the FDCPA to include "first-party" collection actions by health care providers, which means these collectors are not barred from using unfair, abusive, or deceptive collection practices.[24]

14.3.1.2 IRS Rules for Tax-Exempt Hospitals under the Affordable Care Act

The ACA created requirements, implemented by the IRS, restricting the billing and collection practices for tax-exempt hospitals.[25] One provision mandates hospitals to maintain and publicize their financial assistance policies, including the criteria for free or discounted care.

Nevertheless, the IRS rules do not prescribe the method that hospitals must use to establish eligibility for financial assistance, leaving it up to their discretion. Another requirement is that hospitals must limit charges for eligible patients to the "amounts generally billed" to insured patients for emergency or medically necessary care, and they cannot charge gross charges, which are the hospital's full, undiscounted rates. Lastly, the IRS rules restrict nonprofit hospitals from engaging in "extraordinary collection actions" unless they have attempted to determine if the patient is eligible for financial assistance.

There are several gaps in IRS rules' protections against medical debt. First, the rules are underinclusive – they do not apply to the 42 percent of hospitals that are for-profit or government-run or to physician practices.[26] Second, hospitals have complete discretion in determining eligibility for financial assistance, which can be manipulated using restrictive income or asset requirements or difficult application processes. Third, the IRS rules are under-enforced, with no reported sanctions despite the widespread use of extraordinary collection actions and publicized

[23] Letter from 91 Organizations to Rohit Chopra, Dir. of the Consumer Fin. Prot. Bureau (Sept. 26, 2022), https://www.nclc.org/resources/letter-asking-for-rulemaking-to-ban-medical-debt-from-credit-reports/; Letter to Rohit Chopra, Dir. of the Consumer Fin. Prot. Bureau (Mar. 6, 2023), https://communitycatalyst.org/medical-debt-sign-on-letter-to-cfpb-march-6/.

[24] Blake N. Shultz et al., Hospital Debt Collection Practices Require Urgent Reform, Health Affs. Forefront (May 2, 2022), https://www.healthaffairs.org/do/10.1377/forefront.20220429.408324/.

[25] 26 U.S.C. § 501(r). Additional Requirements for Charitable Hospitals, Final Rule, 79 Fed. Reg. 78954 (Dec. 31, 2014), codified at 26 C.F.R. § 1.501(r)-1–1.501(r)-7.

[26] Hospitals by Ownership Type, Kaiser Fam. Found. (2022), https://www.kff.org/other/state-indicator/hospitals-by-ownership/?currentTimeframe = 0&sortModel = %7B%22colId%22:%22Location%22,%22sort%22:%22asc%22%7D; This Memphis Hospital System Flouts IRS Rules by Not Publicly Posting Financial Assistance Policies, ProPublica (May 21, 2021), https://www.propublica.org/article/this-memphis-hospital-system-flouts-irs-rules-by-not-publicly-posting-financial-assistance-policies.

violations.[27] These gaps leave patients with medical debt with inadequate protections and no recourse even if hospitals violate federal tax rules in their pursuit of payment. There is no private cause of action for violations of federal tax rules, even when the patient loses their home, life savings, or creditworthiness.

14.3.1.3 Other Federal Actions That Prevent Creation of Medical Debt

More effective than laws targeting the collection and reporting of medical debts are federal efforts that stop the debts from being created in the first place. The most important of these was the ACA's expansion of Medicaid to nearly all low-income adults earning less than 138 percent of the federal poverty limit (FPL), which has significantly reduced medical debt and racial health coverage disparities.[28] Yet, following the 2012 Supreme Court ruling decoupling a state's decision to expand Medicaid from the state's existing Medicaid funding, many Republican-led states have chosen not to expand Medicaid, leaving about two million low-income and mostly non-White adults uninsured and exposed to medical debt.[29]

Federal public law on medical debt has several key shortcomings: (1) The CFPB's actions to date are nonbinding nudges that rely on voluntary industry practice; (2) the ACA's rules for tax-exempt hospitals are underinclusive, underpowered, and under-enforced; (3) the Supreme Court made Medicaid expansion optional for states, leaving millions uncovered;[30] and (4) none of these federal laws provide consumers with individual remedies in the event their lives are wrongly upended by medical debt.

14.3.2 *State Laws*

Even with federal action on medical debts, states have not abandoned their traditional roles as consumer protectors and policy generators. States have passed laws expanding upon federal protections, filling gaps, and innovating new approaches to the medical debt problem. States have created both public law and private law protections, creating standards for financial assistance policies, applying them to a

[27] Noam Levey, Hundreds of Hospitals Sue Patients or Threaten Their Credit, a KHN Investigation Finds. Does Yours?, Kaiser Fam. Found. Health News (Dec. 21, 2022), https://kffhealthnews.org/news/article/medical-debt-hospitals-sue-patients-threaten-credit-khn-investigation/; Jordan Rau, Patients Eligible for Charity Care Instead Get Big Bills, Kaiser Fam. Found. Health News (Oct. 14, 2018), https://kffhealthnews.org/news/patients-eligible-for-charity-care-instead-get-big-bills/.

[28] Kluender et al., supra note 11; Haynes, supra note 10.

[29] Nat'l Fed'n of Indep. Bus. v. Sebelius, 567 U.S. 519 (2012); Robin Rudowitz et al., supra note 11.

[30] Status of State Medicaid Expansion Decisions: Interactive Map, Kaiser Fam. Found. (Mar. 27, 2023), https://www.kff.org/medicaid/issue-brief/status-of-state-medicaid-expansion-decisions-interactive-map/.

broader range of health care providers, barring certain collection actions, and, in some instances, empowering private individuals to sue to remedy violations.

Several states have implemented laws aimed at ensuring fair medical billing and collection across all hospitals, regardless of their tax status or ownership. For instance, states have limited the amount that hospitals can charge patients who fall below specified income levels.[31] One example is the Hospital Fair Pricing Act in California, which restricts the amount that California hospitals and emergency physicians can charge uninsured patients who earn less than 400 percent of the FPL or insured patients whose medical bills exceed 10 percent of household income.[32] By defining these income and affordability thresholds, states limit hospitals' discretion in determining eligibility for financial assistance and standardize these limits across all hospitals. Most state laws do not extend these financial assistance requirements to nonhospital providers, such as physician groups.

Furthermore, many states have put limits on the medical debt collection practices of health care providers and their debt collectors. At least twenty-one states have laws that restrict providers' medical debt collection practices, including limitations on interest rates, foreclosing or placing a lien on a patient's home or property, wage garnishment, seeking debtors' arrest, credit reporting, or assigning the debt to a collection agency.[33] The scope of these limits varies, with some states applying them broadly to all patients, and others limiting the protections by the patient's income, uninsured status, or eligibility for financial assistance. For example, New Mexico bars any collection actions against patients earning less than 200 percent of the FPL.[34] Maryland requires hospitals to refund patients for amounts wrongly sought in collections from patients eligible for free care.[35] Finally, states can engage in policy innovation, such as Colorado's law prohibiting hospitals from seeking collection of medical debts if they are not in compliance with federal price transparency rules,[36] or Maryland's requirement for hospitals to report on their financial assistance, collection actions by race, ethnicity, and other demographic characteristics.[37]

[31] Andrea Bopp Stark & Jennifer Bosco, An Ounce of Prevention: A Review of Hospital Financial Assistance Policies in the States, Nat'l Consumer L. Ctr. (Nov. 2021), https://www.nclc.org/resources/report-an-ounce-of-prevention/.

[32] Cal. Health & Safety Code §§ 127400–127446 (hospitals), 127450–127462 (emergency physicians).

[33] Christopher T. Robertson et al., New State Consumer Protections against Medical Debt, 327 JAMA 121 (2022); Hospital Community Benefit Program: Community Benefit State Law Profiles Comparison, Hilltop Inst., http://www.hilltopinstitute.org/HCBP_CBL_state_table.cfm (last accessed Sept. 2024); Medical Debt Burden in the United States, supra note 19, at 42–43.

[34] Patients' Debt Collection Protection Act, N.M. Stat. §§ 57-32-1–57-32-10.

[35] Medical Debt Protection Act, Md. Code, Health-Gen. § 19-214.2.

[36] H.B.22-1285, 74th Gen. Assemb., First Reg. Sess. (Co. 2022), codified at Colo. Rev. Stat. §§ 25-3-801–25-3-803.

[37] Medical Debt Protection Act, supra note 35.

To be sure, there can be unintended consequences from overly broad free-care requirements for providers, such as exacerbating financial precarity of less profitable hospitals or service lines.[38] Despite these concerns, states' fair pricing and collection laws have not caused widespread financial strain on hospitals.[39] States have gone farther than federal laws to create standards to protect patients from medical debts.

State law requirements for hospital financial assistance and medical debt collection are forms of public law, enforced administratively by the health department or state attorney general. However, states can provide additional enforcement through a private right of action for individuals aggrieved by unlawful medical billing or collection practices and by strengthening patients' legal defenses in collection actions against them.[40]

Colorado and Connecticut present models for private enforcement of hospital medical debt collection laws. Colorado creates a private right of action for aggrieved patients to sue health care providers that violate the billing and collection requirements individually or via class action for actual damages, statutory damages, and attorneys' fees.[41] Connecticut makes it an unfair trade practice for any provider to demand payment from patients or report debts to credit reporting agencies for prohibited medical bills.[42] Although few patients have prevailed under these laws, in one case, the Connecticut Supreme Court found that a physician's unlawful billing and collection practices violated state unfair trade practice laws, awarding the patient actual and punitive damages and attorney's fees.[43]

The designation of medical billing practices as an unfair trade practice is advantageous in two ways: (1) It provides a private remedy to individuals harmed by unlawful medical billing and collection practices, and (2) attorneys' fees and punitive damages incentivize attorneys to take such cases on behalf of consumers. Nearly all states have an Unfair and Deceptive Acts or Practices (UDAP) law, and state legislatures can reduce legal burdens on patients by classifying medical debt billing and collection practices as unfair trade practices *per se* under their state UDAP statutes.

38 Jill Horwitz & David M. Cutler, The ACA's Hospital Tax-Exemption Rules and the Practice of Medicine, Health Affs. Forefront (Mar. 3, 2015), https://www.healthaffairs.org/content/forefront/aca-s-hospital-tax-exemption-rules-and-practice-medicine.

39 Glenn Melnick & Katya Fonkych, Fair Pricing Law Prompts Most California Hospitals to Adopt Policies to Protect Uninsured Patients from High Charges, 32(6) Health Affs. 1101, 1101–08 (2013).

40 Gianetti v. Siglinger, 279 Conn. 130, 136–37 (2006) (finding in favor of patient in defense against surgeon's billing and collection action that provider's balance-bills violated state unfair medical billing and collection practices and unfair trade practices laws).

41 Colo. Rev. Stat. § 25.5-3-506.

42 Conn. Gen. Stat. §§ 20-7f(b)–(c), 38a-193(c).

43 Gianetti, supra note 40, at 138–39.

14.4 FEDERALISM, PRIVATE LAW, AND MEDICAL DEBT

The pervasive problem of medical debt poses a question of regulatory design – whether consumer protections are best instituted at the federal or state level, using the tools of public law or private law. The policy shortcomings cataloged here demonstrate that the problem requires the combined and concerted action of national and state governments, where states can fill gaps and innovate new policies to build on a federal floor and provide private remedies to supplement inadequate administrative enforcement.

14.4.1 *The Role of Private Law and Private Remedies in Consumer Protection*

The problem of medical debt is a consumer protection problem with both the diffuse harm of unaffordable health care costs borne by the public, employers, and businesses, as well as concentrated harms of medical debts and collection actions borne by individuals and households specifically. Thus, legal solutions for the medical debt problem should combine public and private laws. Nevertheless, extant consumer protections from medical debt tend to focus on public law solutions and neglect private law remedies for individuals. Most of the legal and policy solutions described above focus on regulating conduct of the health care providers, collection agents, and credit reporting bureaus in the creation, collection, and management of medical debt.

Violations of the federal public law on medical debt are enforced, if at all, through administrative penalties, loss of tax-exempt status, or public sanction on the entities, not liability to the affected individuals. In practice, this means that a low-income patient who wrongfully loses their home, is unable to buy food or pay rent, or is unable to fill a necessary prescription due to medical debt has no recourse against the hospital that failed to apply its financial assistance policy or pursued extraordinary collection actions in violation of federal laws. The hospital might lose its tax-exempt status if the IRS were to seek enforcement of the violation, but there is no remedy for the harms suffered by the patient. The combination of inadequate administrative enforcement with the severity of harms inflicted on individual debtors is a prototypical situation for public laws to be supplemented with private enforcement.[44]

Clear and protective standards for consumers could, theoretically, protect the public from unaffordable medical debt if they deterred abusive conduct by creators and collectors of medical debt.[45] Consumer advocacy organizations have called for stronger public law standards: The IRS could specify clearer eligibility standards and blanket prohibitions on harsh collection actions, and CFPB could issue rules

[44] Bagchi, supra note 3, at 240.

[45] Danielle D'Onfro, Error-Resilient Consumer Contracts, 71 Duke L.J. 541, 575 (2021).

eliminating medical debts from credit reports.[46] In June 2024, CFPB issued a proposed rule that would, if finalized, remove all medical debts from credit reports and prohibit creditors from considering medical debts in credit eligibility determinations.[47] Even with stronger rules, the extent of consumer protection depends critically on enforcement, and public enforcement of consumer protection laws against medical debt has been abysmal.[48]

The classic vehicle of consumer protection is the UDAP law, which has been adopted by all fifty states to extend the consumer protections of the Federal Trade Commission through a combination of enforcement by state attorneys general and private parties.[49] Private enforcement of state UDAP laws plays a critical role in supplementing public enforcement, serving a public benefit of deterrence, and expanding states' limited resources. Private enforcement of UDAP laws also creates private benefit by creating legal recourse for affected individuals through reduced burdens of proof, minimum damage recoveries, attorneys' fees, and court costs, which compensate the individual for the harms suffered and enable them to secure legal representation.[50] Consumers struggle to secure legal representation to defend their individual contract disputes with providers over medical bills because these are typically too small in dollar amount for lawyers to take the case and courts are unwilling to aggregate these cases in class action.[51] UDAP remedies thus provide both a private cause of action and increased access to justice by incentivizing attorneys to take these cases.[52]

14.4.2 *Federalism and Private Law Checks against Regulatory Failure*

The biggest challenge for the medical debt policy is not codifying new consumer protections but lack of enforcement. Compared with the federal government, states possess a historic advantage in the creation and enforcement of rights, obligations,

[46] Noam Levey, Medical Debt Affects Millions, and Advocates Push IRS, Consumer Agency for Relief, NPR (Mar. 7, 2023), https://www.npr.org/sections/health-shots/2023/03/07/1161473744/medical-debt-affects-millions-and-advocates-push-irs-consumer-agency-for-relief (describing letters by advocacy organizations to CFPB and IRS on Mar. 6, 2023).

[47] Prohibition on Creditors and Consumer Reporting Agencies Concerning Medical Information, Consumer Fin. Prot. Bureau (June 18, 2024), 89 Fed. Reg. 51682.

[48] D'Onfro, supra note 45, at 576 ("[C]onsumer protection depends on enforcement ... Public enforcement's track record is abysmal").

[49] Dee Pridgen, The Dynamic Duo of Consumer Protection: State and Private Enforcement of Unfair and Deceptive Trade Practices Laws, 81 Antitrust L.J. 911, 911 (2017).

[50] Id. at 937.

[51] Christopher T. Robertson, Medical Bills Are Open-Price Contracts: A Victory for the Little Guy, Harvard L. Petrie-Flom Ctr. Bill of Health Blog (Oct. 3, 2017), https://blog.petrieflom.law.harvard.edu/2017/10/03/medical-bills-are-open-price-contracts-a-victory-for-the-little-guy/.

[52] Ulbrich v. Groth, 310 Conn. 375, 411, 78 A.3d 76, 101 (2013) (noting that Connecticut's Unfair Trade Practice Act "was intended to provide a remedy that is separate and distinct from the remedies provided by contract law when the defendant's contractual breach was accompanied by aggravating circumstances").

and liabilities among private parties, particularly in the areas of health and safety regulation and consumer protection.[53] Private enforcement can fill gaps and supplement public enforcement of consumer protection laws, as illustrated by state UDAP laws.[54] State consumer protection laws enhance consumers' legal protections against medical debt both by supplementing public law with private law remedies and by making the protections more resilient to erosion from federal regulatory failures.

Federal regulatory failure is a growing problem, driven by capture,[55] abdication by presidential administrations,[56] budgetary cuts from Congress,[57] and curtailment of agency authority by the Supreme Court.[58] The primary regulatory agencies in charge of consumer protections against medical debt – the CFPB and IRS – have been prominent targets of the varied forms of administrative evisceration from all three branches of government.[59] Given that federal agency decisions not to enforce are generally unreviewable by courts, states can make up for and check federal regulatory inaction.[60] Concurrent state consumer protection laws with both private and administrative enforcement promote the goals of federalism: policy innovation, diversification of remedies, increased accountability for industry actors and government regulators, responsiveness and superior information of local market conditions and practices, and dynamic regulation.[61]

The recipe for better consumer protections against medical debt combines (1) stronger federal public law standards that operate as a floor for more protective state

[53] Amy Widman, Advancing Federalism Concerns in Administrative Law through a Revitalization of State Enforcement Powers: A Case Study of the Consumer Product Safety and Improvement Act of 2008, 29 Yale L. & Pol'y Rev. 165, 166 (2010).

[54] Pridgen, supra note 49, at 932–33.

[55] Id. at 926 ("[S]tate UDAP enforcement can serve as a check on federal agencies that may be "captured" by their regulatory 'clients'").

[56] Amy Widman, Protecting Consumer Protection: Filling the Federal Enforcement Gap, 69 Buff. L. Rev. 1157 (2021) (describing the abandonment of federal consumer protection enforcement by the CFPB and FTC under the Trump administration).

[57] Emily Cochrane & Alan Rappeport, House Republicans Vote to Rescind I.R.S. Funding, N.Y. Times (Jan. 9, 2023), nytimes.com/2023/01/09/us/politics/house-republicans-irs-funding.html.

[58] Lisa Heinzerling, The Supreme Court Is Making America Ungovernable, The Atlantic (July 26, 2022), https://www.theatlantic.com/ideas/archive/2022/07/supreme-court-major-questions-doctrine-congress/670618/; Lisa Heinzerling, How Government Ends, Boston Rev. (Sept. 28, 2022), https://www.bostonreview.net/articles/how-government-ends/ (describing how the Supreme Court is systematically eroding administrative agencies' authority to govern, exemplified in West Virginia v. EPA).

[59] See Widman, supra note 56, at 1161–6257; Seila Law v. CFPB, 591 US _, 140 S. Ct. 2183 (2020) (holding the for-cause removal protections for the Director of the CFPB unconstitutional, allowing the President to remove the Director at will); Vanessa Williamson, Cutting IRS Funding Is a Gift to America's Wealthiest Tax Evaders, Brookings (Jan. 26, 2023), https://www.brookings.edu/blog/fixgov/2023/01/26/cutting-irs-funding-is-a-gift-to-americas-wealthiest-tax-evaders/ (describing persistent underfunding of the IRS).

[60] Widman, supra note 53, at 167.

[61] Pridgen, supra note 49, at 932–33; Widman, supra note 53, at 167–68.

regulation, and (2) concurrent state consumer protections enforceable by the state attorney general and a private right of action with minimum statutory damages, attorneys' fees, and costs. This recipe reaps the benefits of federalism, public law standards, and private law remedies to provide a fuller set of tools to protect individuals from medical debt. Importantly, these protections would be further enhanced by efforts to provide better health coverage to more people, particularly Medicaid expansion in all states.

Medical debt policy should preserve a meaningful role for states and private law to check against regulatory failure by federal public law solutions. Federalism's separation of powers stems not only from the division of authority between the federal government and the states but also between the levers of public law and private law. An overlapping and mutually reinforcing interplay between federal and state as well as public and private law fosters stronger protections against medical debt for individuals and households.

15

Paying for Health Care and Private Law's Internal Point of View

James Toomey

15.1 INTRODUCTION

American private law is, paradigmatically, judge-made common law.[1] In the century since Legal Realism swept the academy, it is generally considered to be, at bottom, the product of judicial policymaking.[2] From this perspective, the still-persistent conceptual language of common law judging is a façade, obscuring the distributional reasoning beneath. If this is right, we might ask courts to offer comprehensive novel solutions to complex social problems – though wonder why they, beset by well-worn democratic and epistemic limitations, ought to engage in general policymaking.[3]

Against this picture, private law theorists have recently defended an alternative view of private law that takes seriously its language and conceptual structure, from an internal point of view.[4] According to these theories, it *is* possible, and sometimes desirable, to take private law's internal structure seriously, and reason about its basic concepts and commitments.[5] Common law judging may not be general-interest policymaking, but in applying the basic logic and internal language of private law to novel circumstances, courts can sometimes mitigate difficult social problems.

This chapter offers a case study in applying the internal logic of private law to unanticipated social circumstances, drawn from health care finance. Most Americans have health insurance, and the prices charged for their health care are set in opaque volume negotiations between insurers and providers.[6] The relatively small percentage of Americans who don't have insurance, or receive care that their

1 Jeffrey A. Pojanowski, Private Law in the Gaps, 82 Fordham L. Rev. 1689, 1689 (2014).
2 Joseph William Singer, Legal Realism Now, 76 Calif. L. Rev. 465, 467 (1998).
3 David O. Brink, Objectivity in Law and Morals 19 (2000).
4 Andrew S. Gold et al., The Oxford Handbook of the New Private Law (2020).
5 Id.
6 Mark A. Hall & Carl E. Schneider, Patients as Consumers: Courts, Contracts, and the New Medical Marketplace, 106 Mich. L. Rev. 643, 648 (2008).

insurer does not cover, don't benefit from these negotiations. Instead, providers charge wildly inflated "book prices" – the listed prices for services that virtually no one pays.[7] Patients who fail to pay these prices, however, can be sued for breach of contract. What remedy?

Contract law is, at bottom, organized around enforcing agreements.[8] So where parties agree on a price for services, courts will enforce that price as expectation damages.[9] Where they agree to exchange services for payment but fail to specify a price, a court will supply an alternative that approximates what they would have agreed on, a reasonable price.[10] And, as common law courts have increasingly recognized, the prices "charged" by health care providers are not reasonable.[11] Leaving the task of determining a reasonable price to the jury, upon consideration of all relevant evidence, follows from the basic structure of private law and the concepts it deploys.

Of course, this hardly *solves* the many difficulties of health care finance. But courts can legitimately do this themselves (regardless of whether, for institutional, political economy reasons, they are likely to do so). Beyond, regulating health care costs no doubt requires legislative and regulatory intervention, of which there has been a great deal.[12] At the margins, however, private law may play a role.

15.2 CONCEPTUAL REASONING AND COMMON LAW

Conceptual reasoning is famously, or infamously, part and parcel of the "common law method."[13] Judges and juries routinely consider whether novel facts fall within the boundaries of traditional concepts – whether a particular relationship counts as "ownership," whether a certain party's statements are an "offer," etc. They purport to do so by reasoning about the internal structure of the relevant concepts, rather than pursuing the best outcome of the case from an economic or social perspective. To the Legal Realists and conceptual nominalists in Law and Economics and Critical Legal Studies that followed them, this kind of "formalist" reasoning is a façade – a distraction from the policy analysis courts ought to apply in resolving cases, and are anyway.[14]

7 Casey W. Baker et al., Don't Cash That Check! Identifying Risks to Medical Billing and Collection Practices under the Doctrine of Accord and Satisfaction, 16 Rutgers Bus. L. Rev. 308, 309 (2021).

8 Charles Fried, Contract as Promise: A Theory of Contractual Obligation 5–6 (2d ed. 2015).

9 Restatement (Second) Contracts § 347.

10 Id. § 204.

11 Infra Part II.

12 Consolidated Appropriations Act, H.R. Res. 133, 116th Cong. (2020) (enacted); 45 C.F.R. § 180.20 (2023); see also Chapter 14 in this volume.

13 Shyamkrishna Balganesh & Gideon Parchomovsky, Structure and Value in the Common Law, 163 U. Pa. L. Rev. 1241, 1242 (2015).

14 Felix S. Cohen, Transcendental Nonsense and the Functional Approach, 35 Colum. L. Rev. 809 (1935); Duncan Kennedy, Form and Substance in Private Law Adjudication, 88 Harv. L. Rev. 1685 (1976).

Recently, this view has come under sustained attack by theorists of the so-called New Private Law school – a disparate group united by a commitment to taking seriously the language of the law from an internal point of view.[15] These theorists, drawing on different philosophies of language and concepts than legal nominalists, argue that traditional private law conceptual reasoning is possible, often sufficiently determinate, and in principle not coextensive with outcome-oriented policy reasoning.[16] As a descriptive account of private law, if internal reasoning is possible, and judges *act* as though it is largely what they do, then perhaps the burden is on those insisting on the external considerations of economics and social power to prove that private law doctrine is inexplicable without them.[17]

Whatever the outcome of this philosophical debate, if an internal, conceptual account of private law is indeed possible, it might have a number of normative advantages. First, the species of conceptual analysis characteristic of private law reasoning might be epistemically preferable for judges.[18] An individual judge can reason on their own about whether a particular arrangement falls within the concept "contract" but is unlikely to have access to the empirical generalizations required to pursue the best all-things-considered social outcome. Similarly, conclusions about concepts can carry over to cognate domains of law – concluding something is a "corporation," for instance, tells us about both its contractual capacities and tort responsibilities, saving judges from conducting bespoke policy analysis across contexts.[19]

Moreover, taking the language of the private law seriously helps contribute to its coherence. On a nominalist view, since a core private law concept like reasonableness is just a conclusory term for certain distributional consequences, there is no a priori reason for it to have the same content across legal domains, or even cases. In contrast, internal, conceptual theories take the private law as a coherent system – if the same word is being used in various places in the law, the burden is on the skeptic to show that they are not in fact the same concept, as surely the public would be inclined to interpret them.[20]

Finally, a conceptual theory of private law can help make sense of the legitimacy of courts as expositors of private law in a democratic system. Normative questions ought generally to be resolved by democratically responsible representatives.[21] As I have argued at greater length elsewhere, judges are not democratically

[15] Gold et al., supra note 4.

[16] Ernest J. Weinrib, The Idea of Private Law (1995).

[17] Andrew S. Gold, The Right to Redress 18 (2020).

[18] Felipe Jiménez, A Formalist Theory of Contract Law Adjudication, 1121 Utah L. Rev. 1157–65 (2020).

[19] Jeremy Waldron, "Transcendental Nonsense" and System in the Law, 100 Colum. L. Rev. 16, 25–26 (2000).

[20] Ernest J. Weinrib, Corrective Justice 323 (2012).

[21] Fabienne Peter, Democratic Legitimacy and Proceduralist Social Epistemology, 6 Pol. Phil. & Econ. 329 (2007).

responsible, and if the private law is just policy, it isn't clear why we ought to follow judicial pronouncements.[22] But understanding much of private law as the entailments of certain basic concepts or commitments mitigates this problem.[23] We would need to be convinced only that – at least tacitly, or by acquiescence – the people have endorsed that there ought to be a law enforcing agreements and that we've delegated to judges the predominately descriptive work of hashing out what that means.

Importantly, even the strongest defenders of the role of concepts in common law recognize that our private law is not *just* made up of delegated concepts and their entailments. Many rules *are* obviously the result of policy, often tied to a particular time and place – say, the Rule Against Perpetuities.[24] These policy rules are (at least phenomenologically, for many people) qualitatively distinct, often not difficult to distinguish from, and of a less compelling provenance than those derived directly from the basic concepts of the private law.[25]

Finally, although much of the impetus of the Realist critique of conceptualism was motivated by its perceived inability to address modern policy problems, the method has in fact proven quite flexible and adaptable.[26] Concepts are not delimited by their past application – courts can legitimately apply the basic structure of contract law to entirely unanticipated circumstances.[27] And because the policy rules of the common law lack both the systematic role and the democratic legitimacy of its more basic principles, courts act legitimately in preferring the latter to the former where they conflict.[28]

Of course, for all its flexibility, common law conceptual reasoning could hardly resolve all contemporary social or economic challenges on its own. Broader, policy-motivated changes to the private law's basic structure must come from legislatures rather than courts.[29] But common law reasoning can do something, and health care finance offers a case study in what.

15.3 HEALTH CARE PRICING

American health care finance is – perhaps an understatement – odd. Most Americans, some 90 percent, finance their health care in whole or in part with

[22] James Toomey, Property's Boundaries, 109 Va. L. Rev. 131, 145–54 (2023).
[23] Id.
[24] Adolf Reinach, The A Priori Foundations of the Civil Law 131 (John F. Crosby ed. & trans., 2012).
[25] Id. at 131.
[26] Balganesh & Parchomovsky, supra note 13, at 1243; Leslie Y. Garfield Tenzer, Social Media and the Common Law, 88 Brook. L. Rev. 227, 263 (2022).
[27] Andrew S. Gold & Henry E. Smith, Sizing Up Private Law, 70 U. Toronto L. J. 399, 493 (2020).
[28] Balganesh & Parchomovsky, supra note 13, at 1243.
[29] Toomey, supra note 22, at 136.

health insurance.[30] Insurers are, therefore, the primary payors of health care services. Representing many insureds, insurers have substantial bargaining power, and they use it – negotiating volume pricing with health care providers. Thus, most health care is paid for by insurers to providers, on behalf of insureds, based on prices negotiated in the aggregate by the insurer and provider.[31]

But these prices actually paid for most care, nominally volume "discounts" (some portion of which presumably is an actual volume discount), don't appear in the prices that providers ostensibly *charge* for services. That is, although it might be that no insurer is paying more than US$X for a colonoscopy, US$X may be, at least, nominally, a volume "discount" from the provider's "charged" price of US$2X. Or US$5X, why not. If the price to be paid for the vast majority of care has already been negotiated, there's no reason for providers not to "charge" whatever they want.[32] "It is a little game we play. [The providers] put it on the bill, [the insurers] tear up the bill."[33]

The problem is that not *all* care is paid for by insurers. Some 8 percent of Americans do not have health insurance.[34] And, even for those with insurance, insurers rarely agree to pay for *all* of an insured's health care expenses. Most prominently, insurers may dramatically limit the amount they will pay for so-called "out-of-network" care – care received by providers with whom the insurer does not have a preexisting relationship.[35]

This care (like all care) is *billed* at the listed prices. But patients receiving these bills cannot take advantage of the negotiated prices paid by insurers – either they don't have one, or their insurer has not negotiated with this provider. In this example, then, we have an individual patient with a bill for US$2X or US$5X for a colonoscopy – without recourse to any discount – even though overwhelmingly colonoscopies in the United States go only for US$X. Of course, because many people without health insurance are judgment-proof to the tune of US$5X, US$5X

30 Katherine Keisler-Starkey & Lisa N. Bunch, Health Insurance Coverage in the United States: 2021, U.S. Census Bur. (Sept. 13, 2022), https://www.census.gov/library/publications/2022/demo/p60-278.html.

31 George A. Nation III, Contracting for Healthcare: Price Terms in Hospital Admission Agreements, 124 Dick. L. Rev. 91, 94 (2019).

32 George A. Nation III, The Valuation of Medical Expense Damages in Tort: Debunking the Myth That Chargemaster-Based "Billed Charges" Are Relevant to Determining the Reasonable Value of Medical Care, 95 Tul. L. Rev. 937, 942 (2021).

33 Casablanca (Warner Bros. 1942).

34 Keisler-Starkey & Bunch, supra note 30.

35 Matthew B. Lawrence, The Social Consequences Problem in Health Insurance and How to Solve It, 13 Harv. L. & Pol'y Rev. 593, 599 (2019) (other patients that might actually be billed the full list price include international patients, those with "high-deductible" plans, and some tort victims); George A. Nation III, Determining the Fair and Reasonable Value of Medical Services: The Affordable Care Act, Government Insurers, Private Insurers, and Uninsured Patients, 65 Baylor L. Rev. 425, 430 (2013).

rarely ends up getting paid to the provider in these cases either.[36] But such cases nevertheless impose a tremendous amount of stress and hardship on individuals.[37]

This result is perverse, in the sense that it could not possibly be the product of coherent conscious design. Whether as a negotiating position or as an effort to recoup perceived losses on coercive contracts with insurers (particularly Medicare and Medicaid), providers are incentivized to "charge" arbitrarily high prices for their services, with no relationship to the content of the service and almost never paid. Only the un- or under-insured are ever even purportedly on the hook for these prices.

15.4 HEALTH CARE PRICING AND COMMON LAW COURTS

When health care providers proceed to collections for payment of charged prices against a patient, they sue on a contract – a promise by the provider to care for the patient; a promise by the patient to pay. When a contract is breached, contract law generally requires the promisor to put the promisee in the position they would have been in if the promisor had performed – "expectation damages."[38] Where parties have made explicit promises to each other, those promises constitute expectation damages in the event of breach. Following this reasoning, many courts default to enforcing health care contracts as any other contract – holding patients to pay the price charged.[39]

On the other hand, contract law has long held that where parties do not agree on a price but intend to enter into a contract, the court will presume a reasonable measure of expectation damages.[40] And as George Nation has argued, contracts for care between patients and providers are not characterized by meaningful agreement on price.[41] Prices in health care contracts are not prominently disclosed to patients – the form contracts that patients sign consenting to care typically just agree to pay the provider's listed prices, whatever they may be.[42] Even compared to other form contracts, health care contracts much more clearly lack a real promise on the patients' part to pay a particular price.[43]

36 Temple Univ. Hosp., Inc. v. Healthcare Management Alternatives, Inc., 832 A.2d 501 (Pa. Sup. Ct. 2003).

37 George A. Nation III, Hospital Chargemaster Insanity: Healing the Healers, 43 Pepp. L. Rev. 745, 761–66 (2016).

38 Restatement (Second) Contracts § 347.

39 Allen v. Clarian Health Partners, 980 N.E.2d 306 (Ind. 2012); Holland v. Trinity Health Care, 791 N.W. 2d 724 (Mich. App. 2010); Shelton v. Duke Univ. Health Sys., Inc., 633 S.E. 2d 113, 114 (N.C. App. 2006).

40 Restatement (Second) Contracts § 204.

41 George A. Nation III, Healthcare and the Balance-Billing Problem: The Solution Is the Common Law of Contracts and Strengthening the Free Market for Healthcare, 61 Vill. L. Rev. 153 (2016).

42 Nation, supra note 35, at 434–35.

43 Id.

We might, then, expect courts to measure expectation damages in health care cases by seeking a reasonable price, rather than simply the amount charged by the provider. But if the prices charged by health care providers are not presumptively reasonable, how might courts go about determining them?

A growing collection of decisions in tort law where courts have similarly been called on to determine the reasonable cost of health care services offers one method. Tort law generally compensates plaintiffs for negligently caused harms, including medical costs.[44] Just as in contract cases where the parties did not agree on a concrete price, plaintiffs in tort cases are entitled to recover the reasonable cost of their care as the best measure of their actual harm.[45]

But in a world in which most care is paid for by insurers, calculating the reasonable cost of health care is complicated by the so-called collateral source rule. The collateral source rule has a substantive and an evidentiary component. The substantive component holds that plaintiffs are entitled to recover the cost of the harm the defendant's conduct caused, even if they have already been paid for it by a third party; a plaintiff can recover their medical costs even if they have already been paid by their insurer.[46] The evidentiary component of the collateral source rule bars evidence of any payments made on the plaintiff's behalf by third parties, including insurers.[47]

Strictly following the evidentiary component of the collateral source rule, some courts hold that a tort plaintiff is entitled to recover the billed price of their care, refusing to admit evidence, suggesting that the price was or could have been settled by a lower amount by the insurer.[48] But there is an alternative. A growing number of courts in this context charge juries to award "the reasonable value of medical services received by a particular plaintiff in a particular case" upon "consideration of all relevant evidence, notably including the amount billed, the amount paid, and any expert testimony and other relevant evidence the parties may offer."[49] This approach appears to have been pioneered by the Supreme Court of South Carolina in a brief opinion in 2003,[50] and outlined more thoroughly by the Supreme Court of Ohio in 2006.[51] Since then, it has been endorsed by the highest courts of a number of states, and the Eleventh Circuit in maritime law.[52]

44 Restatement (Second) Torts § 924.
45 Restatement (Second) Torts §§ 911 cmt. h, 924 cmt. f.
46 Restatement (Second) Torts § 920A(2).
47 Id.
48 Bonnell v. Carnival Corp., 2015 WL 12712609, at *3 (S.D. Fla. Jan. 20, 2015); Deperrodil v. Bozovic Marine, Inc., 842 F.3d 352, 360 (5th Cir. 2016).
49 Higgs v. Costa Crociere S.P.A. Co., 969 F.3d 1295, 1312 (11th Cir. 2020).
50 Haselden v. Davis, 579 S.E. 2d 293, 294–95 (2003).
51 Robinson v. Bates, 857 N.E.2d 1195, 1200 (2006).
52 Id.; Martinez v. Milburn Enters., Inc., 233 P.3d 205, 222–23 (2010); Stanley v. Walker, 906 N.E. 2d 852, 857 (Ind. 2009); see also Law v. Griffith, 930 N.E. 2d 126, 135–36 (Mass. 2010) (adopting a similar approach); Howell v. Hamilton Meats & Provisions, Inc., 257 P.3d 1130, 1152 (2011) (Klein, J., dissenting) (same).

This procedural mechanism for arriving at the reasonable value of medical care from tort law might be reasonable for contract law.[53] In breach of contract actions, courts could point to this collection of tort cases construing reasonableness and hold that expectation damages are not necessarily the amount the provider charged – they are the reasonable value of the services (that, contract already acknowledges), determined by the jury upon consideration of all the evidence (which it currently does not).

15.5 REASONABLENESS AND PRIVATE LAW THEORY

This move would be consistent with and, indeed, illustrative of, the theory of private law as common law sketched above. Indeed, insisting on reasonable rather than pre-written damages demonstrates the possibility and value of taking seriously the internal logic of private law. First, at a basic level, this approach to calculating the reasonableness of medical expenses illustrates the possibility and value of conceptual reasoning. Next, for this reason, it is consistent with separation of powers. And finally, reasoning in the same way about reasonableness in contract and in tort demonstrates the systematic value of legal concepts.

15.5.1 *The Concept of Reasonableness*

Contract law is, at a basic level, committed to facilitating individuals in ordering their lives according to their aspirations.[54] It therefore enforces the agreements they actually make with one another. And where an individual has not in fact articulated their preferences, the best the law can do is come close.[55] That is where the concept of reasonableness comes in – estimating terms the parties might have agreed to, had they really discussed it.[56] This is the logic of the rule that where parties agreed to a contract but omitted a price term, the law will supply a reasonable one – straightforwardly derived from the basic principles and concepts of contract.

Of course, courts generally presume that the written terms of a contract represent the true agreement of the parties, and enforce them accordingly, prominently under the "parol evidence" and "plain meaning" rules.[57] From this perspective, we might think (and courts have) that health care contracts *do* include price terms, at least

[53] Waldron, supra note 19, at 25–26.
[54] Fried, supra note 8, at 5–6.
[55] Restatement (Second) Contracts § 347.
[56] John D. Wladis, Common Law and Uncommon Events: The Development of the Doctrine of Impossibility of Performance in English Common Law, 75 Geo. L. J. 1575, 1607 n. 153 (1987); J. Gregory Sikak & Daniel F. Spulber, Givings, Takings, and Fallacy of Forward-Looking Costs, 72 N.Y.U. L. Rev. 1068, 1150–51 (1997).
[57] Restatement (Second) Contracts 9 3 Intro. Note. (1981).

incorporated by reference.[58] They are writings; they purport to commit the patient to pay the cross-referenced charged prices of the services to which they consent.

But this rule – taking a writing as the best evidence of the parties' actual agreement – is grounded in policy.[59] Contract law has no *basic* commitment to enforcing writings *qua* writings.[60] It has a *basic* commitment to enforcing agreements, written or unwritten.[61] There are, of course, good policy reasons to take writings in general as the best evidence of the actual agreement.[62] But enforcing writings for their own sake is hardly the point.

Thus, if we take seriously the idea that the common law is built on a distinction between its basic concepts and commitments and a great deal of policy-driven prophylaxis, the health care billing cases offer a case study in their clash – we have a writing containing a purported price term presumably higher than any reasonable parties actually bargaining would agree upon, and no actual agreement on that term. This entails a systematic clash between the basic commitment of contract law to enforce actual or estimated agreements between private parties, on the one hand, and the prophylactic policy rule enforcing writings where they exist on the other. Courts ought not let policy presumptions in favor of writing get in the way of finding a reasonable cost where in fact the parties have not agreed on one, because only the latter is consistent with the basic functions and aspirations of contract law.

Moreover, the concept of reasonableness – everywhere it appears in private law – is not an algorithmic rule of calculation. It is a standard encompassing a range of fair and conceivable outcomes consistent with some mélange of basic morality, community norms, and intuitions.[63] Whether something falls within the concept of reasonableness is generally a question of fact, paradigmatically the domain of the jury.[64] Having concluded that contract damages in health care cases ought to be governed by reasonable prices, then, points toward their being a jury question – to be adjudicated within the jury's prerogative drawing community standards of what is reasonable. This is consistent with how reasonableness is understood throughout private law, rather than, say, courts' adopting an arbitrary mechanical rule that damages reflect some fixed percentage of prices charged or paid, or a penalty default rule designed to incentivize better drafting.[65]

58 Restatement (Second) Torts § 920A(2).
59 Lawrence M. Solan, Contract as Agreement, 83 Notre Dame L. Rev. 353 (2007).
60 Restatement (Second) Contracts § 1.
61 Crescente Molina, The Conceptual Foundations of Contract Formation in Reinach and the Foundations of Private Law (Marietta Auer et al. eds., forthcoming).
62 Restatement (Second) Contracts 9 3 Intro. Note. (1981).
63 James A. Henderson, Learned Hand's Paradox: An Essay on Custom in Negligence Law, 105 Calif. L. Rev. 165 (2017).
64 G. Alexander Nunn, Law, Fact, and Procedural Justice, 70 Emory L. J. 1273, 1284–85 (2021).
65 Wendy Netter Epstein, Price Transparency and Incomplete Contracts in Health Care, 67 Emory L. J. 1 (2017).

This analysis is perhaps even clearer in the tort context. Whatever the logic of the substantive component of the collateral source rule, its *evidentiary* component is policy-grounded prophylaxis – based on the generalization that evidence of third-party payments is more likely to cause greater harm in unreasonably low damages awards than its usefulness in determining reasonableness.[66] Whether or not this calculus and the empirical premises on which it is based are true generally, it is flatly and systematically false in the health care damages context.

The basic purpose of tort law is to redress wrongs.[67] The concept of reasonableness in tort damages plays a similar role as in the contract context – approximating a rough measure of actual damages for injuries that are not algorithmically measurable.[68] And just as there, a theory of private law distinguishing between its basic conceptual commitments and its policy prophylaxis explains why courts in these tort cases legitimately do not permit a strict reading of the evidentiary role of the collateral source rule to systematically frustrate ascertaining reasonable damages.

15.5.2 *Juries, Reasonableness, and Separation of Powers*

Moreover, this kind of conceptual reasoning is consistent with separation of powers. There are, of course, countless policy proposals for limiting the social harm of outrageous medical billing. George Nation, for example, has argued that the cost of medical services should be measured by the "average amount the hospital would be paid by private insurers" plus "between 10% to 15%."[69] Others argue that providers ought to accept the same payment for all patients,[70] or, perhaps, as Wendy Netter Epstein argues, courts should impose penalty default of US$0 in these contracts to incentivize providers to engage in actual bargaining.[71] Of course, maybe health care ought entirely to be paid for by the government.[72] But whether or not any of these are good ideas, they have no basis in the concepts of private law. Contract law's commitment to enforce freely made agreements could not possibly justify capping prices at X percent of some contractually exogenous price. No principle of tort law socializes medicine.

66 Cutsinger v. Redfern, 12 So. 3d 945, 952 (La. 2008); Caylor v. Atchison, Topeka & Santa Fe Ry., 368 P.2d 281, 284 (Kan. 1962); Ellsworth v. Schelbrok, 611 N.W. 2d 764, 767 (Wis. 2000); Restatement (Second) Torts § 920A cmt. a, cmt. b.

67 Steven Schaus, A Simple Model of Torts and Moral Wrongs, 97 Notre Dame L. Rev. 1029, 1030 (2022); John C. P. Goldberg & Benjamin C. Zipursky, Torts as Wrongs, 88 Tex. L. Rev. 917 (2010).

68 Nathaniel Donahue & John Fabian Witt, Tort as Private Administration, 105 Cornell L. Rev. 1093, 1137–38 (2020).

69 Nation, supra note 41, at 189.

70 Uwe E. Reinhardt, The Pricing of U.S. Hospital Services: Chaos behind a Veil of Secrecy, 25 Health Affs. 57, 58 (2006).

71 Epstein, supra note 65.

72 Elenore Wade, Health Injustice in the Laboratories of Democracy, 29 Geo. J. Poverty L & Pol'y 177, 177 (2022).

In contrast, holding that the basic commitments of private law supersede judge-made policy prophylaxis of already-dubious democratic provenance is an entirely legitimate judicial prerogative. And the same goes for recognizing that one of those basic concepts with the same name is in fact getting at the same idea in two distinct areas of private law.

Common law reasoning is a legitimate exercise of judicial prerogative because we have impliedly delegated to the judiciary the authority to apply the basic commitments of private law – we've decided that we want judges to enforce promises, and leave it to them to tell us what that means in particular cases.[73] In contrast, policy rules like the evidentiary role of the collateral source rule are best considered by democratically accountable legislatures.[74] If we reluctantly accept the existence and maybe the necessity of judicial prophylaxis based on policy experience, we can nevertheless insist that those rules be subsidiary to concepts more clearly given to judges.

15.5.3 *Conceptual Reasoning and Common Law Systematicity*

Finally, this move demonstrates the benefits of the systematicity of concepts in a broadly coherent common law.[75] The concept of reasonableness in contract and tort contexts is at least very similar – in both cases, it refers to a range of acceptable rough approximations of something that private law requires the court to measure but which it cannot do easily. If this is right, and the courts giving the question of tort damages to juries are right that theirs is the way to measure the reasonableness of health care prices, it makes sense for the courts to apply the same method of reasoning about the same basic concept in contract cases – admitting all relevant evidence.

After all, it looks like the concept *is* the same in both cases, and what is reasonable in tort is at least presumptively reasonable in contract.

In contrast, if we were to adopt the Realist view that all this just obscures policy reasoning with conceptual words, contract law's drawing on tort law holdings would be epistemically much more demanding – indeed, there is no a priori reason to assume that the policy considerations in both contexts are the same, and the court would have to prove to our satisfaction that measuring contract damages in this way would be as good idea as a policy matter as it is in tort.[76] Maybe it could, but any analogy between the contexts would be an empirically contingent coincidence.

Instead, if the concept of reasonableness is, at a basic level, the same in both places, courts can import conclusions about that concept across contexts without

[73] Toomey, supra note 22.
[74] Id.
[75] Waldron, supra note 19, at 25–26; Gold & Smith, supra note 27, at 492.
[76] Jiménez, supra note 18, at 1155–56.

relitigating policy considerations from the ground up.[77] Of course, there may be circumstances in which the concept of reasonableness might need to be understood differently in different situations, but recognizing the identity of the concept lowers the information costs of reasoning about those kinds of exceptions.[78]

15.6 CONCLUSION

The judicial response to the social challenges of contemporary health care pricing illustrates the mechanisms of taking seriously on its face the conceptual internal logic of private law – both its plausibility and its benefits. Nothing here, again, is offered as a comprehensive solution to the idiosyncrasies of American health care finance. Indeed, for more broader solutions, this understanding of common law tells us to look to legislatures and regulators – as we have.[79]

But the case study also illustrates that a conceptual theory of the common law – often caricatured as rigid and insensitive to complex contemporary problems – is not in fact *powerless* in responding to modern problems, captive to its own precedents. Where the policy rules adopted by those precedents contradict the basic concepts and principles of the private law – especially where courts can draw on similar reasoning about those concepts in related areas – they *can* respond to a variety of social developments and problems, giving us, at least, a private law that is rational, coherent, and democratically explicable.

77 Waldron, supra note 19, at 25–26.

78 Thomas W. Merrill & Henry E. Smith, Optimal Standardization in the Law of Property: The Numerus Clausus Principle, 100 Yale L. J. 1 (2000).

79 See supra note 12.

16

Health Law's Sheathed Sword

Why Hasn't Civil Litigation Dented Health Care Costs?

Jackson Williams

16.1 INTRODUCTION

It is generally agreed that health care costs in the United States are unreasonably high and unsustainably growing, and that these problems are attributable to prices that are excessive, relative to those in peer industrialized nations.[1] High prices, in turn, are frequently attributed to consolidated markets for provider services[2] and other aggressive, extractive practices by providers.[3]

Generally, one might say that three categories of action are available for stakeholders to push back on prices. Health care purchasers – primarily, employers and insurers, can use the carrot of inclusion in a health plan's network to negotiate lower prices.

A second course is seeking legislative or regulatory action to tamp down prices. This can include options such as state-imposed rate setting,[4] or less onerous measures aimed at bolstering purchasers' negotiating leverage.[5]

A third course to pursue is litigation – either initiated by a purchaser or through defense of provider collection suits when a purchaser is willing to challenge bills because it believes the prevailing law is favorable to it.

[1] Gerard F. Anderson et al., It's the Prices, Stupid. Why the United States Is So Different from Other Countries, 22 Health Affs. 89, 102 (2003).

[2] Zack Cooper et al., The Price Ain't Right? Hospital Prices and Health Spending on the Privately Insured, 134 Q. J. Econ. 51 (2019).

[3] Atul Gawande, The Cost Conundrum, The New Yorker (June 1, 2009), https://www.newyorker.com/magazine/2009/06/01/the-cost-conundrum.

[4] Ezekiel Emanuel et al., A Systemic Approach to Containing Health Care Spending, 367 New Engl. J. Med. 949 (2012); Gerard Anderson & Bradley Herring, The All-Payer Rate Setting Model for Pricing Medical Services and Drugs, 17 AMA J. Ethics 770 (2015).

[5] A Tool for States to Address Health Care Consolidation: Prohibiting Anticompetitive Health Plan Contracts, Nat'l Acad. for State Health Pol'y (Apr. 12, 2021), https://nashp.org/a-tool-for-states-to-address-health-care-consolidation-prohibiting-anticompetitive-health-plan-contracts/.

What might be called "cost containment litigation" is not unusual but has been fairly infrequent. One of the most audacious provider overreaches was addressed in an antitrust lawsuit, *UEBT v. Sutter Health*,[6] which was settled in 2019 resulting in a US$575 million disgorgement and injunctive relief to curb the underlying anti-competitive conduct. But this outcome remains an outlier, and the circumstances that make it unique exemplify the dynamics surrounding this type of litigation.

Another practice that provoked an outsize amount of outrage and attention in the second decade of this century was balance billing and other machinations by out-of-network (OON) providers. In particular, hospital-based physicians were able to opt out of all insurance plans because they serve captive clientele within in-network facilities.[7] In 2020, Congress enacted the No Surprises Act in an attempt to finally resolve the problem. But during this period, some modest efforts to invoke private law against rogue providers also proceeded in the courts. As I will explain below, conditions seemed favorable for a litigated solution to the surprise billing problem, yet the coalition of payers and consumer advocates formed to end the abuses chose to concentrate on securing a legislative solution.

Why might it be that this coalition would not, or could not, pursue a coordinated litigation strategy? An impracticability or unwillingness to invoke private-law remedies would give providers and suppliers an edge over purchasers in the struggle to contain the excessive costs of the US health care system. This research project surveyed private-law approaches that have been applied to challenge provider opportunism. The overview of the litigation studied will be presented elsewhere. This article confronts the question of missing-in-action litigation, from political science and economic perspectives.

16.2 WHY TAKE HEALTH CARE COST CONTAINMENT TO COURT?

Two types of provider opportunism seem amenable to court-adjudicated resolution: attempts to collect exorbitant "billed charges," and anticompetitive conduct.

16.2.1 *Background on Billed Charges versus Market Prices*

As a basic framework for understanding legal disputes over healthcare prices, it is helpful to consider the distinction between billed charges and market prices. Billed charges can be thought of as a provider's optimal price for a service free from market constraints, a provider's default "asking price" or "list price." Market prices can be thought of as those prevailing in a competitive market for health care services,

6 UEBT v. Sutter Health, No. CGC 14-538451 (Cal. Super. Ct.).

7 Elisabeth Rosenthal, Costs Can Go Up Fast When E.R. Is in Network but the Doctors Are Not, N.Y. Times (Sept. 28, 2014), https://www.nytimes.com/2014/09/29/us/costs-can-go-up-fast-when-er-is-in-network-but-the-doctors-are-not.html.

emerging from network contracts negotiated by insurers or cash payments by consumers.

While the author strongly believes that patient liability for billed charges has little legal support under the common law, there is admittedly enough legal ambiguity about their status, as well as logistical difficulty in challenging them, that they have had compelling power over payers and consumers.[8] Further, some providers have been able to obtain fees close to their idealized maximum price through consolidation or other anticompetitive practices, reaping amounts that resemble billed charges more than prices that would result from vigorous competition. The following two sections summarize the rationales for challenging these practices in the courts.

16.2.2 *The "Common Law Solution" to Billed Charges*

The substantive law case for litigating billed charges has been articulated by Prof. Barak Richman, who argues that "consumers are already protected by current law – bedrock, rudimentary contract law – and require only its proper application to end harmful chargemaster practices."[9] According to Richman and colleagues, "providers have no legal authority to collect chargemaster charges that exceed market prices for OON services, and thus neither patients nor payers are under any obligation to pay such chargemaster prices."[10]

Richman and colleagues are referring to the doctrine of implied contract, or *quantum meruit*. The Pennsylvania Superior Court applied this doctrine in its decision in *Temple University Hospital, Inc. v. Healthcare Management Alternatives, Inc.*[11] The case involved services provided by a hospital to a health plan's enrollees following expiration of the parties' network contract. The hospital sought its chargemaster rates from the insurer. The court noted testimony from the hospital's CFO that the hospital seldom received its published rates.

The court held that when "there is no express agreement to pay, the law implies a promise to pay a reasonable fee for a health provider's services. Thus, in a situation such as this, the defendant should pay for what the services are ordinarily worth in the community. Services are worth what people ordinarily pay for them."[12] Because the controlling question is "what healthcare providers actually receive for those services," the chargemaster "cannot be considered the value of the benefit conferred

8 See the eleven cases from various jurisdictions holding that paperwork signed by patients can incorporate hospital chargemaster rates cited in Centura Health Corp. v. French, 2020 COA 85, 490 P.3d 780.

9 Barak D. Richman et al., Battling the Chargemaster: A Simple Remedy to Balance Billing for Unavoidable Out-of-Network Care, 23(4) Am. J. Managed Care e100 (2017).

10 Id. at e103.

11 Temple Univ. Hosp. v. Healthcare Management, 832 A.2d 501 (Pa. Super. Ct. 2003).

12 Id. at 508.

because that is not what people in the community ordinarily pay for medical services."[13]

16.2.3 *Private Antitrust Enforcement*

The case for increased private antitrust enforcement in the health care sphere is articulated by Anne Marie Helm, who argues that it "can restore competition, deter antitrust violations, and compensate victims in the markets for health care services and insurance … accordingly, the United States should be looking for ways to optimize it."[14]

Helm acknowledges that plaintiffs face a challenging legal environment. Nevertheless, some supportive case law indicates judicial appreciation of the importance of private enforcement.

Messner v. Northshore Univ. HealthSystem[15] involved a putative damages class action following up on the FTC's unwinding of a hospital merger. The District Court denied class certification on predominance grounds.[16] Observing that "it is important not to let a quest for perfect evidence become the enemy of good evidence," the Seventh Circuit reversed.[17]

Another decision, *Palmyra Park Hospital, Inc. v. Phoebe Putney Memorial Hospital*,[18] permitted a challenge by a competing hospital shut out by a large hospital system's market power. Palmyra had been an in-network provider for Blue Cross Blue Shield of Georgia but lost its in-network status allegedly because Phoebe Putney leveraged its power as sole Certificate of Need permittee for three medical services "to force Blue Cross (and other insurers) to exclude Palmyra from their provider networks. Specifically, Phoebe Putney threatened to demand significantly higher reimbursement rates for those services in its contracts with Blue Cross if Blue Cross included Palmyra in its provider network. Palmyra attempted to contract with Blue Cross on several occasions" but was turned down due to Blue Cross's contract with Phoebe Putney.[19]

The issue in the case was whether a competing hospital is an efficient enforcer of the antitrust laws for purposes of antitrust standing. The district judge believed that the health insurers or consumers were the appropriate plaintiffs. The Eleventh Circuit reversed, observing that such scenarios were unlikely, particularly the former:

[13] Id.

[14] Anne M. Helm, Optimizing Private Antitrust Enforcement in Health Care, 11 St. Louis U. J. Health L. & Pol'y 5, 7 (2017), https://ssrn.com/abstract=3157878.

[15] Messner v. Northshore Univ. HealthSystem, 669 F.3d 802 (7th Cir. 2012).

[16] In re Evanston Northwestern Healthcare Corp. Antitrust Litig., 268 F.R.D. 56 (N.D. Ill. 2010).

[17] Messner, supra note 15, at 808.

[18] Palmyra Park Hosp. v. Phoebe Putney Memorial Hosp., 604 F.3d 1291 (11th Cir. 2010).

[19] Id. at 1296.

> [T]he insurance companies are likely able to pass a large percentage of the higher reimbursement rates on to their policy holders in the form of higher premiums. Thus, they bear relatively little of the cost imposed by the tying scheme. Moreover, an insurance company would risk losing its goodwill with Phoebe Putney if it sued; given that an insurer must include Phoebe Putney in its network to be competitive in southwest Georgia, insurers would be understandably reluctant to anger Phoebe Putney by suing it.[20]

The denouement of this saga, however, shows the weakness of relying on competitors to challenge market power. Phoebe Putney acquired and absorbed Palmyra Hospital over Federal Trade Commission (FTC) objections.[21]

16.3 THE PROMISE AND LIMITS OF COST CONTAINMENT LITIGATION

Victory in litigation over an opportunistic provider can have two types of benefits: a private benefit for the party that brought the suit, and a collective benefit for consumers and payers – that is, the public at large – if the wins change business practices. When a case involves a unique, unusual, or payer-specific practice, the private benefit predominates, and success in the suit, such as a damages award or an injunction, suffices to satisfy the plaintiff's goals.

Use of litigation to achieve a collective benefit is more complex, and when it comes to health care costs that are increasing for every employer, worker, and consumer, due to the same common and pervasive practices, it is the collective good that is implicated. Ideally, success would involve discrete entities subject to controlling legal authority that prohibits an abusive business practice (e.g., the outcome of the recent BCBS antitrust litigation).[22] Realistically, it would more likely result in a few impactful judgments, creating a body of law that convinces the losing litigant that continuing the practice would be economically futile (e.g., the litigation that ended production of the Ford Pinto automobile).[23] To be sure, through the availability of punitive damages in tort suits, treble damages in antitrust suits, and Rule 11 sanctions in civil suits, private law has tools to confront social costs and address collective relief in addition to individual relief; however, no attorney would suggest that these tools are easy for litigants to access.

In the case of the out-of-network hospital-based physician or air ambulance business models, true victory would have meant a sequence of victories spelling out the rights of consumers so explicitly as to make further assertions of balance billing claims frivolous and subject to sanctions. It would have required an

20 Id. at 1305.

21 In the Matter of Phoebe Putney Health System et al., No. 9348 (F.T.C. 2015).

22 In re Blue Cross Blue Shield Antitrust Litig. (MDL No. 2406), 2015 WL 10891632 (N.D. Ala. 2015).

23 Grimshaw v. Ford Motor Company, 174 Cal. Rptr. 348 (Cal. Ct. App. 1981).

orchestrated effort to defend consumers in collection cases (as the author proposed prior to passage of the No Surprises Act).[24]

16.3.1 *The Collective Action Problem in Cost Containment Litigation*

But who, exactly, would bear the costs to achieve this widespread, dispersed collective benefit? A health care system that functions properly in spite of efforts by rogue actors is truly a public good that would be enjoyed by scores of insurers, many thousands of employers, and hundreds of millions of individuals. Some sort of cooperative effort would be needed to achieve it.[25]

Mancur Olson articulated what is known as the Collective Action Problem.[26] While conventional wisdom expects that groups of individuals with common interests would act on behalf of those interests, since they would gain from such cooperation, "they will not act to advance their common or group objectives unless there is coercion to force them to do so," or some separate, distinct incentive is offered to group members individually, conditioned on their help in pursuing the collective aim.[27] Olson's argument is that individual group members, while having common interests, also retain purely individual interests such as saving money, so if it is possible to drop out of paying dues toward a cooperative effort, "the loss of one dues payer will not noticeably increase the burden for any other one dues payer, and so a rational person would not believe that if he were to withdraw from an organization he would drive others to do so."[28]

Consider the sprawling variety of entities that encompass the latent "group" concerned with surprise bills: consumers, who, as patients receive balance bills and as workers experience a significant, but usually invisible, reduction in take-home pay as health benefit costs rise; employers, who in the short run must pay the bills (if self-insured) or higher premiums (if fully insured) but who, over the long run, may be indifferent as to the proportion of employee compensation paid in cash versus health benefits; and insurers, who are most directly on the hook for increased payments but also have interests that may diverge from those of enrollees and clients.

Creating a body of law that would render impotent the out-of-network business model for physician staffing companies would be a public good – a benefit from which no payer or consumer could be excluded.

[24] Jackson Williams, The Persistence of Opportunistic Business Models in Health Care and a Stronger Role for Insurance Regulators in Containing Health Care Costs, 41 Nova L. Rev. 3 (2017), https://nsuworks.nova.edu/nlr/vol41/iss3/3.

[25] Of course, a critical mass of litigation generated for private benefit could have the secondary, incidental effect of deterring a business practice and accomplishing a public benefit, as occurred with the Ford Pinto.

[26] Mancur Olson, The Logic of Collective Action (1971).

[27] Id. at 2.

[28] Id. at 12.

Nevertheless, these diverse interests came together in a Coalition Against Surprise Medical Billing that successfully lobbied Congress to curb balance billing, but they did not jointly pursue a litigation strategy. A fair amount of political science theory and research is available to analyze why groups choose to, or choose not to, seek redress from the courts, which will be discussed *infra*.

16.3.2 *Are Payers Effective Agents of Their Enrollees?*

It is apparent that, unlike other rivalrous dyads in the US economy, providers and payers generally lack an aggressive, two-sided contentiousness. When one compares their network contracting and other interactions to other famously antagonistic dyads – labor versus management, the Association of Trial Lawyers of America and its members versus the US Chamber of Commerce and its members, bulk purchasers for resale versus suppliers – the relationship looks rather amicable. To Dennis Scanlon, "it is somewhat of a mystery as to why insurers and third party administrators (TPAs) have not been able to achieve price reductions through contracting" and "not serving as better agents for their customers."[29]

Surely, a large influence is payers' desire to offer broad provider networks. According to the Kaiser Family Foundation's 2019 Employer Health Benefits Survey,[30] employers were asked what they considered the most important factor in constructing their provider networks. Thirty percent of employers identified the number and convenience of providers as most important.[31] Thirty-nine percent of employers said that they would not reduce network size for cost savings, with 36 percent saying that they would need to realize savings of at least 20 percent to narrow their network.[32] Only 2 percent of firms reported that they or their insurer eliminated a hospital or health system from their provider network during the past year to reduce costs.[33]

Clearly, payers worry about imposing inconvenience on enrollees and see broad networks as attractive to workers. Notably, private insurers have not embraced the role of challenging questionable or fraudulent claims the way that federal health programs have.[34] In Washington, DC, during federal employees' open enrollment

[29] Dennis P. Scanlon, If Reference-Based Benefit Designs Work, Why Are They Not Widely Adopted? Insurers and Administrators Not Doing Enough to Address Price Variation, 55 Health Serv. Res. 344, 344–47 (2020).

[30] 2019 Employer Health Benefits Survey, Kaiser Fam. Found. (Sept. 25, 2019), https://www.kff.org/health-costs/report/2019-employer-health-benefits-survey/#:~:text=The%202019%20survey%20included%202%2C012,the%20cost%20of%20their%20coverage.

[31] Id.

[32] Id.

[33] Id.

[34] Marshall Allen, We Asked Prosecutors if Health Insurance Companies Care about Fraud. They Laughed at Us, ProPublica (Sept. 10, 2019), https://www.propublica.org/article/we-asked-prosecutors-if-health-insurance-companies-care-about-fraud-they-laughed-at-us.

period in 2022, city buses were emblazoned with advertisements from Blue Cross Blue Shield boasting that 96 percent of hospitals and 95 percent of doctors were included in their network. But Amazon and Walmart emphasize broad arrays of products, and this does not deter them from bargaining hard with suppliers. As Scanlon notes, payers should be able to negotiate away unwarranted variations in provider prices until they converge at an appropriate level,[35] as do prices for paper towels negotiated by Walmart.

What incentive do payers have to emphasize provider price reductions over other considerations?

Employers are the largest category of payers in the United States, and many participate in organizations such as Catalyst for Payment Reform and Purchaser Business Group on Health that emphasize cost containment. But one prominent school of thought predicts employers will be largely indifferent to whether compensation is paid in the form of cash wages or health benefits.

> Under traditional economic theory, employer contributions to health insurance premiums are one of many parts of workers' total compensation, and employers offer the combination of wages and benefits that will best help them attract and retain employees ... When health care costs rise, employers can respond ... by increasing worker premium contributions, increasing deductibles or copayment amounts, reducing employment, or increasing their own premium contributions while reducing or limiting wage growth accordingly.[36]

As such, health care costs "come out of workers' wages or other compensation over the long-run," rather than out of employers' profits.[37]

Insurers, meanwhile, may have even less incentive to contain medical costs. Recall the Eleventh Circuit's observations about insurance companies' ability to pass along higher reimbursement rates through higher premiums. Further, insurers are subject to the Affordable Care Act's medical loss ratio (MLR) floor. This regulation requires insurers to issue rebates if claim expenses are less than 80 to 85 percent of premiums. The intention of the law, of course, was to reduce premiums by reducing administrative costs and profits; but the requirement can also be met by holding those elements constant and increasing claim payouts. One study found an increase in claim costs after the MLR law took effect, concluding it was "likely that insurers raised their claims costs from a combination of more comprehensive

[35] Scanlon, supra note 29, at 345.

[36] Laurel Lucia & Ken Jacobs, Increases in Health Care Costs Are Coming out of Workers' Pockets One Way or Another: The Tradeoff between Employer Premium Contributions and Wages, UC Berkeley Labor Ctr. Blog (Jan. 29, 2020), https://laborcenter.berkeley.edu/employer-premium-contributions-and-wages/.

[37] Id.

coverage and reduced cost-containment effort, such as negotiations with providers or claims utilization management practices."[38]

At the other end of the continuum, union health plans established under the Taft-Hartley Act surely have the greatest incentive to curb provider costs since they bargain for the complete compensation package and can quantify the wage/health benefit trade-off literally to the penny per hour worked.[39] Funds that go to high-cost providers can be directly reallocated to wages if the union plan is willing to sacrifice access to some providers.[40] Unlike the situation when the employer alone stewards the health benefit, union leaders can promise definite monetary benefits to be reaped in exchange for dropping, or threatening to drop, a high-cost provider.[41]

And so we see that in the *Messner* antitrust litigation, the Painters District Council No. 30 Health & Welfare Fund was a named plaintiff, while Blue Cross Blue Shield of Illinois filed an affidavit stating that it "did not pay artificially inflated prices" and did not suffer "any injury or damage."[42] This continuum of incentives is concerning, because the payer category with the least incentive has the greatest resources, while the payer category with maximum incentives serves only a small proportion of health insurance enrollees. Payer participation in cost containment activities may rely more on insurers' and employers' executives' sense of unfairness or outrage at excesses than on economic incentives.

The Eleventh Circuit, in the *Phoebe Putnam* decision, also mentioned insurers' incentive to retain goodwill with provider partners.[43] Outside of extreme and exploitative circumstances, insurers surely feel inhibited from confronting providers they need to maintain adequate networks, especially in an era when insurers are asking providers to take on risk. Conversely, unions' mission encompasses vigilance against oppressive business practices, and confrontation is central to their *modus operandi*.

Finally, federal antitrust law prefers plaintiffs to be the direct purchaser of the overpriced service.[44] The victorious cocounsel in *UEBT v. Sutter Health* argues that one reason they secured a settlement in their state-court litigation while a similar federal case yielded a verdict for the defendant was that they sought "direct damages for amounts that self-insured entities allegedly overpaid Sutter for health care services; in the federal case, by contrast, the insured class members sought indirect

38 Steve Cicala et al., Regulating Markups in US Health Insurance, 11 Am. Econ. J. Applied Econ. 71, 101 (2019).

39 Cost Containment and Price Transparency: Hearing before the California Senate Committee on Health (Mar. 5, 2014) (testimony of Ken Stuart).

40 Martha Hostetter & Sarah Klein, In Focus: How Unions Act as a Force for Change in Health Care Delivery and Payment, Transforming Care (newsletter) (Mar. 21, 2019), https://doi.org/10.26099/mx4c-qc89.

41 Noam N. Levey, Not Everyone Has Eye-popping Deductibles: How One Union Kept Medical Bills in Check, L.A. Times (Dec. 17, 2019), https://www.latimes.com/politics/story/2019-12-17/one-union-kept-medical-bills-in-check.

42 Messner, supra note 15, at 822.

43 Palmyra Park Hosp., supra note 18, at 1305.

44 See Illinois Brick Co. v. Illinois, 431 U.S. 720 (1977).

damages for the increased insurance premiums resulting from Sutter's alleged overcharges. Such indirect damages can be harder to prove."[45]

16.3.3 *Examples of Potentially Effective Collective Efforts*

Economic and political science doctrines offer insights into how collective action problems can be solved, and these insights illuminate three categories of litigation, which we might expect to better facilitate challenges to excessive health care costs.

16.3.3.1 Class Actions

Olson argued that one solution to the collective action problem is compulsory participation. Olson cites the tremendous growth of labor unions following enactment of the Wagner Act, which requires that once a majority of workers in a bargaining unit vote for union representation, employers must bargain collectively with the union and that the contract will bind all the workers in the unit.[46]

A certified class action is analogous to a certified bargaining unit – both involve representation of a community of interest, on a mandatory basis, by an entity that will be compensated on a mandatory basis. As with collective bargaining, representation depends upon entrepreneurial activity by that entity, which in turn is conditioned on the union organizer's or plaintiff's attorney's confidence in prevailing.

16.3.3.2 State Attorneys General as Advocates of Lower Costs

Standard neoclassical welfare economic analysis holds that collective benefits, which are non-rivalrous and non-excludable, are public goods that can't be provided by the market and must be provided through government. Successful cost containment litigation that prospectively ends abusive practices fits this description. As such, the most logical plaintiff is not an insurer or a class representative, but the government agencies such as attorney general's offices.[47]

But there are drawbacks to relying on political officeholders to enforce cost containment, including the complexity of health care issues which may intimidate lawyers, the broad range of responsibilities that an Attorney General (AG) must meet with limited resources, and the possibility of regulatory capture of AGs by health care interest groups.

45 Daniel G. Bird & Emilio E. Varanini, Deciphering Sutter Health's State-Court Settlement and Federal-Court Win in Parallel Antitrust Cases, Health Affs. Forefront (May 10, 2022), https://www.healthaffairs.org/content/forefront/deciphering-sutter-health-s-state-court-settlement-and-federal-court-win-parallel.

46 Olson, supra note 26, at 79.

47 Robert A. Berenson et al., Addressing Health Care Market Consolidation and High Prices: The Role of the States, Urban Institute (2020), https://www.urban.org/research/publication/addressing-health-care-market-consolidation-and-high-prices.

16.3.3.3 Patron-Sponsored Litigation

Political scientist Jack Walker charted and analyzed the growth of US interest groups that Olson's theory predicts should not have happened.[48] He found that 60 percent of nonprofit groups and 89 percent of citizen sector groups received startup funding from an outside source.[49] Among nonprofit sector groups, 30 percent reported receiving support from foundations and 29 percent reported support from individual patrons.[50] Among citizen sector groups, 48 percent reported receiving support from foundations and 78 percent reported support from wealthy individuals.[51] Walker concluded: "Patrons stand at the center of a common solution to Olson's collective goods dilemma."[52]

As such, it is not surprising that philanthropies have emerged as a supporter of cost containment litigation in the absence of other collective efforts. The *Wall Street Journal* reported that Arnold Ventures, a foundation with health care costs as a key focus area, is among patrons supporting a number of lawsuits spearheaded by Fairmark Partners LLP.[53]

Note that these collective efforts, with consumers, employers, or the state as plaintiffs, do not implicate the partnership inhibition that seems to neutralize insurers as effective plaintiffs.

At several points *supra*, this article referenced the *UEBT v. Sutter Health* case. This case stands alone as the most – perhaps only – significant victory for payers and consumers over providers. Three notable traits of this case illustrate some of the bolstering elements of cost containment litigation discussed above: (1) a union health plan as plaintiff; (2) structured as a class action; and (3) the AG as a coplaintiff which, according to Bird and Varanini, "may have been significant to the settlement of the state case. Jury research has shown that some jurors are more likely to credit assertions that are backed by an attorney general or similar official."[54]

16.3.4 *Political Science Insights into Collective Litigation*

Walker's study of interest groups included a chapter on their litigation strategies. Interest groups do, said Walker, "file lawsuits to safeguard the interests of their members, promote test cases or class action suits … and file amicus briefs …,"

48 Jack L. Walker, Mobilizing Interest Groups in America: Patrons, Professions, and Social Movements (1991).
49 Id.
50 Id.
51 Id.
52 Id.
53 Melanie Evans, The Billionaire behind a Big-Hospital Battle, Wall St. J. (June 11, 2022), https://www.wsj.com/articles/the-billionaire-funding-a-battle-against-hospital-monopolies-11654920006.
54 Bird & Varanini, supra note 45.

but litigation is generally *ad hoc* and a departure from organizational routines and repertoires.[55]

Over the years, political science scholars have propounded theories explaining why some groups use the courts more than others.[56] Two of these theories suggest that coalitions of payers are unlikely candidates for litigants. The political disadvantage hypothesis holds that groups seek remedies through the courts primarily when they see no way forward via the political branches. Employers and insurers are hardly "out-groups" and their judgment that they could succeed in persuading Congress to curb surprise billing was vindicated. The rights consciousness theory predicts that groups "see[ing] themselves in terms of uncompromising rights" are more likely to seek recourse in the courts.[57] Payers are not citizen groups with this mindset, though some of their coalition partners on surprise billing are.

Meanwhile, two other theories predict that payer groups, having considerable organizational resources and having claims (common law and antitrust) that are quite compatible with and conducive to judicial resolution, would choose to bring litigation.[58]

Walker's own research conclusions suggest several reasons why the payer coalition did not prioritize private-law remedies. First, Walker concluded, litigation is "one of the least popular forms of advocacy pursued by interest groups."[59] Second, "groups engaged in policy areas characterized by intense disputes" – groups with "recurring opponents" or "natural enemies" – are more likely to carry those disputes to court.[60] As noted, payers and providers are opponents only intermittently; more often they are partners. Finally, Walker says, "[G]roups that operate in policy areas that are sensitive to changes in outcomes of national elections are also more likely to resort to litigation."[61] The parties to the "Network Wars" were not aligned with any particular political party or ideology that would complicate passage of a surprise billing law.

16.4 CONCLUSION

It should be noted that, in spite of the foregoing considerations, payer-initiated cost containment litigation *does* take place, albeit not systematically.[62] There seems to be a point at which insurers' frustration can boil over, and a decision is made to invoke

55 Walker, supra note 48, at 158.

56 See id. at 160–61 (summarizing work by Susan Olson, Frank Sorauf, and Karen O'Connor).

57 Id. at 160.

58 Id. (citing Susan Olson).

59 Id. at 171.

60 Id. at 173.

61 Id. at 174.

62 See, e.g., Blue Cross & Blue Shield United of Wis., 152 F.3d 588 (7th Cir. 1998); Bay Area Surgical Management LLC v. Aetna Life Insurance Co., Case No. 15-cv-01416-BLF (N.D. Cal. July 18, 2016); Envision HealthCare Corp. v. United HealthCare Ins. Co., 311 F. Supp. 3d 1322 (S.D. Fla. 2018), French v. Centura Health, 509 P.3d 443 (Colo. 2022).

private law to remedy overreaching. Could these urges be harnessed and institutionalized in some way? Ideally, private law would be a tool to tamp down on provider opportunism that purchaser-side stakeholders utilize as readily as, and complementary to, legislative advocacy or hardball contract negotiations. The author's view, as a lawyer who has advocated before all three branches of government, is that litigation *can* (though not necessarily *does*) produce change more quickly than lobbying Congress.

We would also want insurers and employers deputized as unambiguously committed agents of consumers and workers, and to establish structures to investigate, conceptualize, and prosecute common-law and statutory violations by providers. And we would want employers and insurers to hold themselves to a duty to enrollees similar to that embraced by union health plans.

Not all excessive prices will rise to the level of legal violations, of course, but some instances will merit scrutiny: where provider prices are attributable to antitrust violations, upcoding, claims for excessive billed charges that TPAs paid without regard to prevailing prices, and, perhaps, facility fees and similar mark-ups and upcharges.

One option would be for payers to contribute to a joint legal fund. This could take the form of a small assessment (or "check-off" as it is sometimes called) analogous to those levied on agricultural producers of commodities to support the promotion of their product. Such a fund might be operated under the auspices of existing employer coalitions, which would relieve individual payers from poisoning relationships with providers. It could hire staff to investigate and develop cases or provide grant funding for dedicated positions in state AG's offices. It could ensure that damage awards or settlements are returned to enrollees, and operate as, and be perceived as, a more public-minded litigant than insurers. Seed money from a foundation might help build momentum for such an effort.

Private law could be a powerful sword to wield against health care costs, if an appropriate champion comes forward.

17

The Canary in the Coal Mine

Private Antitrust Law and New Dynamics in Health Care Markets

Jaime S. King

17.1 INTRODUCTION

All is not well in America's health care system. The United States consistently spends significantly more than any other nation on health care goods and services, reaching US$4.3 trillion and nearly US$11,000 per capita in 2021.[1] Despite being an outlier in health care spending, American quality of care metrics and health outcomes lag behind those of other comparator nations.[2] A 2023 report by the Commonwealth Fund found that Americans have the lowest life expectancy at birth, the highest death rates for avoidable or treatable conditions, the highest maternal and infant mortality rates, the highest rates of people with multiple chronic conditions, and among the highest suicide rates of thirteen peer nations.[3]

While numerous factors contribute to American health care woes, a primary cause is the failure of the market-based health care system to protect competition in the ways needed to control prices, promote innovation, and improve quality. Health care markets at all levels are more consolidated and complex than ever

[1] Ctrs. for Medicare & Medicaid Servs., National Health Spending Grew Slightly in 2021, CMS Newsroom (Dec. 14, 2022), https://www.cms.gov/newsroom/press-releases/national-health-spending-grew-slightly-2021; Org. for Econ. Coop. and Dev. (OECD), Health Spending (2023), https://data.oecd.org/healthres/health-spending.htm.

[2] See, e.g., Chih Kuang Liang & Lian-Kung Chen, National Health Care Quality and COVID-19 Case Fatality Rate: International Comparisons of Top 50 Countries, 98 Archives of Gerontology and Geriatrics 104587 (2022); OECD, Life Expectancy at Birth (2023), https://data.oecd.org/healthstat/life-expectancy-at-birth.htm; OECD, Life Expectancy at 65 (2023), https://data.oecd.org/healthstat/life-expectancy-at-65.htm; OECD, Infant Mortality Rates (2023), https://data.oecd.org/healthstat/infant-mortality-rates.htm.

[3] Munira Z. Gunja et al., U.S. Healthcare from a Global Perspective, 2022: Accelerating Spending, Worsening Outcomes, Commonwealth Fund Issue Brief (Jan. 31, 2023), https://www.commonwealthfund.org/publications/issue-briefs/2023/jan/us-health-care-global-perspective-2022) (comparing the US with Australia, Canada, France, Germany, Japan, the Netherlands, New Zealand, Norway, South Korea, Sweden, Switzerland, and the United Kingdom).

before, involving new market structures and actors that often confound and complicate traditional norms of antitrust enforcement. As health care prices continue to increase and quality stagnates, academics and health policy analysts have repeatedly called for stronger enforcement of antitrust laws in health care as well as stronger regulation to control prices.[4] This chapter argues that private antitrust law, the law governing market behavior by and between private actors, has a unique and essential role to play in protecting consumers and competitive markets by identifying and challenging anticompetitive behaviors arising from new dynamics in health care. Private law has an ability to extend, inform, and enhance public law initiatives by state and federal antitrust enforcers.

17.2 THE CURRENT STATE OF HEALTH CARE MARKETS

American health care entities have evolved dramatically over the last fifty years, creating several new dynamics in health care markets, including the rise of health systems and health monoliths, the use of new negotiation and contracting practices, and the introduction of new market actors and business models. The consolidation of American health care markets has occurred through just about any means possible – horizontal, vertical, cross-market, and cross-industry. A recent study found that approximately 95 percent of metropolitan areas had highly concentrated hospital markets, 78 percent had highly concentrated specialist physician markets, and 58 percent had highly concentrated insurer markets.[5] This consolidation has led to the rise of health care systems – jointly owned or managed health care entities, such as physician practices, hospitals, and skilled nursing facilities[6] – and health monoliths – massive health care entities that extend beyond providers to include some combination of payors or insurers, pharmaceutical services, and data management services. Research has repeatedly demonstrated that consolidation drives health care price increases,[7] has minimal quality impacts,[8] and tends to reduce patient satisfaction rates.[9]

4 Leemore Dafny, Addressing Consolidation in Healthcare Markets, 325 JAMA 927 (Mar. 9, 2021); Martin Gaynor et al., Making Health Care Markets Work: Competition Policy for Health Care, 317 JAMA 1313 (Apr. 2017); David Dranove & Lawton R. Burns, Big Med: Megaproviders and the High Cost of Health Care in America 88–95 (2021).

5 Jaime S. King et al., Preventing Anticompetitive Healthcare Consolidation: Lessons from Five States, The Source on Healthcare Price and Competition Rsch. Rep. (June 2020), https://sourceonhealthcare.org/profile/preventing-anticompetitive-healthcare-consolidation-lessons-from-five-states/?portfolioCats=1165%2C1166%2C1167.

6 Nancy D. Beaulieu et al., Organization and Performance of U.S. Health Systems, 329 JAMA 325, 326 (2023).

7 Health Care Industry Consolidation: What Is Happening, Why It Matters, and What Public Agencies Might Want to Do about It, Hearing before the H. Comm. on Energy and Com. Subcomm. on Oversight and Investigations, 115th Cong. (2018) (testimony of Leemore S. Dafny) https://docs.house.gov/meetings/IF/IF02/20180214/106855/HHRG-115-IF02-Wstate-DafnyL-20180214.pdf.

8 Gaynor et al., supra note 4, at 8–9; Nancy D. Beaulieu et al., Changes in Quality of Care after Hospital Mergers and Acquisitions, 982 N. Engl. J. Med. 51, 56 (2020).

9 Beaulieu et al., supra note 8, at 56.

While public antitrust enforcers have had recent success in blocking horizontal health care mergers,[10] they have had significantly more difficulty in preventing consolidation arising in less traditional ways, such as vertical, cross-market, and cross-industry transactions. From 1970 to 2019, the percentage of hospitals that were part of a multi-hospital health system grew from 10 to 67 percent.[11] Many of these multi-hospital systems merged to become multi-market systems spanning sub-state regions (e.g., northern California), states, multi-state regions (e.g. mid-West, South), and the nation. Between 2009 and 2019, 55 percent of the 1,500 hospitals targeted for acquisition were in a different geographic market than the acquiring health system.[12] Historically, public antitrust enforcers have held that such cross-market mergers cannot cause anticompetitive harm, and as such they garnered little to no attention from federal or state officials, allowing rapid growth of multi-market systems. Recent studies now suggest that cross-market mergers can enable hospital systems to raise prices systemwide due to increased market power in contract negotiations with multi-market insurers, a phenomenon known as system power.[13] Despite this evidence, public antitrust enforcers have brought few challenges to cross-market hospital mergers.

Vertical transactions have also unified market actors at different levels of the supply chain, such as payors, hospitals, physicians, pharmacy benefit managers, and health data informatics companies, raising significant questions about foreclosure of competitors throughout the markets.[14] A national study of over 40,000 physicians found that between 2010 and 2018, the percentage of physicians who worked in a practice owned by a hospital increased from 24.1 percent to 45.6 percent.[15] Health system ownership of physician groups typically results in changes in referral patterns and hospital choice, increased prices for both the physicians and hospitals involved, and marginal quality effects.[16]

10 Hearing on Oversight of the Federal Trade Commission before the Comm. on the Judiciary, 117th Cong. 6 (July 13, 2023) (statement of the Federal Trade Commission), https://www.ftc.gov/system/files/ftc_gov/pdf/p210100housejudiciarytestimony07132023.pdf.

11 Brent D. Fulton, Health Care Market Concentration Trends in the United States: Evidence and Policy Responses, 36 Health Affs. 1530 (2017); Michael F. Furukawa et al., Consolidation of Providers into Systems Increased Substantially 2016–2018, 39 Health Affs. 1321 (2020).

12 Brent D. Fulton et al., The Rise of Cross-Market Hospital Systems and Their Market Power in the US, 41 Health Affs. 1652, 1655 (2022).

13 Leemore Dafny et al., The Price Effects of Cross-Market Hospital Mergers: Theory and Evidence from the Hospital Industry, 50 Rand J. Econ. 286 (2019); Matthew S. Lewis & Kevin E. Pflum, Hospital Systems and Bargaining Power: Evidence from Out-of-Market Acquisitions, 48 Rand J. Econ. 579 (2017); Matt Schmitt, Multimarket Contact in the Hospital Industry, 10 Am. J. Econ. Pol'y 361 (2018).

14 Thomas L. Greaney, Navigating the Backwater: Vertical Mergers in Health Care, CPI Antitrust Chron. (May 2019), https://ssrn.com/abstract=3389569.

15 Christopher M. Whaley et al., Physician Compensation in Physician-Owned and Hospital Owned Practices, 40 Health Affs. 1865, 1869 (2021).

16 Vilsa Curto et al., Price Effects of Vertical Integration and Joint Ventures between Physicians and Providers in Massachusetts, 41 Health Affs. 741, 745 (2022); Lawrence C. Baker et al., The

Beyond providers, health care entities have begun to engage in vertical, cross-industry transactions resulting in health care monoliths, like United Health Group (United), which has acquired thirty-five health care companies in the past decade alone. United owns and operates the largest health insurance company in the United States, a network of 53,000 physicians in 15 states, a pharmacy benefits manager (PBM) that processes over a billion prescriptions each year, a health care data analytics company, and a health care claims-editing company. The Department of Justice's (DOJ's) recent unsuccessful vertical challenge of United's acquisition of Change Healthcare, Inc., the leading supplier of claims processing software that serviced many of United's competitors, demonstrates some of the challenges of antitrust enforcement in this area.[17] Overall, the provider, payor, pharmaceutical, and insurance markets in health care demonstrate "textbook conditions" for harm from vertical mergers – high levels of concentration, high and durable barriers to entry, and poor market function – and open the door for merged firms to exclude their upstream or downstream rivals, either by raising their costs or cutting off access to resources.[18] Private market actors, either as consumers, payors, or competitors, can provide insights into the effects of vertical and cross-market consolidation on market function that can inform both future negotiations with health care providers and public antitrust enforcement.

Another major shift in health care markets in recent decades arises from the influx of investment from private equity firms, which have largely been able to consolidate market power in ways that avoid interference from public antitrust enforcers. Private equity investment in the health care industry has increased dramatically in the past twenty years, increasing from US$5 billion in 2000 to US$100 billion in 2018.[19] As of December 2022, one-quarter of all emergency departments nationwide were staffed by private equity-owned emergency medicine staffing companies.[20] While private equity firms have invested broadly across health care markets, they have increasingly acquired specialist physician practices.[21] As a result of their growing market power,

Effect of Hospital/Physician Integration on Hospital Choice, 50 J. Health Econ. 1 (2016); Lawrence C. Baker et al., Vertical Integration: Hospital Ownership of Physician Practices Is Associated with Higher Prices and Spending, 33 Health Affs. 756 (2014); Marah Noel Short & Vivien Ho, Weighing the Effects of Vertical Integration versus Market Concentration on Hospital Quality, 77 Med. Care Res. Rev. 538 (2020).

17 United States, State of Minnesota and State of New York v. UnitedHealth Group Inc. and Change Healthcare, Inc., No. 1:22-cv-00481 at *4 (D.D.C., filed Feb. 24, 2022).

18 Greaney, supra note 14.

19 Eileen Appelbaum & Rosemary Batt, Private Equity Buyouts in Healthcare: Who Wins, Who Loses? 5 (Ctr. for Econ. and Pol'y Rsch., Working Paper No. 118, 2020), https://cepr.net/report/private-equity-buyouts-in-healthcare-who-wins-who-loses/.

20 Leann Adelman, 2023 State of the Emergency Medicine Employer Market, Ivy Clinician (Feb. 2023), https://www.ivyclinicians.io/resources/whitepapers/2023-state-of-the-em-employer-market.

21 Richard M. Scheffler et al., Monetizing Medicine: Private Equity and Competition in Physician Practice Markets, Am. Antitrust Inst., UC Berkeley Petris Ctr., & Wash. Ctr. for

private equity-owned health care entities have been able to demand restrictive employment covenants from contracting providers[22] and payment increases between 8 percent and 18 percent for certain specialist services.[23]

While any entity consolidating market power and demanding anticompetitive contract terms would raise antitrust concerns, private law provides an essential mechanism for consumers and competitors to demonstrate the anticompetitive harms arising from private equity business models and contracting practices, which are relatively new in the health care markets and have typically avoided federal antitrust attention. Private equity firms invest money from wealthy individuals and institutional investors into businesses in hopes of quickly increasing profitability and then returning a large profit to investors before exiting the business.[24] Private equity firms often follow a "buy and build" model that grows an asset through a series of "add on" acquisitions in the same industry.[25] Thomas Wollman termed the practice of building market power through a series of sequential smaller acquisitions that fly under federal antitrust enforcement radar "stealth consolidation."[26] Stealth consolidation is possible in part due to loopholes in the Hart-Scott-Rodino Act (HSR), which requires merging entities to notify the federal government of a proposed merger if the total value of the merger is higher than the HSR reporting threshold, set at US$114.4M for 2023.[27] When a deal does not reach the HSR threshold, the likelihood of a federal investigation drops precipitously.[28] Interestingly, private equity health care acquisitions are often secured for just under the HSR reporting threshold.[29] As a result, private equity firms, as well as other market actors, have been able to make sequential smaller acquisitions and amass market power without public

Equitable Growth 6 (July 10, 2023), https://www.antitrustinstitute.org/wp-content/uploads/2023/07/AAI-UCB-EG_Private-Equity-I-Physician-Practice-Report_FINAL.pdf.

22 See, e.g., Am. Acad. Emergency Med. Phys. Group, Inc. v. Envision Healthcare Corp. et al., No. 3:22-cv- 00421-CRB (N.D. Cal. Dec. 20, 2021) (Envision Complaint).

23 Scheffler et al., supra note 21, at 6. For example, private equity acquisitions have been associated with price increases in specialty practice areas, including oncology (16.4%), gastroenterology (14.0%), OB/GYN (8.8%), ophthalmology (8.7%), radiology (8.2%), and orthopedics (7.1%). When a single private equity firm owned more than 30% market share, the price increases were even greater – gastroenterology (18.2%), dermatology (13.3%), and OB/GYN (16.3%). Id.

24 Erin Fuse Brown & Mark Hall, Private Equity and the Corporatization of Health Care, 76 Stan. L. Rev. 527, 537 (2024).

25 Aslihan Asil et al., Misaligned Measures of Control: Private Equity's Antitrust Loophole, 18 Va. L. & Bus. Rev. 51, 52 (2023).

26 Thomas G. Wollmann, Stealth Consolidation: Evidence from an Amendment to the Hart-Scott-Rodino Act, 1 Am. Econ. Rev. 77, 78 (June 2019).

27 Fed. Trade Comm'n, HSR Threshold Adjustments and Reportability for 2023 (Feb. 16, 2023) https://www.ftc.gov/enforcement/competition-matters/2023/02/hsr-threshold-adjustments-reportability-2023.

28 Wollmann, supra note 26, at 87.

29 Scheffler et al., supra note 21, at 42.

antitrust intervention.[30] In addition, private equity firms have been able to use their market power to engage in other anticompetitive behavior, such as demanding exclusive employment contracts and noncompete clauses that hinder competition.[31] As stated in a 2021 report by the American Antitrust Institute and the Petris Center at UC Berkeley, "when the fundamental characteristics of the private equity business model are combined with the unique structure of the US health care market, the results are potentially catastrophic for patients, payors, and the long-term stability of the health care supply chain."[32]

17.3 THE ROLE OF PRIVATE LAW IN GOVERNING HEALTH CARE MARKETS

Private law offers a complementary pathway to public antitrust enforcement to identify competitive harms arising from new health care market dynamics and test a variety of legal strategies for challenging them. Private law incorporates social norms, national values, and business customs into its purview.[33] From an antitrust perspective, it establishes the market norms and conditions necessary to protect competition and consumers in contracts and other business dealings between market actors. Being adaptable to the ever-changing norms of business, private law grants market participants the ability to enforce those conditions through contractual agreements and challenge breaches of those norms and conditions when violated. As such, it is often the market actors who directly experience the leveraging of market power or the anticompetitive effects of certain contract terms that are in the best position to identify the potential competitive harms arising from new market dynamics and bring an antitrust challenge.

Private antitrust enforcement was always intended to support, inform, and supplement public antitrust enforcement led by the Federal Trade Commission (FTC), DOJ, and state attorneys general. The Clayton Act established a private right of action for individuals who are injured or threatened with injury by the anticompetitive actions of other market actors.[34] Congress further encouraged private antitrust enforcement by awarding treble damages, or three times the damages incurred, to successful private litigants. Having noted that the award of treble damages reflected Congress' intent that consumers and other injured market actors serve as "private

[30] Id. at 91–92.

[31] Envision Complaint, supra note 22, at para. 41.

[32] Richard M. Scheffler et al., Soaring Private Equity Investment in the Healthcare Sector: Consolidation Accelerated, Competition Undermined, and Patients at Risk, Am. Antitrust Inst. & UC Berkeley Petris Ctr. 5 (May 18, 2021), https://www.antitrustinstitute.org/wp-content/uploads/2021/05/Private-Equity-I-Healthcare-Report-FINAL-1.pdf.

[33] John C. P. Goldberg, Introduction: Pragmatism and Private Law, 125 Harv. L. Rev. 1640, 1657 (2012).

[34] 15 U.S.C. §§ 15, 26. The Clayton Act specifically enables a private right of action for violations of the Sherman or Clayton Act. 15 U.S.C. §12(a).

attorneys general,"[35] the Supreme Court stated that "[t]he treble-damages provision wielded by the private litigant is a chief tool in the antitrust enforcement scheme, posing a crucial deterrent to potential violators."[36]

Despite this intent, private antitrust enforcement and private law solutions more broadly, however, have been largely omitted from policy debates and recommendations about how to preserve competitive markets in health care.[37] Scholars and policymakers almost uniformly propose public law solutions to health care market challenges, including transaction notification, review, and approval processes; enhanced public antitrust enforcement; revisions to federal merger guidelines; provider rate caps; and state health care affordability regulations.[38] But public antitrust enforcers and regulatory bodies can only implement those solutions if they have a clear line of sight into market function.

In health care, market dynamics, such as contracting, pricing, employment negotiations, and corporate alliances, are murky at best. Nondisclosure agreements and trade secret protections have become ubiquitous throughout health care agreements, shielding prices and contract terms from view.[39] By witnessing firsthand the impact on consumers and competition, private market actors have the best vantage point by which to identify when new combinations, contract terms, and behaviors can be anticompetitive.

17.4 PRIVATE LAW AS AN ANTITRUST ENFORCEMENT MECHANISM

In the rapidly evolving health care landscape, private antitrust enforcement can draw attention to the kinds of combinations (mergers, acquisitions, and joint ventures) and behaviors that can harm consumers or competition but might otherwise escape public antitrust enforcement scrutiny. Significant strides have been made through antitrust actions from private litigants both in isolation and in partnership with public authorities.[40]

One of the most pivotal health care merger challenges for the FTC was initiated by a private plaintiff and rival, Saint Alphonsus Med. Center – Nampa, Inc., against St. Luke's Health Systems, Ltd., for its attempt to acquire Saltzer Medical Group,

[35] Hawaii v. Std. Oil Co., 405 U.S. 251, 262 (1972).

[36] Mitsubishi Motors Corp. v. Soler Chrysler-Plymouth, Inc., 473 U.S. 614, 635 (1985).

[37] Anne Marie Helm, Optimizing Private Antitrust Enforcement in Health Care, 11 St. Louis U. J. Health L. & Pol'y 5, 6 (2017) (both noting the disregard of private antitrust and arguing in favor of optimizing private antitrust enforcement to improve healthcare markets).

[38] See, e.g., King et al., supra note 5; Brown & Hall, supra note 24; Michael E. Chernew et al., A Proposal to Cap Provider Prices and Price Growth in Commercial Health Care Market, The Hamilton Project 10 (Mar. 2020), https://www.brookings.edu/wp-content/uploads/2020/03/CDP_PP_WEB_FINAL.pdf.

[39] Waters, infra note 54, at 6.

[40] Helm, supra note 37, at 12–13 and accompanying notes (listing numerous cases in which providers, payors, and consumers were plaintiffs in antitrust suits, some of which were joined by public antitrust enforcers).

P.A., the largest independent multi-specialist physician group in Idaho.[41] The FTC and the Idaho attorney general later joined the case, which resulted in the full divestiture of Saltzer's physicians and assets.[42] Although the case was decided on horizontal grounds arising from estimated post-merger concentration levels and price increases in the primary care physician market, St. Alphonsus, as a private litigant, illuminated the risks associated with both the horizontal and vertical aspects of the merger – noting the risk of increases in PCP rates and the foreclosure risks to other hospitals due to the potential for the acquired PCPs to shift referrals to St. Luke's.

Private litigants have also successfully challenged anticompetitive monopolistic behaviors between providers and insurers. In *West Penn Allegheny Health System, Inc. v. UPMC; Highmark, Inc.*, Pittsburgh's second-largest health system sued the dominant health system and insurer for violations of the Sherman Act §§1 and 2.[43] The case highlighted both the opportunities for collusion and competitive harms, such as artificially depressed rates and exclusion of a rival, that can arise from agreements between dominant providers and insurers to protect one another's interests.

Private plaintiffs have generally been more willing than public enforcers to bring novel challenges to anticompetitive behaviors. For example, in *Sidibe v. Sutter Health*, a group of private patients brought the first antitrust challenge to a health care system for using contract terms that leveraged market power across geographic markets.[44] Sutter Health had been strategically acquiring "must have" hospitals and other provider organizations throughout Northern California for many years. The *Sidibe* plaintiffs were the first to certify a class of patients suing for harms arising from a multi-market health system's use of anticompetitive contract clauses and tying behaviors to link providers across geographic and product markets to demand systemwide price increases from multi-market insurers.[45] While the plaintiffs have still not seen resolution of their claims,[46] their arguments laid the foundation for *UFCW and Employers Benefit Trust v. Sutter Health*, which resulted in a groundbreaking settlement for the plaintiffs and the California Attorney General, setting up a wave of follow-on cases.[47]

41 Saint Alphonsus Med. Ctr.-Nampa, Inc. v. St. Luke's Health Sys., Ltd., 778 F.3d 775, 782 (9th Cir. 2015), aff'g 2014 WL 407446 (D. Idaho 2014).

42 Id.

43 West Penn Allegheny Health System, Inc. v. UPMC; Highmark, Inc., 627 F.3d 85 (3d Cir. 2010).

44 Fourth Amended Complaint Demand for Jury Trial at 30, Sidibe v. Sutter Health, 4 F. Supp. 3d 1160 (N.D. Cal. 2022).

45 Order Granting Motion to Certify Class under Rule 23(B)(3) and Denying Motion for Sanctions, Sidibe v. Sutter Health, No. 3:12-cv-04854 (N.D. Cal. July 30, 2020).

46 Sidibe v. Sutter Health, No. 22-15634 Opinion (9th Cir. 2024) (reversing and remanding the district court case for a new trial).

47 UFCW & Employees Benefit Trust vs. Sutter Health, Case No. CGC-14-53-8451 (Cal. Super. Ct. Apr. 7, 2014).

In 2014, the United Food and Commercial Workers (UFCW) union and the United Employers Benefit Trust (UEBT) filed a similar action against Sutter Health for using anticompetitive contract terms and other practices to demand supracompetitive rates.[48] The plaintiffs alleged that Sutter leveraged its presence as the dominant hospital provider in some markets to increase prices for all of its providers and facilities. Sutter accomplished this largely through the use of anticompetitive contract clauses, including "all or nothing" clauses that require insurers and employers to contract with all of Sutter's facilities at elevated rates, or none at all; anti-tiering and anti-steering clauses that prevent insurers from signaling or incentivizing enrollees to seek care from higher value providers; and nondisclosure clauses that prevent health plans from disclosing negotiated rates with employers, patients, or the public.[49] The plaintiffs further argued that these contract terms were mutually reinforcing in ways that strengthened Sutter's market leverage. For example, the all-or-nothing clauses leveraged market power to demand supercompetitive rates, while the nondisclosure clauses and anti-tiering/anti-steering clauses prevented consumers from being able to price discriminate, effectively shielding Sutter from price competition.[50] The plaintiff's claims, which largely mirrored the arguments made in *Sidibe*, brought significant attention to the ability of health systems to leverage market power across product and geographic markets, which had not been previously thought possible.[51]

The case gained even more momentum when the California Attorney General joined, uniting public and private antitrust enforcement and giving credence to the novel arguments made in the case. The Attorney General also contributed new arguments, such as alleging that Sutter also engaged in punitive pricing practices through "de facto all-or-nothing" behaviors.[52] Instead of placing the all-or-nothing provision directly into the contract, a system engaging in de facto all-or-nothing behaviors would impose conditions on an insurer that wants to exclude a newly acquired provider, such as: (1) raising the rates for already contracted providers in future negotiations or (2) preventing the insurer from excluding system providers from the plan by using excessive out-of-network pricing of "must have providers" to essentially force the health plan to accept the system's price and network inclusion demands. In the end, Sutter settled with the plaintiffs for (1) US$575 million, (2) prohibitions on the system's ability to condition pricing on network inclusion of providers and facilities and use of other anticompetitive contract clauses, and (3) the

[48] Id. at paras. 14–18.

[49] Id. at para. 20.a–c.

[50] Id. at paras. 21–22.

[51] See, e.g., Katie Thomas, Sutter Health to Pay $575 Million to Settle Antitrust Lawsuit, N.Y. Times (Dec. 20, 2019), https://www.nytimes.com/2019/12/20/health/sutter-health-settlement-california.html.

[52] Complaint for Violations of the Cartwright Act, People ex rel. Becerra v. Sutter Health, No. CGC 18-565398 (Cal. Super. Ct. Mar. 20, 2018), 2018 WL 1584066, https://oag.ca.gov/system/files/attachments/press_releases/Sutter%20Complaint.pdf.

imposition of cap on out-of-network rates.[53] News of the settlement sent shockwaves through the health care industry, as some of the contracting practices initiated by Sutter had served as a model for other health systems.[54]

The magnitude of the settlement, the novelty of the claims involved, and the eventual alignment of public and private antitrust enforcement in the Sutter case demonstrate the importance of private antitrust actions as a mechanism for identifying and challenging anticompetitive behaviors as they develop in the ever-changing health care landscape. In the wake of the Sutter settlement, private litigants brought several similar actions against multi-market health systems engaging in similar behavior throughout the country, sending out warning signals and changing behavior across the country.[55]

Private litigants have also brought attention to and challenged the market behaviors of private equity investors in health care. For example, in December 2021, the American Academy of Emergency Physician Group (AAEM-PG), a professional association of emergency medicine physicians, sued Envision Healthcare, a multi-specialty physician group and health care management team that includes over 25,000 physicians and 1,600 employees at over 780 hospitals nationwide, for violation of California's Unfair Competition Law and its prohibition of the corporate practice of medicine.[56] Kohlberg Kravis Roberts & Company (KKR), a leading global private equity firm that manages over US$100 billion in assets and has a strategic interest in health care, owns Envision.

The suit alleged significant competitive harm arising from Envision's use of restrictive covenants in physician employment contracts that bar physicians from joining or forming another group of emergency medicine physicians to compete in medical or management services markets serviced by Envision.[57] Such provisions can harm consumers and competition by hindering the growth of existing competitors, limiting market entry, reducing the supply of available emergency physicians,

[53] Amended Order Granting Plaintiffs' Renewed Motion for Preliminary Approval of Settlement at 6–7, 16, UFCW & Emps. Benefit Tr. v. Sutter Health, No. CGC 14-538451 (Cal. Super. Ct. Mar. 10, 2021).

[54] See Rob Waters, California's Sutter Health Settlement: What States Can Learn about Protecting Residents from the Effects of Health Care Provider Consolidation, Millbank Mem'l Fund 6 (2020), https://www.milbank.org/publications/californias-sutter-health-settlement-what-states-can-learn-about-protecting-residents-from-the-effects-of-health-care-provider-consolidation/.

[55] See, e.g., Uriel Pharmacy v. Advocate Aurora Health, No. 2:22-cv-00610 (E.D. Wis. filed May 24, 2022) (alleging use of anticompetitive tying [all or nothing clauses], anti-steering clauses, gag clauses, exclusive contracting practices, and noncompete clauses); Davis et al. v. HCA Healthcare and Mission Health System, No. 21 CV 03276 (N.C. Sup. Ct. filed Aug. 10, 2021) (alleging use of anticompetitive tying [all or nothing clauses], anti-steering clauses, and gag clauses); Brown et al. v. Hartford Healthcare (Conn. Super. Ct. filed Feb. 14, 2022) (alleging use of anticompetitive tying [all-or-nothing clauses], anti-steering clauses, gag clauses, exclusive contracting practices, and noncompete clauses).

[56] Envision Complaint, supra note 22, at para. 20.

[57] Id. at paras. 42–44.

and facilitating price increases. Interestingly, the doctors challenging the case did not ask for financial damages; instead, they asked the court to enjoin Envision from engaging in the corporate practice of medicine, inducing medical groups to include restrictive covenants in their contracts, and providing incentives in exchange for patient referrals. In addition, plaintiffs asked the court to make declarations that the private equity business model in health care, as implemented by Envision and other private equity-owned health care groups in the state, violates competition laws, interferes with providers' clinical decision-making authority and referral patterns, and harms patients.[58] While the case garnered significant media attention and survived Envision's Motion to Dismiss, it has recently stalled following Envision's filing for bankruptcy. The plaintiffs state that they will persist in the suit because of their desire for injunctive and declarative relief.

In modern health care markets, private litigants have a critical role to play in identifying and challenging anticompetitive effects arising from new consolidation strategies, contracting models, market entrants, and investment schemes. Private antitrust enforcement serves as the first line of defense protecting health care market participants, reinforces the business norms of the health care market, and provides insight for the evolution of public antitrust enforcement.

17.5 INFORMING PUBLIC ANTITRUST ENFORCEMENT

Public antitrust enforcers have struggled to keep up with changes in the health care markets for decades. Although they have experienced numerous recent successes in challenging horizontal hospital and insurer mergers, this success has not been replicated with non-horizontal combinations, such as vertical, cross-market, or cross-industry acquisitions. The enforcement challenges have arisen largely from a misalignment between the current realities of health care market dynamics and the norms and assumptions of traditional antitrust enforcement, such as distinct geographic and product markets, direct buyer and seller relationships, price and quality transparency, and a lack of price shielding from third parties. In addition, the relationships between actors in health care markets have become significantly more complex and less transparent.

Private law allows for greater acknowledgment of this complexity by exposing the nature of the relationships between market actors, such as providers and payors, physicians and hospitals, and between health systems and their employees, in ways that reflect use of market power. Furthermore, private health care litigants have proven more willing than public antitrust enforcers to bring cases based on less traditional antitrust claims that have more uncertain outcomes, which is potentially due to less public oversight and fewer resource constraints. As such, the relationships between private actors and the claims brought in private antitrust litigation can

[58] Id. at para. 81.

illuminate both changing dynamics in health care markets, as well as gaps in public antitrust enforcement.

17.6 RECOMMENDATIONS AND CONCLUSION

Paying closer attention to the private law aspects of health care can improve antitrust enforcement and market function. When private law arrangements fail or exhibit evidence of market power abuses, antitrust law should intervene. Antitrust scholars, enforcers, and policymakers should analyze private law contracts, transactions, and relationships between health care entities to better predict the evolution of market function. For example, the FTC and DOJ could replicate its recent listening sessions on the effects of mergers on the health care industry by inviting discussions on the impacts of private contracts and agreements arising from the new dynamics in health care, such as vertical, cross-market, cross-industry, and private equity-based combinations.[59] Policymakers and antitrust enforcers should use this information to improve public and private antitrust enforcement. Several of the insights raised in private antitrust suits or through private contractual relationships between health care entities were recently incorporated into the 2023 Merger Guidelines, which blended guidance for all forms of consolidation (horizontal, vertical, cross-market, and cross-industry) for the first time in decades.[60] For instance, Guideline 5 specifically addresses concerns arising from vertical acquisitions, Guideline 6 addresses concerns potentially arising from cross-market acquisitions that can extend multimarket power, and Guideline 8 permits antitrust enforcers to review a proposed acquisition in the context of being one part of a series of related acquisitions.

As health care markets continue to consolidate across geographic, product, and industry lines, new participants enter the market with goals beyond providing quality health care, and prices continue to increase, both public and private antitrust enforcement must adapt and evolve to address these new market dynamics. Private antitrust enforcement can serve as the canary in the coal mine by identifying anticompetitive behaviors and developing and testing novel strategies and arguments in court in isolation or in partnership with public antitrust authorities.

[59] Fed. Trade Comm'n, FTC and DOJ Host Listening Forum on Effects of Mergers on Healthcare Industry (Apr. 14, 2022), https://www.ftc.gov/system/files/ftc_gov/pdf/FTC-DOJ-Listening-Forum-%20Health-Care-Transcript.pdf.

[60] U.S. Dep't of Justice and Fed. Trade Comm'n, 2023 Merger Guidelines(Dec. 18, 2023), Antitrust Division | 2023 Merger Guidelines | United States Department of Justice.

18

Health Care Finance Law's Relational Bias

Jessica Mantel

18.1 INTRODUCTION

Private health insurers have long played a vital role in financing the US health care system. Yet private insurers' modern role transcends simply paying providers for patient care. Growing recognition of how payment methodologies shape care delivery has generated tremendous interest in leveraging payment reform to address longstanding inefficiencies and quality issues in health care. These problems include health inflation that outpaces general inflation, excessive utilization, fragmented patient care, and preventable medical errors and complications.[1] In response, private insurers increasingly are embracing value-based payment models (VBPMs)[2] that incentivize providers to increase efficiency and better manage patients' health care needs.[3]

[1] See generally Council on Health Care Spending & Value, A Road Map for Action: Recommendations of The Health Affairs Council on Health Care Spending and Value, Health Affs. 18–23 (2023), https://www.healthaffairs.org/pb-assets/documents/CHS_Report/CHS_Report_2022_R5–1675432678.pdf (recommending continued development of value-based payment models).

[2] The term "value-based payment models" and "alternative payment models" often are used interchangeably. In general, VBPMs refer to the broad array of approaches public and private payers use to align financial incentives with approaches to improving efficiencies and patient outcomes, whereas alternative payment models refer to the specific payment mechanisms for implementing these approaches. See Athena Chapman & Samantha Pellón, Medi-Cal Explained: What Are Alternative Payment Models?, Cal. Health Care Found. (May 2022), https://www.chcf.org/publication/medi-cal-explained-what-are-alternative-payment-models/. For purposes of this chapter, the author uses the term "VBPMs" to include alternative payment models.

[3] See Mark B. McClellan et al., Payment Reform for Better Value and Medical Innovation, Nat'l Acad. of Med. (Mar. 17, 2017), https://nam.edu/payment-reform-for-better-value-and-medical-innovation/.

VBPMs reward providers who both improve the quality of care delivered to patients and lower health care spending.[4] For example, pay-for-performance models link providers' payments to their performance on select quality and efficiency measures, rewarding high performers with bonuses or higher payment rates and penalizing poor performers with downward payment adjustments or other penalties.[5] Shared savings and bundled payments reward providers who effectively manage a set of procedures, an episode of care, or all health care services by sharing with the providers all or a portion of any cost savings they generate, coupled with upward or downward adjustments for high or poor performance on quality measures.[6] More advanced population-based payment models, such as per-member-per-month payments or capitation, replace fee-for-service's volume-based payments with fixed prospective payments that cover all or a range of services, with potential adjustments for a provider's quality-related performance.[7]

VBPMs have prompted some providers to pivot to care delivery models that emphasize evidence-based protocols, care coordination, and preventive care, such as accountable care organizations and medical homes.[8] Providers are also exploring care delivery models that take a holistic view of patients' health and consider not only patients' physical needs but also social, economic, and behavioral health needs that impact well-being.[9]

Numerous examples of VBPMs successfully incentivizing quality improvements and efficiency gains have generated confidence that VBPMs can drive providers toward more effective care delivery models.[10] Consequently, private insurers' utilization of VBPMs can increase society's general welfare by improving the overall performance of the health care delivery system. So although private insurers are

4 See U.S. Dep't of Health and Hum. Servs., Assistant Sec'y for Planning and Evaluation, Common Alternative Payment Model (APM) Approaches: Reference Guide (2021) (explaining key features of alternative payment models include financial incentives for providers who meet certain objectives).

5 See Health Care Payment Learning & Action Network, Alternative Payment Model Framework, 23–24, The MITRE Corp. (2017), http://hcp-lan.org/workproducts/apm-refresh-whitepaper-final.pdf (describing the effects of performance on payments received by providers in an APM framework).

6 See id. at 25–27.

7 See id. at 23, 27–29.

8 See Mark W. Friedberg et al., Effects of Health Care Payment Models on Physician Practice in the United States: Follow-Up Study, AMA-RAND 12 (2018), https://www.rand.org/pubs/research_reports/RR2667.html (summarizing the strategies implemented by physician practices in response to VBPMs) (hereinafter "Friedberg Follow-Up Study").

9 See Jessica Mantel et al., Developing a Health Care Workforce that Supports Team-Base Models that Integrate Health and Social Services, 15 St. Louis U. J. Health L. & Pol'y 239 (2022); Nat'l Acad. of Sci., Eng'g, & Med., Implementing High-Quality Primary Care: Rebuilding the Foundation of Healthcare 163 (2021) (discussing interprofessional teams based in primary care practices).

10 See Rachel Werner et al., The Future of Value-Based Payment: A Road Map to 2030 6 (2021) ("The past decade of experimentation with APMs . . . has provided proof-of-concept that if designed well, APMs are capable of driving cost savings and value improvements").

private actors, they arguably undertake a quasi-public role when they employ VBPMs to achieve health care delivery reform.

Yet unlike elected officials and regulators, private insurers perform this role outside the policymaking apparatus of democratically accountable institutions. This state of affairs raises a fundamental question – do the laws overseeing private insurers facilitate their successfully steering the health care system toward improved patient outcomes and reduced spending? This chapter contends that the answer to this question is no. Specifically, it explains that health care finance laws are shaped by private law norms that narrowly focus on relational concerns between marketplace participants and that this results in misaligned payment approaches that hinder providers' adoption of new patient care models. Consequently, policymakers should shift to a public law framework that would mandate coordinated action across payers when acting as value-based purchasers. Alternatively, payment alignment could be achieved through a single-payer health care system.

18.2 THE PRIVATE LAW UNDERPINNINGS OF HEALTH CARE FINANCE

Although the line separating private and public law can be blurred, generally speaking private law governs relationships between private individuals or entities while public law pertains to relations between the state and individuals. Private law thus focuses on the horizontal associations among individuals within familial, commercial, or communal contexts, defining the rights, powers, and duties of private parties vis-a-vis one another.[11] It encompasses not only common law subjects such as tort, contract, and property law but also statutes and regulations that similarly delineate rights and obligations in interpersonal interactions.[12] Conversely, public law's object is vertical, addressing individuals as subjects of the state with individual rights and shared responsibilities. It therefore both defines the state's powers and obligations and individuals' rights against the state, and promotes collective action by obliging individuals to act in concert with one another.[13]

Despite operating in a web of private contracts with patients, providers, employers, and others, private insurers' actions have broad social impact by shaping the contours of the health care delivery system. Consequently, we might expect that the laws governing private insurers would encompass both public and private law principles. The laws of health care finance, however, largely reflect private law norms, namely facilitating cooperative endeavors while securing relational justice.

[11] See Hanoch Dagan & Benjamin C. Zipursky, Introduction: The Distinction between Private Law and Public Law, in Research Handbook on Private Law Theory 2–3 (Hanoch Dagan & Benjamin C. Zipursky eds., 2020); Jeffrey A. Pojanowski, Private Law in the Gaps, 82 Fordham L. Rev. 1689, 1704 (2014).

[12] See Dagan & Zipursky, supra note 11, at 13.

[13] Id. at 2, 12.

In a nod to the influential law-and-economics movement, many twentieth-century scholars argued that private law should structure interpersonal interactions in a manner that maximizes efficiency.[14] Consistent with this aim, numerous laws are designed to support a robust health insurance market. Specifically, they generate market confidence in insurers' willingness and capacity to both provide financial protection for insureds and compensate providers. This is exemplified by strict financial standards for insurers that prevent insolvency, such as minimum capital and reserve requirements. Contract law similarly ensures that health insurers deliver covered benefits to insureds and pay providers promised payments, while consumer protection laws address insurers' unfair trade and claims practices. Health care finance laws also target market failures hampering the efficient functioning of the health insurance sector. For example, various state and federal laws address information asymmetries between private insurers and consumers by requiring clear disclosure of insurance policies' terms and conditions.[15]

The emergence of managed care provoked a public backlash that ushered in a new era of health care finance laws. This backlash coincided with various legal commentators questioning private law's narrow focus on efficiency aims. Scholars such as Hanoch Dagan and Avihay Dorfman argued that private law's interpersonal focus includes structuring private actors' duties, rights, and obligations so that parties relate to one another as equals.[16] Accordingly, private law should remedy significant power imbalances between parties to a transaction and prohibit discriminatory conduct.[17] This in turn ensures that both parties to an interaction can be "self-determining individuals" who "realize their respective freedoms."[18]

The "patient rights" mantra similarly framed managed care debates in relational terms.[19] Proponents emphasized protecting patients from managed care practices deemed unfair, a violation of patient dignity, or an unwarranted interference with the physician–patient relationship. States responded by enacting laws targeting managed care practices that limit patients' access to needed care. These laws include coverage mandates, standards for utilization review, appeal and grievance processes, and network adequacy requirements. Some state laws also protect the physician–patient relationship from interruption or outside influence by requiring that private insurers contract with "any willing" provider or prohibiting insurers use of contractual "gag orders" that restrict the treatment options physicians can discuss

[14] See id. at 7–9.

[15] See, e.g., 29 C.F.R. §2502.102-3 (disclosure requirements for employee group health plans); 42 C.F.R. §156.220 (disclosure requirements for state exchange plans); 28 Tex. Admin. Code § 3.3075 (2014).

[16] Hanoch Dagan & Avihay Dorfman, Just Relationships, 116 Colum. L. Rev. 1395, 1410–17 (2016).

[17] See id.

[18] Id. at 1417.

[19] See William M. Sage, Relational Duties, Regulatory Duties, and the Widening Gap between Individual Health Law and Collective Health Policy, 96 Geo. L.J. 497, 514 (2008) (managed care opponents "frame[d] the debate in relational terms").

with patients. Various state laws also protect providers from unfair insurer practices, such as laws requiring prompt claims payment.

The Affordable Care Act (ACA)[20] took further steps in support of relational justice goals. Notably, the ACA targeted practices that stemmed from private insurers' power advantage over consumers, practices that left many individuals uninsured or underinsured. For example, the ACA prohibits private insurers from rejecting insurance applicants based on their health status, varying premiums based on health status or gender, or excluding preexisting conditions.[21] The ACA also mandates that individual and small group policies cover a comprehensive bundle of "essential health benefits."[22]

The laws addressing private insurers' role as value-based purchasers likewise prioritize relational considerations, namely promoting insureds receiving their promised financial protection against high medical expenses. For example, some states restrict insurers from shifting insurance risk to providers that cannot meet minimum financial viability or solvency standards.[23] Other state laws dictate that private insurers retain ultimate financial risk for covered benefits, thereby protecting insureds from failed risk-sharing arrangements.[24]

This review of health care finance laws reveals a legal regime primarily shaped by private law norms. Its chief aims are relational – keep the economic wheels turning by generating market confidence in health insurers and ensure that their interactions with consumers and providers are fair and just. The law thus regulates private insurers in their *individual* capacity and focuses on their discrete, one-on-one interactions with consumers and providers. Private insurers are not regulated as a *several* engaged in a joint endeavor to reform the health care delivery system through VBPMs.

This narrow focus results in a legal regime that affords private insurers tremendous autonomy in their role as value-based purchasers, as the components of VBPMs – the specific financial incentives and performance measures, patient attribution and benchmarking methodologies, data sharing requirements, and other factors – rarely implicate relational considerations. This leaves the specific terms of VBPMs to private insurers' independent judgment and the voluntary processes of the marketplace. Consequently, while US payment policy is based in part on publicly adopted Medicare and Medicaid payment rules, it also encompasses thousands of decentralized decisions made by private insurers.

In theory, a legal regime that grants private insurers the freedom to develop their own payment policies promotes the public good through market competition. After

[20] Patient Protection and Affordable Care Act of 2010, Pub. L. No. 111-148, 124 Stat. 119 (2010).

[21] 42 U.S.C. §§ 300gg, 300gg-1, 300gg-4 (2023).

[22] 42 U.S.C. §18022 (2023).

[23] 11 N.Y. Comp. Codes R. & Regs. §101.5; Cal. Code Regs. tit. 28, § 1300.75.4.2; Conn. Gen. Stat., ch. 700c, § 38a-479bb(b).

[24] 11 N.Y. Comp. Codes R. & Regs. § 101.4(b); Conn. Gen. Stat., ch. 700c, § 38a-479bb(j).

all, a free-market economy encourages producers of products and services to achieve a competitive advantage through quality improvements, cost reductions, and innovation. Section 18.3, however, shows that in practice, market competition among private insurers undermines the health reform goals of VBPMs.

18.3 VARIATION AMONG PAYMENT MODELS AND ITS ADVERSE EFFECTS

In a competitive marketplace, a private insurer's success depends on it differentiating its health plans from competitors' plans, particularly on factors related to price and quality of care. Payment methodologies are an important source of this competitive differentiation. Individual payers regularly experiment with new and innovative payment approaches as part of their competitive strategies, aiming to achieve for their insureds both lower health care spending and superior quality care relative to their rivals.[25] In theory, then, competition among payers and their experimentation with VBPMs should, over time, propel the health care system toward cost savings and better patient outcomes. In reality, however, VBPMs have yielded mixed results,[26] as few health care providers have fundamentally changed how they care for patients.[27]

Paradoxically, a legal regime that allows private insurers to pursue different payment approaches creates obstacles to VBPMs advancing provider-level reforms. As explained below, a competitive, multi-payer health insurance market results in providers operating in a sea of confusing and conflicting payment rules and incentives. This imposes significant administrative burdens on providers and weakens the business case for their investing in new patient care models.

18.3.1 *Administrative Complexity*

With the US population insured by numerous public and private insurers, health care providers routinely contract with multiple payers. Providers therefore must manage a range of disparate rules, performance measures, and reporting requirements across numerous payment arrangements. As explained below, this creates a

[25] See Kristof Stremikis, All Aboard: Engaging Self-Insured Employers in Multi-Payer Reform 3 (2015) (noting that a health care system with "multiple public and private insurer entities facilities experimentation with a variety of payment structures and quality measurements").

[26] Marina A. Milad et al., Value-Based Payment Models in the Commercial Insurance Sector: A Systematic Review, 41 Health Affs. 540, 546 (2022).

[27] See Hannah L. Crook et al., A Decade of Value-Based Payment: Lessons Learned and Implications for the Center for Medicare and Medicaid Innovation, Part 1, Health Affs. Forefront (June 9, 2021), https://www.healthaffairs.org/do/10.1377/forefront.20210607.656313/ (VBPMs have had only modest impacts because providers have not invested in care transformation).

heavy administrative burden for providers that complicates their operations under VBPMs.[28]

Understanding VBPMs and devising strategies for success requires significant staff time and other resources.[29] Payers' VBPM specifications often are lengthy and require a provider to adjust their workflow and infrastructure.[30] For example, providers may need to redesign their patient care models to incorporate evidence-based protocols, emphasize more preventive care, and integrate behavioral health or social determinants of health interventions. Providers also may be expected to develop new care teams of both licensed and nonlicenced care providers.[31] In addition, providers must redesign their electronic health records systems to accommodate new workflows and build the internal capacity to both analyze their performance under multiple VBPMs and track their numerous requirements.[32] Finally, providers must develop coherent strategies that promote success across VBPM arrangements. Not surprisingly, many providers report confusion and uncertainty over how best to modify their operations.[33]

Providers cite managing an expanding array of performance measures as a particular source of frustration.[34] With each payer adopting distinct performance measures, providers must comply with hundreds of metrics.[35] Doing so complicates providers' data collection and management efforts, including having to configure

28 See generally Jessica Mantel, An Overlooked Argument for a Single-Payer Healthcare System: Eliminating Misalignment among Payment Models, 32 Annals Health L. and Life Scis. 101 (2023).

29 See MedPAC, Report to Congress: Medicare and Healthcare Delivery System 57 (2021) (providers describe VBPMs as requiring "significant investments of time or consultants to understand").

30 See id.

31 See Friedberg Follow-Up Study, supra note 8; see also Mannatt Health, Supporting the Future of Primary Care in California through Aligned Hybrid Payment Models 5 (2021).

32 See Mark W. Friedberg et al., Effects of Health Care Payment Models on Physician Practice in the United States, AMA-RAND 58 (2015), https://www.rand.org/pubs/research_reports/RR869.htm (discussing customizing systems to meet new workflows); MedPAC, supra note 29, at 53 (noting that practices of all sizes reported investing significant resources in building internal capabilities to analyze VBPMs); Friedberg Follow-Up Study, supra note 8, at 12 (commenting on the challenge of keeping track of payment performance details that vary from payer to payer).

33 See Friedberg Follow-Up Study, supra note 8, at 14; Friedberg et al., supra note 32, at 102–03 (providers expressed uncertainty about best strategies for responding to multiple VBPMs).

34 See Friedberg et al., supra note 32, at 64 (physician practices reported "heavy administrative burdens from the growing cacophony of metrics"); Stephanie M. Kissam et al., States Encouraging Value-Based Payment: Lessons from CMS's State Innovation Models Initiative, 97 Milbank Q. 506, 532 (2019) (same).

35 See Tricia McGinnis & Jessica Newman, Advances in Multi-Payer Alignment: State Approaches to Aligning Performance Metrics across Public and Private Insurers, Milbank Mem'l Fund Issue Brief (2014), https://www.milbank.org/publications/advances-in-multi-payer-alignment-state-approaches-to-aligning-performance-metrics-across-public-and-private-payers/ (providers must collect and report "hundreds" of different performance measures).

electronic health records systems to capture all relevant data.[36] In addition, because providers cannot simultaneously tackle numerous metrics, they must decide which ones to focus on and which to ignore.[37] Many providers report struggling with these requirements.[38]

These administrative challenges have slowed providers' adoption of value-based care models.[39] For some providers, the time, effort, and expertise needed to manage disparate payment requirements and performance measures is simply beyond their capacity.[40] For others, the associated administrative costs can outweigh VBPMs' potential financial rewards.[41] These challenges have dissuaded many providers from participating in VBPMs.[42]

For providers who do enter into VBPMs, the administrative challenges can complicate efforts to fundamentally transform their operations. As explained by a practice administrator:

> We're so constrained on staff that the time to investigate [each new payment program], the time to do the thinking, the time to ask questions is hard to come by. And so because of that, I don't think we're doing it as efficiently as we could A) we're not getting everything done that we could get done, and B) we don't have the time to really think about how to do it better.[43]

Relatedly, the administrative cost of participating in VBPMs weakens the business case for providers making significant investments in practice transformation.[44]

18.3.2 *Diluted and Conflicting Financial Incentives*

When providers participate in multiple VBPMs, interactions among payment models can weaken each model's effectiveness in two ways. First, covering only a portion of a provider's patient panel dilutes the financial incentives under each

36 See Friedberg et al., supra note 32, at 52, 102–03 (discussing the investments in data management capabilities made by providers participating in VBPMs).

37 See Friedberg Follow-Up Study, supra note 8, at 64, 93 (explaining that providers filter performance metrics).

38 See id. at 63–64, 95 (confusion over managing many performance metrics is common among small primary care or single-subspecialty practices).

39 See Werner et al., supra note 10, at 8–9 (administrative complexity "dissuades adoption" of VBPMs).

40 See Friedberg et al., supra note 32, at 63 (tracking payment program details "could be beyond the capacity of some practices").

41 See id. at 22, 64 (managing multiple payers' reporting requirements is "a major reason for rising practice expenses," and the cost of complying with certain performance measures can be disproportionate to the financial reward).

42 See Friedberg Follow-Up Study, supra note 8.

43 Id. at 48.

44 Cf. McGinnis & Newman, supra note 35, at 2 (explaining that the "chaos" of facing multiple performance measures "greatly limits the business case for providers to improve specific performance outcomes").

payer's VBPM.[45] For example, if a payment arrangement only covers 15 percent of a provider's patient panel, the arrangement's prospective financial rewards may be of insufficient magnitude to prompt the provider to transform their practice. Now, in theory, alignment across multiple VBPMs could yield sufficiently large financial incentives in the aggregate to motivate practice transformation. Unfortunately, in markets with "many competing payers all going it alone, these conditions are seldom met,"[46] as payers vary in their own readiness to implement specific VBPMs.[47]

Second, when providers treat a combination of patients attributed to VBPMs and fee-for-service arrangements, they face conflicting financial incentives that complicate their transitioning to value-based care models.[48] Fee-for-service incentives that encourage higher volume and care intensity can blunt VBPM incentives to reduce costs, utilization, and intensity.[49] For example, VBPMs that reward a health system's physicians for reducing hospital admissions and ER visits can harm the financial well-being of the system's hospital.[50] Fee-for-service and VBPM arrangements also encourage different clinical care approaches. Specifically, fee-for-service's volume-driven incentives encourage seeing patients quickly,[51] whereas advanced VBPMs require longer patient visits that allow for fully exploring patients' needs and

[45] Sean Cavanaugh & Gregory Burke, A Multipayer Approach to Health Care Reform 4 (2010).

[46] Id.

[47] See Friedberg et al., supra note 32 (describing how practices interested in certain risk-based payment models faced difficulties negotiating contracts with payers who were less interested in those models, especially among payers still focused on fee-for-service payment models).

[48] See Assistant Sec'y for Planning and Evaluation, U.S. Dep't of Health and Hum. Servs., Environmental Scan on Issues Related to the Development of Population-Based Total Cost of Care (TCOC) Models in the Broader Context of Alternative Payment Models (VBPMs) and Physician-Focused Payment Models (PFPMs) 16 (Mar. 3, 2022), https://aspe.hhs.gov/sites/default/files/documents/871a839c1771919499e415b2dae8700a/TCOC-Escan.pdf (noting that it is difficult for providers to "strike a balance" between the incentives under fee-for-service arrangements and VBPMs that shift significant financial risk to providers); Friedberg et al., supra note 32, at 100 ("Some physicians face the 'two-canoe' problem of depending on [fee-for-service] and accompanying incentives to a significant portion of their revenues while working to transition to alternative payment models with conflicting incentives").

[49] See Friedberg et al., supra note 32, at 63 (explaining that when practices participate in both fee-for-service and risk-based contracts, they "faced fundamentally conflicting incentives to increase volume under the FFS contract while reducing costs under the risk-based contract"); see also Nat'l Acad. of Sci., Eng'g, & Med., supra note 9, at 298–99 (explaining that among practices' participating in patient-centered medial home arrangements, their "underlying focus on visit volume" under fee-for-service made it more difficult for them to shift their focus to reducing total spending).

[50] Friedberg et al., supra note 32, at 63.

[51] Collin Couey, Value-Based Care vs Fee-for-Service: The Ins and Outs You Need to Know, Software Advice (Aug. 1, 2022), https://www.softwareadvice.com/resources/value-based-care-vs-fee-for-service/.

providing in-depth patient education.[52] These considerations can greatly weaken the financial rewards of transitioning to new patient care models, as providers who do so may incur declining revenue under their fee-for-service arrangements. Finally, rather than investing in practice transformation, providers with both fee-for-service and VBPM contracts can simply make up any lower VBPM revenue by increasing care volume or intensity for fee-for-service patients.[53]

In sum, while a decentralized approach to health care finance has facilitated payment innovation, this experimentation has not spurred meaningful health care delivery reform. True change instead requires a coordinated approach that harmonizes payment models across payers.

18.4 EFFORTS TO HARMONIZE PAYMENT APPROACHES THROUGH VOLUNTARY ALIGNMENT

Policymakers increasingly recognize the need for payment alignment. Yet this recognition has not produced a public law paradigm for health care finance, with legal mandates used as a tool for coordinating payers' payment approaches. Federal and state agencies instead have developed multi-payment alignment initiatives (MPAIs) that facilitate payers *voluntarily* aligning their VBPMs.[54] For example, payers participating in MPAIs could adopt a common set of performance measures or a uniform patient attribution methodology. Regulators believe that MPAIs can increase the percentage of patients covered by similar payment rules and incentives, thereby lowering providers' administrative burden and improving the business case for participating in VBPMs.[55] Unfortunately, MPAIs are unlikely to achieve these objectives.[56]

[52] See Friedberg et al., supra note 32, at 28–30, 65–66 (quoting a physician practice leader explaining the competing time pressures under fee-for-service and medical home arrangements).

[53] Friedberg Follow-Up Study, supra note 8, at 35–36.

[54] See Stremikis, supra note 25, at 3 ("Multipayer initiatives involve collaboration among public (e.g., Medicaid) and private (e.g., commercial insurance) payers participating in value-based payment and delivery system reforms ..."). Although non-governmental entities can convene MPAIs, collaborations led by private actors risk running afoul of antitrust laws that prohibit coordinated action among competitors, whereas government-led MPAIs can invoke the state action doctrine to protect coordinated action taken pursuant to a clearly articulated state policy and under state supervision. See Barbara Wirth & Mary Takach, State Strategies to Avoid Antitrust Concerns in Multipayer Medical Home Initiatives, Commonwealth Fund (July 2013), https://www.commonwealthfund.org/sites/default/files/documents/___media_files_publications_issue_brief_2013_jul_1694_wirth_state_strategies_avoid_antitrust_ib.pdf.

[55] See Assistant Sec'y for Planning and Evaluation, supra note 48, at 12 (MPAIs can simplify administrative and financial planning for providers, thereby increasing their engagement with VBPMs).

[56] For a more in-depth discussion of factors that frustrate MPAIs' achieving their goals, see Mantel, supra note 28, at 120–25.

MPAIs may appeal to payers seeking to amplify their individual efforts to reform the health care delivery system.[57] Successfully doing so could lead to lower health care spending and higher quality care, boosting participating insurers' profit margins and giving them a competitive advantage over nonparticipating insurers. However, because providers generally treat their patients similarly, any patient care improvements stemming from greater payment alignment would benefit *all* payers, including those not participating in an MPAI. Private insurers participating in MPAIs therefore may derive little if any competitive advantage over other insurers.[58]

Additional considerations may dissuade private insurers from joining MPAIs. The benefits of MPAIs are limited when the participating payers collectively cover too few patients to nudge providers toward practice transformation. This concern can deter potential MPAI participants, creating a vicious cycle. A private insurer also may doubt whether MPAI participants can reach consensus, given marketplace rivalries and likely disagreement over payment strategies.[59] Finally, logistical and financial constraints, such as the burden of switching to new payment methodologies, can further erode the case for MPAI participation.[60] Consequently, MPAIs have had limited success in lowering the barriers to providers adopting value-based care models due to limited payer participation in MPAIs.

18.5 CONCLUSION

Health care finance law, with its private law foundation, largely centers on ensuring that private insurers honor their financial commitments and treat insureds and providers fairly. This narrow relational focus leaves insurers free to develop divergent payment policies based on their own individual priorities and self-interest. In particular, private insurers have embraced a range of value-based payment approaches designed to nudge providers toward more effective patient care models. Unfortunately, these efforts have failed to produce meaningful health care delivery

57 See Stremikis, supra note 25, at 3 ("Successful multi-payer alignment can amplify the impact of payment and delivery reforms by sending consistent incentives to health care providers and aligning performance measurement").

58 See Kissam et al., supra note 34, at 531 (one reason cited by commercial insurers for not aligning with Medicaid VBP models were concerns "that if they invested in a payment model that succeeded in reducing overall utilization and expenditures for a practice's entire patient panel, they would end up subsidizing the care of patients covered by free-riding payers who were not making similar investments in a new payment model").

59 See Mantel, supra note 28, at 121–22 (noting that insurers with a history of competition may struggle to cooperate with and trust one another); Cavanaugh & Burke, supra note 45, at 6 (explaining that a payer's willingness to participate in an MPAI may be influenced by the fact that "[p]ayers differ in their outlook on different models of service delivery reform").

60 See Mantel, supra note 28, at 123 (explaining that some payers may be unwilling to invest in or lack the capacity to adopt new payment methodologies, and that regional or national payers may prefer to standardize their operations across all service areas rather than conform to multiple state MPAIs).

reform, as payers' misaligned payment strategies create obstacles to practice transformation at the provider level. Moreover, various competitive and logistical considerations have impeded attempts to harmonize payment approaches through voluntary payer collaborations.

Efforts to improve the quality and efficiency of patient care through payment reform will prove futile absent greater alignment across VBPMs. Yet a private law approach, with its emphasis on individual rights and bilateral relationships, falls short of eliciting the necessary coordinated action among payers. Public law, however, can transcend this collective action problem by using the law to coordinate payment policies across the health care sector. In addition, a public law paradigm would take a holistic view of the health care system and promote payment policies rooted in collective goals rather than private insurers' self-interest.

A public law approach to health care finance could be achieved in one of two ways. First, regulators could follow the lead of Rhode Island and implement a mandatory cooperative scheme that requires private insurers to operate in concert with one another and with public payers. For example, in order "to ensure consistency in the use of quality measures" across payer-provider contracts, Rhode Island limits insurers to a common set of performance measures.[61] Rhode Island similarly mandates that all insurers pay primary care practices that meet regulatory guidelines for patient-centered medical homes a per-member-per-month fee for care management services and infrastructure.[62] Alternatively, a single-payer system built around a government insurance plan would, by definition, apply uniform payment rules and processes across a provider's patient panel.[63] Choosing between these two options raises complex issues beyond the scope of this chapter, such as questions about comparative institutional competence, value trade-offs, federalism concerns, and political and economic feasibility. Nevertheless, reforming the health care delivery system demands a paradigm shift in our regulatory approach to private insurers, one that moves beyond traditional private law norms. It is thus imperative that future policy conversations about health care finance occur within a public law framework.

[61] 230 R.I. Code R. §20-30-4.10(D)(5).

[62] 230 R.I. Code R. §20-30-4.10(C).

[63] See Mantel, supra note 28, at 127–29 (describing how a single-payer system could address the current payment misalignment under a multi-payer system by paying an individual provider in the same manner across their entire patient panel).

PART V

Private Law Applied

The Pharmaceutical Industry, Nursing Homes, and the End of Life Introduction

Carmel Shachar

This part closes the volume with an exploration of private law within two very different sectors of health care: the pharmaceutical industry and the aging and end-of-life sector. At first glance, it may seem that these two components of the health care field have little in common.

But when the reader has a chance to dive into the four chapters of Part V commonalities emerge, especially in regard to the use and scope of private law. As one of the authors in this part, Barry Furrow, writes, "[p]rivate law can have a powerful role." Three of the chapters in this part speak to opportunities to harness private law to address problematic incentives and profit seeking across the health care field. The last chapter serves as a warning, arguing that private law and organizational choices can undermine public policy and legislation if not properly harnessed. In summation, these chapters provide the reader with a sense of the value of private law in influencing health policy across the field, and the importance of using it well.

In the first chapter of Part V, "Private Equity Firms and Digital Clinical Trials: Tensions between Efficiency and Drug Evidence Access," Chapter 19, Ximena Benavides considers the role of private actors in producing pharmaceutical research. Benavides traces the rise of decentralized clinical trials (DCT), especially during the COVID-19 pandemic. She argues that DCTs make investment in biomedical research particularly appealing to private equity firms. Benavides then argues that private equity firms' profit incentives call into question their ability to support quality research. While Benavides does call for improved regulation, she also notes that private equity firms must accept greater moral responsibility than they have to date.

Rebecca E. Wolitz is likewise concerned with the impact that profit incentives can have on access to pharmaceuticals. She notes that many managers and directors of pharmaceutical companies feel that their investors expect profit maximization, which spurs business decisions that lead to unreasonably expensive prescription drugs. But she notes that for the past several decades shareholders have raised concerns about drug pricing through access to medication shareholder resolutions. Wolitz highlights that the resolutions are a private law tool that can be used to provide a unique perspective and work in tandem with regulatory and legislative efforts to address drug pricing.

The third chapter of Part V, "The Hollowed-Out American Nursing Home: Using Private Law to Police Poor Quality Care and Expand Owner Responsibilities," Chapter 21, shifts the focus of Part V from pharmaceutical research to aging care and nursing homes. Barry R. Furrow, like Ximena Benavides, is concerned with the impact that private equity ownership will have, in this case on nursing homes. Furrow is concerned that the private equity focus on short-term, significant returns for its investors will lead to low-quality care for nursing home residents. He notes, however, that regulatory oversight has been particularly weak for nursing homes, meaning that public law tools may not be optimal for safeguarding nursing home residents. Instead, Furrow offers a model of robust fiduciary duty, using the private law doctrinal framework to better police private equity actors in this space.

The last chapter, "Health Care Organization Policies about the California End of Life Option Act: A Paper Victory of the Medical Aid in Dying Movement," Chapter 22, by Megan S. Wright and Cindy L. Cain, illustrates how private choices can undermine public policy. Wright and Cain focus on the implementation of medical aid in dying (MAiD) in California, calling it a public policy "paper victory" because very few individuals are able to meet its requirements to qualify for MAiD. They flag that private law or organizational choices create a roadblock to meaningful access to MAiD. California allows health care organizations to opt out of providing MAiD, which many religiously affiliated hospitals have chosen to do. Other health care organizations opt into providing MAiD but use internal policies, such as choosing to not publicly post their MAiD policy or require additional appointments and assessments, to limit its use by their patients.

At first glance, Wright and Cain's chapter creates somewhat of a contrast with the work of Benavides, Wolitz, and Furrow, all of whom are arguing for private law tools to address policy concerns. But upon further reflection, Wright and Cain's chapter serves as a warning against ignoring the power of private law. In California, the MAiD legislation did not consider how the choices of private actors could create a "paper victory." Had MAiD advocates understood the importance of private law tools in achieving meaningful access to services for all, they might have found inspiration in the other chapters of Part V, and in the rest of the volume, for ways to harness private law to support their goals.

19

The Financialization of Digital Clinical Trials

Tensions between Efficiency and Scientific Evidence Accessibility

Ximena Benavides

19.1 INTRODUCTION

Over the past two decades, the use of digital technology in clinical trials has proliferated, a shift that has been argued to reach a more diverse and representative trial population more efficiently. Also known as decentralized clinical trials, digital clinical trials (DCTs) saw a vastly increased use amid the COVID-19 pandemic, when remote methods were employed to reach trial participants who could not reach trial sites in person. While improving clinical trial accessibility through decentralized approaches is important, it is also crucial who is leading these efforts in the generation of scientific evidence. This essay re-centers the relationship between private equity (PE) and clinical trials in the analysis of DCTs and the social value of access in the for-profit, private production of scientific evidence. In a highly fragmented biotechnology industry, where PE firms are increasingly acquiring small firms that provide outsourced clinical research services, DCTs and PE firm unions might bring about additional opportunities to increase drug data opacity, compromising the access to the greater production of scientific evidence driving digital technology.

Structured in three parts, the essay examines the current state of DCTs and questions whether PE firms' investment in DCTs is convenient for data generation and access to quality medicine. The first section discusses the exponential growth of DCTs, particularly in the years following the pandemic, and their potential to address challenges of the traditional on-site clinical trial model. The second section examines PE firms' increasing interest in DCTs from a business, law, and policy perspective. The final section discusses the risks of generating scientific evidence through profit-driven models, with a special focus on the issues of publicity in the wider political economy of PE-funded medical research.

19.2 FROM IN-PERSON TO REMOTE CLINICAL TRIALS

Clinical trials are essential for generating the scientific evidence that regulators require to permit and ensure only safe and effective health care innovations leave the laboratory bench and eventually reach the market. In the past decade, private actors, including PE firms, have invested and managed the evidence production endeavor, critical to innovation access. Meeting the appropriate trial enrollment levels has been an important dimension of generating relevant and sufficient trial data that can be used to evaluate the efficacy and safety of medical treatments, drugs, and devices.[1] Yet, finding and recruiting trial participants can often be an operationally limiting and expensive task.

Traditionally, patients had to attend medical research sites in order to participate in clinical trials. This presented a series of problems to researchers. Consider that more than 70 percent of the US population lives at least two hours away from an academic medical research center and that only 50 percent of the US population participates in clinical research.[2] Bringing patients to a facility reduces generalizability[3] and generally implies mobility constraints that could make trial participation expensive or impossible.[4] These difficulties, in addition to participants' communication and the identification of operational constraints, tended to increase the participants' burden, considerably extending trial timelines and inflating costs, particularly in trials involving a large number of participants.[5]

Diversity in trial patient pools is another problem affecting clinical data generation. A recent study of sixty-four trials that led to fifty-nine FDA-approved cancer therapeutics between January 2012 and December 2017 showed an adequate representation of women (56 percent), older adults (24 percent), and racially and ethnically minoritized patients (16 percent).[6] If evidence for new medical interventions is "dominated by data from unrepresentative populations," as independent researchers argue, different disease severities, comorbidities, age groups, geographies, and other

1 Nat'l Acads. of Scis., Eng'g, and Med., Federal Policy to Advance Racial, Ethnic, and Tribal Health Equity (2023).

2 See Andy Coravos, Software-Enabled Clinical Trials, Medium (Sept. 4, 2017), https://blog.andreacoravos.com/software-enabled-clinical-trials-8da53f4cd271.

3 E-mail from Srinivas Murthy to Author (Sept. 15, 2023, 18:33 EST) (on file with author).

4 Dawn Anderson, Digital R&D: Four Ways to Maximize Patient Engagement in Clinical Trials, Deloitte (June 25, 2018), https://www2.deloitte.com/us/en/blog/health-care-blog/2018/digital-rd-four-ways-to-maximize-patient-engagement-in-clinical-trials.html.

5 See, e.g., Thomas Moore et al., Estimated Costs of Pivotal Trials for Novel Therapeutic Agents Approved by the US Food and Drug Administration, 2015–2016, 178 JAMA Internal Med. 1451 (2018) (comparing US$6 million mean cost for a 100-patient trial versus US$77 million for a 1,000-patient trial).

6 Tanvee Varma et al., Metrics, Baseline Scores, and a Tool to Improve Sponsor Performance on Clinical Trial Diversity: Retrospective Cross-sectional Study, 2 BMJ Med. e000395 (2023).

profiling factors will be excluded and users harmed by disparate access to medical treatment.[7]

The decentralization of trials has thus been presented as a way to deal with recruitment and demographic representation obstacles while significantly reducing associated costs and time. Trials conducted entirely virtually can reach a larger, diverse population and their participants no longer need to travel to medical research centers and might not even meet with their study teams.[8] Remote monitoring and real-time oversight of participants can alleviate investigators' and participants' workloads while increasing the opportunities for assessments over extended periods of time.[9] This is expected to accelerate scientific evidence generation, with higher and faster data accuracy and cost controls, and, potentially, contribute to catapulting more products to the market sooner. Technology adds to decentralization improved recruitment, oversight, and the retention of a larger and diverse trial participant pool, data collection and aggregation, and data analytics. Huge growing trial data volumes will progressively be subject to sophisticated analytics and data-driven algorithms, with Artificial Intelligence and Machine Learning in clinical research reshaping drug development.[10]

Although running medical research studies remotely with the assistance of technology has been an ongoing practice for years now,[11] and even captured the attention of the government,[12] it was only by the end of the past decade, with the COVID-19 pandemic, that their decentralization and the use of research digital tools gained popularity. As a result of isolation-based public health measures for the risks of contracting the virus and clinical networks' priorities shifting from research to the treatment of COVID-19 patients, trial enrollment decreased by more than

7 Jennifer Miller & Joseph Millum, Ethical Considerations in International Clinical Trial Site Selection, 7(4) BMJ Global Health e008012 (2022), at 1, 2, n.4.

8 O. T. Inan et al., Digitizing Clinical Trials, 3 NPJ Digit. Med., n.101 (2020).

9 Id. at 2; see also Effy Vayena et al., Decentralised Clinical Trials: Ethical Opportunities and Challenges, 5 Lancet Digit. Health e390 (2023).

10 Greg Licholai, AI in Clinical Research: Now and Beyond, Forbes (Sept. 18, 2023), https://www.forbes.com/sites/greglicholai/2023/09/18/ai-in-clinical-research-now-and-beyond/?sh=2612b1383c85.

11 See Tim McAlindon et al., Conducting Clinical Trials over the Internet: Feasibility Study, 327 Brit. Med. J. 484 (2003) (on knee osteoarthritis studies); Bradly P. Jacobs et al., An Internet-Based Randomized, Placebo-Controlled Trial of Kava and Valerian for Anxiety and Insomnia, 84 Medicine 197 (2005) (on anxiety and insomnia treatments' studies); Pfizer Conducts First "Virtual" Clinical Trial Allowing Patients to Participate Regardless of Geography, Pfizer (June 7, 2011, 5:30 AM), https://www.pfizer.com/news/press-release/press-release-detail/pfizer_conducts_first_virtual_clinical_trial_allowing_patients_to_participate_regardless_of_geography (on Pfizer's FDA-approved REMOTE).

12 See Digital Clinical Trials Workshop: Creating a Vision for the Future, Nat'l Health, Lung & Blood Inst. (2019), https://www.nhlbi.nih.gov/events/2019/digital-clinical-trials-workshop-creating-vision-future.

two-thirds across all therapeutic areas.[13] Remote trials proliferated and the Food and Drug Administration (FDA) required research sites to adjust their safety procedures or switch to digital, waiving Institutional Review Boards (IRB) or FDA approval but still subjecting them to reporting.[14] Remote trials during the pandemic helped to assess the strengths and weaknesses of virtual trials – for example, that studying patients remotely can be safe as long as participants do not have a serious medical condition (e.g., infectious disease or progressive cancer)[15] – and became a regular practice.[16] Since 2021, DCTs have become a "major part of [the industry's] portfolios."[17] Several clinical research organizations (CROs)[18] and academic research and related public–private initiatives[19] have developed products across the decentralized trial spectrum.

19.3 PRIVATE EQUITY'S INTEREST IN DCTS

The US health care industry has been increasingly attractive to PE firms for some time now.[20] Distinctively, the United States reports an average of 2.3 PE health care transactions daily.[21] From hospital and nursing home buyouts in the 2000s, to medical practice acquisitions such as radiology and outpatient care, including

[13] Consolidation in Clinical Research Sites and COVID's Impact, Provident Healthcare Partners (Aug. 2020), https://www.providenthp.com/expertise/consolidation-in-clinical-research-sites-and-covids-impact/.

[14] Conduct of Clinical Trials of Medical Products during the COVID-19 Public Health Emergency: Guidance for Industry Investigators, and Institutional Review Boards, U.S. Dep't of Health & Hum. Servs. (Mar. 2020), https://www.fda.gov/media/136238/download; see also Jacqueline Corrigan-Curay, Conducting Clinical Trials during the COVID-19 Public Health Emergency, U.S. Food and Drug Admin. (Apr. 30, 2020), https://www.fda.gov/media/137496/download.

[15] Podcast: Can Famotidine, a Heartburn Drug, Treat Covid? Health Talk with Tobias Janowitz, Northwell Health (Jan. 23, 2023), https://www.northwell.edu/news/insights/podcast-researcher-talks-famotidine-for-covid-trial.

[16] See also Matthew Libassi, Northwell, CSHL Open Virtual COVID-19 Clinical Trial for Non-hospitalized Patients, Northwell Health (Jan. 27, 2021), https://feinstein.northwell.edu/news/the-latest/-northwell-cshl-open-virtual-covid-19-clinical-trial-for-non-hospitalized-patients (referring to Northwell's post-pandemic trial recruitment strategies).

[17] Marcus A. Banks, In the Wake of COVID-19, Decentralized Clinical Trials Move to Center Stage, 118(47) Proc. Nat'l Acad. Scis. e2119097118 (2021), at 2.

[18] Coravos, supra note 2 (e.g., Science 37, Koneksa Health, Medidata).

[19] Andy Coravos, Decentralized Clinical Trials, Medium (Oct. 15, 2018), https://blog.andreacoravos.com/decentralized-clinical-trials-e9dbde90ea95 (Clinical Trial Transformation Initiative by Duke University and the FDA).

[20] See John Geyman, Private Equity Looting of U.S. Health Care: An Under-Recognized and Uncontrolled Scourge, 53 Int. J. Health Servs. 233 (2003); Anaeze C. Offodile II et al., Private Equity Investments in Health Care: An Overview of Hospital and Health System Leveraged Buyouts, 2003–17, 40 Health Affs. 719, https://www.healthaffairs.org/doi/10.1377/hlthaff.2020.01535.

[21] Data from PitchBook Data Inc., Healthcare Services Report (2022), https://pitchbook.com/news/reports/q4-2022-healthcare-services-report.

urgent care and ambulatory surgery centers and neonatal and trauma units in the 2010s, PE health care investments have increased twenty times their value in the past two decades.[22] PE has also been active in nonhospital-based dermatology, dental, orthopedics, and behavioral health specialties,[23] and medical debt collecting.[24]

Clinical trials, particularly those remote and digital, represent a new business opportunity for PE firms: If a drug can reach the market sooner and at a lower cost, manufacturers will make more profit. By outsourcing the performance of trials to CROs, manufacturers can reduce investment risks and separate the operational costs of running a trial; in turn, CROs can make revenues despite trials failing or if a drug is not approved.[25] The way in which PE firms operate, raising capital and investing it into various privately held companies, often grants them ownership or enough of a stake to gain operational control of their portfolio's companies, appoint company directors, and dictate every aspect of the companies' business and affairs.[26] The decentralization and digitization of trials require infrastructure outside of a research institution and technology tools that are often proprietary. This provides CROs – and the PE firms that finance and manage them – with more opportunity to grow, continue penetrating the space of trials, and build the infrastructure and technology required. Studies found substantial value in employing DCT methods in phase II and phase III of clinical trials, with high returns on investments.[27] Decentralization would be particularly more amenable for "general population drugs," which serve a category of patients with less hospital-based resourcing needs;[28] yet, the industry has expressed interest in the decentralization of trials for rare diseases, too.[29]

Financial stability would make trials a reliable investment for PE portfolios. Business strategies vary somewhat by type of private equity investment, but prioritizing short-term, high profits stays as a primary goal.[30] Unlike other technology-based

22 Eileen Appelbaum & Rosemary Batt, Private Equity Buyouts in Healthcare: Who Wins, Who Loses? 93–94 (Ctr. for Econ. & Pol'y Rsch., Working Paper No. 118, 2020), https://papers.ssrn.com/sol3/papers.cfm?abstract_id=3593887 (from US$5 billion in 2000 to US$100 billion in 2018).

23 Myths v. Facts: Private Equity and Nursing Homes, Am. Health Care Ass'n (Mar. 11, 2022), https://www.ahcancal.org/News-and-Communications/Blog/Pages/Myths-vs–Facts-Private-Equity-and-Nursing-Homes.aspx.

24 Geyman, supra note 20, at 233–34.

25 See Rachana Pradhan, The Business of Clinical Trials Is Booming. Private Equity Has Taken Notice, Kaiser Fam. Found. Health News (Dec. 2, 2022), https://kffhealthnews.org/news/article/business-clinical-trials-private-equity/; Provident Healthcare Partners, supra note 13, at 4.

26 John Morley, Too Big to Be Activist, 92 S. Cal. L. Rev. 1407, 1449 (2019).

27 Joseph A. DiMasi et al., Assessing the Financial Value of Decentralized Clinical Trials, 57(2) Therapeutic Innovation & Regul. Sci. 209 (2023).

28 E-mail from Greg Licholai to Author (Sept. 18, 2023, 22:55 EST) (on file with author) (referring that oncology and rare disease drugs might be less amenable to decentralization).

29 Mercedeh Ghadessi et al., Decentralized Clinical Trials and Rare Diseases: A Drug Information Association Innovative Design Scientific Working Group (DIA-IDSWG) Perspective, 18(1) Orphanet J. Rare Dis. 79 (2023).

30 Geyman, supra note 20, at 234.

industries, trial demand is resilient to inflation and economic declines. Research and development (R&D) of new health technologies can largely be government-backed, which secures low debt levels once entering clinical trial phases. Although these are signs of stable cash flow, some high volatility suggests clinical trials to be risky investments, with already cautionary tales of valuation fluctuation and labor struggles.[31] Science 37, one of the first DCT startups, showed continued and massive share price drops after an oversubscribed offering in 2020 and a major public listing in 2021.[32] Nevertheless, overall, DCTs make financial sense to PE firms that tolerate volatility and can make huge returns provided timely, good planning.[33] The clinical trial space is attractive for businesses; valued at US$16 billion, with an estimated 6.8 percent compound annual growth rate through 2025.[34] Since January 2021, ten PE-backed trial platforms have been acquired or created,[35] yet mostly interested in late-stage trials.[36] No drug studied via remote trials (whether PE funded or not) has been approved yet to date.

From a legal and policy perspective, the outsourcing of pharmaceutical services has not spurred enough regulatory oversight. Generally, PE firms' transactions are not subject to rigorous scrutiny even though they can have large effects on competition.[37] About 90 percent of PE transactions – either buyouts or investments – are exempt from the federal mandatory antitrust reporting threshold,[38] with the

[31] Kyle LaHucik, Two Decentralized Trials Startups Prove They're Not Immune to Broader Wave of Biotech Layoffs, Endpoint News (Aug. 24, 2022), https://endpts.com/two-decentralized-trials-startups-prove-theyre-not-immune-to-broader-wave-of-biotech-layoffs/.

[32] See Science 37 Raises $40 Million to Extend Its Leadership in the Decentralized Clinical Trial Market, PR Newswire (Aug. 20, 2020), https://www.prnewswire.com/news-releases/science-37-raises-40-million-to-extend-its-leadership-in-the-decentralized-clinical-trial-market-301115398.html; Ben Adams, Science 37 Taps a SPAC to Go Public, with Siteless Trial Specialist Valued at a Cool $1B, Fierce Biotech (May 7, 2021), https://www.fiercebiotech.com/cro/science-37-taps-a-spac-to-go-public-siteless-trial-specialist-valued-at-a-cool-1b.

[33] E-mail from Greg Licholai to Author (Sept. 20, 2023, 10:28 AM EST) (on file with author).

[34] Harris Williams, Return on Innovation, Part 6: Clinical Trial Sites (Mar. 2023), https://www.harriswilliams.com/our-insights/hcls-return-innovation-clinical-trials#part-6-full-report.

[35] Id.

[36] See Randal Smith, The Private Equity Firm That Quietly Profits on Top-Selling Drugs, N.Y. Times (July 8, 2017), https://nytimes.com/2017/07/08/business/dealbook/drug-prices-private-equity.html (Royalty Pharma's investment in Soliqua's late-stage clinical trial); David H. Crean, Private Equity Is Making Venture-Style Bets in Drug Development, Cardiff Advisory (Feb. 1, 2023), https://www.linkedin.com/pulse/private-equity-making-venture-style-bets-drug-david-h-crean/ (Blackstone's acquisition of pharma companies with undergoing clinical trials).

[37] Fred Schulte, Sick Profit: Investigating Private Equity's Stealthy Takeover of Health Care across Cities and Specialties, Kaiser Fam. Found. Health News (Nov. 14, 2022), https://kffhealthnews.org/news/article/private-equity-takeover-health-care-cities-specialties/.

[38] The Growth of Private Equity in US Health Care: Impact and Outlook, Nat'l Inst. of Health Care Mgmt. Found. (2023), https://nihcm.org/publications/the-growth-of-private-equity-in-us-health-care-impact-and-outlook (referring to Zirui Song on PE expansion policies); see Statement of Commissioner Rohit Chopra Regarding Private Equity Roll-ups and the Hart-Scott Rodino Annual Report to Congress, Fed. Trade Comm'n (July 8, 2020), https://www.ftc

exception of a few states, such as Oregon and Massachusetts, that monitor health care antitrust activity.[39]

Fragmentation also makes clinical trials a prime target for PE firms. The medical research market includes stand-alone clinics and physician practices performing studies on a part-time basis, commercial sponsors, and CROs. As fragmented as trial activities thus become, it is harder for policies to address trial challenges with specificity, which creates the risk of ignoring the secondary effects of a given policy choice and moving toward contradictory policy goals – like expanding DCTs through PE firms.[40] For PE firms, *fragmentation* also represents the opportunity to consolidate markets and reduce operational costs, which PE firms do to maximize profits.[41] Vertical integration of CROs' service offerings (e.g., recruitment, data collection) allows PE firms to gain operational control over trials.[42] As PE firms acquire independent sites, they become part of larger networks to be sold off once they are rolled up into a business.[43] Following a merger, acquirers tend to prioritize services that are operationally cost-efficient. Recruitment might be one of them. Additionally, former CEOs of pharmaceutical companies are occupying influential seats at PE firms,[44] suggesting new combinations of *small and big* pharmaceutical industry dominance that will demand new private law tools to ensure that consolidations receive increased scrutiny.

19.4 GREATER SCIENTIFIC EVIDENCE AT THE RISK OF MORE OPACITY

Allegedly, PE firms have targeted DCTs as a blooming business opportunity.[45] At least 65 percent of the total clinical research transactions reported until February of 2023 have involved PE firms.[46] Eleven of the twenty-five PE firms

.gov/legal-library/browse/cases-proceedings/public-statements/statement-commissioner-rohit-chopra-regarding-private-equity-roll-ups-hart-scott-rodino-annual.

39 Robin L. Davison et al., A Step Forward for Health Care Market Oversight: Oregon Health Authority's Health Care Market Oversight Program, Milbank Mem. Fund (Mar. 13, 2023), https://www.milbank.org/publications/a-step-forward-for-health-care-market-oversight-oregon-health-authoritys-health-care-market-oversight-program/.

40 Pradhan, supra note 25.

41 Richard M. Scheffler et al., Soaring Private Equity Investment in the Health Care Sector: Consolidation, Accelerated, Competition Undermined, and Patient Risk, Petris Ctr. (May 18, 2021), https://petris.org/soaring-private-equity-investment-in-the-healthcare-sector-consolidation-accelerated-competition-undermined-and-patients-at-risk/.

42 Provident Healthcare Partners, supra note 13.

43 Pradhan, supra note 25.

44 Data with author.

45 Pradhan, supra note 25.

46 Author's examination of Private Equity-Backed CROs Tracker database provided by the nonprofit Private Equity Stakeholder Project (PESP) for this research project. The database collects data from Pitchbook Data Inc. available until February 24, 2023 (on file with the author). Fifty-seven of the eighty-seven research site acquisitions deals reported since 2020 are

identified by PitchBook as health care sector top investors have bought stakes in CROs.[47] Is it beneficial for scientific evidence production that PE firms finance and manage clinical trials, their decentralization, and digitization?

This essay frames this question not as one of ownership but of governance, motivated by concerns around access to scientific evidence produced by private sector actors. PE firms' interest in DCTs is in tension with the original sponsor role of the industry. The FDA first coined the term drug "sponsor" in the 1960s to differentiate research tasks from development, when the labor of clinical investigations was conceived divorced from the industry. The role of drug manufacturers was to promote the merits of a novel product to the regulatory agency until it reached approval for commercialization.[48] The Bayh-Dole Act of 1980[49] opened the door for financialized actors to venture into drug development.[49] In the 1980s and 1990s, pharmaceutical firms underwent a corporate strategy transformation under the rise of the idea of shareholder value maximization (SVM), which distorted the way in which larger, publicly traded pharmaceutical companies generate growth for their shareholders – not on their current profitability but on their potential to deliver future earnings.[50] Although the expansion of financial actors, like venture capital, in the US health care system[51] and biotechnology particularly is not new,[52] as PE firms get more involved in the decentralization and digitization of research, the industry's original sponsor role reaches – yet again – new extremes. It also reinforces the supply-driven approach that has shaped biopharmaceutical innovation, which aligns biopharmaceutical innovation priorities with market demand over the social value of science, leaving the end goal of access to scientific evidence and resulting medicine at the periphery.[53]

private equity-backed. See also PESP 2023 Report, Private Equity in U.S. Healthcare: Trends in 2023 Deal Activity (2023), https://pestakeholder.org/private-equity-healthcare-2023-trends/ (reporting thirty-eight PE-backed deals in 2023).

47 Headlands Research Sites Chosen for Crucial COVID-19 Vaccine Trials, Globe NewsWire (July 16, 2020), https://www.globenewswire.com/news-release/2020/07/16/2063568/0/en/Headlands-Research-Sites-Chosen-for-Crucial-COVID-19-Vaccine-Trials.html.

48 Daniel Carpenter, Reputation and Power: Organizational Image and Pharmaceutical Regulation at the FDA (2014).

49 Arti K. Rai & Rebecca S. Eisenberg, Bayh-Dole Reform and the Progress of Biomedicine: Allowing Universities to Patent the Results of Government-Sponsored Research Sometimes Works against the Public Interest, 91(1) Am. Scientist 52, 52–59 (2003).

50 Victor Roy, A Crisis for Cures? Tracing Assetization and Value in Biomedical Innovation, in Assetization (Kean Birch & Fabian Muniesa eds., 2020).

51 Joseph D. Bruch et al., The Financialization of Health in the United States, 390(2) N. Engl. J. Med. 178 (2024).

52 Gary P. Pisano, Can Science Be a Business, 84(10) Harv. Bus. Rev. 114, 114–24 (2006).

53 Ariel Katz, Pharmaceutical Lemons: Innovation and Regulation in the Drug Industry, 14 Mich. Telecomm. & Tech. L. Rev. 1, 8 (2007).

Scholars have raised concerns about PE firms' investment in health care based on negative outcomes in the delivery of medical care: decline in safety and efficacy[54] and higher prices.[55] Clinical trials bring forth their own set of risks, too. Two areas of concern are the ethics of trial participants' engagement (including data privacy protections, inclusivity, and participants' rights and safety)[56] and the opportunities to skew or produce faulty data in uncontrolled environments.[57] In these cases, private law tools like torts are available to enforce data privacy obligations. But having new financialized actors like PE firms, private by nature, directly involved in a considerable and rising number of trials that generate critical scientific evidence that supports the release of new health technologies into the market, might affect *all and everyone* as potential science users, beyond trial participants, and subject to less transparency regulations.

Crucially, DCTs are expected to generate greater data volume and data diversity. As PE firms engage in ambitious DCTs, they will gain access to a larger number of patient data sources, leverage data management tactics with sophisticated digital tools, and be able to obtain more critical clinical data. For instance, a 2021 Tuft CSDD report evidenced that phase III clinical trials already generated an average of 3.6 million data points, three times the data collected by late-stage trials ten years ago.[58] These numbers are expected to continue to grow as trials are digitized. Now, more data has not always led to better scientific evidence for quality drugs. The clinical evidence that the industry currently produces and delivers to the FDA in order to assess the safety and efficacy of drugs is either incomplete or not as transparent and accessible as needed. There is no indication that PE firms' involvement in the generation of scientific evidence will fix the information problem clinical trials face – to the contrary, the risk of opacity may even increase under PE leadership due to their opportunistic business model.

PE firms generate scientific evidence that is essential for regulators to exercise oversight over drug development, improve treatment guidelines, incentivize better

54 See Robert T. Braun et al., Association of Private Equity Investment in US Nursing Homes with the Quality and Cost of Care for Long-Stay Residents, 2 JAMA Health F. e213817 (2021), https://doi.org/10.1001/jamahealthforum.2021.3817.

55 Yashaswini Singh et al., Association of Private Equity Acquisition of Physician Practices with Changes in Health Care Spending and Utilization, 3(9) JAMA Health F. e222886 (2022), https://jamanetwork.com/journals/jama-health-forum/fullarticle/2795946.

56 See Vayena et al., supra note 9; Pradhan, supra note 25; Tessa I. van Rijssel et al., Ethics Review of Decentralized Clinical Trials (DCTs): Results of a Mock Ethics Review, 27(10) Drug Discovery Today 103326 (2022); Carlo Petrini et al., Decentralized Clinical Trials (DCTs): A Few Ethical Considerations, Front Public Health (2022), https://pubmed.ncbi.nlm.nih.gov/36590004/.

57 Banks, supra note 17, at 2.

58 Tuft Ctr. for the Study of Drug Dev., 23 Rising Protocol Design Complexity Is Driving Rapid Growth in Clinical Trial Data Volume (2021), https://f.hubspotusercontent10.net/hubfs/9468915/TuftsCSDD_June2021/pdf/Rising+Protocol+Design+Complexity+is+Driving+Rapid+Growth+in+Clinical+Trial+Data+Volume++++++++++.pdf.

innovation, and shed light on and correct bad industry practices. Data publicity is also important to bioethicists, who aim to reduce risks to trial participants and drug users; to health economists, to better direct health care spending to safe and effective treatments; and to independent researchers, advocates, and citizens at large for data reevaluation and accountability.[59] The FDA, which "houses the largest known repository of clinical data" in the world,[60] plays a gatekeeping role, with a primary function of information generation and validation.[61] This function is essentially frustrated when all information about drugs obtained in clinical trials is not made available or a part of it remains secret. *All* information includes both the positive and the negative data generated at trials. The burden to provide evidence of any negative effects is on firms.[62] However, drug developers have insufficient incentives to generate and share negative information as they want drugs to be approved, affecting validation.[63] A free rider problem leads to an information production and data publicity problem that PE firms could hardly overcome due to their appetite for maximizing profits in line with their fiduciary duty to create value for their investors in return for their entrusted money. This transactional PE–investor relationship silences other stakeholders' interests (e.g., developing science for the benefit of the community) and makes more socially oriented goals, such as making complete drug evidence accessible, be perceived with disbelief.[64]

Different trials produce different types of data. Metadata is essential for interpreting clinical trial results.[65] They include the study protocols that set forth investigators' statistical analysis plans and the endpoints a clinical study will evaluate. The FDA requires metadata for drug assessment and approval;[66] independent researchers use them to run a reanalysis of studies and identify probable misleading studies generating flattering results.[67] Summary data include clinical trial summaries,

59 Christopher J. Morten & Amy Kapczynski, The Big Data Regulator, Rebooted: Why and How the FDA Can and Should Disclose Confidential Data on Prescription Drugs and Vaccines, 109 Calif. L. Rev. 506, 506–09.

60 U.S. Food and Drug Admin., Driving Biomedical Innovation: Initiatives to Improve Products for Patients 22 (2011).

61 Amy Kapczynski, Dangerous Times: The FDA's Role in Information Production, Past and Future, 102 Minn. L. Rev. 2357, 2357–58 (2018); Jorge L. Contreras, Leviathan in the Commons: Biomedical Data and the State, in Governing Medical Knowledge Commons 19–45 (Katherine J. Strandburg et al. eds., 2017).

62 W. Nicholson Price II & Timo Minssen, Will Clinical Trial Data Disclosure Reduce Incentives to Develop New Uses of Drugs?, 33(7) Nature Biotech. 685, 685–86.

63 Id. at 2363–64; Morten & Kapczynski, supra note 59, at 509.

64 Jeanne A. Markey & Raymond M. Sarola, Private Equity, Health Care, and Profits: It's Time to Protect Patients, STAT News (Mar. 24, 2022), https://www.statnews.com/2022/03/24/private-equity-health-care-profits-time-to-protect-patients/.

65 Morten & Kapczynski, supra note 59, at 512.

66 See, e.g., 21 C.F.R. §314.50(d)(6) (2019) (requiring nondisclosure agreements to contain a statistical section).

67 See, e.g., Yale Collaboration for Rsch. Integrity & Transparency, Promoting Transparency in Clinical Research: Why and How 9 (2017) (referring to the Paxil case).

prepared by manufacturers and submitted to the FDA, that highlight key trial results. Although not routinely disclosed by the FDA, summary data can jeopardize medicines' permanence in markets.[68] Another set of valuable data for reanalysis is individual patient-level data. On a voluntary basis, raw and granular data collected per trial participant is made available in analyzable form and used to identify discrepancies, for example, in summary data.[69] A drug is safe only if its known therapeutic benefits outweigh its known risks;[70] thus, because "safety can only be understood in relation to efficacy and vice versa,"[71] and the safety and efficacy of drugs must be determined together, it is absolutely necessary that all trial data – metadata, summary data, individual patient-level data, and others – are not omitted, but disclosed and shared. The hidden data and existing opacity practices over privately produced evidence have already translated into grave examples of unsafe medicine. Vioxx led to tens of thousands of cardiac deaths,[72] whereas Paroxetine (Paxil) caused suicidal thoughts in a substantial portion of young patients who used the antidepressant during pediatric treatment, despite studies showing their risks clearly.[73]

PE firms' profit incentive schemes continue to put the prioritization of safety maximization at risk. The absence of PE-backed trials and approved drugs to date makes it hard to run a comparative analysis between trials with and without PE support. During the pandemic, the New York-based private equity firm Headlands Research established in 2018, which provided outsourced COVID-19 vaccine decentralized trials to pharmaceutical firms (such as Pfizer, Moderna, AstraZeneca, and Johnson & Johnson), grew by buying established trial sites and opening new ones in the United States and Canada under the promise of boosting underrepresented racial and ethnic minority trial representation.[74] Many of their acquired locations promptly closed, and it remains unclear whether the enrollment targets set for

68 Id. at 12–13 (referring to the Avandia case and the 2007 independent reanalysis of data that was possible due to a high-profile litigation settlement).

69 Joshua D. Wallach et al., Updating Insights into Rosiglitazone and Cardiovascular Risk through Shared Data: Individual Patient and Summary Level Meta-Analyses, 368 Brit. Med. J. 1 (2020).

70 FDA's Drug Review Process: Continued, U.S. Food and Drug Admin. (2015), https://www.fda.gov/drugs/information-consumers-and-patients-drugs/fdas-drug-review-process-continued.

71 Morten & Kapczynski, supra note 59.

72 David J. Graham et al., Risk of Acute Myocardial Infarction and Sudden Cardiac Death in Patients Treated with Cyclo-Oxygenase 2 Selective and Non-Selective Non-Steroidal Antiflammatory Drugs: Nested Case-Control Study, 365 Lancet 475, 280 (2005); Harlam Krumholz et al., What Have We Learnt from Vioxx?, 334 Brit Med J. 120 (2007).

73 Joanna Le Noury et al., Restoring Study 329: Efficacy and Harms of Paroxetine and Imipramine in Treatment of Major Depression in Adolescence, 351 Brit. Med. J. h4320 (Aug. 3, 2015).

74 Pradhan, supra note 25 (some of these sites were in McAllen, Texas; Houston, Texas; Metro Atlanta; and Lake Charles, Louisiana).

COVID-19 vaccine trials were ever met. The drug company sponsor was the only entity that had access to the multisite aggregated clinical data.[75]

Considering the growing risks of clinical data opacity, PE firms should voluntarily commit to not only advocate for-profit maximization but simultaneously pursue the social value of generating scientific data. Different mechanisms to pursue social value may include targeting socially conscious executive compensation and multiple stakeholder board representation.[76]

19.5 CONCLUSION

PE investment in remote, digitized clinical trials promises to improve operational, technological, and financial trial inefficiencies. Securing trial participant safety can be ensured by demanding PE firms have higher standards of care, enforced by private law tools. Yet, leaving the production of substantial scientific evidence to PE-backed trials deserves greater scrutiny. It is access to evidence that allows safe and effective health technologies to reach the market. The publicity concerns present today in drug development already indicate a free rider problem and low incentives to generate and disclose all and necessary privately generated evidence. As PE firms with financial opportunistic interests encroach upon DCTs, the tension between profit maximization and evidence and drug safety and efficacy maximization will only become greater. Resolving this tension requires greater moral responsibility from the industry and closer monitoring and critical analysis of PE activity from regulators.

[75] Id.

[76] Emilie Aguirre, Beyond Profit, 54 U.C. Davis L. Rev. 2077 (2021).

20

Shareholder Resolutions and Access to Medications

Rebecca E. Wolitz[*]

20.1 INTRODUCTION

The unaffordability of prescription medications remains an issue of moral and practical importance. To address this issue, scholars, politicians, and activists dominantly focus on "external" regulation – that is, the public law tools of legislative and regulatory reform, such as the Inflation Reduction Act's (IRA) Medicare provisions.[1] "Internal" governance dynamics of drug manufacturers and associated opportunities for private ordering, however, are underexamined aspects of access to medications (A2M) discussions.[2]

A standard narrative blames high drug prices on shareholders and corporate fiduciary obligations to "maximize profits."[3] Yet, *for nearly half a century*, shareholders of large drug manufacturers have put forward shareholder resolutions, or proposals, raising concerns about drug manufacturers' pricing practices. Resolutions are submitted in accordance with regulations under the Securities Exchange Act[4] and are a tool uniquely available to shareholders. Resolutions have demanded pricing

[*] For their helpful feedback, thank you to Jacob Madden, Efthimios Parasidis, Paul Rose, Ric Simmons, workshop participants at Harvard Law School's Petrie Flom Center and audience members at PORTAL. Thank you to Addie Becker, Kat McCarthy, and Stephen Whitney for research assistance.

[1] Inflation Reduction Act of 2022, Pub. L. No. 117-169, 136 Stat. 1818 (2022).

[2] Carly J. Goeman, The Price Isn't Right: Shareholder Proposals as Opportunities for Institutional Investors to Restore Firm Value and Reduce Pharmaceutical Prices, 2017 Colum. Bus. L. Rev. 748 (2017); Rebecca E. Wolitz, A Corporate Duty to Rescue: Biopharmaceutical Companies and Access to Medications, 94 Ind. L.J. 1163 (2019). Compare Yaniv Heled et al., Why Healthcare Companies Should Be(Come) Benefit Corporations, 60 B.C. L. Rev. 73, 78 (2019).

[3] Wolitz, supra note 2, at 1176.

[4] 17 C.F.R. § 240.14a–8 (2023).

restraint, transparency and reporting about how drug prices are set, and justifications for a range of activities.

These shareholder efforts may not unseat the standard narrative but do add complexity. Not all shareholders accept the serious externalities imposed by drug manufacturers' pricing practices. Moreover, shareholder proposals raise existential questions about corporate purpose and faithful agency. Discordance may exist between what drug manufacturers say and what they do when it comes to being patient centric. Further, drug manufacturers often seek to exclude resolutions or issue statements in opposition.

This chapter asks: can shareholder efforts achieve public-spirited reform? What are shareholder resolutions' relative strengths and weaknesses as compared with public law efforts? Are shareholder proposals uniquely well-suited to certain aspects of A2M problems?

Ultimately, shareholder proposals can be an important part of a multi-prong approach that complements "external" legislative efforts. They may also have purchase for overlapping governance matters perhaps better suited to private ordering. Yet, as this chapter shows, shareholder resolutions confront several limitations, and the pursuit of A2M resolutions may be more an opportunity of necessity than choice.[5]

This essay proceeds as follows. Section 20.2 provides background on shareholder resolutions and applicable law. Section 20.3 turns to drug-pricing and A2M proposals, tracing their evolution and then focusing on three kinds of proposals: executive compensation, mission misalignment with political spending, and patenting practices. Section 20.4 reflects on and analyzes themes from these shareholder efforts to address the main questions identified above. Section 20.5 concludes.

20.2 SHAREHOLDER RESOLUTIONS IN A NUTSHELL

A corporation's board is endowed with the power to manage the corporation's business and affairs.[6] Historically, with the separation of ownership and control, shareholders though nominal owners have enjoyed limited control rights.[7] Shareholder voting is one important vehicle for participation in corporate governance. Under state law, shareholders typically have rights to vote on director elections and major transactions. They can also make "proposals on a variety of issues,

5 See Chapter 1 in this volume.

6 Del. Code Ann. tit. 8, § 141(a) (West 2020).

7 Stephen M. Bainbridge, Revitalizing SEC Rule 14a-8's Ordinary Business Exclusion: Preventing Shareholder Micromanagement by Proposal, 85 Fordham L. Rev. 705, 707 (2016). But see Harwell Wells, A Long View of Shareholder Power: From the Antebellum Corporation to the Twenty-First Century, 67 Fla. L. Rev. 1033, 1098 (2015) (shareholder power ebbs and flows).

including general corporate governance and social interest matters."[8] Shareholder proposals have been analogized to state constitutional ballot initiatives.[9] Shareholder proposals, however, are typically advisory. They are opportunities for shareholders to communicate their preferences.[10]

For public companies, shareholder proposals are subject to federal securities law, which regulates their default inclusion on the corporation's proxy materials at the corporation's expense.[11] As one might imagine, however, not every shareholder proposal must be included. The U.S. Securities and Exchange Commission (SEC) makes case-by-case exclusion determinations,[12] and proposals must clear multiple hurdles. For instance, among other eligibility and procedural requirements, proposals have a word limit and only shareholders holding securities for specified continuous lengths of time and value can submit a proposal.[13]

Regulations further permit a company to exclude a proposal if it qualifies under one of the enumerated substantive exclusions. The ordinary business exclusion – exclusion based on a proposal "deal[ing] with a matter relating to the company's ordinary business operations"[14] – is among the most popular and contentious. This exclusion's rationale is to embed and be deferential to "the bedrock state corporate law principle" that a firm's ordinary business operations is the proper purview of directors and officers and not shareholders.[15]

Drug manufacturers are consistently resistant to drug-pricing proposals,[16] and the ordinary business exclusion is a commonly sought refuge.[17] That said, though some proposals have been ensnared by this exclusion, the SEC has determined that many drug-pricing and A2M proposals cannot be excluded from proxy materials on this basis because they transcend such matters.[18] This is an important exception to an otherwise excludable proposal: Even if a proposal *relates* to a company's ordinary business, the proposal *may not be excluded* if it focuses on "sufficiently significant

8 Paul Rose, Shareholder Proposals in the Market for Corporate Influence, 66 Fla. L. Rev. 2179, 2186 (2014).

9 Id. at 2185–86.

10 Id. at 2186–87; 17 C.F.R. § 240.14a–8(a) (2023).

11 17 C.F.R. § 240.14a–8 (2023); see also Alan R. Palmiter, The Shareholder Proposal Rule: A Failed Experiment in Merit Regulation, 45 Ala. L. Rev. 879, 893–95 (1993–94).

12 See, e.g., Palmiter, supra note 11, at 905 n.112.

13 17 C.F.R. § 240.14a–8 (2023).

14 17 C.F.R. § 240.14a–8(i)(7) (2023).

15 Bainbridge, supra note 7, at 720; see Amendments to Rules on Shareholder Proposals, 63 Fed. Reg. 29106, 29107 (May 28, 1998) (amending 17 C.F.R. § 240.14a–8).

16 See, e.g., Goeman, supra note 2, at 759.

17 17 C.F.R. § 240.14a–8(i)(7) (2023).

18 See, e.g., Goeman, supra note 2, at 768; Jill E. Fisch, From Legitimacy to Logic: Reconstructing Proxy Regulation, 46 Vand. L. Rev. 1129, 1158 (1993).

social policy issues."[19] Proposals that raise such issues "transcend the day-to-day business matters" and are "appropriate for a shareholder vote."[20]

The ordinary business exclusion is highly relevant to drug-pricing proposals, but it is one among many exclusions comprising an intricate system. Thus, there are two big-picture points to highlight among these preliminaries. First, as a practical matter, when it comes to A2M proposals, as with any proposal, proponents must navigate these regulations with skill and strategy. Misjudgment of support or missteps in one proxy season can impact not just an individual proposal but the inclusion of future proposals as well.[21]

Second, federal proxy rules have empowered shareholders to take a more active role in overseeing corporate conduct through "shareholder democracy."[22] Contested shareholder proposals involve different factions of the corporate ecosystem vying for power with a federal agency inserting itself as arbiter over whether a proposal is sufficiently meritorious to be put to a shareholder vote.[23] However, so long as an investor meets regulatory criteria, investors of all kinds – from the individual "gadfly" to large institutional investors – have the opportunity for their voices to be heard.[24]

20.3 DRUG-PRICING AND A2M PROPOSALS

Since at least the 1970s, shareholders have sought proxy access to raise concerns regarding drug-pricing and A2M. Over the years, shareholders have run the gamut from small retail investors to large institutional shareholders.[25] Proponents have included individuals,[26] health systems,[27] asset managers,[28] social justice

19 Amendments to Rules on Shareholder Proposals, supra note 15, 29108.

20 Id. Interpretation and application of this exception is fraught. See, e.g., Bainbridge, supra note 7.

21 17 C.F.R. § 240.14a–8(i)(12) (2023); see Goeman, supra note 2, at 770.

22 See, e.g., Palmiter, supra note 11, at 879.

23 See generally id. Submission of proposals can yield three outcomes: inclusion, withdrawal, or omission. Kobi Kastiel & Yaron Nili, The Giant Shadow of Corporate Gadflies, 94 S. Cal. L. Rev. 569, 580–81 (2021).

24 Kastiel & Nili, supra note 23, at 572; Rose, supra note 8, at 2197.

25 Proponents often are religiously affiliated.

26 See, e.g., Gilead Sciences, Inc., 2014 Proxy Statement 34 (2014), https://www.sec.gov/Archives/edgar/data/882095/000119312514112507/d690615ddef14a.htm (proposal submitted by Mr. Michael Weinstein).

27 See, e.g., Eli Lilly and Co., 2023 Proxy Statement 95–96, 101 (2023), https://www.sec.gov/Archives/edgar/data/59478/000005947823000120/lly-20230317.htm (proposals submitted by Trinity Health and CommonSpirit Health).

28 See, e.g., AbbVie Inc., 2023 Proxy Statement 83 (2023), https://www.sec.gov/Archives/edgar/data/1551152/000155837023004204/abbv-20230505xdef14a.htm (proposal submitted by Friends Fiduciary Corporation); Johnson & Johnson, 2023 Proxy Statement 136 (2023), https://www.sec.gov/Archives/edgar/data/200406/000020040623000023/jnj-20230313.htm (proposal submitted by Mercy Investment Services, Inc.).

organizations,[29] and pension plans.[30] During the 2023 proxy season, for example, lead filers have included Friends Fiduciary Corporation, Mercy Investment Services, Trinity Health, Oxfam, the Service Employees International Union, and the Boston Common ESG Impact US Equity Fund.[31]

A2M resolutions commonly express twin themes of concern. First, proposals register concern for how a drug manufacturer's pricing and related decisions impact shareholders' investments, given their invitation for regulatory response.[32] Second, they note concern for potential negative externalities imposed upon patients and society.[33]

Historically, resolutions have sought price-setting information and requested pricing "restraint."[34] A pre-Hatch-Waxman Act 1976 proposal, for instance, expressed concerns over disparities between US and foreign pricing and generics access. This proposal requested that shareholders receive "[a] breakdown of prices of and corporate profits from antibiotics sold in five representative countries ..."[35] It also sought information about the corporation's anti-substitution law lobbying.[36]

Likewise, in the early 1990s, citing an environment with "little market pressure on manufacturers to set fair and reasonable prices," the imposition upon patients of "cruel choice[s]," and skepticism of management's claims that research costs were causing increasing prices, shareholders of Eli Lilly and Company requested that the Board "seek input on pricing policy from consumer groups, and adopt a policy of price restraint ..."[37] According to shareholders, Eli Lilly's excessive pricing was "bringing us to the brink of federal action to control drug prices."[38] Other proposals sought price-setting transparency through a report on "overall pricing policy."[39]

29 See, e.g., Merck & Co., Inc., 2023 Proxy Statement 91–92 (2023), https://www.sec.gov/Archives/edgar/data/310158/000119312523089525/d277607ddef14a.htm (proposal submitted by Oxfam America, Inc.).

30 See, e.g., Eli Lilly and Co., supra note 27, at 91 (proposal submitted by SEIU); Vertex Pharmaceuticals Incorporated, 2015 BL 116062 (Feb. 25, 2015) (proposal submitted by UAW Retiree Medical Benefits Trust); Eli Lilly and Co., SEC No-Action Letter, 2007 BL (Jan. 5, 2007) (proposal submitted by Minnesota State Board of Investment).

31 See, e.g., AbbVie Inc., supra note 28; Johnson & Johnson, supra note 28; Eli Lilly and Co., supra note 27; Merck & Co., supra note 29; Regeneron, 2023 Proxy Statement 106 (2023), https://www.sec.gov/Archives/edgar/data/872589/000130817923000728/lregn2023_def14a.htm (proposal submitted by Boston Common ESG Impact US Equity Fund).

32 See, e.g., Ed Silverman, SEC Greenlights Shareholder Proposals for Several Big Drug Makers over Pricing, STAT (Mar. 26, 2018), https://www.statnews.com/6harmalot/2018/03/26/sec-shareholders-drug-prices.

33 See, e.g., AbbVie Inc., supra note 28.

34 Cf. Goeman, supra note 2, at 752.

35 Schering-Plough Corp., SEC Staff No-Action Letter, 1976 BL [Sisters Sorrowful Mother-Mgmt Serv.], *1–2 (Mar. 4, 1976).

36 Id.

37 Eli Lilly and Co., SEC Staff No-Action Letter, 1993 BL [Wadsworth], *5–6 (Feb. 25, 1993).

38 Id. at *6.

39 Eli Lilly and Co., SEC Staff No-Action Letter, 1993 BL [United Senior Action], *4 (Dec. 23, 1992).

Shareholders articulated that Eli Lilly should act with "the highest standards of responsibility and fairness to the consumers who rely on our products."[40] Given enduring opacity, proposals from the 2010s continued to seek transparency about numerous price-setting factors.[41] Recently, with COVID-19 vaccines, shareholders have inquired about the role of federal funding.[42]

Recent proxy seasons include a multitude of proposals pursuing new directions. Some raise questions about management's incentives. Others, arguably, raise existential questions about drug manufacturers' underlying corporate purpose and guiding norms. Three approaches are briefly discussed below. These proposals regard (1) the links between drug-pricing and executive compensation incentives; (2) the potential misalignment between corporate mission, values, and political spending; and (3) reporting on patenting procedures.

20.3.1 *Executive Compensation*

The size and setting of executive compensation is a contentious topic that has not escaped Congressional notice or the public's attention. Moderna, for instance, generated headlines when its CEO made US$398 million in 2022.[43]

Large salaries juxtaposed with A2M challenges generate a slew of questions, and generally, accross sectors, there has been "growing demand for executive compensation metrics linked to stakeholder welfare."[44] Linking executive compensation in this manner is thought to benefit various non-shareholder stakeholders (such as patients) and address the critique of stakeholderism that managers lack incentives to act in the interests of these non-shareholder groups.[45]

Recent drug-pricing proposals reflect these broader trends. Some proposals express concern about A2M and how these issues intersect with executive

[40] Id. at *3–4.

[41] See, e.g., Gilead Sciences, Inc., SEC No-Action Letter, 2015 BL 116210, *22 (Feb. 23, 2015).

[42] Pfizer, Moderna, Johnson & Johnson, Merck Shareholders Must Vote to End Unequal Access to COVID-19 Vaccines and Medicines, Oxfam (Apr. 27, 2023), https://www.oxfamamerica.org/press/press-releases/pfizer-moderna-johnson-johnson-merck-shareholders-must-vote-to-end-unequal-access-to-covid-19-vaccines-and-medicines/ [https://perma.cc/RDL5-L5U5]; Johnson & Johnson, supra note 28, at 130.

[43] Bob Herman & Damian Garde, Moderna CEO Made $398 Million in 2022, but Still Pledges to Give Most to Charity, STAT News (Mar. 17, 2023), https://www.statnews.com/2023/03/17/moderna-stephane-bancel-compensation/ [https://perma.cc/T2JG-DPD9]; Daniel Gilbert, Moderna's Billionaire CEO Reaped Nearly $400 Million Last Year. He Also Got a Raise, Wash. Post (Apr. 29, 2023, 6:00 AM), https://www.washingtonpost.com/business/2023/04/29/modernas-billionaire-ceo-reaped-nearly-400-million-last-year-he-also-got-raise/ [https://perma.cc/7TQ9-W36H].

[44] Lucian A. Bebchuk & Roberto Tallarita, The Perils and Questionable Promise of ESG-Based Compensation, 48 J. Corp. L. 37, 44 (2022).

[45] Id. at 42. "Stakeholderism" is a view of corporate purpose that holds directors should serve non-shareholder constituencies as well.

compensation.[46] Consequently, proposals have sought greater information about how drug-pricing strategies (and associated risks) figure into the pay incentives for senior executives to be provided through a shareholder report. A proposal submitted to Pfizer, Inc., is illustrative:

> RESOLVED, that shareholders of Pfizer, Inc. ("Pfizer") urge the Compensation Committee ... to report annually to shareholders on the extent to which risks related to public concern over drug pricing strategies are integrated into Pfizer's incentive compensation policies, plans and programs ("arrangements") for senior executives. The report should include, but need not be limited to, discussion of whether (i) incentive compensation arrangements reward, or not penalize, senior executives for adopting pricing strategies, or making and honoring commitments about pricing, that incorporate public concern regarding prescription drug prices; and (ii) such concern is considered when setting financial targets for incentive compensation arrangements.[47]

The supporting statement identified concerns about the association between drug-pricing practices such as chronic price increases (a "key risk") and short-term financial performance as undermining long-term value creation.[48] Shareholders noted that the Trump administration singled out Pfizer for these increases, writing "[i]n our view, excessive dependence on drug price increases is a risky and unsustainable strategy, especially when price hikes appear to drive large senior executive payouts."[49] The disclosures sought would permit shareholders to "better assess the extent to which compensation arrangements encourage senior executives to responsibly manage risks relating to drug-pricing and contribute to long-term value creation."[50]

Pfizer sought to omit this proposal from its proxy materials under the ordinary business exclusion but was unsuccessful.[51] According to the SEC, disclosure of how drug-pricing risks "are integrated into senior executive compensation decisions[] transcends ordinary business matters" as drug-pricing strategy is a significant issue,

46 An earlier example is a 2014 proposal requesting that the Board "adopt a policy that incentive compensation for the Chief Executive Officer . . . should include non-financial measures based on patient access to the Company's medicines." Gilead Sciences, Inc., supra note 26, at 34.

47 Pfizer Inc., 2019 Proxy Statement 115 (2019), https://www.sec.gov/Archives/edgar/data/78003/000093041319000953/c93082_def14a.htm. See also Abbvie Inc., SEC Staff No-Action Letter, 2019 BL 74951, *17 (2019); Johnson & Johnson, SEC Staff No-Action Letter, 2019 BL 74937, *19 (2019) (each with substantially similar proposals).

48 Pfizer Inc., supra note 47, at 115.

49 Id.

50 Id.

51 Pfizer Inc., SEC Staff No-Action Letter, 2019 BL 75180, *1–2.

and the proposal further failed to micromanage the company.[52] Though this proposal garnered a significant response (40.2 percent approved), it did not pass.[53]

20.3.2 *Purpose and Politics*

Another area of recent focus is the congruency of political spending with purported corporate purpose. Drug manufacturers often have lofty, public-spirited, patient-centric mission statements.[54] AbbVie's website, for instance, says: "our life's work is to improve lives."[55] Likewise, Pfizer states: "[o]ur purpose ensures that patients remain at the center of all we do."[56]

However, in 2022, pharmaceutical and health products companies spent a record US$372 million on federal lobbying, with most aimed at undermining the IRA's efforts to lower drug prices.[57] After PhRMA (a trade association), which spent US$29.2 million, Pfizer was the second-largest individual spender at US$14.9 million.[58] Pfizer's spending exceeded previous years and occurred when the COVID-19 vaccine maker planned to quadruple the vaccine's price.[59]

Thus, reconciling what drug manufacturers say and how they act has been the subject of a series of proposals. A proposal filed with Gilead, for instance, provided:

> RESOLVED: Shareholders request that the Board of Directors commission and publish a third party review within the next year ... of whether Gilead Sciences, Inc. lobbying activities (direct and through trade associations) align with its Vision statement, "To create a healthier world for all people" and in particular its Policy Position Statement that "the price of medicines should never be a barrier to access, and we work domestically and globally to ensure that patients who need our products are able to obtain them." The Board of Directors should report on how

[52] Id. at *2–3.

[53] See Pfizer Inc., Current Report (Form 8-K) (Apr. 29, 2019), https://www.sec.gov/Archives/edgar/data/78003/000007800319000018/a8_kxvoting2019.htm.

[54] See Elizabeth Pollman, The History and Revival of the Corporate Purpose Clause, 99 Tex. L. Rev. 1423 (2021) (observing contemporary charters stating "for any lawful purpose" have pushed mission statements elsewhere).

[55] Positions & Views, Abbvie, https://www.abbvie.com/who-we-are/our-principles/positions-views.html [https://perma.cc/SF22-AZHK] (last accessed Oct. 9, 2024).

[56] Our Purpose, Pfizer, https://www.pfizer.com/about/purpose [https://perma.cc/77MR-HDH5] (last accessed Aug. 3, 2023).

[57] Inci Sayki, Despite Record Federal Lobbying Spending, the Pharmaceutical and Health Product Industry Lost Their Biggest Legislative Bet in 2022, Open Secrets (Feb. 2, 2023, 1:58 PM), https://www.opensecrets.org/news/2023/02/despite-record-federal-lobbying-spending-the-pharmaceutical-and-health-product-industry-lost-their-biggest-legislative-bet-in-2022/ [https://perma.cc/Y9VD-DN5U]. Drug manufacturers are now litigating the IRA.

[58] Id.

[59] Id.

> it addresses the risks presented by any misaligned lobbying and the company's plans, if any, to mitigate these risks.[60]

The supporting statement noted Gilead's contributions to PhRMA, and that its CEO sat on PhRMA's board.[61] According to these shareholders, however, PhRMA has "systematically opposed" any attempt to improve A2M through drug-pricing reforms.[62] In a similar proposal filed with Eli Lilly,[63] shareholders observed that given the company's "extensive direct and indirect lobbying *against* measures that would make drugs more affordable, investors need to better understand the balance Lilly is striking between its commitments to innovation, on the one hand, and access and affordability, on the other."[64] The proposals at Gilead and Eli Lilly each failed to pass but received 49.8 percent and 22.4 percent of votes, respectively.[65]

20.3.3 *Patenting Practices*

A2M resolutions periodically raise questions about intellectual property policies. Recent proposals have focused on intellectual property and the related issue of anticompetitive conduct.[66] While proposals regarding tech transfer in the context of COVID-19 vaccines are noted later, this section highlights proposals focusing on secondary and tertiary patenting.

Secondary patents – those patents pertaining to a product other than its original active ingredient – and tertiary patents – those pertaining to drug delivery devices – have increasingly caught the attention of academics and policymakers.[67] Not only

60 Gilead Sciences, Inc., 2022 Proxy Statement 90 (2022), https://www.sec.gov/Archives/edgar/data/882095/000120677422000832/gild3988061-def14a.htm#d3988061a041.

61 Id.

62 Id.

63 Eli Lilly and Co., supra note 27, at 101.

64 Id. (emphasis added).

65 Gilead Sciences, Inc., Current Report (Form 8-K) (May 5, 2022), https://www.sec.gov/Archives/edgar/data/882095/000110465922056435/tm2213708d1_8k.htm; Eli Lilly and Co., Current Report (Form 8-K) (May 4, 2023), https://www.sec.gov/Archives/edgar/data/59478/000005947823000165/lly-20230501.htm. Notably, under Gilead's rules, abstentions count as a vote against, otherwise the "for" votes would have received 50.2 percent of the votes. Gilead Sciences, Inc., 2022 Proxy Statement, supra note 60, at 99. While precatory, if a proposal receives a majority of "shares cast," proxy advisors may recommend voting against a board that fails to implement it. ISS, United States: Proxy Voting Guidelines Benchmark Policy Recommendations 13 (2023), https://www.issgovernance.com/file/policy/active/americas/US-Voting-Guidelines.pdf.

66 See, e.g., Pfizer Inc., SEC Staff No-Action Letter, 2022 BL 80621 (Mar. 8, 2022); AbbVie Inc., SEC Staff No-Action Letter, 2022 BL 88092 (Mar. 11, 2022); Eli Lilly and Co., SEC Staff No-Action Letter, 2022 BL 80626 (Mar. 7, 2022).

67 Reed F. Beall & Aaron S. Kesselheim, Tertiary Patenting on Drug-Device Combination Products in the United States, Nature Biotech. (Feb. 6, 2018), https://www.nature.com/articles/nbt.4078.epdf?author_access_token=k19w_aka6yYXhVtkaCGFOdRgNojAjWel9jnR3ZoTvoMGOAdGITA-e4stuwIqLoZGEo–17DL5n2Qg8u7csdohGlFGwUWdjvieJtiDwzfoldY3_E4HS6rf7YbpkcyvI2u [https://perma.cc/JQ97–6TKN].

do these patents extend a drug manufacturer's market power by delaying generic competition, but such patents can also be weaker, meaning they are more frequently invalidated.[68] Concerns about drug manufacturers' utilization of these practices to stymie competition motivated President Biden to direct the U.S. Food and Drug Administration and the Patent and Trademark Office to collaborate on addressing these issues.[69]

Concurrent to these regulatory efforts, shareholders requested that drug manufacturers report on their patenting practices and how concern for A2M is incorporated. A proposal filed with AbbVie is illustrative:

> RESOLVED, that shareholders of AbbVie Inc. ("AbbVie") ask the Board of Directors to establish and report on a process by which the impact of extended patent exclusivities on product access would be considered in deciding whether to apply for secondary and tertiary patents The report on the process should be prepared at reasonable cost, omitting confidential and proprietary information, and published on AbbVie's website.[70]

The resolution's supporting statement noted that one of AbbVie's products, Humira, had undergone 27 price increases and is protected by 130 patents.[71] The requested report, in the proponents' view, "would ensure that AbbVie considers not only whether it can apply for" these patents "but also whether it should," given the perception of "abusive patenting practices."[72] A significant minority – 28.9 percent – of AbbVie shareholders supported this proposal.[73]

20.4 REFLECTING ON THESE EFFORTS

Submission of shareholder proposals has increased over time, as has the weight they hold among management and boards.[74] Shareholder proposals today are considered a "powerful tool" for influencing corporate governance and conduct.[75] Yet, what makes a shareholder proposal "successful"? For A2M advocates, what are its relative

68 Doni Bloomfield & Aaron S. Kesselheim, Biden Can Lower Drug Prices without Congress Doing Anything, Wash. Post (Jan. 5, 2021), https://www.washingtonpost.com/outlook/2021/01/05/drug-prices-patent-office-generics-biden/ (referencing work of Michael Frakes & Melissa Wasserman).

69 Exec. Order No. 14,036, 3 C.F.R. 609 (2022); FDA, Letter from Janet Woodcock, M.D., Acting Comm'r of Food and Drugs, to Andrew Hirshfield, Performing the Functions and Duties of the Under Sec'y of Comm. for Intell. U.S. Pat. & Trademark Off. (Sept. 10, 2021), https://www.fda.gov/media/152086/download [https://perma.cc/X5UR-VPFQ].

70 AbbVie Inc., supra note 28, at 83.

71 Id.

72 Id.

73 AbbVie Inc., Current Report (Form 8-K) (May 10, 2023), https://www.sec.gov/Archives/edgar/data/1551152/000110465923058520/tm2315162d1_8k.htm.

74 See Rose, supra note 8, at 2191.

75 Kastiel & Nili, supra note 23, at 579.

strengths and weaknesses as a reform tool? Are there aspects of these issues that shareholders are uniquely positioned to address through proposals?

20.4.1 *What Counts as Success?*

If "success" means getting onto the proxy *and* getting a majority vote, then drug-pricing and A2M shareholder proposals appear a fruitless exercise. No such proposals put to a vote at the 2023 annual meetings, for instance, appear to have passed.[76] A majority vote, however, is a sufficient but not necessary condition for success.

Shareholder proposals are attractive for their ability to facilitate direct corporate engagement. Indeed, the filing of resolutions often occurs when initial dialogues break down.[77] Withdrawn proposals and proposals that secure a significant, albeit non-majority vote can also signal success as shareholder proposals offer important leverage with management and the board.[78] The value of shareholder resolutions thus may most reside not in any "'short-term voting results,'" but in their "long-term ability" to foster dialogue that generates reassessment and reform.[79]

Regarding withdrawn proposals, parties negotiate after resolution filing. Through these negotiations, shareholders might be able to procure satisfactory concessions. As one shareholder explains, resolution withdrawal "typically means" dialogue "about moving the company into a better position; the company has agreed to further discussions; or the company has made changes in response to the shareholder request."[80]

Likewise, if a proposal attracts significant minority support, corporations often view this as an important signal.[81] With "say-on-pay" votes, for example, if 20 to 30 percent of shareholders object, companies will "reconsider and revise their compensation packages."[82] Many drug-pricing and A2M proposals have attracted substantial minority votes, including those discussed in this essay. For these reasons, drug-pricing resolutions appear to enjoy some degree of success.

76 Rebecca E. Wolitz, Drug Pricing and Access to Medications Shareholder Proposals for 2023 Annual Meetings (Aug. 6, 2023) (hand-collected data on file with author).

77 See, e.g., Shareholder Resolutions, Mercy Investment Services, Inc., https://mercyinvestmentservices.org/our-approach/shareholder-advocacy/shareholder-resolutions/ (last accessed Aug. 3, 2023).

78 See, e.g., Goeman, supra note 2, at 784–85 (discussing the significance of withdrawal as indicating success).

79 Goeman, supra note 2, at 785.

80 Why We Withdraw Resolutions, Mercy Investment Services, Inc., https://www.mercyinvestmentservices.org/why-we-withdraw-resolutions.aspx [https://perma.cc/G3W6-XLGQ] (last accessed Aug. 3, 2023).

81 Kastiel & Nili, supra note 23, at 626–27.

82 Id.

20.4.2 *Strengths and Weaknesses*

As a tool for improving A2M, shareholder proposals have comparative and intrinsic strengths and weaknesses. Comparatively, legislation is often the reform tool of choice. Yet, legislative reform frequently proceeds at a glacial pace, stymied by gridlock and special interests.[83]

Shareholder proposals, by contrast, may be nimbler, permitting relatively fast and direct engagement with drug manufacturers. Corporations pay attention to their shareholders, and so long as a proposal does not qualify for an exclusion, the issue *must* go on the proxy. Following an annual cadence, shareholder proposals are generally filed in the fall.[84] If there is friction with the company, SEC no-action letters are sought in winter.[85] The season concludes with voting on proposals at annual general meetings in the spring.[86] Rather than waiting decades for legislative reform, change could occur within a year.

Legislative reform and shareholder proposals can be complementary strategies. Shareholder proposals can, for instance, mirror legislative agendas. Consider California's passage of SB 17 in 2017. State legislative agendas at the time included drug price transparency laws, and SB 17 mandates notice and the collection of information pertaining to certain prescription drug price increases.[87] Concurrent to this legislative activity, shareholder resolutions were advanced at numerous drug manufacturers seeking corporate reporting on "product price increases, their rationale, and associated risks."[88] As another example, shareholder proposals focusing on potential anticompetitive activity and corporate patenting practices reflect similar themes of present interest to legislators and regulators.

Further, shareholder proposals – even when they mirror topics of external regulatory interest – are not merely redundant. They are symbolically important as the messenger's identity matters. An intrinsic strength of A2M shareholder proposals is that their critique of drug manufacturers' conduct is bound up with corporate self-determination. It matters that at least some shareholders are concerned about these

[83] States may be more agile than the federal government but must navigate additional barriers. Rebecca E. Wolitz, States, Preemption, and Patented Drug Prices, 52 Seton Hall L. Rev. 385 (2021).

[84] Laura D. Richman & Michael L. Hermsen, Proxy Season Legal Update, Harv. L. Sch. F. on Corp. Governance (Oct. 16, 2017), https://corpgov.law.harvard.edu/2017/10/16/proxy-season-legal-update/ [https://perma.cc/23NA-XLCG].

[85] See id.

[86] Laura D. Richman & Michael L. Hermsen, 10 Tips for Upcoming Annual Shareholder Meetings, Harv. L. Sch. F. on Corp. Governance (Apr. 11, 2018), https://corpgov.law.harvard.edu/2018/04/11/10-tips-for-upcoming-annual-shareholder-meetings/ [https://perma.cc/8WSX-JVNP].

[87] Rebecca E. Wolitz, Litigation Watch: California's Drug Pricing Transparency Bill SB-17, Stan. L. Sch. (Jan. 6, 2018), https://law.stanford.edu/2018/01/06/litigation-watch-californias-drug-pricing-transparency-bill-sb-17/ [https://perma.cc/APP3-MDH5].

[88] Wolitz, supra note 2, at 1211.

corporations' conduct. Even if the public-minded end goal is the same as would-be legislation, the questions posed by shareholders versus non-shareholders concerned about A2M have an inherently different orientation. Shareholders can ask *themselves* and those who serve the corporation: who do we want to be as a company? What norms, values, and codes of conduct ought we to comply with? Even if, for instance, the law permits secondary patenting, should we participate? These questions are distinct from those of the regulator charged with determining which constraints best serve the public.

Consequently, shareholder proposals may be uniquely positioned to address those aspects of A2M challenges overlapping more squarely with internal governance questions.[89] Some view shareholder proposals as an economic accountability mechanism and agency-cost corrective.[90] Similar accountability issues, however, arguably could be at play for nonfinancial (or, not purely financial) considerations as well. If shareholder proposals are conceived as a tool to discipline the relationship between principals and agents, then they would appear to be particularly well targeted to those places where A2M challenges intersect with matters seemingly more appropriate for private ordering. There may be no "pure" such examples. Executive compensation proposals, however, might serve as candidates for further consideration. Given firm specificity, providing individualized incentives to executives to improve A2M may be more appropriately the dominion of shareholders for some degree of oversight rather than regulators.[91]

The distinct orientation of these considerations intersects with three weaknesses of shareholder proposals as a mechanism for drug-pricing reform.[92] First, to be included in the proxy, shareholder resolutions must navigate a complex regulatory scheme sensitive to the division of labor between boards and shareholders. Thus, proposals frequently take the form of requesting increased transparency through a report. While increased transparency and information gathering are crucial, those seeking immediate bold reforms might view such constraints as tepid, rendering this tool substantively weaker. Second, in contrast to external regulation, this vehicle is only available to shareholders and reform takes place company by company. While there appear to be coordinated efforts, shareholder proposals are not an efficient tool for systemic, industry-wide regulation. There are differences in how corporations react to such proposals and distinct shareholder voting patterns on nearly identical proposals.[93] On proposals for reporting on political spending, for example, the

89 The line between "social" and "governance" proposals can be blurry. See, e.g., Rose, supra note 8, at 2208.

90 Id. at 2217.

91 There are considerable criticisms, however, of this approach. See, e.g., Bebchuk & Tallarita, supra note 44, at 40–42.

92 Additionally, the SEC's no-action letter determination is not devoid of politics.

93 See, e.g., Goeman, supra note 2, at 782 (tabulating voting on 2015 proposals). Some corporate engagement, further, might forestall filing a proposal.

proposal at Gilead received 49.8 percent of votes and Eli Lilly received 22.4 percent. Regarding individualized responses, with secondary patenting proposals filed with AbbVie and Amgen, both companies initially sought SEC no-action letters. The AbbVie resolution went to a vote, but the Amgen resolution was "[w]ithdrawn due to agreement with company."[94]

The third weakness of shareholder proposals as a reform tool is that to the extent the goal is *societal* drug price reform in the public interest, shareholder proposals offer an awkward fit. Although pragmatists might think, "well, whatever gets the job done," there are significant underlying questions of allegiance, authority, and expertise. Shareholders of drug companies are generally private actors with divided interests; they are not elected officials charged with protecting and promoting the public good. That the lives, health, and fate of so many should depend upon a shareholder vote is unsettling, if not inappropriate.

The example of COVID-19 vaccine equity highlights this point. Given that many throughout the world have lacked access to COVID-19 vaccines, Oxfam submitted proposals to Moderna and Pfizer requesting feasibility studies of transferring pertinent intellectual property.[95] Such knowledge transfers would ideally expand worldwide manufacturing capacity and save lives.[96] In an "unprecedented" move, the WHO Director-General even backed the Moderna resolution and spoke on its behalf at the annual meeting.[97] Though a significant contingency (24 percent and 27 percent of shareholders at Moderna and Pfizer, respectively) supported the proposals, the resolutions failed.[98]

Though these losses seemed like a public health failure, they put pressure on the tool itself.[99] As Els Torreele notes, despite there being well-meaning investors, "the key issue is that pharmaceutical companies and their investors should not . . . hav[e] the power to decide about public health issues . . . It painfully shows, once again, how financial interests pursued by private companies, investors, asset managers, and speculators eclipse decision-making informed by public health experts, even during

[94] Shareholder Resolutions: Amgen, Inc., Mercy Investment Services, Inc., https://www.mercyinvestmentservices.org/shareholder-resolutions-detail.aspx?bid=400815 [https://perma.cc/9E2B-KDB3] (last accessed Aug. 3, 2023).

[95] Jonathan Josephs, Investors Lose Vote to Share Covid Know-How, BBC (Apr. 29, 2022), https://www.bbc.com/news/business-61262065 [https://perma.cc/93XD-22ZD].

[96] Els Torreele, Global Health Should Not Be Determined by Pharma Investors and Shareholders, STAT (May 3, 2022), https://www.statnews.com/2022/05/03/pharma-investors-shareholders-should-not-determine-global-health/ [https://perma.cc/4FTB-V37E].

[97] Josephs, supra note 95.

[98] Id. Proxy advisor ISS supported these proposals (Glass Lewis only supported Moderna). Hannah Kcuhler, Pfizer and Moderna Urged to Share Vaccine Technology With Developing World, Irish Times (Apr. 19, 2022), https://www.irishtimes.com/business/health-pharma/pfizer-and-moderna-urged-to-share-vaccine-technology-with-developing-world-1.4856720 [https://perma.cc/Z4ZH-QDY9].

[99] Torreele, supra note 96.

the biggest global health crisis of our lifetime."[100] In other words, relying on shareholder proposals to pursue A2M reform emerges from a context of failed public institutions and failed framing. If public institutions charged with protecting and promoting the interests of each of us to equitable A2M were successful, there would be no need for private actor intervention. Patients would not look toward the private "largess" of some shareholders to be drug-pricing reformers and rely on their talents to convince the majority of shareholders who are not.

20.5 CONCLUSION

Matters of important public policy should not be vulnerable to the whims of shareholders. While this background critique looms large, the foregrounded question is what shareholder resolutions offer by way of drug-pricing and A2M reform. Despite indications of some general shareholder population ambivalence about A2M, given voting outcomes and the limitations discussed above, shareholder proposals have many comparative and intrinsic strengths. They add important voices seeking improved A2M and may be particularly well suited to address certain corners of these issues. At the very least, these shareholder efforts complement external reforms, and the existence of such proposals signals a more complicated narrative of shareholders' relationship to drug-pricing challenges.

[100] Id.

21

The Hollowed-Out American Nursing Home

Using Private Law to Police Poor Quality Care and Expand Owner Responsibilities

Barry R. Furrow[*]

21.1 INTRODUCTION

The United States has more than 26,000 nursing homes, caring for more than 1.4 million residents.[1] About 70 percent of nursing homes are now operated by for-profit corporations, 24 percent are not-for-profit, and 7 percent are government-owned, while 58 percent are operated by corporate chains.[2] Private equity firms own about 11 percent of nursing facilities nationwide. By 2050, up to 30 million people in the Americas will require long-term care services. Most of these nursing home residents are or will become exceptionally vulnerable, but the quality of their daily lives may well be shortchanged by their nursing home owners – particularly private equity (PE) owners. Nursing home care is an industry built on "market" solutions to end-of-life care for the elderly.[3] The advent of Medicare and Medicaid was not based on a model of nonprofit nursing homes. As Leslie King writes: "[l]awmakers instead allowed the growth of a system of large, for-profit, chain nursing homes."[4] Early advocates of such privatization argued that a private ownership system could be more efficient – providing quality services at a lower cost.[5] For-profit corporate

* Many thanks to participants in the Petrie-Flom Conference on Private Law at the Harvard Law School for their helpful suggestions, and particularly Lauren Roth.

1 Abby McCain, 25 Insightful Nursing Home Statistics [2023]: Residents, Locations, and Long-Term Care, Zippia (Mar. 20, 2023), www.zippia.com/advice/nursing-home-statistics/.

2 These Administrative Actions Would Improve Nursing Home Ownership and Financial Transparency in the Post COVID-19 Period, Health Affs. Blog (Feb. 11, 2021), https://www.healthaffairs.org/content/forefront/these-administrative-actions-would-improve-nursing-home-ownership-and-financial.

3 Leslie King, How Government Created and Shaped the U.S. Nursing Home Industry, 46 Critical Socio. 881, 897 (2020).

4 Id.

5 John B. Goodman & Gary W. Loveman, Does Privatization Serve the Public Interest?, Harv. Bus. Rev. (Nov.–Dec. 1991), https://hbr.org/1991/11/does-privatization-serve-the-public-interest.

entities would strive to maximize their bottom-line goals for shareholders, but the great engine of the "market" in an industrial economy would also deliver benefits for consumers.

The market, however, fails when PE ownership exists: PE owners are a special class of financial entity driven toward intense opportunistic behavior in order to hit high rates of return promised to investors within a short time frame.[6] PE firms – blessed with captive residents, guaranteed federal reimbursement, and poor regulation – pillage nursing homes with impunity.

Flaws and externalities in for-profit businesses can normally be counteracted by regulation, shifts in consumer shopping, and private litigation. The nursing home industry, however, is poorly regulated for several reasons. First, annual surveys of nursing homes are backlogged, leaving too many homes uninspected and sanctioned.[7] Second, serious problems are underreported because state inspectors fail to identify quality problems or rate them as less severe than they are.[8] Third, states fail to act to force institutions to correct violations, rarely imposing financial penalties. And even if corrections are mandated, there is rarely follow-up by state surveyors.[9]

The NAS 2022 report is striking: "[d]espite significant measures to improve the quality of nursing home care in OBRA '87, the current system often fails to provide high-quality care and underappreciates and underprepares nursing home staff for their critical responsibilities."[10] Government enforcement needs a partner – private law litigation – to force transparency of ownership, improve remedies for families of injured residents, and formalize a fiduciary standard of ownership that uses equitable tools to claw back excess profits and constrain bad nursing home management.

My argument is in three steps. First, I examine the unique financial incentives baked into the PE model of profit-maximizing ownership. Second, I examine the development of the corporate negligence doctrine. Third, I develop a model of a robust fiduciary duty, coupled with equitable remedies. My goal is to build a private law doctrinal framework to better police the waste, fraud, and pillaging of assets by PE owners of nursing home systems.

6 Eileen O'Grady, Understaffed, Unlicensed, and Untrained: Behavioral Health under Private Equity, Private Equity Stakeholder Project 2 (Sept. 2020), https://pestakeholder.org/reports/understaffed-unlicensed-and-untrained-behavioral-health-under-private-equity/.

7 Letter from Robert Casey, U.S. Senator of Pa., to State Survey Agencies (Sept. 13, 2022) (noting that 71 percent of nursing homes nationally had gone at least sixteen months without a standard survey).

8 Nina A. Kohn, Nursing Homes, COVID-19, and the Consequences of Regulatory Failure, Geo. L. J. Online 8 (2021), https://www.law.georgetown.edu/georgetown-law-journal/wp-content/uploads/sites/26/2021/04/Kohn_Nursing-Homes-COVID-19-and-the-Consequences-of-Regulatory-Failure.pdf.

9 Id.

10 Nat'l Acads. of Sci., Eng'g, and Med., The National Imperative to Improve Nursing Home Quality: Honoring Our Commitment to Residents, Families, and Staff 2 (2022).

21.2 PRIVATE EQUITY AS OPPORTUNISTIC FIDUCIARY: PIRATES WITH MBAS[11]

Private equity investment involves acquisition of a total or partial ownership interest in an entity that is not publicly traded.[12] The playbook of PE is actively antithetical to the operation of a quality nursing facility.[13] The profits are intended to satisfy investors first, not to provide quality resident care.[14] I will show that the financial playbook of PE risks poor quality for nursing home residents[15] – as well as draining the Medicare and Medicaid budgets through strategies of revenue inflation.[16] Patients suffer from neglect caused by a cost-cutting PE ownership mode of finance.[17] The PE strategies are cumulative and opportunistic, striving to capture and extract excess profits from every aspect of a nursing home system.[18] Consider the playbook of PE firms that acquire nursing homes:

21.2.1 *High Rates of Return in a Short Time Horizon: Fast Bloodletting*

PE demands a rate of return in three to five years of around 20–30 percent, and typically a firm moves on at that point, selling the new consolidated firm after having extracted value from the firm and often leaving it in poor condition.[19]

[11] For the use of "pirate" to describe private equity owners, see Brendan Ballou, Plunder: Private Equity's Plan to Pillage America (2023).

[12] Lisa Lilliott Rydin, Private Equity, Venture Capital, and Hedge Funds, Harv. L. Sch. Libr. (Aug. 17, 2022), https://guides.library.harvard.edu/law/private_equity.

[13] Private Equity Ownership of Nursing Homes Linked to Lower Quality of Care, Higher Medicare Costs (Nov. 19, 2021), https://news.weill.cornell.edu/news/2021/11/private-equity-ownership-of-nursing-homes-linked-to-lower-quality-of-care-higher; Robert Tyler Braun et al., Association of Private Equity Investment in US Nursing Homes with the Quality and Cost of Care for Long-Stay Residents, 2 JAMA Health Forum e213817 (2021).

[14] Richard M. Scheffler et al., Soaring Private Equity Investment in the Healthcare Sector: Consolidation Accelerated, Competition Undermined, and Patients at Risks, Petris Ctr. (May 18, 2021), https://publichealth.berkeley.edu/wp-content/uploads/2021/05/Private-Equity-I-Healthcare-Report-FINAL.pdf.

[15] See Eileen Appelbaum & Rosemary Batt, Financialization in Health Care: The Transformation of US Hospital Systems, Center for Economic and Policy Research 58 (2021), https://cepr.net/wp-content/uploads/2021/10/AB-Financialization-In-Healthcare-Spitzer-Rept-09-09-21.pdf; Commercial Real Estate Investor & Private Equity Liability, First Nat'l Realty Partners (Mar. 2, 2022), https://fnrpusa.com/blog/commercial-real-estate-investor-private-equity-liability/.

[16] David C. Grabowski et al., Low-Quality Nursing Homes Were More Likely Than Other Nursing Homes to Be Bought or Sold by Chains in 1993–2001, 35 Health Affs. 907 (2016).

[17] Yasmin Rafiei, When Private Equity Takes over a Nursing Home, The New Yorker (Aug. 25, 2022), https://www.newyorker.com/news/dispatch/when-private-equity-takes-over-a-nursing-home.

[18] See generally Robert I. Field et al., Private Equity in Health Care: Barbarians at the Gate?, 15 Drexel L. Rev. 821 (2023).

[19] Private Equity Industry Overview, St. of Walls Blog (2013), https://www.streetofwalls.com/finance-training-courses/private-equity-training/private-equity-industry-overview/.

21.2.2 *Debt as a Profit Tool: Starving the Nursing Home*

PE loads up acquired firms with high levels of debt and then leverages this debt on the firms acquired in order to pay themselves and other shareholders dividends – in the order of magnitude of billions of dollars.[20] The acquired company must then manage these high levels of debt.[21] The result often is a high number of bankruptcies;[22] one study found that nearly 20 percent of PE-owned companies have filed for bankruptcy, ten times the rate of public companies.[23] Nursing homes end up reducing worker wages and cutting other resources, further increasing the risk of bankruptcy.[24] Nursing homes end up with little money for resident care improvements[25] and the long-term health of the nursing home suffers.[26]

21.2.3 *High Rates of Churn in Ownership: Instability as Byproduct*

Frequent shifts in nursing home ownership destabilize both residents and staff.[27]

21.2.4 *Staff Reduction Programs: Blood from a Turnip*

Cost-cutting is a central PE tool, used aggressively to allow firms to hit their rate-of-return metrics. Cutting billing, legal, and human resource departments reduces "wasteful" overhead. The PE ownership toolkit in particular drains nursing home assets and reduces needed spending on nurses and aides.[28] For-profit nursing homes routinely determine staffing levels based on census and reimbursement as opposed to resident acuity – for-profit facilities have 16 percent fewer staff than nonprofits after accounting for differences in residents' needs.[29]

20 Eileen O'Grady, Dividend Recapitalizations in Healthcare: How Private Equity Raids Critical Health Care Infrastructure for Short Term Profit, Private Equity Stakeholder Project (2020), https://pestakeholder.org/wp-content/uploads/2020/10/PESP-HC-dividends-10-2020.pdf.

21 Id.

22 See Everything Is Private Equity Now, Bloomberg: Businessweek (Oct. 8, 2019, 4:10 PM), https://www.bloomberg.com/news/features/2019-10-03/how-private-equity-works-and-took-over-everything?embedded-checkout=true.

23 See Brian Ayash & Mahdi Rastad, Leveraged Buyouts and Financial Distress, Fin. Rsch. Letters, Forthcoming 4 (July 19, 2019).

24 O'Grady, supra note 20.

25 Id.

26 Jordan Rau, Nursing Home Owners Drained Cash While Residents Deteriorated, State Filings Suggest, NPR (Jan. 31, 2023), https://www.npr.org/sections/health-shots/2023/01/31/1139783599/new-york-nursing-home-owners-drained-cash.

27 Grabowski et al., supra note 16.

28 Robert I. Field et al., When Worlds Collide: The Effects of Private Equity on Health Care, 15 Drexel L. Rev. 101 (2023).

29 Charlene Harrington et al., Time to Ensure Sufficient Nursing Home Staffing and Eliminate Inequities in Care, 7 J. Geontol. Geriatr. Med. 99 (2021).

21.2.5 *"Related Party Transactions": Skimming the Till*

For-profit nursing facility executives develop new financial streams by creating complex ownership and management structures – this creates tax advantages and allows companies to move capital from one entity to another. Nursing home chain owners often outsource goods and services to multiple entities in which they also have ownership, and these entities then allow ancillary clinical services to be fragmented and spun off under the corporate umbrella.[30] Such services may include laboratory, radiology, pharmacy, and specialty medical services.[31] PE nursing homes may also make referrals to PE-owned home health care, hospice, mental health, emergency room staff services, and specialty clinics.[32]

These ownership structures are not a search for market efficiencies and cost-savings: to the contrary, "... the owners can establish highly favorable contracts in which their nursing homes pay more than they might in a competitive market. These profits are then siphoned off, not recorded in nursing home accounts, and hidden in affiliated companies."[33]

21.2.6 *Multilevel Corporate Structures: Deceiving and Dodging*

Complex layers of entities also shield the enterprise from liability by making it difficult for plaintiff lawyers to pursue a defendant with assets. Such strategies often involve deception in financial statements to conceal real income and assets among a myriad of subsidiaries.[34] Without data and visibility, plaintiff lawyers and regulators are all blinded.[35]

The cumulative effect of the PE playbook is poor quality care and high mortality rates – PE ownership increases 90-day mortality by 2.4 percentage points, or 15 percent of baseline mortality among Medicare residents, adding up to approximately 20,150 deaths over the course of 12 years according to a recent study.[36] Costs to the

30 See Melea Atkins, The Impact of Private Equity on Nursing Home Care: Recommendations for Policymakers, Roosevelt Inst. 5–6 (Apr. 2021), https://rooseveltinstitute.org/wp-content/uploads/2021/04/RI_NursingHomesandPE_IssueBrief_202104.pdf.

31 See Gary M. Kirsh & Deepak A. Kapoor, Private Equity and Urology: An Emerging Model for Independent Practice, 48 Urologic Clinics N. Am. 233, 234 (2021).

32 Id.

33 Jordan Rau, Care Suffers as More Nursing Homes Feed Money into Corporate Webs, N.Y. Times (Jan. 2, 2018), https://www.nytimes.com/2018/01/02/business/nursing-homes-care-corporate.html.

34 Yao O. Dinizulu & Jennifer Matta, The Multi-Level Nursing Home Corporate Structure: Transparency, Accountability and Common Sense, 12 Nursing Home Litig. Rep. 3 (2009).

35 David E. Kingsley & Charlene Harrington, Financial and Quality Metrics of a Large, Publicly Traded U.S. Nursing Home Chain in the Age of Covid-19, 52 Int'l J. of Health Servs. 212 (2022).

36 Atul Gupta et al., Does Private Equity Investment in Healthcare Benefit Patients? Evidence from Nursing Homes, NBER Working Paper No. 28474 (2021), https://www.nber.org/system/files/working_papers/w28474/w28474.pdf.

federal and state governments of paying for Medicaid and Medicare services are also inflated with no benefit accruing to residents.

21.3 HEALTH CARE AS AN ENTERPRISE: CORPORATE NEGLIGENCE

The origins of corporate negligence in health care settings began with hospitals.[37] Courts began to notice that hospitals were big businesses – running aggressive marketing campaigns, managing their medical staff and other professionals, and generally acting like the central provider of health care.[38]

21.3.1 *Corporate Negligence: Responsibility of the "Enterprise"*

The doctrine of corporate negligence starting in the 1960s noted that the modern hospital as an enterprise is no longer just a shell for physicians to use.[39] Hospitals have gone from small not-for-profit religious systems to large systems run on corporate principles of revenue maximization.[40] More than half of American jurisdictions have now adopted the corporate negligence doctrine in some form.[41]

Corporate negligence, in the Pennsylvania case of *Thompson v. Nason Hospital*,[42] requires a hospital to uphold a standard of care to "ensure the patient's safety and well-being while at the hospital." *Thompson*'s corporate negligence doctrine mandates four distinct duties for institutional providers: (1) reasonable care in the maintenance of safe and adequate facilities and equipment; (2) selection and retention of competent physicians; (3) oversight of all persons who practice medicine within its walls as to patient care; and (4) formulation, adoption, and enforcement of adequate rules and policies to ensure quality care for patients. These duties are nondelegable.

Corporate negligence views the modern hospital as a complex corporate management structure with responsibilities to its patients, measured by its own internal practices as well as those of other similar hospitals.[43] Hospitals can in fact be just as opportunistic as any business, susceptible to the temptation to engage in self-

37 Sword v. NKC Hospitals, Inc., 714 N.E.2d 142 (Ind. 1999) (and cases cited).

38 Clark v. Southview Hosp. & Family Health Ctr., 628 N.E.2d 46 (Ohio 1994) (promotional and marketing campaign stressed the emergency departments); Gragg v. Calandra, 696 N.E.2d 1282 (Ill. App. Ct. 1998) (patients assume that hospital physicians are employees).

39 Alex Stein, Toward a Theory of Medical Malpractice, 97 Iowa L. Rev. 1201, 1229 (2012).

40 Thomas L. Hafemeister & Joshua Hinckley Porter, Don't Let Go of the Rope: Reducing Readmissions by Recognizing Hospitals' Fiduciary Duties to Their Discharged Patients, 62 Am. Univ. L. Rev. 513, 546 (2013).

41 See Larson v. Wasemiller, 738 N.W.2d 300 (Minn. 2007) (adopting corporate negligence for Minnesota, the court noted that more than half of the state courts have adopted the tort, and it has support in Restatement (Second) Tort sections such as sections 320 and 411).

42 Thompson v. Nason Hosp., 591 A.2d 703 (Pa. 1991).

43 See Barry R. Furrow, The Limits of Current A.I. in Health Care: Patient Safety Policing in Hospitals, 12 NE. Univ. L. Rev. 1 (2020).

interested behavior when their financial interests conflict with those of the populations they serve.[44] The evolution of the corporate negligence doctrine reflects judicial awareness that health care institutions owe enhanced duties to their beneficiary patients.[45] Corporate negligence has been a large step toward a vigorous fiduciary obligation to care for patients.

21.3.2 *The Corporate Negligence Model Expands*

Thompson, decided in 1991, was at first applied only to hospitals. Next, in *Shannon v. McNulty*,[46] Health Maintenance Organizations (HMOs), acting as the primary decision-makers with respect to their subscribers' care, were subject to corporate liability. In *Hyrcza v. West Penn Allegheny Health*,[47] medical professional corporations were added, on the basis that such entities, if they take responsibility for their patients' total health care like hospitals, are liable for failing to fulfill institutional duties.[48] Finally, in 2012, the Pennsylvania Supreme Court applied corporate negligence to nursing homes in *Scampone v. Highland Park Care Center*.[49] The court held that nursing home facilities and their parent corporations were subject to corporate negligence liability for patient harms. This new duty intensifies nursing home incentives to improve the quality of their care to avoid liability.[50]

21.4 CREATING A PRESUMPTIVE FIDUCIARY DUTY FOR NURSING HOME OWNERS

A second source of private law is fiduciary law. Courts can use fiduciary duties plus equitable powers to constrain nursing home opportunism, creating a presumptive fiduciary duty that eliminates the need for plaintiffs to make a particularized factfinding in each case.[51]

This nursing home fiduciary duty is built on three foundations.

44 Danielle Ofri, Why Are Nonprofit Hospitals So Highly Profitable?, N.Y. Times (Feb. 20, 2020), https://www.nytimes.com/2020/02/20/opinion/nonprofit-hospitals.html.

45 Barry R. Furrow, Patient Safety and the Fiduciary Hospital: Sharpening Judicial Remedies, 1 Drexel L. Rev. 439 (2009).

46 Shannon v. McNulty, 718 A.2d 828 (Pa. Super. Ct. 1998).

47 Hyrcza v. West Penn Allegheny Health, 978 A. 2d 961 (Pa. Super. Ct. 2009).

48 McClure v. Parvis, 294 F.Supp.3d 318 (E.D. Pa. 2018) (physician practice groups were added, as entities responsible for a patient's health).

49 Scampone v. Highland Park Care Ctr., LLC, No. 16 WAP 2011.

50 R. Tamara Konetzka et al., Malpractice Litigation and Nursing Home Quality of Care, 48 Health Serv. Res. 1920 (2013) (finding "... significant increases in registered nurse-to-total staffing ratios in response to rising malpractice threat, and a reduction in pressure sores among highly staffed facilities").

51 See, e.g., Zaborowski v. Hosp. Care Ctr. of Hermitage, Inc., PA. Dist. And Cty. Ct., 2002 WL 32129508 (2002).

21.4.1 *Medicaid as a Fiduciary*

Medicaid is the primary federal payer of nursing home expenses. Sara Rosenbaum and her coauthors have argued that Medicaid has a fiduciary duty standard, based on statutory state plan requirements for medical assistance requiring "… such safeguards as may be necessary to assure that eligibility for care and services under the plan will be determined and such care and services will be provided in a manner consistent with simplicity of administration and the ***'best interests of the recipients.'*** [Italics mine.]"[52] This "best interests of the recipients" standard is analogous to ERISA's fiduciary duty standard.[53] Since state programs certify and regulate all owners of nursing home chains, whether nonprofit or for-profit, this "best interests" standard of fiduciary duty obligates states and their nursing home managers and owners.

21.4.2 *The Resident as "Vulnerable"*

Fiduciary law establishes a norm of special obligations, creating higher expectations than we normally allocate to others in contractual relationships.[54] As Rothman writes, "the fiduciary concept brings law closer to the human condition by anticipating potential problems that exist in certain forms of interaction characterized by power imbalances and vulnerability and prohibiting their development through the entrenchment of strict principles on fiduciaries."[55] This concept of fiduciary law fits the nursing home relationship between owners/managers and residents perfectly.[56] The court in *Schenk v. Living Centers-East* emphasized the unique vulnerability of residents in nursing homes:

> Residents are in the care and custody of the home on a 24–hour basis, with all their needs necessarily supplied by the facility. Residents are almost invariably in poor physical and/or mental health; they are frequently incompetent and unable to comprehend much less protest any mistreatment or neglect; their families likewise are not in a position to readily know whether injuries are caused by genuine accidents or whether they result from neglect or abuse. [] These various factors make such residents particularly vulnerable to neglect and a variety of possible abuses with detection arguably difficult … unlike the situation where a presumably

[52] Sara Rosenbaum et al., Medicaid and Health Information: Current and Emerging Legal Issues, 28 Health Care Fin. Rev. 21 (2006–07).

[53] Id.

[54] Leonard I. Rotman, Understanding Fiduciary Duties and Relationship Fiduciarity, 62 McGill L. J. 975, 1003 (2017).

[55] Id. at 46.

[56] Petre v. Living Centers-East, 935 F. Supp. 808 (E.D. La. 1996).

competent person seeks a consultation with a physician for a particular problem or even requires hospitalization for a particular malady.[57]

The *Schenck* court then builds a conceptional foundation for the fiduciary duty count in the plaintiff's complaint:

> [M]any if not most nursing home residents are in a vulnerable physical and/or mental state. Placing a loved one in such a facility necessarily entails trust on the part of the family as well as the resident. Since the residents reside in the home, the family has comparatively limited access and opportunity to learn if the resident is neglected or otherwise mistreated. *If entrusting one's money to a receiver or conservator created a business relationship, one would hope at least in principle that entrusting a valued family member to the care of a business entity such as a nursing home would carry similar responsibilities.* [Italics mine.][58]

The *Schenk* court acknowledges the realities of nursing home care: Most residents are vulnerable physically, lack the cognitive skills in many cases to protect themselves, did not "choose" their home, and need a heightened level of personal attention and care.[59] The *Petre* court observed that no relationship better fits "the description of the fiduciary capacity than the relationship between a nursing home and its residents."[60]

21.4.3 *Anti-Opportunism: Fiduciary Controls over "Self-Interest Seeking with Guile"*

The third leg of nursing home fiduciary duty is built on the extreme opportunism of PE ownership in health care, as shown in Section 21.4.1. The generally accepted definition of opportunist behavior in fiduciary law is that of Williamson. His definition is as follows:

> By opportunism I mean self-interest seeking with guile. This includes but is scarcely limited to more blunt forms, such as lying, stealing and cheating. Opportunism more often involves subtle forms of deceit . . . More generally, opportunism refers to the incomplete or distorted disclosure of information, especially to calculated efforts to mislead, distort obfuscate, or otherwise confuse.[61]

Fiduciary law strives to control such opportunistic behavior: Smith defines "opportunism" as "behavior that is undesirable but that cannot be cost-effectively

57 Schenck v. Living Centers-East, Inc., 917 F. Supp. 432 (E.D. La. 1996).
58 Id. at 438.
59 See generally Joachim Boldt, The Concept of Vulnerability in Medical Ethics and Philosophy, 14 Phil., Ethics, and Human. in Med. 6 (2019); see also D. Gordon Smith, The Critical Resource Theory of Fiduciary Duty, 55 Vand. L. Rev. 1399, 1404 (2002).
60 Petre, supra note 56, at 812.
61 Oliver E. Williamson, The Economic Institutions of Capitalism: Firms, Markets, Relational Contracting 47–48 (1985).

captured – defined, detected, and deterred – by explicit ex ante rulemaking ... It often consists of behavior that is technically legal but is done with a view to securing unintended benefits from the system, and these benefits are usually smaller than the costs they impose on others."[62]

Private equity acts knowingly and opportunistically through its financial playbook – deliberate pillaging of nursing home, residents, and government payers. Actions by PE owners of nursing homes are "intentional" – the core strategies discussed in Section 21.4.1 are intended to load nursing homes with debt, build structures to inflate charges to Medicaid and Medicare, and cut staffing and other costs with the predictable results of poor care and fraud on Medicaid.

21.5 EQUITABLE POWERS TO CONSTRAIN PRIVATE EQUITY OWNERSHIP

Fiduciary law, coupled with a court's equitable tools, provides a far more muscular approach to nursing home bad actors than does either tort or contract law limited to damage remedies.[63] Fiduciary law offers future-looking equitable tools to change the PE calculus for those who invest in and run nursing homes.[64] It identifies opportunistic power used against the vulnerable. It allows vulnerable beneficiaries and their families to demand honesty and selflessness of their fiduciaries.[65]

21.5.1 *Coupling Fiduciary Duties and Equitable Remedies*

Imposing a fiduciary duty on an organization raises the baseline for conduct and the measurement of failure and breach of duty. Fiduciary doctrine can create a presumption of wrongdoing for this class of relationships.[66] Fiduciary law creates legal rights grounded in equity for those who need protection, allowing tolling of statutes of limitation and easing a plaintiff's burden of proof. And fiduciary law can draw on a range of equitable remedies. Equity imposes harsh sanctions against fiduciaries for failing to conform to the fiduciary concept's high standards: These may include *inter alia* the disgorgement of profits or amounts equal to losses avoided, equitable compensation, a constructive trust, an injunction, or an accounting of profits.[67]

62 Henry E. Smith, Why Fiduciary Law Is Equitable, in Philosophical Foundations of Fiduciary Law 267 (Andrew S. Gold & Paul B. Miller eds., 2014).

63 Id.

64 Kingsley & Harrington, supra note 35.

65 O'Grady, supra note 20.

66 Rotman, supra note 54.

67 For a full list of fiduciary remedies, see generally David F. Johnson, Remedies for Breach of Fiduciary Duty Claims (Aug. 7, 2020).

21.5.2 *Examples of Fiduciary Powers*[68]

21.5.2.1 Disgorgement

In *Rohlfing v. Manor Care, Inc.*,[69] the executor of a nursing home resident's estate sued Manor Care, the nursing home operator, its parent, and the related pharmaceutical company for antitrust violations, fraud, and breach of fiduciary duty. His goal was to recover excessive fees the resident was forced to pay because of the nursing home's pharmaceutical policies, as well as attorney fees. The court allowed class certification for antitrust and Racketeer Influenced and Corrupt Organizations Act (RICO) claims, the Illinois Consumer Fraud Act (ICFA), and the breach of fiduciary duty.

Manor Care owned a network of 179 facilities in 28 states, offering a spectrum of services to residents – from "high acuity" (intensive) nursing care to custodial care and assisted living arrangements. Manor Care owned an 82.3 percent interest in eighteen of the facilities, which were required to get their pharmaceutical services from Vitalink Pharmacy Services, Inc. (Vitalink). Vitalink also provided consulting services for Manor Care residents, such as monitoring potential drug interaction problems and reviewing patients' drug administration records.

The court expanded on the nature of fiduciary duty: "A fiduciary duty exists in relationships where 'there is confidence reposed on one side and a resulting superiority and influence on the other.' [citations omitted] ... It is certainly true that 'many, if not most nursing home residents are in a vulnerable physical and/or mental state,'[*Schenk*], which could place their caregivers in a position of confidence and influence."[70]

The court in *Rohlfing* held that the plaintiff, Rohlfing, had alleged a proper claim for breach of fiduciary duty.[71] The plaintiff in *Rohlfing* alleged that Manor Care charged him excessive prices for pharmaceuticals, thus breaching their fiduciary duties. The court found that Rohlfing had alleged a claim for breach of fiduciary duty, quoting *Quist v. Dorn*: "Courts of Equity will scrutinize with jealous vigilance the transactions between parties occupying fiduciary relations toward each other ..."[72]

Manor Care is an example of the abuse of *related-party transactions*, specifically use of a pharmacy service owned by the nursing home system to extract high prices

[68] Samuel L. Bray, Fiduciary Remedies, in The Oxford Handbook of Fiduciary law (Evan J. Criddle et al. eds. 2019).

[69] Rohlfing v. Manor Care, Inc., 172 F.R.D.330 (N.D. Ill. 1997).

[70] Id.

[71] Id. (the court did make a specific finding of several elements that justified imposing a fiduciary duty in the case).

[72] Quist v. Dorn, 301 Ill.App. 264, 22 N.E.2d 729, 732 (1939).

for drugs and drug services. If such a case goes to trial, a plaintiff can seek disgorgement of excess gains – to be returned to nursing home residents.

21.5.2.2 Fiduciary Duties of Corporate Owners

In *Isby Brandon v. Beverly Enterprises, Inc.*,[73] defendants were the corporate owners of the nursing home – the administrator was not a defendant. The District Court considered whether a fiduciary breach could be claimed against nondiverse defendants, the corporate owners of the nursing home. The court stated the elements of a fiduciary duty. A contractual relationship may give rise to a fiduciary duty when: "(1) the activities of the parties go beyond their operating on their own behalf, and the activities for the benefit of both; (2) where the parties have a common interest and profit from the activities of the other; (3) where the parties repose trust in one another; and (4) where one party has dominion or control over the other."[74]

The *Isby Brandon* court held that patients could prove a fiduciary duty at trial as a matter of Mississippi law. It recognized the resident status as "vulnerability" in a nursing home, by analogy to the "ward" of a fiduciary. The patient, says the court, is "usually permanently invalid and subject to the nursing home." The court continued: "[T]he parties obviously repose trust in one another and has been said above, the nursing home as fiduciary has dominion and control over the nursing home patient."[75]

This case, drawing on fiduciary law analysis, opens a judicial path to plaintiff's pursuit of owners who are not the onsite managers but rather the corporate owners of the nursing homes. It offers state courts the power to unravel complex ownership structures created by PE firms, imposing a fiduciary duty through the mechanism of private law.

21.5.2.3 Accounting for Profits

An accounting orders an inquiry into the defendant's handling of money or property, usually to ascertain the defendant's gains so they may be paid to the plaintiff. Such an accounting is typically given against a fiduciary. One recent example: New York's Attorney General has asked a state court to force the owners of a Syracuse nursing home to answer questions about "pocketing" US$37.6 million in Medicaid funding from related-party transactions.[76] A private litigant can make the same

[73] Isby Brandon v. Beverly Enters., No. 1:06CV280-P-D (N.D. Miss. Apr. 6, 2007).

[74] Id. at 2.

[75] Id. at 3.

[76] See Jessica R. Towhey, NY Brings Fresh Allegations for a For-Profit Nursing Home "Pocketing" Medicaid Funds, McKnights Long-Term Care News (June 13, 2023), https://www.mcknights.com/news/ny-brings-fresh-allegations-of-a-for-profit-nursing-home-pocketing-medicaid-funds/.

demand for an accounting if the state court invokes the equitable powers available to someone victimized by a fiduciary.

21.5.2.4 Unwinding Remedies

One of the specialties of equity is unwinding and undoing. "Equity, one might say, delights in erasing and not by halves."[77] Judicial orders may include cancellation of documents, avoidance of contracts, reformation, and equitable rescission.[78]

21.5.2.5 Injunctions

As fiduciary scholars write, fiduciary law offers robust remedies that "... must be more severe than against garden variety actors. One method of conforming to this requirement is to employ injunctions against suspected opportunists, and also to withhold injunctive relief from opportunists."[79]

21.6 CONCLUSION

Vulnerable nursing home patients can benefit from the use of private law tools to move the regulatory focus back to the nursing resident as the beneficiary of a fiduciary owner.

Fiduciary duties coupled with corporate negligence duties harness private law to force PE owners toward more demanding fiduciary duties toward their nursing home residents. Private law can have a powerful role in expanding the duties owned by PE firms to vulnerable nursing home patients.

77 W. Hudson R. Unger, Equity Delights to Do Justice and Not by Halves, 33 Dick. L. Rev. 248 (1929).

78 Bray, supra note 68, at 459.

79 Kenneth Ayotte et al., Safety Valve Model of Equity as Anti-Opportunism 30–31, Nw. L. & Econ. Rsch. Paper, Paper No. 13–15 (2013), https://papers.ssrn.com/sol3/papers.cfm?abstract_id=2245098.

22

Health Care Organization Policies about the California End of Life Option Act

The Paper Victory of the Medical Aid in Dying Movement

Megan S. Wright and Cindy L. Cain

22.1 INTRODUCTION

Law and society research demonstrates that law in practice is often different than law on the books and that organizational policy matters for the construction of law. Laws are often vague, ambiguous, or silent on important matters, and so organizations subject to the laws may respond by creating policies that define terms, resolve ambiguities, or fill gaps.[1] Organizations that most directly shape health law include hospitals, health care systems, health insurance programs, pharmacies, and professional associations. When constructing policies, organizations mediate the impact of law and may even create the law if courts or legislatures later rely on the organization's policies to decide legal questions, a process known as legal endogeneity.[2]

This process has not been studied in the context of health care organizational policy about medical aid in dying (MAiD) laws in the United States. Since the mid-1990s, eleven US jurisdictions have legalized MAiD.[3] In the United States, MAiD is an end-of-life option wherein a competent adult patient with a terminal illness may voluntarily request a prescription medication that, when self-administered, will end

[1] Lauren B. Edelman, Legal Ambiguity and Symbolic Structures: Organizational Mediation of Civil Rights Law, 97 Am. J. Soc. 1531 (1992); Frank Dobbin, Inventing Equal Opportunity (2009).

[2] Lauren B. Edelman et al., The Endogeneity of Law: Grievance Procedures as Rational Myths, 105 Am. J. Soc. 406 (1999).

[3] Oregon Death with Dignity Act (1994); Washington Death with Dignity Act (2008); Vermont Patient Choice and Control at the End of Life Act (2013); California End of Life Option Act (2015); Colorado End of Life Options Act (2016); D.C. Death with Dignity Act (2016); Hawai'i Our Care, Our Choice Act (2018); New Jersey Medical Aid in Dying for the Terminally Ill Act (2019); Maine Death with Dignity Act (2019); New Mexico Elizabeth Whitefield End-of-Life Options Act (2021); see also Baxter v. Montana (2009 MT 449) (decriminalizing medical aid in dying).

their lives.[4] Although more Americans live in jurisdictions that have legalized this end-of-life option,[5] very few terminally ill individuals use MAiD.[6] Those individuals who choose MAiD tend to be white and highly educated.[7] Low use of MAiD could reflect preferences, but low use may also reflect lack of access, despite legalization.[8]

Lack of access could be due, in part, to health care organizations' responses to MAiD laws, where existing statutes may not adequately address eligibility and procedural questions about this end-of-life option and where hospitals and health systems may address ambiguity through policies that ultimately restrict access to MAiD. Restrictive policies can reflect organizational "opt out" of MAiD participation on behalf of the institution and affiliated health care providers. But even organizations that "opt in" can adopt policies that require providers to follow specific processes beyond what the law mandates, which may result in reduced access to MAiD. Hospitals and health systems can enforce compliance with organizational policy through employment contracts or medical staff privileges and medical staff bylaws, and thus private law choices and agreements mediate public laws.

This chapter builds on an ongoing study of health care organizations' policies adopted in response to the legalization of MAiD in California in 2015 and highlights how despite the seeming success of "right to die" social movements in convincing voters and legislatures that MAiD should be legal, legalization of MAiD in the United States is mostly a "paper victory." By this we mean that the "law appears to advance [an] agenda but in reality it does no such thing."[9] In this case, the law on the books should result in individuals who meet statutory requirements being able to choose MAiD, but in practice, MAiD is often not an option at all.

This chapter proceeds as follows. First, we will briefly describe the data and methods of the parent study from which this chapter draws. Second, we will show

4 There are other procedural and eligibility requirements as well. For a description US MAiD laws, see Megan S. Wright, Equality of Autonomy? Physician Aid in Dying and Supported Decision-Making, 63 Ariz. L. Rev. 157 (2021).

5 Twenty percent of Americans now live in a jurisdiction where MAiD is legal. Compassion & Choices, Medical Aid in Dying, https://www.compassionandchoices.org/our-issues/medical-aid-in-dying (last accessed Apr. 10, 2023).

6 See, e.g., California Dep't of Public Health, California End of Life Option Act 2021 Data Report 4 (July 2022), https://www.cdph.ca.gov/Programs/CHSI/CDPH%20Document%20Library/CDPH_End_of_Life%20_Option_Act_Report_2021_FINAL.pdf (reporting that in 2021, between 448 and 642 individuals died using MAiD, and only 772 prescriptions were written).

7 See, e.g., id. at 5 (reporting that in 2021, 85.65 percent of individuals in California who died with medical assistance were white, and 76.7 percent had some college education). Only 35 percent of individuals in California are white. Hans Johnson et al., California's Population, Public Pol'y Inst. of Cal. (Jan. 2023), https://www.ppic.org/wp-content/uploads/JTF_PopulationJTF.pdf.

8 Mara Buchbinder & Cindy L. Cain, Medical Aid in Dying: New Frontiers in Medicine, Law, and Culture, Ann. Rev. L. & Soc. Sci. 195, 199, 204–05 (2023).

9 Jaclyn Greenberg, A Right of Appeal under Ontario's Health Care Consent Act: A Paper Victory Is No Victory at All, 44 Ottawa L. Rev. 433, 461 (2012–13).

how the text of the California MAiD statute ensures that few individuals will qualify for MAiD. Third, we will show how the implementation of the law also ensures that even fewer individuals qualify. In this section, we will focus on two health care organizations' policies and demonstrate how they restrict access to MAiD for otherwise eligible individuals. We will conclude by discussing how MAiD in the United States is not a true victory for the "right to die" movement but is instead a "paper right."

22.2 DATA AND METHODS OF LARGER STUDY

The California legislature passed the End of Life Option Act (EOLOA) in 2015, effective 2016.[10] The EOLOA, like most other US MAiD laws, includes a provision that health care professionals and health care organizations can choose not to participate. Additionally, because the law is silent on several implementation questions, health care organizations can write their own policies on MAiD practices. Policymakers and scholars in California began researching how the law was implemented and after two years, recommended that health care organizations be more transparent about their policies.[11] In 2021, the legislature amended the Act, effective January 1, 2022, to require "health care entit[ies]" to "post on the entity's public internet website the entity's current policy governing medical aid in dying."[12] This public regulation does not mandate a particular organizational policy, which preserves organizational autonomy and private ordering, but instead attempts to promote patient autonomy by mandating that patients have access to information that may be important to their medical and end-of-life decision-making. Adopting a requirement that health care entities be transparent about their EOLOA policy also makes it possible for researchers to collect and analyze the policies.

In March 2023, we obtained a list of all licensed health care entities in the state of California from the California Department of Health Care Access and Information.[13] We limited our focus to general acute care hospitals. We then went to each hospital's website and searched for the hospital's EOLOA policy. As we report elsewhere,[14] very few hospitals are compliant with the legal mandate to publicly post their EOLOA policies on their public-facing institutional website, but there is no enforcement mechanism for this EOLOA provision included in the statute. We analyzed available policies for whether organizations choose to

[10] Cal. Health & Safety Code §§ 443–443.22 (West 2023).

[11] Cindy L. Cain et al., Hospital and Health System Policies Concerning the California End of Life Option Act, 23 J. Palliative Med. 60, 65 (2020).

[12] Cal. Health & Safety Code § 443.15(i) (West 2023).

[13] California Health and Hum. Servs. Open Data Portal, OSHPD Healthcare Facilities, https://data.chhs.ca.gov/dataset/oshpd-healthcare-facilities (last accessed Feb. 18, 2024).

[14] Megan S. Wright & Cindy L. Cain, Hospital Compliance with the California End of Life Option Act Transparency Requirements (Working Paper, forthcoming) (reporting that about a third of hospitals posted their EOLOA policy).

participate in MAiD and whether organizations add restrictions to or conditions of participation for health care providers or patients that are not contained in the text of the law.

We report on an analysis of these policies elsewhere but will briefly summarize our main findings here.[15] We found that (1) organizational policies vary in how they restrict patient and provider participation in MAiD, including adopting no policy, using the text of the law as policy, restricting provider participation only, restricting patient participation only, or adding conditions to participation for both providers and patients; (2) the predominance of religiously affiliated hospitals means that many hospitals "opt out" because MAiD is inconsistent with religious doctrine; and (3) organizations that "opt in" may burden patients seeking MAiD with onerous requirements and organizations that "opt out" may not actually preclude access to MAiD, although neither physicians nor patients may recognize this.[16]

For the purposes of this chapter, we use a subset of organizational policies to illustrate reasons why MAiD is only a paper right. First, however, we focus on how eligibility and procedural requirements in the law, ignorance of the law, and functional eligibility requirements such as financial resources, limit access to MAiD. We then illustrate how private organizational policies, even for organizations that opt in, can make MAiD a "paper option" for many individuals who otherwise may desire MAiD.

22.3 LEGAL REQUIREMENTS LIMIT ACCESS TO MAID

As others have reported elsewhere,[17] the strict eligibility requirements in MAiD laws prevent many individuals from using MAiD. Only residents of states where MAiD is legal can avail themselves of this option.[18] Further, only adults with decisional capacity can access MAiD,[19] which excludes terminally ill individuals with cognitive

[15] Megan S. Wright & Cindy L. Cain, Mediating Autonomy (Working Paper, forthcoming).

[16] Id.

[17] See, e.g., Mara Buchbinder & Thaddeus M. Pope, Medical Aid in Dying in Hawaii: Appropriate Safeguards or Unmanageable Obstacles?, Health Affs. (Aug. 13, 2018), https://www.healthaffairs.org/do/10.1377/forefront.20180808.14380/; Amanda M. Thyden, Death with Dignity and Assistance: A Critique of the Self-Administration Requirement in California's End of Life Option Act, 20 Chap. L. Rev. 421 (2017).

[18] Recent lawsuits in Oregon and Vermont contesting residency restrictions have resulted in changes in these jurisdictions. Elizabeth Castillo, Oregon Settles Lawsuit Challenging Residency Requirements for State's Death with Dignity Law, NPR (Mar. 30, 2022), https://www.opb.org/article/2022/03/30/oregon-settles-lawsuit-challenging-residency-requirement-for-states-death-with-dignity-law/; Lola Fadulu, To Die on Her Own Terms, a Connecticut Woman Turns to Vermont, N.Y. Times (Mar. 29, 2023), https://www.nytimes.com/2023/03/29/nyregion/connecticut-vermont-medical-assisted-death.html.

[19] See, e.g., Cal. Health & Safety Code §§ 443.2(a) (West 2023), 443.1(e) ("'Capacity ...' means ... the individual has the ability to understand the nature and consequences of a health care decision, the ability to understand its significant benefits, risks, and alternatives, and the ability to make and communicate an informed decision to health care providers").

impairments such as moderate dementia.[20] The terminal illness requirement excludes from using MAiD those who are suffering from serious and incurable illnesses but who do not meet the terminal illness definition,[21] and the self-administration requirement may exclude individuals with disabilities that make it impossible to self-administer the medication.[22] And waiting periods imposed by law can also mean someone dies or becomes incapacitated between the first and second requests,[23] thus losing the opportunity to die with MAiD.

Aside from these eligibility requirements, the law also imposes significant paperwork burdens on physicians and patients. Physicians have to make referrals to other health care providers and complete legally required forms and submit them to the state.[24] And patients have to complete a written form that is witnessed by two people, neither of whom can be their current health care providers and one of whom cannot be a family member.[25] Individuals at the end of life, especially if institutionalized, may not be able to satisfy these requirements. These burdens are especially significant, given that people seeking MAiD are very ill and have limited life left.

In brief, existing public law requirements may result in very few people qualifying for MAiD, regardless of subsequent private policy choices of health care organizations, making this end-of-life option a paper right.

22.4 IGNORANCE OF LAW LIMITS ACCESS TO MAID

Even assuming an individual satisfies the legal eligibility requirements for MAiD, many individuals may not know about MAiD. This is in part due to silence in many states' MAiD laws about whether physicians can initiate a discussion about MAiD with their patients. In this statutory and regulatory silence, some private professional organizations have adopted recommendations suggesting that physicians not bring up MAiD with their patients to not unduly influence patients to hasten death.[26] Such recommendations from private organizations can be considered "soft [private]

[20] But see Wright, supra note 4 (arguing that disability law may facilitate access to MAiD for some individuals with cognitive impairments).

[21] See, e.g., Cal. Health & Safety Code § 443.1(r) (West 2023) ("'Terminal illness' means an incurable and irreversible disease that ... will ... result in death within six months").

[22] See, e.g., id. § 443.1(q).

[23] State laws authorizing MAiD require two requests separated by a waiting period, which typically was fifteen days. However, some states chose to have a longer waiting periods (e.g., twenty-one days), and California recently reduced its waiting period to forty-eight hours. Id. § 443.3.

[24] Id. §§ 443.8, 443.9. Requiring the participation of multiple physicians may also create barriers.

[25] Id. § 443.3.

[26] See, e.g., Bonnie Reagan, Conscientious Practice, in The Oregon Death with Dignity Act: A Guidebook for Health Care Professionals 12, 12 (Sept. 2007), https://www.wsha.org/wp-content/uploads/Death-with-Dignity_Death-with-dignity-guidebook.pdf ("We believe that the attending physician should not initiate the discussion, because if he/she does, the patient may feel pressured ...").

law," which although not legally binding, may become very influential in practice. Following this guidance means that patients who are not well informed about end-of-life options may not know about MAiD.

Another way in which individuals may be ignorant of the law occurs when information about the law is not available in multiple languages. When we were researching California health care entities' websites, it was not uncommon to find hospital policies and forms in both English and Spanish (e.g., advance directive forms), but never did we find an EOLOA policy posted in a language other than English.[27]

Ignorance means that end-of-life decision-making rights are not exercised.

22.5 HIDDEN HEALTH CARE ORGANIZATION OPT IN LIMITS ACCESS TO MAID

Another way access to MAiD is limited in states where it is legal occurs when health care organizations opt in but hide this information from their patients and the public. In our research, we found several instances in which organizations had an opt-in policy, but this was not easily found using the hospital website search function or that had a policy that could be found elsewhere online but not on the hospital's webpage. Organizations that are not transparent about opting in make it less likely that their patients will use MAiD, but this hidden opt in may serve other organizational (i.e., private law) preferences, such as maintaining the status quo of low MAiD rates, resisting controversial change, reducing administrative burden on providers, and reducing risk of liability.

22.6 FUNCTIONAL INELIGIBILITY LIMITS ACCESS TO MAID

An individual may desire MAiD but not be able to afford this end-of-life option. Often the MAiD medication is not covered by health insurance.[28] This means that patients who choose MAiD must pay for the medication out of pocket. That cost is often from US$700 to over US$3,000 and has increased over time as more states legalize MAiD.[29] This may be cost-prohibitive for lower-income individuals, making them functionally ineligible for MAiD. Further, using MAiD is not an option

[27] Wright & Cain, supra note 14.

[28] David Grube & Ashley Cardenas, Insurance Coverage and Aid-in-Dying Medication Costs, 3 JAMA Oncology 1137 (2017); Veena Shankaran et al., Insurance Coverage and Aid-in-Dying Medication Costs – Reply, 3 JAMA Oncology 1138 (2017). However, in California, Medicaid covers many of the costs associated with MAiD, but Medicaid does not cover all low-income individuals. California Dep't of Health Care Servs., End of Life Option Act Services (Aug. 2020), https://files.medi-cal.ca.gov/pubsdoco/Publications/masters-MTP/Part2/eloa.pdf.

[29] JoNel Aleccia, Terminally Ill, He Wanted Aid-in-Dying. His Catholic Hospital Said No, Kaiser Fam. Found. Health News (Jan. 29, 2020), https://kffhealthnews.org/news/when-aid-in-dying-is-legal-but-the-medicine-is-out-of-reach/ (noting that the cost of one aid-in-dying drug is over

through the Department of Veterans Affairs (VA),[30] and so veterans who receive health care through the VA will not have access to this end-of-life option, even in states where MAiD is legal.

It may also be the case that pharmacies do not have MAiD medications,[31] which means that patients will not be able to use this end-of-life option.

Lack of financial resources or lack of access to the aid-in-dying medication makes the right to die illusory for some otherwise eligible individuals.

22.7 HEALTH CARE ORGANIZATION OPT OUT LIMITS ACCESS TO MAID

More significantly for limiting access to MAiD, however, is the law's facilitation of individual health care provider and organizational opt out of participation. The law states that "[p]articipation under this part shall be voluntary. . . . A person or entity that elects, for reasons of conscience, morality, or ethics, not to participate is not required to participate."[32]

The law directs that "a health care entity may prohibit its employees, independent contractors, or other persons or entities, including health care providers, from participating under this part while on premises owned or under the management or direct control of that health care entity or while acting within the course and scope of any employment by, or contract with, the entity."[33] Consequences for violating an organization's policy can include "[l]oss of privileges, loss of membership, or other action authorized by the bylaws or rules and regulations of the medical staff"[34] and "[s]uspension, loss of employment, or other action authorized by the policies and practices of the health care entity"[35] among other potential penalties.[36] Health care entities are not permitted to prohibit health care provider or employee participation in the EOLOA when not acting within the "course and scope" of their

US$3,000); UCSF Health: FAQs End of Life Option Act at UCSF Health, UCSF Health, https://www.ucsfhealth.org/education/faq-end-of-life-option-act-at-ucsf (last accessed May 1, 2023) (stating the cost of the medication is US$700 plus "delivery fees"); Katie Engelhart, I'm the Doctor Who Is Here to Help You Die, The Atlantic (Mar. 1, 2021), https://www.theatlantic.com/health/archive/2021/03/aid-dying-lonny-shavelson/618139/ (describing how some physicians have opened MAiD specialty practices, which are expensive for patients); Veena Shankaran et al., Drug Price Inflation and the Cost of Assisted Death for Terminally Ill Patients – Death with Indignity, 3 JAMA Oncology 15 (2017).

30 Dep't of Veterans Affs., VA Fact Sheet for Healthcare Staff 3 (Sept. 2010), https://www.ethics.va.gov/docs/pandemicflu/Ethics_and_Pandemic_Flu_Fact_Sheet_508_2010-09-30.pdf.

31 Aleccia, supra note 29.

32 Cal. Health & Safety Code § 443.14(e)(1) (West 2023).

33 Id. § 443.15(a).

34 Id. § 443.15(c)(1).

35 Id. § 443.15(c)(2). Physicians can be fired for noncompliance with health care employer policy. See, e.g., Aleccia, supra note 29.

36 Cal. Health & Safety Code §§ 443.15(c)(3), 443.15(c)(4).

employment or independent contracting duties with the entity and when not on the facility's premises.[37]

When a health care organization, such as a general acute care hospital, decides that its employees, and physicians on its medical staff, are not participating in MAiD, patients who receive their end-of-life care from the organization and affiliated personnel will likely struggle to access MAiD. In theory, patients could transfer their care to seek MAiD, but in practice, providers may not accept a new patient solely to facilitate the patient's death through MAiD.[38] Additionally, patients may be physically unable to seek new care because they are actively dying or institutionalized, or the patient may not be able or want to leave their home to search for MAiD providers that may be geographically distant.

Religious hospitals constitute a significant share of private nonprofit hospitals,[39] and many religious hospitals have declined to participate in the California EOLOA.[40] Many of these hospitals are part of a large health system, which means that patients receiving care through the system will not have access to this end-of-life option. For this chapter, we use the case of one health system that has complied with the legal requirement to post its EOLOA policy publicly – Dignity Health – to demonstrate the effect of organizational opt out on access to MAiD.

Dignity Health system's goal is "to create environments that meet each patient's physical, mental, and spiritual needs," and it is "made up of more than 60,000 caregivers and staff who deliver … care to … communities in 21 states. Headquartered in San Francisco, Dignity Health is the fifth largest health system in the nation and the largest hospital provider in California."[41] Dignity Health started with one Catholic hospital and has since grown to include thirty-nine hospitals, of which twenty-four are Catholic.[42]

Not surprising, given the Catholic church's opposition to MAiD,[43] Dignity Health hospitals opted out of the EOLOA, and this opt out extends to other services

[37] Id. § 443.15(d).

[38] See, e.g., FAQs: End of Life Option Act at UCSF, UCSF Health, https://www.ucsfhealth.org/education/faq-end-of-life-option-act-at-ucsf (last accessed Apr. 13, 2023) ("At this time, only established UCSF patients are eligible to pursue EOLOA with UCSF.").

[39] Maryam Guiahi et al., Patient Views on Religious Institutional Health Care, 2 JAMA Network Open e1917008 (2019) (reporting that nearly 20 percent of hospitals are religiously affiliated as of 2016, most of which are Catholic); Aleccia, supra note 29 (reporting that 1/6 US patients receives health care from a Catholic hospital).

[40] Cain et al., supra note 11.

[41] About Us, Dignity Health, https://www.dignityhealth.org/about-us (last accessed Apr. 13, 2023).

[42] Our History: Rooted in Kindness, Dignity Health, https://www.dignityhealth.org/about-us/our-organization/mission-vision-and-values (last accessed Apr. 13, 2023).

[43] U.S. Conf. of Catholic Bishops, Ethical and Religious Directives for Catholic Health Care Services 20–22 (6th ed. 2020), https://www.usccb.org/about/doctrine/ethical-and-religious-directives/upload/ethical-religious-directives-catholic-health-service-sixth-edition-2016-06.pdf.

such as hospice and home health.[44] Indeed, the system's opposition to MAiD is explicit in its Statement of Common Values: "Death is a sacred part of life's journey; we will intentionally neither hasten nor delay it. For this reason, physician-assisted suicide is not part of Dignity Health's mission."[45] This language is also copied in its official hospital policy, where it asserts that "[t]he mission, values, and philosophy of care of Dignity Health compel us to reject participation in physician aid in dying."[46]

Dignity Health's EOLOA policy begins with a statement that the organization is committed to providing "excellent palliative care," is opposed to MAiD, and wants to ensure that everyone is aware that Dignity Health is exercising its legal right to opt out of participating in MAiD.[47] Dignity Health then specifies the following with respect to MAiD:

> B. It is the policy of Dignity Health that its facilities, programs, staff, and related operations shall not be involved in physician aid in dying, including:
> 1. Providing or securing an "informed decision" as defined by the Act.
> 2. Providing or completing the written and oral request as provided by the Act.
> 3. Providing any medication with the specific purpose of ending a human life as contemplated by the Act.
> 4. Being present at the time of administration of the medication by the patient.
>
> C. Patients, families, nurses, physicians, and other providers are encouraged to fully explore and discuss care and treatment options for terminally ill patients. As part of that discussion, Dignity Health recognizes that requests for physician aid in dying will occur within the context of the physician-patient relationship. Dignity Health respects the rights of patients and physicians to discuss and explore all such treatment options, but fully expect that patients and physicians will respect and adhere to the Dignity Health's position as set forth in this policy while undergoing and providing treatment in Dignity Health facilities, programs, and services.[48]

Interestingly, Dignity Health's website refers individuals with questions about the EOLOA to their primary care providers and the Coalition for Compassionate Care of California (CCCC), which is an organization that "promotes high-quality,

[44] See, e.g., Dignity Health Operations, Dignity Health Administrative Policy and Procedure, Physician Aid in Dying (Physician Assisted Suicide) 140.1.019, 2 (June 9, 2016), https://www.dignityhealth.org/content/dam/dignity-health/socal/pdfs/Dignity-Health-System-Policy-Physician-Assisted-Suicide.pdf.

[45] Dignity Health, Statement of Common Values 3, https://www.dignityhealth.org/content/dam/dignity-health/pdfs/our-1dh-missionintegration-standards-indicators2014.pdf (last accessed Oct. 9, 2024).

[46] Dignity Health Operations, supra note 44, at 1.

[47] Id. at 2.

[48] Id. at 3.

compassionate care for everyone who is seriously ill or nearing the end of life"[49] and is officially neutral about the CA EOLOA. Although it is neutral, the CCCC website includes a wide range of information about all end-of-life decisions, including the EOLOA. The CCCC website also includes a link to the American Clinicians Academy for Medical Aid in Dying, which connects interested individuals to physicians willing to assist them in accessing MAiD.[50]

Dignity Health has twenty-nine hospitals across California,[51] and thus its opt out significantly affects access to MAiD.

While this section focused on a religiously affiliated health system as a case of organizational opt-out of MAiD, other health systems in California have also opted out, despite no religious reason. Such opt outs also preclude patient access to MAiD, especially when the hospital is the only hospital in a rural region.

22.8 HEALTH CARE ORGANIZATION OPT IN WITH ADDITIONAL REQUIREMENTS LIMITS ACCESS TO MAID

It may seem that when health care organizations decide to opt into the CA EOLOA, patients will have access to MAiD if they meet the legal requirements as outlined in the statute. However, many organizations that opt in create policies with additional requirements that may impede access to MAiD.[52] This section will focus on the CA EOLOA opt-in policy of the University of California San Francisco (UCSF) Medical Center to highlight organizational requirements that may restrict patient choice at the end of life.

One way that UCSF may make it more difficult for patients to obtain MAiD is by requiring that patients meet with two additional clinicians beyond the attending and consulting physicians required by law. The UCSF policy directs that patients inquiring about MAiD be referred to a social worker for information.[53] If the patient decides to move forward with the process, their attending physician to whom they make their initial request for MAiD must refer them to a mental health specialist for a capacity assessment and to ensure no mental illness is affecting their decision to

[49] About Us, Coal. for Compassionate Care of California, https://coalitionccc.org/CCCC/CCCC/About/Mission.aspx?hkey=f520866d-3c6d-4407-8445-3026cb0d9026 (last accessed Apr. 13, 2023).

[50] Key Facts about the End of Life Option Act for Patients & Families, Coal. for Compassionate Care of California, https://coalitionccc.org/CCCC/Resources/Consumer-Information-on-EoLOA.aspx (last accessed Apr. 13, 2023).

[51] Our Locations, Dignity Health, https://www.dignityhealth.org/ourlocations (last accessed Apr. 13, 2023).

[52] See Wright & Cain, supra note 15.

[53] UCSF Health & UCSF Med. Ctr., The California End of Life Option Act (Patient's Request for a Drug for the Purpose of Ending Life) Policy 6.06.16, 4, https://www.ucsfhealth.org/-/media/project/ucsf/ucsf-health/pdf/end-of-life-option-act-policy.pdf (last accessed Apr. 2022).

pursue MAiD.[54] UCSF justifies their policy on the basis of protecting patients with impaired decisional capacity, including from mental illness.[55]

With these requirements, UCSF's policy is trying to ensure that patients' decisions are truly informed and voluntary and thus autonomous.[56] However, requiring additional appointments and assessments slows the MAiD process, and because patients are terminally ill, they may die before the process is complete, frustrating their autonomy. Further, meeting with two additional providers, neither of whom the patient may have met before, can constitute a significant privacy burden and provides an opportunity for strangers to veto the patient's decision, given that UCSF's policy is not to prescribe aid-in-dying medication if health care team members have concerns about whether the patient is making a voluntary request.[57]

Other parts of UCSF policy may also reduce patient access to MAiD. For example, aid-in-dying medication cannot be dispensed or ingested on the premises.[58] Patients who cannot be discharged from the hospital will not be able to use MAiD. Further, UCSF will not accept patients only for MAiD. UCSF will only facilitate MAiD for current patients.[59] Patients must also be able to communicate in the absence of familial support as UCSF policy requires that physicians discuss the EOLOA with their patients alone,[60] and this can negatively affect those who prefer to make decisions with family or who need decision-making assistance.[61] Moreover, there are additional requirements that physicians must meet in order to participate in MAiD at UCSF, such as obtaining UCSF Medical Staff EOLOA privilege[62] and making reports to UCSF risk management,[63] which may decrease physician willingness to participate, given how many burdens are on their time in everyday

54 Id. at 7.

55 Id. at 8.

56 The meeting with the social worker can be helpful to patients whose physician does not participate in MAiD because the social worker will connect the patient to a physician who does participate. Id. at IV.G. Some research has found that UCSF's mental health evaluation adds no benefit beyond the assessment of patient capacity that the attending and consulting physicians perform, however. Jordie Martin et al., UCSF End-of-Life Option Act 2016–2019: A Retrospective Chart Review Pilot (SC1923), 61 J. Pain Symptom Mgmt. P682 (Mar. 2021).

57 UCSF Health & UCSF Med. Ctr., supra note 53, at 5.

58 Id. at 4.

59 Id. at 4.

60 Id. at 7.

61 See Megan S. Wright, End of Life and Autonomy: The Case for Relational Nudges in End-of-Life Decision-Making Law and Policy, 77 Md. L. Rev. 1062 (2018) (describing how many individuals prefer to make end-of-life decisions in consultation and collaboration with their family members); Megan S. Wright, Dementia, Autonomy, and Supported Healthcare Decision Making, 79 Md. L. Rev. 257 (2020) (describing supported health care decision-making); Wright, supra note 4 (describing how supported decision-making can facilitate autonomous use of MAiD for individuals with cognitive impairments).

62 UCSF Health & UCSF Medical Center, supra note 53, at 4.

63 Id. at 2–3.

medical practice and are added just through complying with the statutory EOLOA requirements.

In brief, even when organizations opt into MAiD, their policies do not guarantee that statutorily qualified individuals will be able to use this end-of-life option.

22.9 DISCUSSION AND CONCLUSION

Our research demonstrates that health care organizations, most of them private, mediate medical decision-making rights granted by the state. Employment contracts with health care professionals and medical staff bylaws and staff privileges for physicians constrain involvement in MAiD and affect the physician–patient relationship. Thus, the spread of MAiD across the United States may be only a symbolic victory for patients' rights advocates because in practice, this option is not available to many patients due to health care organizations' policies. Indeed, statistics reflect that only the most privileged patients are receiving MAiD. Organizational policies thus limit patient autonomy, which California's EOLOA law was meant to increase, but such limits will primarily be experienced by rural patients, low-income patients, and patients with low health literacy.